THE HOPE FOR HOLINESS

GOD'S DIVINE ENDGAME

A FRESH CONSIDERATION OF EPHESIANS 4:17-24

PAUL F. EVANS

TO

WYATT

May God guide and guard your steps

Ps. 37:1-9, 18-19, 23-24, 25-26, 39-40

This publication is designed to provide accurate and authoritative information in regard to the subject matter covered. It is provided with the understanding that neither the author nor the publisher is engaged in rendering legal, financial, medical, or other professional services. While the author and publisher have used their best efforts in preparing this book, they make no representations or warranties with respect to the accuracy or completeness of the contents. The advice and strategies contained herein may not be suitable for your specific situation. You should consult a qualified professional where appropriate. Neither the author nor the publisher shall be liable for any losses or damages resulting from the use of this information.

Book Cover by Logan Tudor (Billy Logan Creative)

First edition 2026

Pastor Paul's Book Sales (imprint)

ISBN-13: 979-8-9954215-1-1 (sc)
ISBN-13: 979-8-9954215-0-4 (e)

Unless otherwise indicated all Scripture references and quotations are taken from the New International Version Grand Rapids, MI: Zondervan, 2011.

Unless otherwise indicated all New Testament Greek quotations and references are taken from The Greek New Testament: SBL Edition. Lexham Press: Society of Biblical Literature, 2011—2013, by Michael W. Holmes.

Contents

PREFACE

In *The Hope for Holiness,* my aim is to provide an exposition of Ephesians 4:17-24 without resorting to systematic theology or propositional dogmatics. As much as possible, where theological terms or ideas are used, I hope that their meaning, consistent with sound biblical exposition, will be clear. Ideas like *justification, reconciliation, righteousness, salvation, sanctification, soteriology, eschatology* and so forth, are used as handy short-hand to reference concepts. My precise meaning ought to be made clear by context, or by the laying out the underlying biblical perspectives that give them content – which hopefully will be received by the reader as soundly New Testament and Pauline.

Sparse references to historical doctrinal camps or positions serve to set some of my conclusions drawn from this passage, very loosely speaking, in the tradition of the church, but are not supposed to offer definitive representations of those positions or traditions. They serve as a foil against which to offer a rationale for why we ought to understand the text better. Much confusion exists over the biblical concepts of *holiness, sanctification, righteousness, sin,* and *sinfulness* in human nature, a great deal of it arising from early church controversy and developing doctrinal positions. Theological debates have been like a snowball rolling down hill, gathering more and more material and momentum, so that we often lack the will to confront it, and many will not stand in front of it for fear of being rolled over, misunderstood, or worse, branded "doctrinal dissenters" of their tradition.

My hope is that by ignoring some of accumulated material, and going back to the text, we might be able to take a more objective approach to understanding the Pauline perspective on holiness, its role in the

Christian life, and what constitutes it in the life of the believer. Part of that process will be taken up in the lengthy, and some may say a disproportionate, early treatment of Ephesians as a letter from Paul the Apostle, to the church at Ephesus, which he established after initially meeting a number of disciples of John the Baptist on his arrival, as recorded in Acts 19. It is, I believe, the same church in the city to which Paul sent Timothy to stabilize the believing community there because of controversy and infighting among its members. There was, at the very least, a danger of things degenerating into disunity. Paul had predicted that problems would arise when he called a meeting of the leaders and elder prior to going to Jersualem, and before he was arrested. He told them he would never see them again, so Timothy became the apostle's surrogate at a difficult time for the church. John, who ended his life in Ephesus, wrote to the same church, and warned them against their attrition away from an early zeal (Rev. 2:1-7). Ignatius, also writing to the Ephesians, encourage them to make an effort to seek unity among themselves.[1] A pattern emerges.

Although there are indications in the letter that Paul may not have known or had direct relationships with some of the first recipients, for whatever reason (maybe because churches in the various locations were made up of a number of independent congregations), we accept the early church's judgment that Paul is the author, and the Ephesians as the original and initial recipients. That having been said, our historical knowledge of the church from Acts, Ephesians, 1 and 2 Timothy, Revelation, and references to Ephesus and Asia in 1 Corinthians permits us to establish the credible thesis that Paul is addressing potential inside threats to the unity in the church, as well as mitigating the effects on their relationships from perennial outside pressure from Ephesian society, and so encourages his readers to see to it that they *make every*

---

[1] Ignatius to the Ephesians chapter III-V.

effort to maintain unity through peace by the Spirit (Eph. 4:3). Uprightness and godliness of character and conduct, which Paul treats in our passage as something they had learned about earlier from him, is the key to this unity, in that it promotes the kind of unselfishness that supports an interconnectedness between believers by which they are beneficiaries of the grace of God, as well as freely acting as suppliers of its richness to one another (Eph. 4:16). His later instructions on how this might look in terms of practice and church life presupposes that the members of the church are committed to the moral transformation at work in them through God's renewing power, by which they are to act in one another's best interests rather than selfishly (Eph. 4:3, 13-16).

There is, in Paul's treatment of godliness in Ephesians 4:17-24, where character and conduct are in view, a striking allusion to the divine endgame, which he previously mentions in the context of church unity in verse 13, that through moral and spiritual development the saints and the church are on course to becoming a representation of the imago Dei (Eph. 4:13). That the new life God has created in them at initial salvation has been imprinted with the true holiness and righteousness of God is an indication that God intends to reestablish as his goal, in a redeemed humanity, the reflection of his character back into a renewed creation. This redeemed humanity is to be made up of saints from every conceivable ethnic and social background to become one church, an eschatological temple in which God will dwell by his Spirit in eternity, and that will be a representation of God to the new creation in the coming eschaton (Eph. 2:11-22).

While I have made general historical references from time to time to theologians or historical doctrinal positions, I have not sought to shape my exposition of the text to support or to discredit them, except where a plain understanding of the text makes some point clear. Since I am a Wesleyan-Pentecostal, and I am interested in whether my own tradition and ideas, shaped by exposure to doctrine and teaching over decades, have sound and defensible foundations in the text, and in the general teaching of the New Testament as a whole. Therefore, I have avoided the use of language found in doctrinal statements with which I am familiar, in favor of expressing my conclusions using content and language consistent with a perception of the meaning and original intent of the text. An evaluation of doctrinal statements against the text is for another time. Besides, I have already attempted some of that in an earlier book, *Holiness Reconsidered* (2016), and it is not necessary to repeat it here. My goal is to unpack the text, not attempt dogmatic alignment or doctrinal polemics. Nevertheless, in my conclusion, I break away into a historical treatment that has more to say to my own constituency, than it may to other readers of this book. For that reason, chapter five, especially the summary near the end, stands as the proper expository conclusion to this book.

Finally, I offer this work, not as a polemic for a doctrinal tradition (even if I believe that the text may speak particularly poignantly to my own). It is a treatment of biblical holiness, and in particular of the Pauline development of a model for holiness that is connected to the divine purpose for the life of the believer, the divine endgame for personal redemption, and an eschatological trajectory for the moral transformation, and growth of the saints.

INTRODUCTION

Few believers stop to think about the endgame of their faith in Christ for salvation, beyond a rather shallow consideration that they might end up in heaven one day. But is this the most important thing to God, for believers, saved by the power of Christ's shed blood on the cross, to simply *end up in heaven*? Even if we should end up in heaven, what does that really mean in terms of eternal life? It is way too easy to miss the New Testament's emphasis on the quality of eternal life, over and against quantity, how long it will last, especially as believers glibly speak to one another about *eternal life* with respect to the unsaved (cf. John 3:16-18; Rom. 6:23).[2] In describing the incarnation of the Word as flesh, John spoke about *light being* life, that is kn*owing God* has something to do with what it means to *be truly alive* (John 1:4-5). Jesus made the telling statement that he had come "...that you might have life, and have it more abundantly," which the NIV translates "have it to the full" (John 10:10).[3] John captures Jesus meaning when he uses the adverb abundantly, extraordinarily, profusely, going far beyond "normal" and ordinary life as we now know and experience it (περισσὸν ἔχωσιν).[4]

Later, as he prepared for the cross, Jesus told his disciples that he was concerned that their "joy might be full" (πληρωθῇ), meaning to have it increase to its greatest extent. He had something in mind concerning their present conscious experience, that their acquaintance with him should come to a complete and full knowledge of God, a satisfying fellowship with God, and with his One and Only Son (John 15:11; 16:20-

---

[2]Cf. Chadwick, The Way to Pentecost, 1932, 110-111.

[3] *The New International Version*. (John 10:10) (2011). Zondervan.

[4] Arndt, W., Danker, F. W., Bauer, W., & Gingrich, F. W. (2000). *A Greek-English lexicon of the New Testament and other early Christian literature* (3rd ed.). Chicago: University of Chicago Press, 805.

22; 17:13, cf. Luke 10:21; John 3:29; Rom. 14:17).[5] For John the apostle, that was the theme of the opening of his first epistle, that his disciples might enter with one another into satisfying and fulfilling fellowship with God, and experience the full joy it implied (1 John 1:1-7). Jesus' high priestly prayer just before his crucifixion, makes this explicit when he rehearsed to the Father that life was to *know the one and true God and the one he had sent, Jesus Christ (*John 17:3).[6] To know (γινώσκωσι), here, probably emphasizes the experience of coming to know something or someone through acquaintance, exposure, or interaction. It is experiential and experimental knowledge of God and of Christ through a close relationship and fellowship.[7] In his epistles, Paul emphasizes *knowing* and *understanding* God, where in his opening remarks in Ephesians, he expresses his aspiration that his readers might know and understand God, his wisdom and provision for them (cf. Eph. 1:8-10, 15-23; Col. 1:9-12). For Paul, the purpose and goal of coming to know God was for knowledge and fellowship to deepen and increase over time, indeed into eternity (cf. Phil. 3:8-11).

To the Philippians, Paul remarks that his goal was to know Christ by sharing in his suffering so that at the coming of the Lord, he might also know the power of God in resurrection with Christ, and to be found having the righteousness of Christ impressed upon his life and character (Phil. 3:12-14). This was something he had already begun engaging through faith and obedience, and in his fellowship with God who was

---

[5] Arndt, 2000, 828.
[6] Γινώσκω here implies the acquisition of knowledge, coming to know God and Christ, who are the personal objects of the verb. Life consists in getting to know or coming to know God, in the sense of developing a deeper relationship with him over time (cf. Arndt, W., Danker, F. W., Bauer, W., & Gingrich, F. W. (2000). *A Greek-English lexicon of the New Testament and other early Christian literature* (3rd ed.). Chicago: University of Chicago Press, 200-201).
[7] Cf. Arndt, 2000, 199.

already at work in him. But he freely admitted he had not yet experienced it fully in the way he anticipated in the eschaton. He anticipated a greater degree of knowledge of God and a deeper experience of fellowship with God in eternity, of which his present experience was merely a beginning or a foretaste (Phil. 3:12). For Paul, walking in the Spirit now meant that the glorious life of the coming eschaton had already begun in the present, of which it was a downpayment or preemptive experience in anticipation of the fullness yet to come (Eph. 1:13; 14; 4:30, cf. Rom. 8:23; Cor. 5:5). Although he had already come to know God, he anticipated his experience of God exploding into a deeper and fuller knowledge of God on the day of the Lord.

Nevertheless, Paul implies that there was not a *qualitative* difference in his experience of God through the Spirit in the present, and life following the return of Christ. He excepted its extent and magnitude to increase exponentially into eternity in terms of depth and intimacy with God, beginning with an explosive resurrection. However, he considered himself to have already gained access to this new life through faith and the grace of God because of justification and reconciliation, and especially through his experience of the power and indwelling of the Spirit (cf. Rom. 5-8). It was not length of life Paul celebrated as the *gift of eternal life,* but its expanding quality in connection to his relationship and fellowship with God in eternity. By the same token, Paul saw his present life and experience of God to be essentially made of the same *substance*, bearing the same nature and properties as the life he anticipated in the future at the return of Christ, and so he characterized his experience of the indwelling Spirit as a foretaste of that life, a downpayment or deposit, guaranteeing the full realization of its future fullness when Christ comes (Eph. 1:13-14; 2 Cor. 1:20-22; 5:5).

Eternal life is not merely everlasting existence for Paul, but possessing and enjoying a quality of conscious knowledge of God, and experiencing a relationship with him that consists of close fellowship, mutually appreciated, interactive, and loving, with rich shared communion (cf. Gen. 17:7; Ex. 6:7; 25:8; 29:45-46; Lev. 11:45; 15:31; 22:33; 25:38; 26:11-12; Num. 15:41; 35:34; Deut. 12:5; 29:13; Ps. 27:4; 101:6; Isa. 51:16; Jer. 11:4; 30:22; 31:31-34; 32:38; Ezek. 11:19-20; 14:11; 34:30; 36:28; 37:23, 27; Hos. 1:9-11; Hag. 2:5; Zech 2:11; 8:8; Rom. 8:14-17; 2 Cor. 6:16; Heb. 8:18; John 1:14; Rev. 21:1-7). Such a life engaged in the present produces intimacy with God, that Jesus calls *unity* in his high-priestly prayer prior to his crucifixion. Unity with God is fellowship. It is no more mysterious than that. It is a relationship with him to which no interruption and disruption can be or will be admitted. We become one with God when we live in fellowship and harmony with him.

Jesus went on to say that unity also admits fellowship and harmony between his disciples. An important sign of harmony with God and fellowship with him is similar mutual love and fellowship between the saints, one that admits no interruption or disruption (John 17:20-26). Life, then in the New Testament sense, consists not of existence, but of a relational quality and worthwhileness of intimacy and fellowship with God through Jesus Christ, and that is begun now, in the present, through the indwelling Spirit (John 1:4, 9, 12, 14-18; 14:9-11). We are called through faith in Christ, Paul says, to live in fellowship and communion with God, and this is the definition of new life, of living (1 Cor. 1:9; 3:16; 2 Cor. 6:14-18; 13:14; Eph. 2:22; 3:17, cf. 1 John 1:3, 6, 7; Rev. 21:3). Jesus was undoubtedly concerned about the quality of his disciples' experience of the new life he was offering them through the gospel (John 10:10), and that it should culminate in their coming to know God in an ongoing, deepening relationship (John 17:20-26). For Jesus, salvation was not about getting to heaven as much as it was getting to know God in genuine and growing intimacy. So, just as he called God *Father*, he encouraged his followers to develop a similar intimacy with God (cf. Matt. 6:9).

Everywhere in the New Testament, believers are challenged concerning the quality of their faith, their joy, their spiritual lives, their commitment to God, their conduct, their maturity, and progress toward fully developed, mature godliness. As well as their relationship to God, believers are encouraged to have right attitudes toward one another, and to serve one another out of genuine and sincere love (cf. 2 Cor. 6:6; 1 Tim. 1:5; 1 Pet. 1:22). These are qualities of the newly transformed life arising from salvation. No one reading the Bible objectively and with sensitivity, could possibly conclude that the quality of one's life morally, spiritually, or physically for that matter, is somehow incidental to God's concerns. The quality of Christian living is at the core of what it means to be a disciple of Christ, to being saved. That quality of life is wrapped up in knowing God, obeying him, serving him, and pleasing him, all while also loving and serving others (cf. 1 John 1:5-10; 2:4; 3:4-10; 4:7-8; 5:18). The life of the believer is not so concerned with duration as much as with its quality.[8]

Part of the character of new life in Christ consists in righteousness, the moral and upright quality of the nature of God reflected in the life and disposition of the disciples of Jesus Christ. Holiness was from the start God's commission to Adam and Eve, and an essential part of the relationship by which, in partnership with God, they were to reflect his image and likeness back into creation as his representatives (Gen. 1:26-28). This was to take place in the temporal and physical sphere of their lives and existence, and it is at the heart of the psalmist's observation that God made man lower than the angels, but crowned him with glory,

---

[8] Cf. Chadwick, The Way to Pentecost, 1932, 110-111.

because he invested his rule and purposes in humanity as his emissaries and ambassadors (Ps. 8:1-9, cf. Gen. 1:26-28). To represent God, human beings must accurately reflect the character and nature of God as they rule in his behalf. Under the terms of the new covenant, Paul reengages this idea in a number of passages, in what has been traditionally called the *imago Dei.* He reminded the Romans that the real goal of justification is to be conformed to image of God's Son, Christ Jesus (Rom. 8:29-30). And in Philippians he reminded his readers that they were lights in a darkened sky, among a perverse and crooked generation of people opposed to the rule of God (Phil. 2:14-16). These themes then converge at the intersection of important notions of righteousness and holiness, and form part of God's purposeful plan for fallen humanity. They are not incidental. Rather, at the heart of God's purposes and redemptive work, righteousness and holiness are critical for humanity, at first for the sake of the restored relationship at justification, where pardon is required for reconciliation. Second, they are also essential for ongoing fellowship with God because sin alienates from God, and those waking in darkness cannot claim to enjoy fellowship with him (cf. Rom. 5:1-2; 1 John 1:5-9). Third, God's plan is for those who belong to him to resume their role as his representatives to creation, and to eventually rule with Christ in the future ages (Rom. 8:15-17).

Paul challenged the notion rather strongly, that someone who had come to justifying and reconciling faith in God through Christ might henceforth trade on the grace of God, and continue to live in habitual sinning (Rom. 6:1-2, 15). So, begins a long discourse on what has sometimes been called *sanctification*, a life of consistent moral and spiritual uprightness that reflects the moral character and nature of God in the disposition, character, and conduct of the those who have been saved and claim to belong to him. The exercise of God's grace in justification does not clear the decks for the believer in Christ to go on living in habitual sin (Rom. 6:1-2), or to return to the sinning of the old life. In other words, is justification a morally transformative reconciliation to God through grace and faith? Can salvation exist without having a profound effect on the disposition, character and conduct of those who have put their faith in Christ, or as Paul prefers, are now (relocated) *in Christ* (Rom. 5:1-11; 6:1-10, cf. 1 Cor. 6:21; 2 Cor. 5:17)?

Such changes to the inner environment of the heart and nature arising from justification and regeneration are bound to affect disposition and conduct, Paul concluded, and must result in new life. The conditions following morally-transformative justification are bound to produce a definitive inner moral transformation, which must be followed up by a new moral impetus through the indwelling Spirit (Rom. 8:1-17). Salvific changes, Paul maintains, are not just positional ones; when faith in Christ is initially exercised, they involve a death of the old life and a resurrection to new life morally and spiritually (Rom. 6:1-11; 2 Cor. 5:17; Eph. 4:22-24).[9] These are critical ideas that John and Charles Wesley grappled with in a pessimistic Reformation theological environment, where at the heart of the conversation was the question of to what extent are we to expect holiness in the life of the believer? In terms of the new life that proceeds from justification, there is bound to be an effect on conduct and lifestyle, because there has, in fact, been a change made to nature, Paul argues, with the goal of producing righteousness of character, as well as of *practical* godliness as conduct (Rom. 6:3-4, cf. 2 Cor. 5:17). Both the justification *and moral change* are the grounds upon which the relationship with God moves forward and deepens, with right character affecting right conduct. It begins with an initial transformative work of Christ in justification, but it is continued

---

[9] Paul's logic undercuts the debate over positional or imputed righteousness versus imparted righteousness. Paul says yes, both.

spiritually and morally through the activity of the Spirit in us (cf. Rom. 6-8). Salvation, then, will and must produce a change in behavior and character, and consists not merely of a change of position with God. It will affect conduct in very practical ways because of a changed nature, but it should also go on to develop integrity of character as a result of maturing godliness (cf. Eph. 4:12-16).

The basis for Paul's repudiation of a hypothetical believer remaining ethically unchanged after coming to know Christ consists in the moral and spiritual transformation inherent in justification, where there has been an exercise of God's grace on account of faith – the result is not only reconciliation to God, but a new creation, a new person raised by the Spirit to new life (Rom. 5:1-2; 6:1-18; 2 Cor. 5:17). No one coming to Christ is morally and spiritually the same person they used to be before coming to know him. Therefore, life, its conduct, and its habits must, and inevitably will change.

Once reconciled to God, there is potential for an ongoing relationship with him, growing in intimacy. Paul argues that at the most fundamental level a call to live in resurrection newness, forsaking and leaving the old life of sin behind to embrace a new life of holiness, with resolute and decisive faith, is fundamental to justification (being made right with God) (Rom. 6:11-14). Justification is far more than a mere change in status or position with God. By positively embracing Christ with decisive faith, Paul envisions that the old life controlled by sinful desires crucified with Christ, and a new life of holiness and righteousness brought into existence through a personal experience of resurrection with Christ (Rom. 6:1-14, cf. Rom. 5:3-7; 2 Cor. 5:16-17).[10] The result, then, is a radical change in lifestyle and behavior for the one who has come to know God through Christ. In this world, they are bound

---

[10] Cf. Noel Brooks Fingertip Holiness, 3-15.

to exhibit the holiness of God through right conduct as evidence of a transformed nature (cf. Matt. 5:13-15; Gal. 5:16-25).

In his letters, Paul often explains the role of the Spirit. Those who have come to know Christ now surrender to his leading and make use of their bodies differently (1 Cor. 6:19-20). They go on to righteousness (obedience to God) through the leading of the Spirit (Rom. 6:11-23; Gal. 5:16-25). Paul's overarching thesis concerning the life of the believer, which shows up continually in his epistles, is that as a result of pursuing righteousness consistently and habitually (through the leading of and active surrender to the Spirit), God will perfect godliness or holiness in them as character and disposition, leading to final, fully mature godliness, while more immediately resulting in godly conduct in the present age (Rom. 6:15-23; 8:1-17; Gal. 5:13-22; Eph. 4:11-16; Co. 3:1-11).[11]

Paul sees grace in Romans 5:1-2, as something in which we "now stand." It is the new spiritual environment of operations for soul and life after believing in Christ. In this new environment, the believer is capable of producing the fruit of righteousness through daily living, ethical practice, right conduct, and maturing character – this will result over time, through building inner integrity, in the uprightness of the righteous man. It is an idea first anticipated in the Old Testament under the law, but now fully revealed and made possible through the Spirit, resulting in the possibility of actively maturing godliness for the saints.[12] It is Paul's

---

[11] Cf. Wright, N. T. *After You Believe*.

[12] Paul's statement is emphatic, in that he alludes to the new state in which they find themselves through justification by faith, as "having access to grace in which they are standing" (δι᾽ οὖ καὶ τὴν προσαγωγὴν ἐσχήκαμεν τῇ πίστει εἰς τὴν χάριν ταύτην ἐν ᾗ ἑστήκαμεν). With respect to their new lives in Christ, those who have been justified through faith in Christ, now have peace with

application of the new covenant promised by God in Jeremiah (31:31-34), linked to Ezekiel's cleansing from sin and the removal of the old heart of stone, to be replaced by a new heart and new S(s)pirit (Ezek. 32:22-28). [13] Paul's new covenant theology of justification, moral transformation, and subsequent right conduct and obedience to God, followed by the impartation of the Spirit, is clearly rooted in the prophetic promises found in Jeremiah and Ezekiel, which he ties to the advent of Christ's death and resurrection. In Pauline theology, the death and resurrection of Christ, as well as the impartation of the Holy Spirit, whom Christ also promised his disciples upon his departure, are the means by which God fulfilled his earlier promises and predictions to his old covenant people.

The environment of grace in Romans 5:1-2 is expanded by Paul in the logic of his argument in Romans 5-8 beyond morally transformative justification, to embrace the power and presence of the indwelling Spirit in the life of the believer. By way of analogy, the temple, where God dwelled among his people, to be their God and they his people, God now dwells with, among, and in the lives of his people who have surrendered to Christ by faith, so that even their physical bodies may legitimately be called the *temple of God* (1 Cor. 3:16-17; 1 Cor. 6:19; 2 Cor. 6:16). God no longer dwells in a temple constructed by Israel, but among his people, and in them personally because of the terms of the new covenant. His indwelling presupposes and builds on a personal inner change to the moral environment of those who are saved, in terms of their attitude and nature (Jer. 31:31-24). Paul went further to say that not

---

God as a result, and stand and live in a new environment of grace, where the power and freely given provision and resources of God is constantly accessible to them in order to assist and equip them go on to Christian growth and the development of godly character.

[13] Cf. Fee G. D., 1994, 14-32.

only does God dwell among his people, as in his temple, but he dwells in them personally, that is in their bodies, their inner personal lives, and in their nature so that their bodies become his temple through the Holy Spirit (1 Cor. 3:16-17; 6:15, 19 2 Cor. 6:16). God's presence through the Spirit indwells the personal and daily lives of the saints who are sanctified by the grace of God in Christ, thereby producing obedience and right conduct (Rom. 8:1-4; Gal. 5:16-25).

The great hope for the future, for those who persevere in their experience of salvation, is that one day God will produce the full quality of godliness in them that reflects his own righteousness and holiness (Rom. 5:3-5; 8:29-30; 1 Cor. 1:8; 15:2, 58; 2 Cor. 1:24; Gal. 5:1; Eph. 4:13-16, 22-24; Phil. 2:14-16; 3:7-11; Col. 1:9-14, 21-23, 28-29; 2:6-7; 3:1-4; cf. Gen. 1:26-28; Heb. 3:6; 6:11, 19; 1 Pet. 1:13). Paul claims that the outworking of grace in the lives of those who are justified and reconciled to God by grace will ultimately produce character, mature godliness, and that developing character gives rise to hope for the consummation of the purpose of God for which they were redeemed and reconciled to him in the first place (Rom. 5:4-5; 8:18-25; 28-30, cf. Gal. 5:5, 22-24). It is because they are saved by grace, and then empowered to live a holy life in and by the indwelling Spirit, that not only is initial salvation critical, but the ongoing sanctification of God's people by grace is paramount. If holiness ultimately comes about by the provision of God through the activity of the Spirit, it is by grace that their character and conduct are perfected, and not by works. Salvation then is by grace/faith first to last (Rom. 1:17). This is what Paul means by standing in grace after initially being reconciled to God by grace (Rom. 5:1-2). For Paul, *hope* in the present anticipates the full realization of what awaits us in terms of God's ultimate plans for his redeemed people (Rom. 8:18-24a, 24b-c, 25). And that plan is to raise the moral and spiritual renewal and reformation of those who are in Christ to the level of mature godliness in the context of a deepening and ongoing fellowship with him in eternity.

Paul is explicit in Romans 8 about the nature of this hope, that it is the expectation of the future culmination of a present process involving the development of hope-raising character (Rom. 5:1-11). The process of maturing godly character gives rise to hope for its future full realization. It anticipates final consummation of our salvation in terms of the redemption of our physical bodies, bringing to full realization what the present moral and spiritual transformation of initial salvation and its ongoing development promises, and that the gift of the indwelling Spirit guarantees (Rom. 8:14-17; 22-25; 29-30; Eph. 1:13-14; 2 Cor. 1:20-22; 5:5, cf. 1 Cor. 15:50-58). Resurrection, according to the New Testament, will bring together the final perfection of body and character in the believer, in order that God might reflect his holiness and righteousness back into his creation through them (Rom. 8:19, 29-30), which is what he originally intended at creation (cf. Gen. 1:26-28).[14] Speaking of the consummation of salvation in our bodily resurrection, and of final mature godliness, Paul reminds the Ephesians they will spend eternity discovering and coming to a greater understanding of the love of God, in terms of its infinite dimensions in every conceivable direction, as well as the glorious riches available to the saints even now through Christ by the Spirit, but unveiled even more perfectly and freely in the eschaton (Eph. 1:7-10, 17-23; 3:7-12, 14-19). It will be a fellowship with God we presently have no capacity to imagine. In this way, the consummation of character development and bodily resurrection are bound up in God plans for an ongoing and eternal fellowship with his people, a fellowship that involves an experience of a growing and deepening knowledge of God, and appreciation of him throughout eternity.

Paul links the hope for the consummation of salvation not only to the resurrection of the body, but to the development of the integrity of

---

[14] Cf. (Beale, We Become What We Worhip: A Biblical Theology of Idolatry, 2008).

character into mature and final godliness that reflects the holiness of God (Rom. 5:4-5; 8:29-30; 2 Cor. 3:18; Eph. 3:10-13, Ps. 8:6-11). It is critical not to overlook this aspect of Paul's soteriology (theology of salvation). Elsewhere, in his epistles, Paul, in agreement with the New Testament generally, makes the point that the consummation of salvation relies on faith remaining fully engaged until the end of the process, and not on merely making an initial confession of faith (cf. Matt. 24:13; Mark 13:13; 1 Cor. 1:8; Gal. 6:9; Phil. 1:6; 2 Tim. 2:12; Heb. 3:6, 14; 6:11; 12:25; 1 Pet. 1:9). Salvation comes to its completion in and for those who exercise their faith in Christ *until the end* (cf. 2 Tim. 4:6-8). A consummation of faith leading to bodily resurrection is joined to a similar consummation of faith in terms of mature godliness, the full expression of the righteousness that God is looking for in his people (cf. Rom. 8:1-4, 29-30; Gal. 5:22-25; Eph.4:13-16). The future resurrection of the body depends, therefore, on faith remaining engaged until the end, when the maturity and godliness that God desires for his people reach their final and full expression through the Spirit (cf. Gal. 5:5:16-25).

The kind of eternal life God has in mind consists of his people engaging in fellowship and partnership with God in his eternal enterprises (Rev. 21:3-4, cf. Isa. 6:7a; John 14:3b; 1 Thess. 4:17b; Rev. 19:4, 6). But this kind of life requires holiness and righteousness of character, a removing of every impediment to the ongoing relationship with God (Heb. 12:10). This is what the writer of Hebrews meant when he said without holiness no one will see God (Heb. 10:14). He did not refer to a *discrete experience of initial sanctification,* but of character forged in us by God through the Holy Spirit applying the saving and sanctifying power of the cross to us, as well as Jesus' resurrection (Rom. 6:1-11). Salvation initiates this new life through transformative justification, but it must go on to the development of maturing character, with its goal to ultimately break into a full expression of godliness at the return of Christ (Rom. 8:22-24, cf. 1 John 1:7-2:2; 3:1-3). We were designed to reflect that godliness of God back into his creation as his representatives (Gen. 1:26-28). Transformative justification is the first step, growth and development in holiness is the process that follows, and resurrection or glorification is the consummation of it, in terms of both physical body and character (cf. Phil. 1:6; 3:8-14). In other words, salvation is telic, oriented toward a goal, to bring believers to full spiritual and moral maturity, where final resurrection to a new glorified body and eternal fellowship with God will become its fullest expression and greatest fulfillment (Rom 8:29-30; Phil. 3:8-14; Rev. 21:1-7).

The purpose of God, then, his goal for salvation, is far higher than "getting to heaven," whatever that means to some people. Our narrow view of what heaven might be like under the covenant of a new heaven and new earth is sometimes laughably small and shallow. The scope of God's future purposes, while beyond the purview of this book to discuss in detail, is immense and certainly overruns the boundaries of typical western, Christian thinking or many of the sermons we typically hear about heaven, death, resurrection, and eternal life. For this reason, we want to take a close look at the hints given to us in a passage in Paul's epistle to the Ephesians, where he remarks that the new man, his view of which he fully lays out in Romans 6, has been created after the likeness and image of God (Eph. 4:22-24). Paul's statement implies that there is a new state of existence and life that God has implanted in those who have been reconciled to God by grace, and that he intends to develop its characteristics to its fullest expression and realization in preparation for the eschaton and beyond.

CHAPTER ONE

PAUL'S EPISTLE TO THE EPHESIANS

Students of the New Testament, and not a few preachers, are sometimes guilty of jumping into a passage of scripture without considering its context, not literarily nor historically. Paul's letter to the Ephesians, like other epistles found in the New Testament, is occasional. It has a context, and that context is important to a proper understanding of what Paul intended to say when he wrote. He wrote for a specific purpose, and to address specific people and circumstances. Without at least some appreciation for the historical context of Paul's letters and how they are composed, it is likely that we will find ourselves arriving at conclusions about their meaning and application that says more about our imagination than his intention, or the intention of the Holy Spirit when he inspired what Paul set down on paper. We assume that Paul wrote purposefully, that his epistles are intentional, and self-consciously communicate meaning, correction, instruction, and teaching about the issues, situations, people, and circumstances he addresses.

Most of the time, his letters are transparently clear. Paul rarely shrinks from naming names or calling out the offending parties. For that reason, we are hardly in the dark about what Paul is addressing most of the time, even if the minutiae are sometimes a little murky. For us to benefit from what God intended to say through Paul, some 2,000 years later, we'll need to pay attention to those historical contexts, so that we do not twist or apply what Paul says differently than the Spirit intended when Paul wrote. For us this is a safeguard against misapplying scripture or reading into it meaning that is not there, and was not intended by God in the first place. In reading scripture, we must ask first, what did the writer intended to say to his original audience, and what would they have understood by what he said or wrote. Our application of scripture to our own Christian lives and circumstances must be consistent with its original and intended meaning, otherwise we will violate God's word, or worse, make it say what we want it to say and mean.[15]

Furthermore, Paul's letters are characteristically well-argued, often depending on cascading logic coming to clear and well-supported conclusions. For this reason, we must pay attention to the literary context, how arguments flow, and the overall effect of his letters on theology, if we are to come to right conclusions about what Paul intended to say in some particular passage. Since, as many grammarians argue, the Greek of the New Testament communicates meaning mainly through the paragraph or periscope, and not through isolated words, phrases, clauses, or sentences, it is extremely important to understand how a particular periscope functions as part of the whole, and then how the elements of the pericope work together to communicate meaning. In summary, it is vitally important to have some understanding of the historical background to each New Testament book we are studying, and of its flow, purpose, and conclusions, as well as of how the various elements work and function together to advance their message and meaning. We seek at first the author's intended meaning before we make an application to ourselves or our circumstances, not to mention before we develop doctrine and theology.

This line of reasoning does, of course, beg the question, why are we so concerned with the author's intended meaning? In every attempt to

---

[15] This reversal, reading back into the text our "sense" of what it means, or layering different levels of meaning, as with Origen, and the early church, is what leads to theological and doctrinal error, disputes, and wrong practice.

communicate, whether spoken or written, the originator assumes that the receptor desires to comprehend *their intended meaning*. We do not ordinarily engage in communication with the intention of leaving the interpretation of meaning open to the receptor. On the contrary, we fully intend for the receptor to comprehend our intended meaning, especially when it is critical or urgent. If someone shouts, "The place in on fire!" in a concert hall, it is critical to know what the context of the remark is, so that, if necessary, we might immediately evacuate the building, rather than interpret the warning as an observation on the quality of the music, or musician's skill! We do this instinctively and without much thought most of the time and unconsciously look for intended meaning from context. Indeed, we are confused by communication without context, because without it, it is hard to discern the intended meaning, which we assume is inherent in the communication itself.

If we are to have meaningful interaction with the Bible, we must assume God *intends* to communicate something objectively meaningful about himself, his intentions, his requirements, about salvation, and our responsibilities or expected response to him. Under no circumstances are we free to make up the meaning, or interpret the Bible without regard to his intention, not if we want an accurate knowledge of God. The number of Bibles that have been created around contemporary agendas, and that dial back or paper over traditional theologies of sin, judgment, wrath, the need for salvation, as well as other doctrines distasteful to "enlightened" western humanity, are testaments to this latter impulse, and instinctively we know that they have violated the rules of good communication to make nonsense of what God intended to say to us.

Human interaction through any means of communication would utterly break down, and relationships would be impossible, if meaning is entirely self-derived, and disconnected from the intention of the originator. In every act of communication, whether as originator or receptor, on both sides we take for granted that there is intention on the part the one who seeks to convey something important to the receptor. This meaning, from the communicator's perspective, is important enough to be properly and accurately understood, or else there is no reason to communicate it in the first place. As I write this book, these principles are at work, because I feel like what I have to say about holiness is worth saying and being understood by others as I have understood it myself. Of course, the receptor will need to evaluate what I write, and decide whether I succeed or am accurate.

Without understanding the intended meaning of the communicator, the act of communication fails. Therefore, theories of derived and entirely subjective imputation of meaning to communication fail, and produce nonsense with no objective value, and that bear no relationship to the author's original intention. They fail because they eliminate the essential element of authorial intention as part of the successful transfer of meaning from one person to another. Transfer of meaning is the central purpose and object of communication. Communication, by definition, is the transfer of meaning. As an act, communication is a two-sided affair, with one party originating the communication and another party receiving it. The goal of the process is that the intended meaning of the originating party might be understood, and properly comprehended by the receiving party. If the receptor may take the originator's words and interpret them freely or construe them as they wish, then communication has *not occurred* at all, and the intended meaning of the originator is lost. Whatever has happened at that point, it is no longer communication. If we want to understand Paul's perspective on salvation and holiness, then we have to comprehend his meaning, and by extrapolation, the intended meaning of God, who through the Spirit inspired his words and the content of what he had to say (1 Tim. 3:16-17, cf. 1 Pet. 1:19-21).

PAUL'S INTENTION

Paul's purpose for his epistles, some may think, are merely religious pedantry, holding forth generalities concerning the Christian faith and belief in God. Rather, the apostle seeks to communicate truth with instruction to his readers and hearers, and to affect a response from them in connection with his intended meaning. In other words, his epistles are occasional, something has come up that has elicited Paul's desire to write and to provide help, guidance, instruction, correction, encouragement, or occasionally a rebuke. We see this especially when Paul is correcting problems in his churches or setting up an offering that he intends to take back to Jerusalem. In those contexts, he seeks to persuade them to adopt a viewpoint, course of action, to take a position on an issue, to believe something, or to lay something aside. In order for Paul to accomplish this, he must successfully convey, through his letter, his intended meaning, and the receptor must accurately apprehend that meaning and respond to it appropriately, by complying, or reordering their conduct or behavior, and meeting his expectations. If Paul is to feel like he has accomplished his intended purpose for preaching and writing, the response of his readers and churches must conform to Paul's instruction by complying with the meaning of what he has communicated. In a stunning example of Paul's vulnerability, Paul wonders at the reception of his first letter to the Corinthians, and how they had received it. Did they accurately comprehend his concerns? In his second letter he muses and reflects on his apprehension, that maybe they had *not* received it well, had taken it wrongly or badly (2 Cor. 7:1-16). He hoped they would not misunderstand his motives, or understand his meaning imperfectly, and reject it and him as their apostolic leader. First and Second Corinthians give us insight into Paul's expectations when writing to his churches.

Finally, Paul declared success for his first epistle to the Corinthians, when in the second epistle, after some initial doubt about how they at first might have received it (2 Cor. 7:6-7, 13-16). He struggled to explain his bold tone toward them, that it was not as an angry, authoritative leader he confronted them, but as a father who is concerned for his children (cf. 1 Cor. 4:15-17; 2 Cor. 10:1-2). His boldness in seeking to correct the problems in Corinth required a straightforward communication style, which Paul hoped would not be rejected. Paul feared he might come across as overbearing and be rejected by his readers. What Paul did not expect was that the Corinthians would *misunderstand* the meaning of that he said. On the contrary, he was afraid that the meaning would be so plain, that they would be offended, and his instruction might be rejected in favor of the more easy-going teaching and approaches of the "super-apostles", who seemed to have gained some traction among them (2 Cor. 10:7-11:11). They fully understood to what he was referring, and might well feel that he was interfering too closely in the affairs of the church, and some even expressed that he was acting too heavy-handedly (2 Cor. 10:1-2), particularly now that they had formed new relationships with those itinerate leaders whose outward style seemed to appeal to some of them more favorably (2 Cor. 11:12-18; 12:5-11). He feared their response might be to reject his plain talk, and even more, his plain meaning. He did not sugar-coated any of it. It was not a misunderstanding Paul feared, but that his Corinthian readers would understand him all too well, including his invectives over certain practices in the church community.

At the time he began writing, Paul had been anxious to hear from Titus about how things had gone since receiving his earlier, corrective missive (2 Cor. 2:12-13, 7:6, 13). When he heard affirmation of their love toward him, acceptance of Paul's apostleship, and that they had endeavored to comply with his instructions, he was greatly relieved and overjoyed (2 Cor. 7:5-13). They had understood Paul and responded positively to his message. Paul went on to explain the strategy of his first letter, that he intended the letter to shake them up, to cause them to respond to his correction with sincere godly sorrow (2 Cor. 7:8-13). Paul relied on the Corinthians to fully appreciate, not only his meaning, but the tone of the communication, and the apostolic authority that stood behind it. Yet he hoped they would also perceive the deep love from which it originated. The Corinthians we supposed to discriminate not only the meaning of Paul's words, but the nuances of purpose and motivation behind them, that the letter was designed to be both corrective *and* loving.

It would have done Paul no good at all to write them obscurely, mysteriously, in riddles, or with enigmatic propositions. To do so would defeat his purpose and make reconciliation impossible. The key to Paul's letters in general, and to the Corinthian church in particular, is an accurate understanding of his meaning, to be clearly perceived from the contextual/occasional nature of Paul's written communication, with respect to the issues and circumstances he addressed. Without that, the letter would have at best been ineffective, at worst it might have sealed the fate of the relationship between them. We see in the Corinthian letters, and in the letter to the Galatians some of Paul's most passionate defense of his gospel, and aspects of the life and practice of the church. In both cases, it is clear communication of his intended meaning that carries the purpose of the letter and elicits an appropriate response.

For this reason, with Paul's letters and the Bible generally, a collection of writings about by God about himself, we are fully justified in assuming two things. First, the writers intend to communicate their understanding of God from the events that occurred in their experience and in the course of coming to know God as a result. Secondly, these writers framed their communication in ways that it might reflect their God-centered worldview, their knowledge of God from his revelation of himself to them, and that this revelation that came about in the context of their circumstances in time, geography, culture, ancestry, and tradition. If we are to go back and fully appreciate what it is that God revealed, and what the writers then communicated to us in that historical context, we must seek to know something of that background and context, or at least have a fundamental grasp of it.

Another component to scriptural communication is what we call literary style. Each writer betrays a unique personal style by how he writes, the vocabulary he uses, his grammatical competency, and the adoptive style of the communication (poetry, prose, narrative, gospel, letter, wisdom literature, etc.). This requires the contemporary reader to pay attention to how things are phrased, how the entire work or sections of it are structured, arranged, and interdependent on one another, because the flow of the thing as a whole helps to carry the overall meaning, and that in turn affects the meaning of the constituent parts. Some part of a biblical book cannot be lifted out and correctly understood without reference to the parts around it, or the flow of the entire book. Biblical books reflect various levels of literary or academic competency, and exhibit characteristic personal style in communication that reflects the personality of the writer. In which case, where we have more than one work from the same author, we might expect some consistency in characteristics and modes of expression. These can be compared to shed light on difficult passages or turns of phrase.

However, we must remember that occasions for writing may betray a difference in approach, even by the same writer, and such differences, all things being equal, are not a reason to reject the authorship of a particular book, as is sometimes done with the traditionally ascribed letters of Paul and Johannine writings. A writer may adapt or alter his style, and may even change modes of expression as time passes, especially as in Paul's case when more than two decades are involved from the earliest to the latest letters. The occasion and purpose of writing may indeed cause a writer to adopt a different style, forms of expression, or elicit differences in framework and approach, just as contemporary writers may write in a variety of styles, depending on their purpose or chosen literary genre. All this being said, internal literary considerations are important to consider when seeking to understand the meaning of the text, and authorship is critical for mapping theology.

Biblical writers wrote from their own worldview, historical circumstances, geography, culture, ancestry, and traditions, which differ significantly from our own contemporary, western literary forms. As a result, we cannot assume automatically that we understand their meaning, without taking care not to view their communications cavalierly, through the lens of *our* personal experience, time, geography, and culture, and assuming that it surely could not be that different from our own. Comprehending New Testament communication will fail to the extent our determination or lack thereof, to closely examine its meaning with these considerations in mind. Our goal ultimately is to understand the author's intended meaning because it is through the inspired author God had communicated the revelation of himself to us.

To be guilty of reading back into biblical communication what *we* think and how *we* view God or the world around us, rather than allowing the original writers to communicate what *they* wish for us to know about him, will only result in circular reasoning, that is reinforcing our own views, without giving us any confidence that we have discovered anything truly objective about God, or anything else for that matter. This is called *eisegesis* (reading meaning back into the text). We assume, therefore, that as students of Paul's letters, we are interested in what Paul has to say, and that we wish to clearly understand *his* meaning. That is our goal. This is called *exegesis,* deriving meaning *out of* or *from* the text. As faithful Bible students, we are not interested in a circular process that yields the product of *our own* views, prejudices, theology, and thinking, which we have read back into the text. We prefer to understand what the writers, inspired by God through the Spirit, sought to reveal and communicate to us about him from their unique and advantaged positions, because they were the eyewitnesses and ambassadors commissioned by God to pass on the truth revealed to them in their historical context (cf. 2 Tim. 3:16-17; 1 Pet. 1:10-12; 2 Pet. 1:16-21).

The essence of biblical interpretation is to discover the intended meaning of the text, that is, the author's meaning. The final step is to determine how it applies in our contemporary setting, or how we should react to its significance in our context, as contemporary readers. We can do this with the conviction when through the ancient writers and the preserved text, in which God has *chosen* to make himself known, we have confidence in the accuracy of the revelation, and that we properly understand what is being *communicated* by the Bible to us. In our context and consideration of Ephesians 4:17-24, we intend to apply these principles to the notions of *righteousness* and *holiness* found there. Whatever our understanding of these ideas right now, there ought to be openness to having them challenged, changed, or enlarged by a thoroughgoing investigation into the intended meaning of the text, and then a willingness to sincerely apply what we learn to our contemporary setting and lives. Our work then is set out before us. First, understand Paul. Second, consider how it might impact us with respect our lives and theology. Until that is done, we cannot possibly know what God is seeking from us. In that case, then, Paul's letter to the Ephesians as a whole is where we must start.

AUTHORSHIP

Questions about the Pauline authorship of Ephesians are relatively recent, dating from the late 18th century and gaining in popularity up through the early 20th century.[16] F. J. Long notes that doubt over Pauline authorship of Ephesians is relatively late, beginning with F. C. Baur's conjecture that it was written in the early second century.[17] "This claim [of Pauline authorship] is confirmed by the testimonies of Irenaeus, Origen, Polycarp, Tertullian, and Ignatius, who in his own epistle to the Ephesians alludes to the frequent and affectionate mention made by Paul of the Christian state, privileges, and persons of the Ephesians."[18] Why should we take a letter seriously as the revelation of God, that claims to be written by Paul, if in fact it is not? Authorship or claims to authorship are likely to be the first hurdle to having confidence in what has been written about God.

Some of the chief reasons for contesting Pauline authorship of Ephesians are listed by Wood in *The Expositor's Bible Commentary,* volume 11, on Ephesians. They are that Ephesians contains a style not characteristic of known Pauline epistles, what it shares in common with or where it overlaps Colossians, and that Ephesians contains *too much* material that is shared with other known epistles of Paul.[19] About a hundred words occur in no other Pauline letters, but they do occur in other New Testament books, and this is thought to demonstrate that Paul is not likely its author.[20] These factors have led some to conclude

---

[16] Wood, A. S. (1981). Ephesians. In F. E. Gaebelein (Ed.), *The Expositor's Bible Commentary: Ephesians through Philemon* (Vol. 11). Grand Rapids, MI: Zondervan Publishing House, 3.
[17] Long, F. J. (2016). Ephesians, Letter to the, Critical Issues. In J. D. Barry, D. Bomar, D. R. Brown, R. Klippenstein, D. Mangum, C. Sinclair Wolcott, ... W. Widder (Eds.), *The Lexham Bible Dictionary*. Bellingham, WA: Lexham Press.
[18] Elwell, W. A., & Comfort, P. W. (2001). In *Tyndale Bible dictionary* (p. 432). Wheaton, IL: Tyndale House Publishers.
[19] Wood, 1981, 6.
[20] Wood, 1981, 5, cf. Merkle B. L., 2016, 2.

that Ephesians is a compilation of known Pauline works, based mainly on Colossians.[21]

Another major factor for regarding Ephesians as not genuinely Pauline is the lack of personal references to the Ephesians themselves, such as are common in other known Pauline letters. Paul spent a great deal of time in Ephesus, several years, more than two (Acts 19:10). The closeness of the relationship that he had with the church and its leaders is eminently demonstrated in his farewell speech at Miletus, and the reaction of the elders to his assertion they would never see him again (Acts 20:17-38). Paul quite freely mentions people and addresses them in his letters, but in Ephesians, there is, it is thought, a conspicuous lack of such personal references and ending salutations.[22]

To these objections are added theological objections, that Ephesians represents theology of a more sophisticated kind than found in other epistles.[23] This argument is patently absurd because it assumes that the record of development in Paul's thought and understanding over time must necessarily be linear, not allowing for the fact that Paul may communicate principles of different complexity and sophistication on different occasions as circumstances require. It also assumes that theological sophistication, as we conceive it, forms the standard by which Paul's theological ideas are to be gauged. This is contemporary intellectual snobbery. It is also circular, in that it assumes that one or another of the features of Pauline theology cannot reflect his own thinking, because they do not reflect known Pauline theology in other epistles. For example, the similarity of the material in Ephesians with other known epistles is evidence of non-Pauline authorship. Plainly, these arguments demonstrate a certain amount of question-begging. It

---

[21] Merkle B. L., 2016, 2.
[22] Wood, 1981, 6.
[23] Wood, 1981, 6, cf. Merkle B. L., 2016, 2.

may well turn out that these are arguments *for* Pauline authorship. This objection is incoherent. Ben Merkel notes that arguments against Pauline authorship have been soundly answered by scholars.[24]

So, what is the case for Pauline authorship? First, Pauline authorship of Ephesians was accepted until the 18th century when questions were raised on *internal grounds* and not external witnesses. A. S. Wood notes that external, historical witness to Pauline authorship of Ephesians is "incontestable" and poses an "insurmountable barrier" to arguments from internal data.[25] He calls the evidence from vocabulary and style for Pauline authorship "impressive internal testimony."[26] He cites the *different themes addressed* in Ephesians as a reason for words not appearing elsewhere in the Pauline corpus.[27] Although Wood admits the style is somewhat different, he notes that Paul seems not to be addressing a particular church, that the letter shows evidence of being a general epistle, that may have been intended as a circular correspondence among the churches. This is a departure from Paul's other letters, which are personal and occasional. That Paul adopted a different style of writing, or mode of communication, or addresses a general audience, rather than a specific church or person, is not reason enough in itself to preclude Pauline authorship, or to cast suspicion on a letter that, does after all, contain a personal reference to ministry and administration of the gospel that is known from other undoubted Pauline epistles (cf. Eph. 3:1-13). Paul is making this claim about himself, and it would be a major discreditation of the epistle if the passage has been fabricated to give cover for pseudoanonymity.

---

[24] Merkle B. L., 2016, 4.
[25] Wood, 1981, 7.
[26] Wood, 1981, 7.
[27] Wood, 1981, 7.

There is no text-critical evidence to suggest that this letter ever did not bear the name of Paul, in the first, as its writer or that it bore another author's name. In a similar way, arguments made against Pauline authorship based on disputes over the recipients falls flat. Even if the destination, Ephesus, is disputed on textual grounds, the letter's claim to Pauline authorship from the earliest times is not. Doubt over the letter's destination does not automatically translate into doubt over its author. Indeed, if the early absence of references to Ephesus is grounds for throwing the letter's original destination and intended recipients into doubt, early and universal attestation to Pauline authorship should be grounds for confidence that he was indeed its writer. The opening (Παῦλος ἀπόστολος Χριστοῦ Ἰησοῦ διὰ θελήματος θεοῦ τοῖς ἁγίοις τοῖς οὖσιν) or similar openings is typical of known Pauline epistles, and no example of Ephesian from the earliest manuscripts omits it.

We note here some internal indications of Pauline authorship from content. For example, references to imprisonment and chains are similar to references found in Philippians and Colossians. The writer calls himself an "ambassador in chains" (πρεσβεύω ἐν ἁλύσει) (Eph. 6:20). Here he means that he is constrained by his circumstances as a prisoner for the sake of the gospel (τοῦ εὐαγγελίου ὑπὲρ οὗ). This is typical Pauline language when referring to his imprisonment for the gospel's sake (cf. Eph. 3:1; 4:1, 10; 6:20; Phil. 1:7, 13, 14, 16, 17; Col. 4:3, 18; 1 Tim. 1:8, 16; Philm 1, 9, 13, 23). Repeated imprisonment for the sake of the gospel was a particular characteristic of his apostolic ministry over against the other apostles. Paul "bragged" to the Corinthians that imprisonment was one of the signs of his genuine apostleship, serving as proof to overrule the claims of other "super apostles" who competed with him for the loyalty of the Corinthians, but who had not suffered the same level of inconvenience and deprivation for the sake of the gospel (cf. 2 Cor. 11-13). Being chained for the gospel was a self-conscious designation of his identity as a genuine apostle of Jesus Christ and a servant of God. This Pauline turn-of-phrase "in chains" is so characteristic of the apostle, it is tough to imagine anyone else making such a claim without being confused with Paul, in the absence of some other clarification of their identity (cf. Rom. 16:7; 2 Cor. 11:23). Certainly, we know of no one who, like Paul, at this time suffered such multiple imprisonments and beatings for the gospel, and who could make this "brag" as a confirmation of their identity and apostleship.

It would be disingenuous to add personal details like this into a letter that is a deliberate pseudonymous compilation of Pauline material, and to portray it as a genuine epistle. It would be deceptive on two counts, in the claim to Pauline authorship, and by attempting to give the impression that it is an authentic Pauline epistle by addressing a specific church and its current circumstances, in order to imitate a known Pauline letter to a congregation he planted. This sort of obfuscation is unworthy of works that were considered inspired scripture early on in church history. It is antithetical to what we know about the compilation of the New Testament, and how the early church operated. It seems doubtful that when the ancient church decided its canon, often based on apostolic authorship or association, that it overlooked serious concerns over Pauline authorship, and "accidently" passed over a pseudonymous work. Surely, if doubts or questions existed, they would have come up in the early church writings, and it is likely they would have disqualified Ephesians or put it into the same provisional acceptance as, say Hebrews or even Revelation. Ephesians was never considered one of the disputed epistles. It is, of course, the height of anachronistic snobbery to assume that we know better, from our vantage point of nearly 2,000 years after the fact, based on a "superior" *scientific approaches* and internal analysis of Ephesians, than those who knew Paul personally, or were disciples of those who did!

Surely, another mark of internal attestation to Pauline authorship is Paul's treatment of the theme of the mystery of the gospel, the knowledge of which he claims to be the *particular recipient by the ordination of God himself* (cf. Eph. 3:2-6, cf. Gal. 1:11-12). This is a quintessential Pauline claim, made by no other early apostles or writers. Being a claimant to a particular revelation of the gospel and to have knowledge of its mystery is uniquely Pauline. Not only that, but the nature of that mystery is described as the joint fellowship of Gentiles and Jews in redemption through Christ, by-passing the law and tradition of Israel. This is a theme that is repeated over and over in Paul's known letters.

The word *mystery* (ἐν τῷ μυστηρίῳ τοῦ Χριστοῦ)[28] is used 28 times in the New Testament, 27 of which are characteristically Pauline.[29] Paul was self-consciously called by God to be the apostle to the Gentiles, something that the church in Jerusalem recognized and endorsed with their blessing and commission (Ga. 2:6-10). Paul, above all the other letter writers, employs the notion of *mystery* to refer to hidden workings of God's redemptive plan under the old covenant, now revealed through the incarnation, death, and resurrection of Christ in the new covenant to his apostles and prophets in the early church (Eph. 3:5). The mystery consists in the hitherto unknown purpose of God to combine Jews and Gentiles under one plan of salvation through Christ, and to create from this unity one redeemed people for God. While Peter reaches for this idea in Acts 11, after his visit with Cornelius, it is Paul who develops the full theological implications of Gentile inclusion in salvation through faith in Jesus Christ. He does so in repeated explanations of the idea in

---

[28] Holmes, M. W. (2011–2013). *The Greek New Testament: SBL Edition* (Eph 3:4). Lexham Press; Society of Biblical Literature.
[29] (Burer & Miller, 2008), 365.

his known epistles, and that becomes an internal authenticating feature of his letters.

Ephesians clearly contains a supreme example of a Pauline excursion into the mystery of Gentile inclusion, and does not appear to be a disjointed or stitched in passage. Rather, it concludes a careful and reasonable argument for the basis of unity in the church that began in chapter one with God's purpose to unify all things in Christ, and where Jews and Gentiles both share fellowship in the one church, the body of Christ, as a result of their common faith in Christ (Eph. 2:1-11). All of this is consistent with what we know of the circumstances of Paul's ministry in Ephesus from Acts, where the church began with Jewish and Gentile believers, and soon after resistance arose from the Jews, Paul withdrew to a lecture hall, at which time Jewish and Gentile believers went with him (Acts 19:8-10). Riots broke out when enthusiasm for the gospel let to burning $12,650,000 worth of books, by today standards, because the gospel was growing so rapidly (Acts 19:19-20). The tensions with the Jews and Gentiles alike strained relationships between the communities, who sought a common enemy in Paul (Acts 19:32-34). It also testifies to a church born out of controversy and tensions, and this may have something to do with what we read later of Paul's instruction to Timothy concerning argumentations and philosophical wrangling among the members in Ephesus, and his warnings to the leaders at Miletus, all of which are consistent with an Ephesian provenance for this epistle, and help to mitigate claims that the letter shows no internal connection to the church as Ephesus.

Mystery, as a term, is characteristic of Paul, where he uses it 16 times in his epistles, including Ephesians. By *mystery*, throughout his writings, Paul refers either to the overall revelation of what was hidden before Christ's advent or aspects of God's redemptive purpose that have now been made clear since Christ's incarnation, death, and resurrection (Rom. 11:25; 16:25; 1 Cor. 2:7; 15:51; Eph. 1:9; 3:3, 4, 6, 9;

6:19; Col. 1:26-27; 2:2; 4:3; 1 Tim. 3:16). Ephesians is built around this theme and climaxes in chapter two with a theological statement about the church consisting of Jews and Gentiles sharing equally in the provision of salvation through Christ's crucifixion, and of the Spirit, so that there is unity in the church, which is the body of Christ (Eph. 2:11-4:16). These themes of unity, and the church as the body of Christ, with Christ as the head, are distinctly Pauline metaphors, characteristically Pauline analogies. They are among other features in Ephesians, like locative language "in Christ" or "in him", particularly in chapter 1, that are particularly Pauline in nature and style. These themes can be also found in the later letters, like Romans, as well as earlier letters like 1 and 2 Thessalonians and 1 Corinthians, probably written from Ephesus.

Ephesians does not show evidence of being "stitched" together from other Pauline material, where the seams would surely show. We might have expected to hear from the redaction critics at this point showing these supposed divisions, since they found such convincing evidence at one time in the gospels of such compilation. But of course, no compelling demonstration of these supposed divisions is forthcoming. The epistle does, in fact, hang together as a closely reasoned whole, with logic and style characteristic of other known Pauline epistles (long sentences with elided words, and scarcity of finite verbs). The extended opening in chapter one with one sentence composed of a series of clauses and phrases using participles, relative pronouns and prepositional phrases piled upon one another is a remarkable example of Pauline style and of spontaneous dictation, rather than the cobbling of disparate statements drawn from multiple sources (Eph. 1:3-12). Furthermore, it is hard, if not impossible to imagine any of the ancient writers, other than Paul, being able to compose such a masterpiece of expression, given what we know about extant examples of the Christian writing from the second century, which some claim to be the time Ephesians was written.

There are other unique Pauline signatures, ideas, or themes in Ephesians. For example, οἰκονομίαν, management, or governance, is a word Paul employs six times, three in Ephesians. In 1 Corinthians 9:17, Paul appears to use οἰκονομίαν of the stewardship of preaching the gospel. Elsewhere, however, οἰκονομίαν refers to the governance of God over redemption, the work of the gospel to which Paul had been called, or the overarching plan toward which God is working (Eph. 1:10; 3:2, 9; Col. 1:25; 1 Tim. 1:4). Two occurrences outside of Ephesians have similar semantic properties to the three in the epistle, referring to the governance of God over the work of the gospel and the plan of redemption. Luke is the only other New Testament writer using οἰκονομίαν to refer to the management responsibilities of the unfaithful steward in Jesus' parable, where its meaning is entirely unlike known Pauline usage of the same word (Luke 16:1-15). Furthermore, it is inconceivable that a redactionist, cobbling together an epistle to pass off as written by Paul, would take the similar wording from Colossians, ἧς ἐγενόμην ἐγὼ διάκονος κατὰ τὴν οἰκονομίαν τοῦ θεοῦ τὴν δοθεῖσάν μοι[30] and render it εἴ γε ἠκούσατε τὴν οἰκονομίαν τῆς χάριτος τοῦ θεοῦ τῆς δοθείσης μοι εἰς ὑμᾶς,[31] thereby altering its original sense, especially when he appears to make a similar point using similar phrases and construction, but by reworking the syntax in the different places (Col. 1:25; Eph. 3:2). Why not just reproduce the whole expression as it is rendered in Colossians if Ephesians is a compilation? Although they are similar, they do actually show evidence of expressing related but different ideas to suit different contexts or purposes for writing. Paul does this elsewhere, using similar ways of expressing himself, but reworking syntax to suit the context, especially when speaking on

---

[30] Holmes, M. W. (2011–2013). The Greek New Testament: SBL Edition (Col 1:25). Lexham Press; Society of Biblical Literature.

[31] Holmes, M. W. (2011–2013). The Greek New Testament: SBL Edition (Eph 3:2). Lexham Press; Society of Biblical Literature.

related issues. *It is, then, a characteristic in the Pauline corpus that he sometimes uses similar but adapted expressions, and it is not an argument against Pauline authorship in and of itself.* Indeed, these features may be arguments in favor of it. We can probably view features like this in the New Testament as characteristically Pauline.

The idea of *adoption*, υἱοθεσίαν, is entirely Pauline (cf. Rom. 8:15, 23; 9:4; Gal. 4:5; and Eph. 1:5). It appears nowhere else in the New Testament. Paul uses the idea of adoption differently in different contexts, for example of inclusion into the family of God as children and heirs of Christ (Rom. 8:15), of the full consummation of the redemption of the physical body at final salvation (Rom. 8:23), of the privilege of Israel's adoption and possession of the message of salvation to the world (Rom. 9:4), of transfer from sin or condemnation of the law into the family of God as children (Gal. 4:5-6), and of inclusion into the company of those who belong to God in Christ by a transfer from one state to another (Eph. 1:5). Adoption as a motif is characteristically Pauline. The notion of belonging to God as the result of an adoptive transfer into a new relationship with God is a Pauline concept, although the idea of transfer *from the world of sin and rebellion against God into the kingdom of God* is found elsewhere in the New Testament (cf. Acts 26:18; Eph. 5:8; Col. 1:13; 1 Thess. 5:5; 1 Pet. 2:9). Paul's favorite idea is that we have become free children of God through justification, and are now relocated, as far as the realm of our new lives is concerned, in Christ. Jesus' idea of regeneration emphasizes the moral changes that occur through the power of God, calling it being born again. Paul's adoption metaphor does not compete with Jesus' metaphor, but views redemption from a different perspective, the advantage we now have by being adopted out of the family in which we once lived as slaves to sin, and into a life of holiness as true children of God. Regardless, adoption is a uniquely Pauline motif in the New Testament.

Lastly, we observe that the tenor of the argument and the ideas in the passage we are examining are unique to Paul. Although we will explore this at length below, we ought to harness this feature as evidence of Pauline authorship. Ephesians 4:17-24 hinges on the idea of rejecting the old life and taking up the new life that his readers now have in Christ as a result of justification (created in them by God) (Eph. 4:24). By laying aside the old life, they open the door to God working in them to produce the holiness and righteousness he is seeking from them. Furthermore, the development of the new life into mature godliness depends on the renewing power of God, which Paul specifically says has to do with ongoing changes to the spirit of their minds (Eph. 4:22-24). In Romans 6, Paul specifically and in detail addresses these issues under the figure of a participation in the death and resurrection of Jesus, by which the old life is crucified, and they are raised to new life in connection with their new relationship God in Christ (Rom. 6:3-4). Furthermore, they are to engage their minds in the enterprise of laying aside the old life and taking up the new in service to going on to righteousness and holiness (Rom. 6:11), alluded to by repeated references to state of the mind of the Gentiles in Ephesians 4 (17-19). In Romans 12:1-2, Paul presents his argument, which one might construe as recapitulated in Ephesians 4:17-24, that by a surrender of themselves to God, through a transformation of their nature by the ongoing renewal of their minds, they are to resist the world's attempts to squeeze them back into its culture. The parallels are striking, and clearly Pauline.

RECIPIENTS

To whom was Ephesians written? Does it matter? The words "in Ephesus" do not appear in the oldest manuscripts, and the evidence is quite strong for their omission until after the second century.[32] Wood notes that a few manuscripts similarly omit "in Rome" from the epistle to the Romans (Rom. 1:7).[33] This evidence may not be decisive in whether or not this letter was originally addressed to the Ephesian church. It is not hard to imagine letters copied for circulation excluding the original recipients in order to give them broader appeal to the congregations to which they were read. We know that Paul even requested that his letters and instructions be exchanged between churches and that they were to be circulated among them (Col. 4:16). Peter seems to confirm the wide circulation of the Pauline letters with his remarks about Paul's writings, the contents of which he was aware, and were well enough known generally to have been the subject of attack by enemies of the gospel (2 Pet. 3:15-16). Copies that have addressees, that are extant, have “in Ephesus”. That there are copies with no addressees and later copies with “in Ephesus”, with no other early or later copies with other addressees is not conclusive for the omission. On balance external evidence is inconclusive regarding destination, but by no means rules Ephesus out altogether.[34] Bruce Metzger, who gives “in Ephesus” a “C” rating, notes that, even if the letter was an encyclical, Ephesus may appear as its chief target, so the committee of the USB 3rd edition retained the words.[35]

---

[32]Wood, 1981, 9.

[33] Wood, 1981, 9.

[34] Although a few important early mss, Codex Sinaiticus (א*) — original hand, Codex Vaticanus (B), Papyrus 46 (𝔓46, c. 200 AD), do not have “in Ephesus”, the words are present in Codex A (Alexandrinus) (Alexandrian text type other than the gospels, and in Codex D (Claromontanus) (and example of the Western Text), as well as the majority text tradition. Some early church writers either note, or demonstrate a knowledge of omission in early mss. Cf. ChatGPT https://chatgpt.com/c/69a0c765-7014-8326-99e3-30d9be326b53.

[35] Metzger, 1971, 601.

The argument made against Pauline authorship of Ephesians assumes that if this were a genuine letter to Ephesus, Paul would have included personal remarks to a church with which he had the highest affinity, and he would mark it with personal touches, as he often does elsewhere. In any case, the absence of the words ἐν Ἐφέσῳ is not ultimately an argument against Pauline authorship, but rather for a lack of confidence in knowing the original recipients. What cannot be argued is that the lack of personal remarks and the words "in Ephesus" rule out the destination as we have it handed down to us, and the lack of knowledge of the destination excludes Pauline authorship. At some point, the argument becomes circular and self-defeating. The early church certainly took the letter as a Pauline epistle to the Ephesian church, founded by the apostle.

Arguments mustered to deny that Ephesians was originally written to the Ephesian church, make use of the lack of personal references to provide confirmation of his relationship with the church as we know it from Acts. [36] A similar thing could be said of the conclusions to Galatians, 1 and 2 Thessalonians, or could be construed as strong confirmation that Hebrews is a Pauline letter! So how *impersonal* is Ephesians really? As we saw earlier, the argument that the letter is impersonal, by itself, does not vacate the epistle's historical or occasional nature, considering all things on balance. We do have historical or circumstantial references, along with allusions in the epistle that correspond broadly and even closely the Ephesians. These commended themselves to us internal evidence (see below).

There are clues in the epistle that require thoughtful consideration, before setting the letter aside from the Pauline corpus or dismissing the tradition that the letter was indeed written to the church at Ephesus, founded by Paul. Some of these may indeed show the epistle to have

---

[36] Cf. Merkle B. L., 2016, 2.

been aimed at the churches in Asia generally, and to congregations in and around Ephesus in particular. For example, Tychicus, who is to carry the letter to the churches, is listed as a companion to Paul and as being from the province of Asia (Acts 20:2-4, cf. Eph. 6:19-21). Paul sent him back there with this letter and a letter to the church at Colossae, with similar instructions to inform the churches about his circumstances (Col. 4:7-9). Colossae was situated to the east, on the main road to Ephesus in the west.[37] He was traveling with Onesimus, who had fled from his master, Philemon, and had become a believer under Paul's preaching in Rome (Col. 4:9).[38] Onesimus was to return to his master in Colossae in Asia and to make amends so that his future disposition might be decided by Philemon (Philm 12-16).

Paul claims to have previously instructed the Ephesians closely on his theology of sanctification, that they learned it from him, and that he had taught them (λέγω καὶ μαρτύρομαι... εἴ γε αὐτὸν ἠκούσατε καὶ ἐν αὐτῷ ἐδιδάχθητε, καθώς ἐστιν ἀλήθεια ἐν τῷ Ἰησοῦ).[39] He implies very clearly that they had learned personally from him how to conduct themselves in Christ, that they were to lay aside the old life of sin, to take the new life of obedience to God, and that his was the basis for a renewed call to holiness and righteousness (Eph. 4:17-24). It is inconceivable that such a direct and personal claim of association has been fabricated, especially since the previous instruction is offered at the basis for the reminder and enjoinder that they ought to follow through and make the decision. The imperatives (see below) are premised on a personal relationship with and knowledge of the writer's teaching, and that the readers can identify and know who the writer is,

---

[37] Elwell & Comfort, 2001, 299.

[38] Wood, 1981, 16.

[39] Holmes, M. W. (2011–2013). *The Greek New Testament: SBL Edition* (Eph 4:17, 20-21). Lexham Press; Society of Biblical Literature.

that he carries the requisite authority and has a close enough connection to make such demands of them.

Let's consider some other reasons for concluding that Ephesians is personal and specific in character, and that it provide evidence Paul a had genuine relationship with its recipients.[40] Paul references being *in chains* (Eph. 3:1, 13; 4:1; 6:20), as if his predicament would have been of genuine concern to his readers, and then calls on them to pray for him, asking that they pray he will represent the gospel well when he is put on trial, and not fail the coming test (Eph. 6:18-20).[41] The strongly worded section about the unity of Jews and Gentiles in the church through a common relationship with and experience of Christ (Eph. 2:11-22), and the equally strong imperative that they *make every effort to keep the unity of the church, which the Spirit has created,* implies he knows relationships may well be strained or tense, particularly between the Jewish and Gentile factions (Eph. 4:3). This accords with what we know of the church in Ephesus, made up of Jews and Gentiles, where strong tensions existed between the communities in the city, and where Paul warned, on his departure, that factionalism would develop in the church, and he sent Timothy to Ephesus to put a lid on it (see below). That the writer addresses threats to unity head-on, with apostolic

---

[40] We are seeking to show that the claim Ephesians is nor personal, and that the writer has no specific readership in mind, and that there is not a close connection between them is demonstrably false.

[41] It is inconceivable that a pseudonymous letter writer would seek to reproduce the illusion of a fictitious relationship of such intimacy as represented here, and consider their conscience "clean" in perpetrating such a deception (even if the assumed motive is the "exhortation" of the saints). It is inconsistent with the whole tenor of the New Testament writers that good can come from or that God might out of such deception. Remember, on the premise of pseudonymity, the request for prayer for Paul would be entirely contrived, and therefore a bold misdirection.

authority, and with confidence that surely comes from his close connection to the church, and exhibits no fear, as with the Corinthians, that his intervention might be rejected.

The mystery of the gospel given to Paul concerning Gentile inclusion along with Jews in God's redemptive plan (Eph. 3:1-13), is an especially appropriate message for the Ephesians church, under the circumstances mentioned above, where unity is premised on a shared redemption in Christ and fellowship with God in his church, through the Spirit, as his temple. Maintaining unity in the church appears to be paramount, where the constituent groups of the church come from such disparate backgrounds and religious traditions (Eph. 4:1-16), that Paul follows up his theological foundation with a significant portion of the letter dedicated at unpacking the practical implications in how they ought to relate to one another under various circumstances. These speak of a personal knowledge of the recipients consistent with what we know of the Ephesian church and its situation from Acts, as well as Paul's relationship with them.

The section dealing with the God's goal of maturing the moral and spiritual nature of the saints, and hope that they come to a fuller understanding and experience of God, demonstrate a deep concern and intense desire for the spiritual success of the recipients of the letter. How ever we might describe Paul's early sentiments in chapters 1 and 2, indifference is not an option. There is nothing impersonal about any of it. In the expansive section about the lifestyle and conduct for believers in Christ, which appears to be aimed mainly at the Gentile faction of the church (Eph. 4:17-6:9), and that he evokes application of the armor of God in service of their wrestling and struggling against principalities and powers that resist the gospel and the work of the ministry, Paul betrays deep concern for the spiritual success and perseverance of these saints, who are also readers of this letter. Incidentally, that Paul reminds them they are not wrestling against flesh and blood but against spiritual wickedness in high places, is particularly apropos for the church in Ephesus under external pressure from outside the church, in a way that it is not for Paul's other churches, with the possible exception of Thessalonica (Eph. 6:10-12). Much of this is consistent with what we know about Paul's relationship with the Ephesians, people with whom he spent the longest time in one place, who prevented him from offering himself to the wrath of a belligerent crowd in full riot (Acts 19:28-31), and who wept bitterly at his final departure (Acts 20:36-38). There is deep concern and tenderness in how this letter addresses its readers.

The writer's genuine concern for the spiritual health and welfare of these saints, as well as for their ongoing praxis, is certainly not indicative of a contrivance. These elements are not likely to signal a passing acquaintance, and definitely not a total lack of one. That Paul launches a very a personal appeal for prayer from his readers, where he makes himself transparent with respect to his "fears", cannot be ignored as evidence of a relationship (Eph. 6:19-20).[42] Paul gave some background about his personal struggle, which he was facing in prison, as he prepared for a trial, to people whom knew him would remember him in prayer out of their concern and love.[43] This appeal has the feeling of something that trades on a very personal and genuine connection between Paul and his readers. It cannot be said with a straight face, that the absence of greetings at the end of this letter betrays that it is impersonal and lacks warmth, as though the writer had no relationship

---

[42] Sometimes, material that can be construed as "embarrassing" is adduced as supporting the authenticity of the content or text in New Testament studies. That Paul makes himself vulnerable surely confirms that there is intimacy between the writer and the readers.

[43] Alford, H. (1865). *The New Testament for English Readers: Containing the Authorized Verson, with Revised Text; Marginal References; and a Critical Explanatory Commentary* (Vol. 2). Cambridge, UK: Deighton, Bell, and Co., 44.

with its recipients. On the contrary, the depth of the connection is readily apparent.

Summary on Authorship and Recipients: Unless it is argued, and can be conclusively proven, that these elements have been inserted into the text of the epistle by a redactor, it is hard to account for them in a letter purportedly written after Paul's death. If inserted then we must conclude the epistle was deliberately passed off as authentic when, in fact, it was not. The whole character of the epistle as truth and *God's Word* is thrown into doubt if these personal remarks are not genuine, because they indicate duplicity on the part of the compiler. Nothing in Ephesians, however, even on close examination, suggests we should doubt the authenticity of these very personal elements. Still, how helpful might a deceptively created letter be for exhortation and correction? Why would the church refuse recognition to other inauthentic, or doubted early works and not this one, if it readily appeared to be a fabrication?[44] Indeed, it was included in the canon because of confidence in its apostolic authorship, by Paul. Is it possible the early church could have been so thoroughly fooled for so long? That is not likely. Questions about the generally accepted provenance of Ephesians were not raised until the age of skepticism and enlightenment. If substantiated, such claims would impact our understanding of inspiration, canonicity, and scriptural authority. As we have said, Ephesians does not bear the marks of being stitched together from disparate sources. On the contrary, it exhibits a remarkable unity,

---

[44] The snobbery of the assumption that the early church could not tell the difference, but we can from our more advanced and literarily adroit perspective is supremely arrogant. Afterall, some of the early fathers were aware of the problems with the addressees, but did not reject either its Pauline authorship not its provenance as a letter to the church at Ephesus. It made its way into the canon unchallenged and remained there for almost 2,000 years.

cohesion, and flow of thought throughout the letter, from its theologically lofty beginning to its practical conclusion. Logically and smoothly transitioning between its parts organically, and without appearing forced, the development of its central theme, arguably unity, builds. There is no categorical or unambiguous internal indication that this letter is anything but what it appears to be, an epistle of Paul written to one of his churches, to readers he personally knew, and judging by the only addressed copies, to the Ephesians, since no other addressees exist in the manuscript tradition (except for an unreliable mention by Marcion, that it was addressed to the Laodiceans).

This is not quite the same, however, as saying that it is entirely proven that Paul wrote to the Ephesians specifically, but that creditable reasons can be given to support that thesis. Walter Elwell conjectures that although the letter was written to churches in the Ephesian region, and Paul seems to have purposefully left off the address *in Ephesus* (ἐν Ἐφέσῳ), presumably to give it broader appeal (Eph. 1:1).[45] As we noted above, the prepositional phrase, ἐν Ἐφέσῳ, was almost certainly not present in the earliest copies of the manuscripts.[46] This absence neither conclusively confirms nor disproves that the original recipients were in the Ephesian church or were churches of the Ephesian region. The idea that this letter was aimed at a greater number of congregations than in the city proper, or to a wider audience in the Ephesian region, may explain the paucity of personal references and greetings as well. If we are correct, most of those to whom the letter was written would have almost definitely known of Paul, some more intimately than others, no doubt (cf. Acts 20:13-37). Alford notes that a pattern exhibited in Paul's writing may contradict the conclusion that a lack of personal references supports unknown recipients. Paul seems to include more personal

---

[45] Elwell & Comfort, 2001, 432.

[46] Wood, 1981, 9; Elwell & Comfort, 2001, 432.

references in letters to congregations like those in Rome and Colossae whom he had not met, compared to churches with which he has close relationships.[47] This is arguably because Paul is anxious to create a connection with the readers in a church where a personal connection may not exist (cf. Rom. 16). Whereas, with churches he had a close relationship it was not as necessary to do so. If this is true, we might conclude that fewer personal references, like in Ephesians, is possibly evidence of a closer relationship between the apostle and his readers and not the absence of one. Nonetheless, there are enough personal touches and indications of close connections in this letter to be consistent with the notion that Paul did know his readers, and they knew him.

These are a few of the details in the text of the letter that demonstrate that it was written to a real and specific church (composed probably of several congregations), suffering from real church issues. Paul's letters are what Gordon Fee calls *occasional*, and Ephesians appears, though different from some, to also be *occasional.* [48] Ephesians seems to address a real church, people, and situations requiring advice, correction, and instruction; this is the meaning of the term *occasional* in this context. On balance, then we confidently affirm that Paul knew the original and primary recipients of this epistle, and that furthermore, he knew them well. Even if the letter was intended to be encyclical, shared by several congregations, Paul seems to have written the letter primarily to people of churches in Asia with which he was familiar, probably in the region around Ephesus. Paul specifically addresses issues he wished to broach with its recipients, about which he appears to have close knowledge, and which also seem to impinge on the need to maintain unity, where possible ethnic and cultural

---

[47] Alford, 1865, 40-41.
[48]Fee, G. D. (1994). God's Empowering Presence: The Holy Spirit in the Letters of Paul. Peabody, MA, USA: Hendrickson Publishers Inc., 803-804.

diversity has led to the development of stress points between Jewish and Gentile believers.[49] There is good reason from internal evidence to think that the letter was indeed intended initially for Asia, and to be read in Ephesus first, even if it was later circulated and read elsewhere.

Other Possible Recipients in Ephesus Not Know to Paul and Confirmation of Intimacy: A comment in chapter one seems to indicate that the letter was addressed, at least in part, to some believers he may not have known personally, and that it appears that he may not have been directly responsible for their coming to Christ (Eph. 1:15). He refers to having *heard of their faith* (Eph. 1:15). Henry Alford addresses this objection, saying that Paul may not even be referring to the initial conversion of the Ephesian saints at the time of the church's founding, but to a report of their continued faith or faithfulness to God of which he had heard subsequently in his absence.[50] He says something similar to the Romans in the church at Rome, where he expresses his intention to visit them, and that he had as yet not met them personally, and to the Colossians (Rom. 1:9-10, 11-13; 16:23; Col. 1:4). From Acts we know that, although there were believers in Ephesus when Paul arrived, he explained Jesus to them more fully, baptized them, prayed over them for the reception of the Spirit, stayed in Ephesus teaching a considerable amount of time, and left after a tearful and deeply moving farewell to their leaders (Acts 20:13-37). If any church was a Pauline church, Ephesus was. It appears that Paul is addressing his letter to people he both knows and others of which he has indirect knowledge, somehow navigating the line between the two so that his letter might have a broad

---

[49] Elwell & Comfort, 2001, 432.

[50] Alford, 1865, 44.

appeal. As Elwell notes, this would account for why many scholars believe Ephesians to have the characteristics of an encyclical.[51]

Ephesians is not the only letter in which Paul addresses issues of the powerful disincentives he faced for the gospel, and expressing his wish for the supportive prayers and loyalty of those who knew him (2 Cor. 1:10-11; Phil 1:19; Col. 4:3; 1 Thess. 5:25; 2 Thess. 3:1-2; Philm. 22). In these instances, he writes to people he considers friends enough that he can ask for earnest prayer as he faces threats posed by the authorities, imprisonment, and his own personal fears and dread at the prospect of being put on trial or executed (cf. Eph. 6:18-20). He seems to feel the need for the loyalty and support of those who know him best, and he petitions them for that support on the grounds of their close relationship to one another.[52] Paul makes himself vulnerable to those who know him best, surely, because he knows his readers sufficiently to be open with them.

From all of this, if we accept Pauline authorship, we ought to conclude that Paul does, in fact, know the recipients of the letter, well enough that he is comfortable in soliciting prayer for himself while in his captivity, and asking them particularly to intercede for his courage and determination to hold out under the pressure of his suffering. Paul asked them to pray that he will proclaim the gospel as boldly and freely as he ought, where the subjunctives hint at a contingency, that there is certain to be intimidation connected to his imprisonment and trial (ἵνα

---

[51] Elwell & Comfort, 2001, 432.

[52] We see something similar in the garden in the interaction between Jesus and his disciples. In his dread at the prospect of the cross, Jesus sought the support of his closest friends. What we can say about this is that in the crisis Paul seems to be calling on those who know him and care enough to pray for him and support him in what he believes are going to be his last sacrificial acts of service for the gospel.

ἐν αὐτῷ παρρησιάσωμαι ὡς δεῖ με λαλῆσαι).[53] Paul wants to make a good presentation of himself in the presence of Caesar and his court, and for that he needs courage (παρρησιάσωμαι). The characteristic exposure of vulnerability is another mark of authenticity in Paul's genuine epistles. 2 Corinthians is a particular example, along with Philippians. Paul comfortably exposes his feelings and vulnerabilities to churches and people he counts among his friends, some of his misgivings or concerns, deepest aspirations, or struggles, and even his abortive attempts to visit with them (cf. Rom. 1:13;1 Cor. 15:32; 2 Cor. 9:4; Gal. 4:12-16, 19-20; Phil. 4:10-20; Philm. 7, 8-10; 2 Tim. 4;9-18). His remarks in Ephesians are typically Pauline, seeming to confirm both authorship and connection, even a close relationship, with his readers.

A mention of dispatching Tychicus, who is from Asia, and who is going to take a letter from Paul to Colossae, as well as to accompany Onesimus to meet his master in Colossae, sets the recipients of Ephesians in the geographic region where Paul had his longest ministry, and closest relationships in Asia. Tychicus is the Asian link between Paul and the Asian recipients of letters to the Ephesians and Colossians. Tychicus will be able to authenticate a missive from Paul. Naming Tychicus as the bearer of the correspondence *dates the letter to the time of Paul's ministry,* as well as his imprisonment (57-62 AD), and mitigates arguments of a later compilation of Pauline teaching.[54] The letter assumes that Paul's readers are sufficiently concerned about his welfare under the current circumstances of his imprisonment, that word

---

[53] Holmes, M. W. (2011–2013). *The Greek New Testament: SBL Edition* (Eph 6:20). Lexham Press; Society of Biblical Literature.

[54] If this is not so the letter is deliberately deceptive and not worthy of consideration for the canon. The early church would not have stood for such a deceptive element in what purported to be a genuine letter of the apostle. This is not a compilation at all, but a genuinely personal piece of writing to known or at least partially known recipients.

from Tychicus would be of comfort to them, maybe putting their minds at rest (Eph. 6:21). The reference to Tychicus provides powerful evidence that a close relationship existed between Paul and his readers, and stands as an example of the *personal remarks* demanded skeptics. It is much more likely that by sending Tychicus to report to them on his circumstances, the letter was intended for a specific congregation, or a known readership, disciples of Paul's acquaintance, rather than serving entirely as an encyclical, which scholars seem to assume are largely unknown to him. Evidences like these seem to undermine much of this line of reasoning, and do not leave the impression that Ephesians is impersonal, or contrived. Even if Paul did not know *everyone* in Ephesus, he certainly knew a great many of them, and had a close enough relationship with them that marks of authentic relationship can be detected throughout the letter.

Finally, we ought to recall that a church in a particular "city" or "region" did not consist of a single congregation, meeting in a church building, in the way we think of it today. Churches designated by city names consisted of more than one congregation, meeting usually in the homes of the wealthier members. We can see, then, how an epistle might have circulated among a number of congregations, which together constituted the church in that location. It may even have copied and circulated, and despite being intended for a particular church in a specific city or location at first, enjoyed wider distribution in the region, and later throughout the empire (i.e., Gal. 1 Cor. 16:1). A remark in the letter to the Colossians confirms the practice (Col. 4:16). Tychicus was to make the rounds among the congregations in the region around Ephesus, to whom this letter was first written (whether he went to Ephesus first or not), to encourage them, as well as inform them about how Paul was getting along. Tychicus was also dispatched with other letters for Asian churches or recipients, with instructions to inform them of his welfare, including letters to the Colossians Laodicea, and Philemon (cf. Col, 4:7, 9, 13, 16). Paul's instructions in Colossians, a church not planted by him, do not give expression to Paul's vulnerability or exhibit a similar closeness as his connection to the Ephesians, although Philemon, a close Pauline friend, is among them members of that church (cf. Col. 4:9). Paul didn't seem to have sent letters by Tychicus to churches with which he was less familiar requesting prayer in quite the same intimate or vulnerable way as he does in Ephesians. Details like these in the Ephesian epistle are indicative of specific addressees rather than unknown or vaguely familiar ones, close friends rather than unfamiliar readers.

Paul demonstrates knowledge of the church to which the letter is written, implying he has a specific congregation or city church nexus in mind. Ephesians gives us this clear impression, even if the letter is intended secondarily for wider circulation in the region. Such knowledge is undoubtedly based on the authentic dynamics of a relationship with the congregations who are the first and primary recipients of the letter, that is, the ones with whom Tychicus *first* leaves the epistle. Rather than wooden, general, and disparate exhortations, Paul's reasoned logic is developed along lines that encourage unity in the church, and may indicate that a need existed for such exhortations due to some tendency for division or tension among his recipients (Eph. 2:11-22; 4:1-16).[55]

Relational Dynamics among the First Recipients of the Letter: One might argue that chapter one and the first half of chapter two presses the ground of grace for salvation for everyone, Jew and Gentile, and that the later part of chapter two follows it up with a declaration of equality and unity as God's eschatological scheme of redemption for his people, to form a unified church, body, or temple for his indwelling (Eph. 1:4-2:22). Chapter three addresses this mystery as the intended purpose of

---

[55] It certainly seems to this writer that unity is a major and persistent theme throughout the epistle, focused particularly on the unity of Jews and Gentiles.

God, and chapter four asserts this unity in the nature of salvation, and in the fully functioning body of Christ, which is the church (Eph. 3:1-13; 4:1-16). Our passage falls in this vicinity, where Paul is discussing the purposes of God for his church and believers in terms of their continued moral and spiritual development, with an allusion to his eschatological endgame. After this comes a treatise on critical elements of practical interaction between members of the believing community. This emphasis on relationships, right treatment of and the obligation to serve one another in order to promote unity in the church, may well hint at fissures and schisms among the intended readers, not something unheard of in other churches (i.e., Corinth, Rome). Such an emphasis betrays an intimate knowledge of particular congregational dynamics and a specific group of people.

The subtle use of the plural personal pronouns *you* and *we* in which Paul appears to refer to Jews and Gentiles, respectively, who are also believers in Christ, may indicate that Paul is addressing some tendency for division. There are indications that the epistle to the Romans addresses a similar problem, where tensions caused by stark cultural differences between Jewish and Gentile believers became a source of tension and difficulty when it came to table fellowship in particular, in the mode of the first century church (Rom. 14:1-15:13, cf. Acts 2:42-47; 4:32-37; 1 Cor. 10:14-11:34). The historical and purposeful progress of gospel preaching is brought out in Paul's treatment of the *mystery* of which he was the particular apostolic representative. In statements he made about his strategy, Jews first and then Gentiles, Paul was aligning himself to the divine strategy by which God first approached Israel with the good news of salvation, fully intending to offer it to Gentiles as well (Isa. 42:6; 49:6, cf. Rom. 1:16; 2:9-10). Both, Paul says, are included in Christ, and equally sealed with the Holy Spirit regardless of their ethnic circumstances before coming to Christ (Eph. 1:11-14; 3:1-13; Col.

3:11).[56] That his readers must not allow divisions over ethnic scruples, is a recurring Pauline theme, and references to God's intended unity in the church may be an indirect way for Paul to make the point he overtly expresses in chapter 4 and verse 3; it is their responsibility to maintain that unity by every effort within their power. A seemingly trivial feature of interchange between pronouns, as is the case many times in Paul's introductory remarks, may be an indication of the direction the letter is going and of the issues he is intending to address.

In any case, by the end of chapter two, Paul concludes Jews and Gentiles as one body of believers through the sacrifice of Christ, where all distinction and demarcation is lost through its removal by the cross and the sacrifice of Christ's flesh (Eph. 2:11-22). This develops into a discussion of the mystery of the gospel of which Paul is particularly its chief messenger to the early church. God always intended to bring Jews and Gentiles together in salvation through Christ to form one people of God (Eph. 3:1-13). Paul often develops themes of unity, and their implications, because of the practical needs of the church to address the harmony of relationships between believers. Following a spontaneous outburst of praise to God for the wonder of his redemptive plan, which turns into a doxology celebrating its magnificent devising and execution, Paul conspicuously returns to the importance of unity in the church (Eph. 4:1-16). The purpose of that unity is to ensure the growth of the church and the to support the welfare of each individual believer in order to bring them to full maturity in Christ (Eph. 4:11-16).

The letter has an elegant flow to it, and it seems to build on the theme of unity, at first focusing on the relationship between Jews and Gentiles but moving to the importance and implications of unity for everyone (cf. Eph. 5:21-6:9). Paul appears to be aware of the potential for tension arising from the dual ethnicity of his churches. Indeed, he

---

[56] Paul will develop this idea more fully in Romans chapter 2 and 3.

engaged a strategy that necessarily guaranteed that it would be so (Acts 9:20; 13:5, 14; 14:1; 17:1-2, 10; 18:4, 19, 26; 19:8; 28:23-31). Unity between the ethnic parties was critical for the churches' survival and success, so he often addressed the need for unity. In Ephesians he does so from a theological angle at first, and then from a practical perspective. Romans seems to follow a similar pattern addressing unity between Jews and Gentiles in the church. Beginning in chapter one with implications of the prior ethnic starting points for salvation, and ending with the eschatological implications of God's redemptive plans for both classes of people in one redemptive action. In Romans, Paul also addressed practical considerations, chapters 14 and 15. It is a Pauline strategy, by which he not only instructs the church in its doctrinal underpinnings, but in the practical implications of their shared faith in Christ with respect to their relationships with one another (cf. Rom. 1-2; 9-11; 14-15).

Unity that leads to maturity and growth for the church and its members has moral implications, Paul says, something which he takes up in the next section of the epistle (Eph. 4:17-20). He is about to make his case through practical instruction about how they are to interact with one another, and to engage serious efforts to maintain unity with one another. This is going to require that they address character and their relationship with God, to surrender to his ongoing renewal and development of godliness in them, which will serve as the foundation for unity, and practical right treatment of one another. After addressing character, integrity, renewal, and maturing in godliness, Paul notably zeros in on unity again, this time in terms of practical interaction between the saints, showing that their spiritual and moral integrity are critical to relationships in the body. In chapter five he provides instructions on submissiveness and proper attitudes in relationships between husbands and wives, believing slave owners and slaves, children, and their parents. These are the kind of interactions that have to do with the household and family, the fallout of which most naturally affects the relational environment of the church, particularly since the home is where congregations typically gathered in Paul time (Eph. 5:21-6:9).[57] If there are tensions in the church or among the saints, Paul does not address them with instructions and directives, until at first he has reminded his readers of what is implied by their new relationship with God through Christ, and how that ought to affect their attitudes towards one another.

THE REMOTE CONTEXT

So much for the historical context. We now must consider the literary context, the book as a whole and the more immediate context and argument in which our passage is found. Having established to some degree of satisfaction that Paul is the author, the reasons he wrote, and arguably who the original recipients were, it is time to consider the flow of Paul's themes and arguments. A discussion of the literary and theological context seeks to set the passage in the context of its flow in the letter, and in Paul's theology or the logic of his reasoning as a whole, to correctly discern it meaning.

Literary Context: We have already remarked to some extent on the content of this epistle as an indication of its occasional nature, addressed to real people, comprising a real church, of which Paul had knowledge, and with which he enjoyed a relationship. In this section, we will not labor those points again, except to remark on the apparent purpose of the epistle as a means for the moral appeal of which our passage is a part. While a unifying theme may not be apparent upon a

---

[57]Cf. Witherington, The Problem with Evangelical Theology: Testing the Exegetical Foundatiuons of Calvinism, Dispensationalism, Welseyanism, and Pentecostalism, 2016, 91-93; Liefeld, 1997, 141-153; Keener, Galatians: New Cambridge Bible Commentary, 2018), 166-170; Keener, Paul, Women & Wives: Marriage and Women's Ministry in the Letters of Paul, 2004.

cursory reading of Ephesians, Paul does address unity in the church as a primary concern. Whereas it was once common for scholars to see Paul's letters as divided into theological and practical "halves," the thematic unity of his writings is now much better appreciated through an awareness of characteristic Pauline techniques and styles of writing, by which he overlays his central concerns across content divisions.

SUPPOSED THEOLOGICAL VERSUS PRACTICAL INSTRUCTION IN PAUL: Even if Paul characteristically does deal with his themes on a more theological footing at first and goes on to draw out the practical implications later, we often see in the "practical" sections the same thematic concerns raised, and theological implications or underpinnings reaffirmed and honed for conduct. For example, Romans 9-11 and 14-15 address the eschatological implications of Israel's rejection of Christ, where Paul is anxious to demonstrate God's final purpose to bring about the repentance and salvation of the Jews as far as that is possible. In this, Paul is anxious to establish the theological implications of God covenant faithfulness to Israel, even if ultimately there is only a remnant that responds to the gospel and to Christ. He considers himself to be part of that remnant, and, therefore, representative of those of his own people who will be saved through Christ (Rom. 9-11). From Paul's theological perspective, this remnant of Jews responding to the gospel will be greatly increased near the end when God renews his focus on Israel, immediately prior to wrapping up his redemptive purposes in this age (Rom. 11:25-32). He appears to be basing his assertions on the overall tenor of Old Testament scriptures that promise a reconstitution of Israel as the victorious people of God, who will ultimately be confronted by Jesus as their pierced redeemer and Messiah (Zech 12:10). Then under national conviction and repentance, they will turn to him in final recognition (Zech 14:1). These ideas are commonly found in the Old Testament prophetic tradition, where the warnings issued to Israel in the midst of its apostacy are balanced by promises of future restoration to God, and of the kingdom of Israel. These Paul views fulfilled in Christ and his rule over all of God's creation, as well as over Israel (cf. Rom. 11; 1 Cor. 15:20-28; Col. 1:15-20).

This is Pauline theological methodology. For example, he renders his eschatology, in Romans, in a context largely focused on his concern for unity in the church, because the church is the representation of that kingdom in the present age (cf. Rom. 14-15). *Weak* and *strong* brethren in the church seemed to be divided by food laws, ethnic origins, tribal rivalries, or cultural backgrounds, most especially when it comes to Jewish scruples and engaging in table-fellowship with Gentiles (cf. Rom. 14). Paul argues for unity on the basis of the superiority of the principles of the kingdom of God, which consist not in meat and drink (religious customs, scruple, laws, cultural background, or ethnic worldviews), but of the commonly shared principles of righteousness, peace, and joy in the Holy Spirit (Rom. 14:17). Paul affirms the central idea that the righteousness at which the law took aim, but failed to achieve because of a flaw in human nature, God has accomplished through the impartation of the Holy Spirit into the lives of believers, by an act of the grace commensurate with their justification and forgiveness (Rom. 6-8; Gal. 5:16-25).

Paul's references to the Holy Spirit in connection with the moral and spiritual success of godliness and Christian life are not casual. In Romans they join with Paul's arguments elsewhere concerning the source of righteousness being found in Christ by faith (Rom. 3:21-26), through the power of God at work in the believer's life, and they are why law-keeping and Jewish cultural traditions for attaining righteousness have been thoroughly rejected (cf. Rom. 6-8). In The Roman church context, consisting of Jewish and Gentile brothers in Christ, they must not now allow differing cultural customs or views divide them or undermine their relationships and unity, because for both it is in Christ their justification and ultimate attainment of righteousness rests. In

Galatians, Paul states that he cannot allow Judaizers to establish a law-keeping tradition among the Gentile believers there, because it would undermine faith in God, not just for initial justification, but also for the final perfection in godliness (Gal. 3:1-6, 10-14; 5:1-6, 16-25, cf. Rom. 1:17; 8:1-4; Eph. 4:17-24). Tolerance, love, and grace are required for fellowship, Paul argues. In the church, attitudes and conduct of the believers toward one another depends on everyone being clear that righteousness is from God, through grace, and by the power of the Spirit, whether you are a Jewish or a Gentile (Rom. 14). There cannot be any confusion about how God will affect his purposes in and for his people. They are same for all who are saved, regardless of background or ethnicity. The whole practical argument for mutual respect and proper treatment of one another in the church is supported by Paul's theological convictions concerning God's redemptive actions are that by the same grace all people are saved, and by that same grace, and sacrifice of the cross, they are perfected in godliness by the Spirit working in them (cf. 1 Cor. 1:8-2:16). So, Paul makes the eschatological point that God's concerns for Israel places Jewish believers under the same plan as Gentiles, so he might act consistently according to his promises and covenants, and those Jews who are willing to be saved through Christ, and should they remain faithful to him until the end, will come into the inheritance of Israel promised in the scriptures (Eph. 3:1-16, cf. Rom. 9-11).

His theology, then, leads him to a consideration of the challenges to fellowship and unity faced by Gentiles and Jews in the present, who serve God in the same congregations of the early church, prior to the consummation at the eschaton, where cultural and religious scruples and differences present barriers and hurdles that need to be overcome. His solution is grounded in a theology of the right interpretation of Old Testament scripture. The Jewish believers may be experiencing difficulty with the idea of "abandoning" the law as a means of seeking righteousness, but Paul makes the point that God openly revealed, while still working under cover of the old covenant, his future intention of establishing a new covenant to supersede it (cf. Heb. 10:7-13). Along with his expressed intention of including Gentiles in the redemption that he purposed to enact through his chosen servant (Messiah) (cf. Isa. 42:1-6; 49:6), he planned to unite Jews and Gentiles in Christ, a mystery once hidden now revealed (Eph. 3:1-16). By employing the same means of salvation for both (Eph. 2:11-13), God purposed to create one new people of God, consisting of Jews and Gentiles, reconciled to himself by Christ's shed blood, the blood of a new covenant (Eph. 2:11-3:16, cf. Luke 22:20; 1 Cor. 11:25; 1 Cor. 3:6; Heb. 8:6-8; 9:15: 12:24, and Isa. 42:6; 49:6; Jer. 31:31-34). This new covenant would consist of a moral and spiritual change taking place in their nature, something the law could not affect, so that righteousness might arise out of the rewriting of his law in their hearts and minds, and by the replacement of the old heart and spirit, with a heart of flesh and a new S(s)pirit, all in connection with the forgiving of their sins and the pardon of their wickedness, so that they might stand justified with God and morally cleansed, having been sprinkled with clean water (Jer. 31:31-34; Ezek. 36:22-28). Paul takes great trouble to clearly demonstrate that when it comes to justification and reconciliation to God, and attainment of godliness, that those Jews and Gentiles, who make up church, are drinking from the same wells of salvation, faith in Christ, and the operation of God grace through the Spirit, and that God intentionally made it that way (cf. Eph. 2:1-10).

In his epistles, Paul seems compelled, because of the mixed ethnic composition of the early church, to clarify Israel's historical and eschatological position with respect to the covenants that God made with the nation as part of his plan of salvation (Rom. 9:3-5). Israel's national rejection of Christ did not imply that all Jews were lost and without hope of salvation, certainly not if they were prepared to put their faith in Christ (Rom. 9:30-33). On the contrary Jews and Gentiles are both saved by grace and faith in God on account of Christ (Rom. 9:6-18; 10:8-13). Romans 9-11 deals with the eschatological question of how the covenants and promises of God will carry forward historically for the nation in the light of Israel's national rejection of their Messiah. Paul declares that national rejection will not prevent God from bringing about his purpose to offer and accomplish salvation among his covenant people. He will do it through Christ, and in that way bring his promises to fulfillment in a redeemed remnant. Their rejection is temporary, and made way for the salvation of the Gentiles (Rom. 11:1-32). If Israel's historical rejection of the Messiah opened the doors to Gentile salvation, Paul says, you can only imagine what their eschatological recognition of Christ at the *Parousia* will mean for them, when one last chance for salvation will be offered, it seems (Zech. 12:10; Rom. 11:11-12, 15, 23-25; 28-32). Still, more importantly, Israel's national rejection of Christ, Paul argues, does not prevent God from fulfilling his covenants and promises to Israel through those who accept and surrender to God for salvation in Christ. By and in them God will, in the end, have brought to fulfillment his covenant with Israel (Rom. 11:26). These will become the remnant that make the whole holy, the yeast that works through the whole batch of dough (Rom. 11:16). Paul envisions those among Israel who are saved through Christ, vindicating the promises, prophecies, and covenants of God with Israel, and as representing the whole nation (Rom. 11:16).

Romans 9-11 deals with these eschatological themes concerning Israel's national rejection of Christ, whereas chapters 14-15 explain how Gentiles are to make practical provision for the ethnic scruples of their Jewish brethren in the context of the table-fellowship and corporate worship of the early church in the present age. Both Gentile and Jewish believers must learn to live with one another in unity, and work past what divides them, because they are part of one church and the body of Christ, because of the grace of God and the cross of Christ. Both groups are to resist judgmentalism against their brethren, especially with respect to sincerely held convictions or lack thereof (cf. Rom. 14:17). They are, as a matter of principle, to treat one another with patience and grace based on the theological implications of their shared experience of salvation through grace and faith in Christ, and of the prospect of perfection in holiness accomplished through the power of the Spirit in the life of believing saints (and not by law keeping or religious tradition) (Rom. 5:1-2; 8:1-4; Gal. 2:17-21). In this way, Paul intertwines theological principle and practical requirements, along with vigorous, sometimes authoritative instruction, where the theology and practice are not entirely separated from one another, even when he is focused on those practical issues of conduct and fellowship between Jews and Gentiles, especially in light of their shared eschatological future.

UNITY AS A THEOLOGICAL THEME WITH PRACTICAL IMPLICATIONS: In a similar way, Paul advocates for unity in the Ephesian church, using similar arguments, declaring that the religious, traditional, and the cultural wall separating Jews and Gentiles has been torn down by Christ to form one people of God, united in their mutually experienced salvation through the sacrifice of his body on the cross (Eph. 2:11-22). Like Romans, Ephesians gives evidence of Paul's concern for unity, particularly between Jewish and Gentile believers. Their social interactions are sometimes hindered by radical differences in Jewish and Gentile culture or traditions. Coming to Christ from different ethnic or cultural background, they sometimes faced obstacles in fellowship with one another. Jewish food scruples, and religious traditions placed obstacles in the path for sincere table-fellowship between believers, particularly since Gentiles had no capacity for appreciating the depth of conviction their Jewish fellow believers experienced. Paul pleaded for tolerance and latitude on both sides. However, he rooted his appeal for unity in his theological convictions linked to a shared experience of salvation by faith in Christ, and the action of God's grace (Eph. 2:5, 8-9, Eph. 2:11-3:12, cf. Rom. 5:1-21). Paul's appeals for unity to the Ephesians are framed by theological arguments that come out of the implications of the gospel message of salvation by grace for all people, Jew or Gentile. As we approach our passage, we must recognize that its context is Paul's command that they "...maintain the unity of the Spirit through the bonds of peace," and that he describes the church as the body of Christ supported by its interconnectedness, believer with believer, in Christ (Eph. 4:1-16).

Our passage is woven into Paul's treatment of the theme of unity, and seems to address the purpose of God for his body, that it might be healthy and thriving. The church is made up of believers in fellowship with one another, and its fellowship and community are to be supported by vigorous mutuality between members, caring for and encouraging one another (Eph. 4:13-16). The foundation of mutual care and support is the personal integrity and ongoing moral development of the saints themselves (Eph. 4:17-24), which in turn will affects how they related to one another in practical ways and everyday situations of family, church, and society life, while also determining the kind of witness for the gospel they will become (Eph. 4:25-6:9). The overarching purpose of Christian mutuality of fellowship and concern is the upbuilding of the church, its growth, not just in size, but in character and quality of love for one another to reach the stature of the fullness of Christ, that is to reflect the character of God back into the world (Eph. 4:13). Far from being incidental to the purpose of God, unity in the church is integral to the purpose of God, a reflection of the character of God back into the world by his people.

So, in our passage is language that speaks of God's holiness and righteousness being imaged (created – cf. Gen. 1:26-28) in his people, and that they are to lay aside conduct that reflects the flesh or their former life of sin, out of which they have come, and the world where the children of disobedience still live in rebellion against God (Eph. 2:1-3; 4:17, 22). They are to be made new in the attitudes of their minds (ἀνανεοῦσθαι δὲ τῷ πνεύματι τοῦ νοὸς ὑμῶν) (Cf. Rom. 12:2).[58] The goal is to put on the new self, to fully embrace the change that has occurred as a result of transformative justification, and to realize that they have become new creations who are to reflect the righteousness and holiness of God back into the world around them (2 Cor. 5:17, cf. Rom. 6:1-23). Their unity with one another is an important part to achieving God's purpose in this respect (something Paul addresses in almost every one of his epistles in some way). The key to witness and representing God to the world around them is their own full acceptance of the implications of moral and spiritual changes that have occurred in them as a result of coming to know Christ (Eph. 4:22-24). These moral and spiritual changes form the contextual rationale for the practical instructions following our passage (in order to affect unity in the church, its full development into a temple for the habitation of God in the coming ages, the body as a reflection of the character of God back into creation, concern for the upbuilding and encouragement of the saints, so that the saints and church thrive).

Paul's premise, therefore, in Ephesians appears to be that unity in the body (Eph. 4:1-12) has implications for spiritual maturity and growth both in the church and among the saints themselves (Eph. 4:11-16). His readers should conduct themselves practically, that is on a personal and corporate level toward one another (as well as to the world), with integrity as a reflection of the character of God, *because* they have been created, through justification, into his image (Eph. 4:17-6:9). Success in holiness and coming to mature godliness will similarly be impacted by how they relate to one another, because disunity disrupts the flow of the resources of the body that grow and sustain the saints in their personal lives (Eph. 4:13-16). They are in some way dependent on one another for

---

[58] Holmes, M. W. (2011–2013). *The Greek New Testament: SBL Edition* (Eph 4:23). Lexham Press; Society of Biblical Literature.

success in godliness. Unity in the church is crucial for their thriving and that of the church as a whole. The church is the body of Christ, and is supported by leadership, which God gifted to the church, to equip a unified membership to care for one another and build one another up (Eph. 4:7-12). But Paul also makes the point that unity in the church it is supported by personal spiritual and moral development that lays aside the works of the flesh and the former life, to embrace the radical transformation that has occurred in their nature through justification and coming to know Christ (Eph. 4:17-22). Paul views these dynamics as having reciprocal power. A unified membership in fellowship with and ministering to one another, produces growth and maturity in Christ, the goal of which is progress in the godliness, holiness, and righteousness that God seeks from his people, while at the same time personal growth in these attributes contributes to the unity and thriving of the church (Eph. 4:1-4; 10-12, 13-16, 22-24).

Our passage seems to fall into the part of the argument where Paul is giving expression to the goal of unity with respect to facilitating spiritual growth in the church, in a context where unity is integral to the free flow of resources from the Spirit to the saints, because they are vital for their thriving (Eph 4:16). Paul will later turn this into practical instruction by citing specific examples of right conduct, of family relationships, and social interactions, including husband and wife, parents and children, and slave owners and slaves, especially where all parties share a faith in Christ. In that section, Paul expands his concern beyond unity of Jewish and Gentile believers, to include other relationships typically found in the Gentile Roman world, where the same spiritual obligations and implications for unity exist that ought to bind Jewish and Gentile believers to one another in selfless concern and mutual love. No ethnic, social, or societal division, nor any religious convention, as far as Paul is concerned, should be allowed to disrupt unity or hinder close, caring relationships among the saints.

UNITY AS THE UNIFYING THEME – Ephesians is not, as some think, athematic or composed of several themes stitched loosely together. There *is* a unifying thematic principle throughout; it is the unity of believers in the church, with implications drawn out in terms of how they are to live practically together with one another, especially Jews with Gentiles. In the course of the discussion, Paul uses examples drawn from typical social interactions in Roman and Greek cultural contexts in the empire, to illustrate to unbelievers how it might look if the gospel were to influence them, or should they find themselves entering the church or community of believers (Eph. 5:21-6:9, cf. Philemon). In that case, they would submit themselves to one another, that is to value the intrinsic worth of other believers in the church, without regard for social standing in empire culture, and serving each other selflessly, even if slave owners and slaves found themselves worshipping in the same congregation. For that matter husbands and wives, or parents and children, regardless of Roman society's views on subservience, would value one another with genuine respect, and act selflessly in their relationships (Eph. 5:20).

Notions of mutuality and even service to one another was, for imperial culture and tradition, radically countercultural.[59] Roman society's honor/shame codes and divisions, the ones with which Paul's converts would have been all too familiar, and in which every conscious thought would have been steeped, might not be easily overcome in their thinking, even after initial conversion. So, Paul appeals for the church to pay special attention to sustaining unity among believers, and that is

---

[59] (Witherington, The Problem with Evangelical Theology: Testing the Exegetical Foundatiuons of Calvinism, Dispensationalism, Welseyanism, and Pentecostalism, 2016) 91-93; (Keener, Paul, Women & Wives: Marriage and Women's Ministry in the Letters of Paul, 2004), 139-224.

going mean fully taking hold of the new and transformed life of Christ God has created in them.

The apostle set out the reasons for maintaining unity, which he bases on certain theological, even eschatological considerations. These are mostly found at the front end of the letter, but are also scattered throughout the more practical sections. It is Paul's writing and rhetorical style to do it this way, so that the theme is not contained in a discreet section of the letter, but interwoven into every part. His overarching concern appears to be laying down a strategy and rationale for how the church is to move forward in light of their common experience of Christ, particularly by establishing genuine unity of fellowship among believers, so as to have them support and encourage one another (Eph. 4:3, 13-16). The theological first reason given for unity is God's eschatological plan to bring all things into reconciliation to himself in Christ (Eph. 1:13-23), and that the church, God's redeemed community consisting of Jews and Gentiles, is one church, one body, and one temple of God, even now, but will ultimately be the dwelling place of God through the Spirit in eternity (Eph. 2:11-22, cf. Rev. 21:1-8).[60] The strategy requires, among other things, a full recognition of the moral and spiritual implications arising from their experience of salvation (Eph. 4:17-24). The plan cannot succeed without a radical change in human nature as it came to be following the fall, steeped in sin and rebellion against God (Eph. 2:1-3). Our passage stands at the

---

[60] We should note here the expansive redemptive purpose of God to be God among his people in fellowship with them, beginning in the garden, with Abraham, Israel in the wilderness and then in the land, in the tabernacle, then in the temple, lost during the exile, restored at the incarnation of Christ, poured out as promised at Pentecost as the Spirit, his indwelling the body of believers and church as if they are his earthly temple in the present, and an intended restored intimacy of the garden, only better, in a new heaven and new earth, to last into eternity without ceasing or interruption.

heart of exhortations for believers to fully embrace the moral and spiritual transformation of their nature that took place at justification, when God created in them a new man, capable now, in the present of following and being disposed toward the true holiness and righteousness of God, which God intends to perfect by his Spirit through constant ongoing renewal throughout the rest of their lives (Eph, 2:22-24). Unity in the church, and between believers, flows from these moral changes and the operation of God in believers, with the goal of developing mature godliness in his people and a perfect church without blemish and defect (Eph. 5:25-27, cf. 2 Cor. 11:2). Unity requires a critical recognition of the moral-spiritual implications of coming to know Christ. Believers must act in a Christ-like manner toward one another, reflecting the character of God back into the community of faith and the world. They are not at liberty to act in ways that are sinful or governed by the motivations and desires of the old life, that much Paul had taught them when he was with them before his arrest (ὑμεῖς δὲ οὐχ οὕτως ἐμάθετε τὸν Χριστόν) (Eph. 4:17-20).[61]

We may even be more specific than this. Paul introduces his theme of unity by at first exploring their (his and the Ephesians) common experience of salvation through a shared knowledge of God, as well as his provision of the shared blessings of salvation foreordained to all those who come to Christ regardless of previous backgrounds (Eph. 1:3-10). Then he introduces the idea that those who first believed in Christ, the Jews, compared to the Ephesians who came to faith later, as Gentiles, have different backgrounds, and yet share in a common experience of salvation in Christ (Eph. 1:11-13; 2:1-3). By this, the apostle seems to introduce his theme of unity in the church, essentially as part of the opening remarks of his epistle. Both groups are recipients

---

[61] Holmes, M. W. (2011–2013). *The Greek New Testament: SBL Edition* (Eph 4:20). Lexham Press; Society of Biblical Literature.

of the common blessing of God foreordained for those who believe in Christ, and who are sealed by a common experience of the Holy Spirit's power (Eph. 1:13-14). The same sacrifice of Christ on the cross provides salvation to both Jew and Gentile, so that there is no difference between them in the eyes of God (Eph. 2:11-22). Both are *in Christ* as a result of the working of God himself, according this own design and purpose to create one church, one people of God out of Jews and Gentiles (cf. Ps. 45:12; 87:4; Isa 2:2-5; 19:25; 26:18; 42:6; 45:14; 49:6; 55:5-13; Micah 4:1-3; Zech. 8:22; Luke 2:29-32). When he wrote this, it might not be too much to say that Paul had in mind for this opening the theme of promoting unity in the Ephesian church, particularly between Jewish and Gentile believers. The theme comes to an early the theological climax in the statement of unity in Christ, and the eradication of separating barriers in Ephesians 2:11-22. After this, Paul turns to the eschatological context in God overarching redemptive, asserting that this was God plan all along, and that it will be vindicated fully to his own satisfaction in the end (Eph. 3:1-16).

In chapter three, Paul sets the foundation for his appeal for unity, particularly between Jewish and Gentile believers, in the mystery of the gospel *revealed*, especially to him as the apostle to the *Gentiles* (cf. Gal 1:11-12, 17; 2:1-2), and which was fully contained prophetically in the old covenant scriptures, even if a little cryptically (Eph. 3:2-3). The revelation of this mystery has come to light in the incarnation of Christ as the fulfilment of God purpose and earlier prophecy (Eph. 3:1-6). At the core of this revelation is that God always intended to provide salvation to Jews and Gentiles on the basis of the same sacrifice of Christ on the cross, and by faith in him (Eph. 3:6, cf. Gen 12:1-3; Isa. 42:6; 49:6). Both must come to Christ in the same way, and on the same basis of faith and reliance on God's grace (Eph. 3:4-6; 7-13, cf. Rom. 5:1-2; Eph. 2:5, 8-9). Paul insists that their common experience of salvation through faith in Christ, means that they must be united in their fellowship and life together in the community of faith, the body of Christ

(Eph, 4:3, 13-16). Chapter four reinforces the idea of unity and its implications, first by asserting the primacy of unity, and the need for believers to support other believers with every effort that it is possible for them to engage toward one another (Eph. 4:3, 16). He goes on to demonstrate that unity is critical to the ongoing health, growth, and maturation of believers personally, and of thriving for the church corporately (Eph. 4:8-16). The latter part of chapter 4 and on into chapter 5 deals with what unity looks like in terms of conduct and attitudes among believers, and moves beyond the narrower Jew-Gentile context.

At first in this section, beginning after the doxology closing chapter 3, Paul alerts them to God's goals for unity, namely maturity into godliness of character, and the thriving of the church as the body of Christ (Eph. 4:1-16). God has given them leaders to equip them for unity and to ensure the church does in fact thrive (Eph. 4:8-16). He underscores what maturation looks like for believers in the church, a reflection of the holiness and righteousness of God back into the world (Eph. 4:17-24, cf. Gen. 1:26-28; Phil. 2:14-16). In the later part of this section, going through the early part of chapter 6, Paul further develops this theme of unity by addressing some critical elements of Christians living in community with one another (Eph. 4:25-6:9). These are the practical implications, with respect to unity and his theology of the gospel, of God overarching purpose for reconciliation, of the mystery revealed to him as the apostle to the Gentiles, of the common and shared experience of all believers in Christ, Jew, or Gentile, and of salvation through faith in Christ – all of that. Later in chapter 5, and the first half of chapter 6, Paul speaks of the implications of living in this kind of community of faith with one another, particularly with respect to specific social relationships believers might have with one another in Roman society outside of the church – such as husbands and wives, slaves and slave owners, parents, and children (Eph. 5:20-6:9). Paul is concerned throughout the letter with how his readers will navigate their relationships with one another in the church or community of faith, and as citizens surrounded by imperial Roman culture, among whom they must live and conduct their lives daily with different attitudes and moral values, since now they belong to the kingdom of God (Eph. 4:17-19, cf. Phil. 2:14-16; 3:17-21; Col. 1:13-14). The values of the world around them cannot govern how they relate to and treat one another (Eph. 4:17-23). On the contrary, they must conduct themselves toward one another in ways that are consistent with the principles of the kingdom of God, and that reflect the righteousness and holiness of God back into fallen society around them (Eph. 4:24, cf. Phil. 2:14-16).

Regardless of how world around them work or acts, believers must relate to one another ways consistent with having been morally transformed by the grace of God, and are now members of the body of Christ (Eph. 2:8-9). In the church graciousness rules, and unity of relationships through selfless love must be preserved above all things. To value one another through mutual service and caring, sincere love is required (cf. Rom. 12:3, 4-5; 13:8, 10; 14:13-21; 16:17-18; 1 Cor. 13:1-13; 16:15-16; Gal. 5:13; Eph. 4:12; Phil. 2:5-11, 17), as they go on helping one another to maturity in godliness and character (Eph. 4:13-25; 22-24). The enterprise of the moral and spiritual maturation for the saints is in fact vitally and integrally connected to unity in relationships in the church, with service and encouragement at the heart of shared life and fellowship (Eph. 4:16, cf. Rom. 14:19; 15:2; 1 Cor. 8:1; 14:12; 10:8; 13:10; Eph 4:29; 1 Thess. 5:11).

Although the last part of chapter 6 appears to move away from the main theme of unity, it actually supports it. Though the famous armor of God passage is viewed almost "materialistically" by the contemporary church or as a mystical "spiritual" exercise in one's personal devotions, it is actually allegorical, depicting the elements of Christian character and practice that contribute to the unity of the church because of spiritual discipline in the lives of the saints (Eph 6:10-18). It is a concrete expression of what characteristics of the Christian life Paul had in mind, when he spoke of holiness and righteousness, and the sorts of moral qualities envisioned in putting on the new man. In this passage, Paul shows that objective personal and spiritual attributes, the kind coming out of the new life they have in Christ, and which God is bringing to maturity, do have a practical role to play in the lives of the saints as they engage themselves against the temptations and hardships in the world, particularly where the opposition to the enemy in at work to discourage and sabotage them (Eph. 6:10-18). To preserve the unity of the church and support other believers through fellowship, to engage the practical instructions laid down by Paul, believers will need to engage these spiritual and moral attributes, represented by the armor, as a matter of consistent faith and practice. Elements of the armor include spiritual virtues, attributes and supports for the work of God in the believer's life through the working of the Spirit. They are, like the new man, to be consciously and deliberately engaged by faith through the Spirit in the daily living of Christian life. They are to characterize how believers interact in fellowship with one another, as well as how they conduct themselves in the context of the world around them, resisting pressure to conform to Gentile culture of society at large (Eph. 4:17; 6:10-18). When engaged, these elements become specific "mechanisms" that support right conduct and thus lead to the development of godly character. Habitual practice of these things leads to a deepening of Christian character and integrity.[62] Surely, it is clear that, far from being separate instruction, Paul is still addressing the issue of Christian character in the context of relationships in the church, which he has just described in some practical detail.

For example, to mention just two, they are to be truthful with one another – stand firm with the belt of truth firmly affixed around them

---

[62] Wright N. T., 2012, 154-159.

(Eph. 6:14). This promotes unity and is a moral virtue leading to integrity (Eph. 4:15; 5:9; cf. Rom. 12:9; 1 Cor. 5:8; 13:6; 2 Cor. 6:6; 8:8; Eph. 6:5; Col. 3:22). Righteousness as practical conduct coming from the internal integrity is critical, because where each of them behaves appropriately toward God and one another, it leads to growth in authentic godliness and character for others. Righteousness has a horizontal dimension to it, not just a vertical one. It is relational, and evidence of the kind of selflessness that lies at the heart of how Paul views relationships working between believers in the church.

SUMMARY: Paul did not come to the idea of unity as mutual concern ex-nihilo, but stood in continuity with the expressed concerns of God in the old covenant of the law, where his people in right relationship with him must care for one another selflessly, Israelite for Israelite. One of the particularly prominent ideas in the Old Testament is righteousness, not right conduct towards God alone, but as right conduct towards, and the proper treatment of others (cf. Lev. 19:18; Deut. 6:4). The law required that those who were able must care for the disadvantaged and needy. The poor and needy, disadvantaged, and aliens were not to be ignored. Righteousness is something Paul often emphasizes in his letters, that it is was the original impetus behind the old covenant idea for mutual concern and love for your neighbor, but is now is greatly increased by the grace of God in salvation, as a result of the power of the indwelling Spirit given to believers in connection with transformative justification, and because of the renewal of their nature in Christ that establishes godly love as the underlying foundation for relationships in the community of faith (Rom. 8:9-17; 2 Cor. 5:17). The spontaneous outbreak of this in the early church, immediately after Pentecost is a testament to its generations as a result of new life in Christ, brought to bear on the converts from the inception of their new and continued experience as believers (Acts 2:42-47; 4:32-37). It is as though love and concern for one another erupted like a great and involuntary explosion of grace.

Right relationships and proper, compassionate, and gracious treatment of fellow believers in the believing community of the church is paramount for Paul. Even elements of the *armor of God*, play their part as critical for Christian life and character, which, when deliberately and purposefully embraced, increase and promote fellowship in the church. At the same time, their increasing (maturing) presence in the life of the believer has a protective role to play that will preserve their lives against opposition and temptation, leading to future hope, as well as to personal maturity (Rom. 5:3-8). Peter argues that continued development in Christian character provides for victory and safety, as they stand against the spiritual wickedness that is at work in the world, an idea Paul endorses with his exhortations to persistence in the pursuit of godliness (2 Pet. 1:3-11, cf. Eph. 6:10-12). As Paul views it, where the saints are thriving in their own spiritual lives, they are at the same time receivers of the resources of God at work in the church, by means of their connection to others, and through fellowship, as suppliers of resources the saints with whom the share fellowship, all *their* strengthening and edification (Eph. 4:16). Ideas of mutuality in the church are at the heart of Pauline theology of the church, and of practical relationships between believers in the community of faith.

As the last of chapter 6 closes with personal remarks and greetings, which critics complain do not exist, or are not extensive enough to suit their criteria for proof of Pauline authorship, as is usual, Paul closes his letter warmly, relationally, by emphasizing their shared experience of Christ. He blesses them with peace, and exalts the exchange between them of their love and faith from God, as well his concern for his readers, that they not be overly anxious for him, acknowledging that their concern for him is a demonstration reciprocal and genuine love for him (Eph. 6:19-23). He had already called on his readers to pray for him, and invited them to be *united* with him through prayer for his efforts to share the gospel publicly in connection with his trial (Eph. 6:19-20). The invitation itself is a call to be joined in unity with him in the great enterprise of the gospel. So, even the final remarks make use of the idea of connection, and thus underscore unity. Paul informs his readers that he is sending Tychicus to tell them about what is going on with him, while at the same time, Paul might offer encouragement to them through him (Eph. 6:21-22). Even in this, Paul models reciprocity, supporting the theme of unity in the work of the kingdom of God, and the body of Christ.

Mutuality or unity is demonstrably a, if not the, key theme in Ephesians. For that reason, we see that our passage which focuses on character reflecting the holiness and righteousness of God, builds on Paul's call for unity in the church, and serves as the foundation, and even the rationale for making every effort to preserve the unity which the Spirit has established through his application of the saving grace of God in their lives (Eph. 2:5, 8-9; 4:3).

Theological Context: In *Help for Holiness,* I included a lengthy discussion of the concepts of *righteousness* and *holiness* in both the Old Testament and epistles of Paul, which I do not propose to repeat here.[63] We will take time here only to summarize a few of the most pertinent points.

In Ephesians 4:22-24, Paul refers to *holiness, righteousness,* and *being created like God,* that is in the image of God. They are allusions to Old Testament concepts with which Paul was eminently familiar as a former Pharisee. Important elements of Paul's theology were not snatched out of the air without connection to the Old Testament. Although he invests them with significance in the context of the advent of Christ's incarnation, death, and resurrection, Paul's theology does not appear *ex nihilo* (cf. Rom. 9-11). Indeed, Paul is at pains to show how Christ provides fulfilled of Old Testament expectations with respect to

---

[63] Evans, P. F. (2018). Help For Holiness: Rediscovering God's Resources for Practical Sanctification in Galatians 5:16-25. Bloomington, IN, USA: WestBow Press, 6-133.

holiness and righteousness (Rom. 1:2-6), and how God made provision for Isreal under the new covenant to live successfully as a righteous and holy people through the power of the Spirit (cf. Rom. 8:1-4 Gal. 3:1-6; 5:16-25). For God's new covenant people, starting with the Jews (cf. Rom. 1:16-17) just as he promised, the Holy Spirit came to take over the Old Testament role of the law as the guide and instigator of righteousness for God's people (Rom. 7:1-8:17, cf. Gal. 3:1-5:25). Through regenerative and transformative justification, which Paul discusses in Romans 5, 6 and 7, God made provision for success in righteousness by imparting of the Spirit to work in partnership with new life, created in those who come to faith in Christ (Eph. 4:24, cf. Rom. 8:1-17).[64] Paul sees righteousness through the Spirit as affecting both right conduct and right character, making ongoing fellowship with God, and moral development in godliness possible (cf. Rom. 6:1-23; Gal. 5:1-25).

The purpose of the law in the Old Testament was to provide God's people with the support they needed to go on to godly conduct and character, and so to honor God as his people and provide a witness to a godless world.[65] Furthermore, consistent righteousness as integrity and right conduct was a condition of Israel's continued relationship and fellowship with God, personally as far as relationship was concerned, but critically corporately in the context of covenant blessings (cf. Lev. 11:44-45; Deut. 28; Isa. 1, 58; Mal. 2-3; Jer. 31:31-34; Ezek. 36:22-28). Under the new covenant, as predicted in Jeremiah for the future, the law was to be written on the hearts of God's people, which is a way of saying what Ezekiel also promised, that God would cleanse his people and give them a new heart and new S(s)pirit[66] leading to godliness (Jer. 31:31-34;

---

[64] Cf. Keener, Galatians: New Cambridge Bible Commentary, 2018, 22.
[65] Cf. Keener, Galatians: New Cambridge Bible Commentary, 2018, 19.
[66] To adopt the Gordon Fee scheme, whereby the combination of the upper and lower case "s" in this way signifies the interconnectedness of the

Ezek. 36:22-28). Where law had failed because of a flaw in human nature (as Paul discusses in Romans 7), God promised a new working principle which would produce the righteousness he was looking for. This law was to be written into their nature as a result of pardoning their sins and remembering their wickedness no longer (Jer. 31:34). God was, in essence, promising a transformation in their nature, which Jesus called new birth, and Paul calls "newness of life," or resurrection after the crucifixion of the old self (cf. John 3; Rom. 6; 2 Cor. 5:17).

For later Wesleyans in the mid-nineteenth, all the way into the twentieth centuries, following the influences of the post-civil war holiness movement, and particularly the doctrinal developments of the Pheobe Palmer movement, focus shifted to more narrowly construe outward appearance and conduct as marks of holiness. Leading to widespread legalism, the practice of *holiness* sometimes overshadowed God's purpose, expressed in the Old Testament, that right conduct must first of all come from a right, transformed heart, and ongoing renewing of the mind, as Paul put it (Eph. 4:22-24; Rom. 6:1-11; 12:1-2, cf. 1 Sam. 10:9; Ps. 51; Ezek. 18).[67] Paul saw the impartation of the indwelling-Spirit under the new covenant as the means by which God would fulfill his promise to establish righteousness in and among his people, to write on their hearts and minds. What eluded Israel under

---

operation of the Holy Spirit with the human spirit under the transformative dynamics of grace in the new covenant, where justification and righteousness are by faith, leading to godliness and obedience. The impartation of the Spirit to perfect righteousness in God's people comes as fulfillment of the Old Testament promises concerning the impartation of the Holy Spirit to God's people in the end times as a sign of the imminent coming of the kingdom of God (cf. Jer. 31:31-34; Joel 2:28-29; Rom. 5:1-2; 8:1-4).

[67] Peters, Christian perfection and American Methodism, 1995, 130, cf. 112-122.

the law and the old covenant was to be made possible in God's people going forward through the gift of the Spirit as part of the new (Jer. 32:31-34; Ezek. 36:22-28).

THE SPIRIT OF HOLINESS: God predicted and promised this dimension of the Spirit for his future people, as well as pardon for their sins, and cleansing from the moral impurity of their wickedness, all as part of a new covenant in Jeremiah, and moral transformation in Ezekiel (Jer. 31:34b; Ezek. 36:25). Moral power from this new relationship with the Spirit would make it possible for the people of God to gain victory over the human impulse to habitually sin (what Paul would later call carnality or the flesh) (cf. Gen. 6:5, Ps. 14:1-3; Jer. 17:9). The need for moral renewal and a new moral dynamic to secure it, is due to Israel's repeated moral failure under the old covenant based on the law, and provides the rationale behind the promise in Jeremiah of a coming *new covenant* (cf. Jer. 31:31-34), and in Ezekiel of a *new heart* and *S(s)pirit* (Ezek. 36:26). It is the inauguration of this new covenant through Christ's incarnation and sacrifice (Rom. 1:1-3), that brought about the arrival of the kingdom of God into the present age, signaled particularly by the outpouring of power of the Spirit, working just as God promised he would, producing holiness and righteousness in his people (cf. Rom. 8:1-17; Gal. 2: 19-21; 3:1-6; 5:16-25; Eph. 4:22-24; et al.). For Paul, the gift of the Spirit is the already-realized dynamic of the eschatological kingdom of God, which is at work in the church now, connecting disciples who serve Christ in this age to the power of God and the future glory of the age to come (2 Cor. 1:22; 4:1-12; 5:5; Eph. 1:11-14; 4:20, cf. Gal. 5:16-25; Rom. 8:1-17; Eph. 4:22-24).

If the kingdom of God is breaking into the world, it is breaking in at the point where God's people are living by the power of the Spirit in true holiness and righteousness, because that is how the image of God, and his likeness are to be reflected back into the world around the church (cf. Gen. 1:26-28; Eph. 4:22-24; Phil 2:14-16). If the church is in any way reflective of the rule of God in the present, it is by and through the outwardly manifested operation of the Spirit in and among his transformed people, regulating their conduct and producing righteousness in their lives as a witness to this godless age (Phil. 2:14-16). God's people are to image God to this age, shining as lights in a darkened sky in full sight of a perverse and crooked generation, to represent God (Phil. 2:12-16). Only through the indwelling Spirit, Paul believes, can that be possible (Rom. 7:21-25; 8:1-4; Gal. 5:16-5; Eph. 4:24; Phil. 2:14-17, cf. Matt. 5:13-16). What God intended for Israel with the support of the law, namely to provide a witness to the people around by them by living morally different lives that reflected his character and image, is now at work more powerfully and successfully than ever in the church through the Spirit, so that God's New Testament people might image him to the people of this present age, as a true witness of God's holiness.

The effect of implanting a new principle of life in God's people is the same in Jeremiah as the cleansing and renewal of heart and S(s)pirit in Ezekiel. It provides the grounds for producing and perfecting righteousness in conduct and character for God's people, based not an external law, but on the inward work of God in their nature (cf. Jer. 31:31-34; Ezek. 36:24:29a). The Old Testament's promise of the Spirit to God's people in the age to come had for Paul a moral dimension to it, which he connected to Jeremiah's assertion that the new covenant would bring transformation of nature, and which Ezekiel linked to cleansing leading to inner regeneration.[68] For Paul, the Spirit was the internal dynamic or principle promised by God then, now at work in the church through

[68] This is the often-overlooked dimension for Pentecostals, where we emphasize the *power of the Spirit,* along with charismatic manifestations, but overlook almost entirely the role of the Spirit in God's plan for moral transformation and success in righteousness (i.e., maturity into godliness).

Christ, creating morally and ethically new lives for his people. Their regeneration may begin with morally transformative justification (cf. Rom 5-6; 2 Cor. 5:17), but it will be brought to full moral maturity in godliness through the power of the indwelling Spirit, working in them over time (Gal. 5:16-25; Eph. 4:13-24).

The signature mark of God's presence and of the kingdom of God in the world, that God dwells among his people (the church), is the godliness he is developing in them, where it is evident by a difference in their character and conduct (cf. Phil. 2:14-16, cf. Ex. 29:45; Num. 23:21; Deut. 4:7; Jer. 24:7; 31:33; 32:38; 43:1; Ezek. 11:20; 14:11; 34:30; 37:27; 39:22; Zech. 8:8; 12:5; 2 Cor. 6:16; Heb. 8:10; Rev. 21:3). In this way, the church now represents God through the Spirit in true righteousness of character and image, reflecting his character and nature back into creation in the present age (cf. Gen. 1:26-28; Phil. 2:14-16). The inward principle or dynamic promised in the Old Testament, Paul boldly asserts, is *already* at work through the gift of the Spirit which has been given to believers, the disciples of Jesus Christ (Rom. 8:1-4, 13-17, cf. 2 Cor. 5:17). The age of the new covenant has come.

Paul believes that where believers are indwelt by the Spirit of God, and so long as they maintain an attitude of faith and surrender to God, they will be guided by the Holy Spirit into righteousness of conduct, and the development of godly (mature) character (Rom. 8:1-14; Gal. 5:16-25). As a result, Paul assures the Galatians, the desires of the flesh are denied the opportunity to raise themselves to concrete action in their bodies, that is as sinful conduct, whenever they walk in the Spirit, are led by the Spirit, and keep in step with the Spirit (cf. Rom. 8:1-8; **Gal. 5:16**, 18, 24-25). It is in this sense, that the Holy Spirit affects holiness in God's people.[69] It is God's daily interaction and fellowship with his reconciled people, justified by grace, and at peace with God through Jesus Christ, that allows the Spirit to regulate and guide conduct and mold character. Paul views the saints as those who are sealed with the Spirit of promise, the anticipation of which is final and mature godliness (Eph. 1:13-14; 4:22-24). He considers their bodies to be temples of the Spirit, a sanctified dwelling place for God, out of which concrete expressions of practical righteousness must and should arise in the present age to "...glorify God in your bodies" (2 Cor. 6:14-18).

THE HOLY SPIRIT AS A DOWNPAYMENT OF WHAT IS TO COME: The experience of the indwelling of Spirit, to produce righteousness and to regulate conduct, is an anticipation of the full reality of the future kingdom of God in the coming age, when the moral authority of God will reign over his entire creation without opposition (cf. Col. 1:15-20). Paul calls the impartation of the Spirit into the lives of the saints, the seal of the Spirit, a downpayment, a deposit in the present that guarantees the final redemption (retrieval at the return of Christ) of what God has already "purchased" and belongs to him (Rom. 8:23; 2 Cor. 1:22; 5:5; Eph. 1:13-14). Paul stresses vehemently in his letters and preaching that the dynamic power of the kingdom of God through the Spirit is already operating in the church and the lives of God's people. He argues, holiness and righteousness are already in process and under development for those who belong to Christ, even now in the present age as we serve God, and their experience of the Spirit serves as a taste of future glory in the age to come (Eph. 1:13-14; 2 Cor. 1:20-22; 5:5, cf. Phil. 3:7-14). The power of the Spirit, working in our character and conduct, is not somehow held in abeyance for the future, for the "article

---

[69] Employing the very dynamics anticipated by Jeremiah and Ezekiel and involving the anticipated gift of the Spirit to mark the commencement or arrival of the eschatological age of the kingdom of God.

death," Welsey observed, against the Calvinism of his day. Rather it must be worked out in us in the present, so as to represent God to a sinful generation (Phil. 2:12-16).

This Pauline idea of God at work in the present for holiness in his people was at the foundation of Wesley's theology of a second blessing, or sanctification. Through grace and faith in Christ, by the outworking of God's grace through the presence and power of the Spirit, we already belong to and participate in the "future" kingdom of God, but in the context of our daily, somewhat mundane, lives in this present. Nevertheless, Paul contends, the dynamics of the future kingdom, including righteousness, are already at work in and through us because of the Spirit (Phil. 3:20-21). The kingdom has come into the present age with the arrival of the Spirit, although its full realization awaits a future full manifestation. It is both now and not yet. Our participation in the kingdom of God now, nonetheless, is real and authentic as the rule of God in present is worked out through surrender to the Spirit. The Spirit has set about producing in us what God has been looking for all along from his people, righteousness, and holiness.

MORE ON CONTINUITY BETWEEN OLD COVENANT RIGHTEOUSNESS IN THE NEW – There appear to be three fundamental aspects of Old Testament righteousness that carry forward in the theology of Paul, which are enlarged by his understanding of the Christ advent and the operation of the kingdom of God in the present age through the Spirit. N. T. Wright remarked in a podcast that *righteousness* in the Bible is like a barge going downriver, or a ship going from port to port picking up cargo as it goes – righteousness has picked up a great many nuances of meaning over the centuries. However, three principal ideas resonate in the redemptive context of God's dealings with his people. They are righteousness as godly character and right standing with God (*being* right with God subjectively, in heart and conduct, integrity, coupled to objective rightness with God by his reckoning), righteousness of right conduct (behavior and action, obedience, *doing* what is right by God reckoning), righteousness in the sense of moral uprightness of one's disposition (attitude and disposition of holiness, the deposit of godliness imparted by God, and maturing in one's nature, character that improves over time through a relationship with God).[70] Properly speaking, the latter two are aspects of the former and speak to what the Bible calls integrity, the correspondence of inward nature and character to outward practice. Sometimes righteousness can mean vindication or consistent obedience to God, even after past moral failure, as in the example of King David (cf. Ex. 34:6-7; Ezek. 18:1-32). Nevertheless, aspects or nuances of righteousness are emphasized by context when the term is used in the Old Testament.

Righteousness for Paul also consists in the just judgment of God on sin and the persistent sinner, something also rooted in the Old Testament. Righteousness, as a term, seems to represent something of a spectrum of elements, all critical to the concept, but individually significant in context. Righteousness sometimes expresses the existential side of Christian life for God's people, in that it seems to unite right character with right conduct as the work of the Spirit in believers

---

[70] Of course, these overlap, but are nuanced by context in scripture. The subjective and objective aspects rightness with God are often blended into criteria or evidence a right standing with God. Together the full spectrum of elements in righteousness correspondence to the character and action of God himself, which he aims to reproduce in his people as a reflect of his image and likeness. Moral transformation at justification, implies an obligation to go on habitual rightness with God, consist with both right character and conduct (in the Old Testament integrity/obedience). From our point of view as new covenant servants of God, righteousness requires reconciliation to God by grace through Christ, where past sins are pardoned by God followed by a commitment to the habitual pursuit of righteousness by faith through power of the indwelling Spirit at work in us (Rom 1:16-17; 5:1-2; 6:1-8:17; Gal. 2:19-21; 6:16-25).

(cf. Gal. 5:1-25; Eph. 4:22-24; Col. 3:1-14). These essentials of righteousness carry over from the old covenant into the new, but with the with the critical role of the Spirit's power enable meaningful moral success (Jer. 31:31-34; Ezek. 36:22-28; Rom. 8:1-8; Gal. 5:16-25). Our standing with God matters, how God views us morally and spiritually as a result of salvation and pardon. But the development of right character as increasing maturation in godliness, leading to obedience matters as much. The latter flows out of the former through the operation of the Spirit in us. After justification and becoming new creations in Christ, righteousness is expected to grow and mature (Rom. 6:1-11; 2 Cor. 5:17).[71] The advent of personal salvation or conversion is not divorced from God's requirement for obedience, uprightness of character and right conduct in his people (Rom. 6:1-2; Eph. 2:1-3; 4:17). So, just as Israel often got in trouble with God, following his redemptive initiative in Exodus, because of persistent sin, disobedience, and a failure to acknowledge and repent for wickedness in their character that marred their witness, so the New Testament people of God are called to go on to embrace new life in Christ and growth for mature godliness through the power of the Spirit, and to avoid falling back into sin (Eph. 4:17-19). He warns the Romans of the danger of being squeezed back into conformity to the world (Rom. 12:1-2), or of trading on the grace of God by re-engaging in habitually sinful conduct (Rom. 6:1-2). The book of Hebrews is the magnum opus of the New Testament on this theme.

Jesus' own perspective was that his life and ministry fulfilled the scriptures so that the law and the prophets stood in continuity with the plan of God at work in his ministry and sacrifice, toward which God was

---

[71] For example, Romans 6 deals with right conduct following transformative union with Christ in justification. There Paul uses the terms righteousness and holiness to refer to character and conduct in alignment, where that is the trajectory of the progressive logic of his argument (cf. Rom. 6:1-2, 15, 8:1-4, also Gal. 5).

working when he promised a new covenant to accomplish what never materialized consistently out of the old (Matt. 5:17-20). He came to bring to completion and fulfillment what God had revealed in the scriptures, but through the fresh dynamic of the good news of the kingdom's arrival, and therefore a new power from God to equip his people for righteousness (Jer. 31:31-34). Jesus saw the righteousness of the kingdom of God, which he came to establish through faith in God, by transformative repentance, as superior to the righteousness of the law and adherence to Jewish tradition. He often drew attention to this, especially in light of the self-designated *law-keepers, the* champions of rule-keeping, the Pharisees (cf. Matt. 23-24).

Jesus defended a righteousness that stood in continuity with Old Testament righteousness, by which God desired to produce a people for himself, a people who love God and obey him from a right heart producing right conduct (Matt. 5:20, 21-48; 12:35). He passed on this idea of righteousness of conduct *out of character* (the idea of integrity in the Old Testament) to his disciples. They in turn imparted it to the church. Paul the Apostle notably took up the theme and explored it in terms of the theology of grace and of the Holy Spirit's role in the life of the believer. The theology of righteousness found in the New Testament stands in continuity with righteousness in the Old Testament, and as a fulfillment of the scriptures, where God stated his intentions and purposes for his people, in terms of a new approach and a new covenant, moving on from the law (cf. Jer. 31:31-34; Ezek. 36:22-28). Using his personal experience as a law-abiding Jew Paul explores this idea in Romans 7, and in the process identifies a problem, an underlying flaw in human nature that makes law-keeping impossible without the power of God to break the power of indwelling sin. God's people need both relief from the power of sin to enslave them to habitual sinning, Paul concluded, as well as moral empowering from God to go on to right practice, and the development of right character (Rom. 7:21-8:4).

Jesus spoke of the coming dynamic of the Spirit as part of the arrival of the kingdom of God into this present age (cf. Luke 24:25-31; 36-49; Acts 1:3-8). From the Old Testament we discover that this new dynamic is connected to God applying morally transformative pardon for sins to his people as part of a new covenant, of which in both Jeremiah and Ezekiel speak (cf. Jer. 31:31-34; Ezek. 18; 36). David's confession in Psalm 51, makes it clear that even under the old covenant, certain dynamics of repentance, faith, the power of the Spirit, and of reconciliation and fellowship with God are critical to righteousness and relationship with God. The new covenant extends and expands those dynamics more explicitly, by applying them under the terms of the sacrifice of Christ, and through the moral application of his resurrection (Rom. 6:1-11), thereby making not just moral transformation possible, but equipping the believer with the power of grace through the Spirit to go on to the consistent and habitual pursuit of righteousness (Rom. 5:1-2; 8:1-4; Gal. 5:16-25). In terms of the new covenant, the operation of the Holy Spirit in the people of God is the stated mark of the arrival of that kingdom, with its moral power and dynamic influence to bring about holiness for God's people, and to prepare them for the coming new creation, the final realization of God's supreme reign and purpose (Rev. 21:1-6). The dynamic moral power of the Holy Spirit, indwelling God's people and in the church, is at the heart of Pauline theology of righteousness. And the Holy Spirit's power and presence in and among God's people, affecting moral change and making them different in character and conduct from the people of this present age, is the sign of God's activity bringing about his eschatological purposes for his people and future creation.

Paul's Explanation to The Galatians: After his dramatic conversion, Paul saw in Christ the fulfillment of Old Testament promises and prophecies, and he worked out his understanding of the implications of the scriptures in light of Christ through a significantly long period of reflection and study while away from Jerusalem (Gal. 2:1). Sometime later, Paul subjected his theology and conclusions to the critical judgment of the leaders in Jerusalem for their affirmation or possibly correction (Acts 9:26-31; 11:25-26; Gal. 1:11-2:10). The Jerusalem leaders and apostles not only whole-heartedly endorsed Paul's understanding of Christ but affirmed him to be particularly the apostle to the Gentiles (Gal. 2:6-10). They added nothing to *his gospel* (the gospel he had been preaching), and they offered no alteration of correction (Gal. 1:11; 2:6).[72] Paul points to this as a sign of its acceptance by the apostles and leaders of the Jersualem church, an endorsement of his theological and doctrinal positions on the gospel as he currently preached and applied it among the Gentiles.[73] His preaching and application of the gospel, which in Ephesians 3 he explains as a revelation from God, arose from divine light shed on the Jewish scriptures in connection with the incarnation, the life and resurrection of Christ, and based on the promises and prophecies made under the old covenant that found their fulfillment in him. Paul's

---

[72] For a critical analysis of this phrase *"added nothing to me"* (ἐμοὶ γὰρ οἱ δοκοῦντες οὐδὲν προσανέθεντο), see Moises Silva, *Interpreting Galatians,* ((Silva, 2001), 143-158).

[73] Moises Silva points out that any differences in approach between Paul, the apostles, or prominent leaders (τῶν δοκούντων εἶναί τι) in the Jersualem church, was the result of context and relationship to cultural and historical Judaism, and that Paul did not expect Gentiles to embrace the scruples and practices of Judaism in order to fully belong to the community of believers in the church. Nevertheless, Paul is aware of the difficulties between the two with respect to engaging in table-fellowship in particular and encouraged each group to exercise temperate attitudes toward one an another (cf. Rom. 14), non-judgmentalism, and grace in churches where there are mixed congregations. What Paul would not allow was that Gentiles should be forced to adopt specifically Jewish practices and rituals (i.e., circumcision) as a condition of their inclusion in the church, or to be considered entirely saved. He reminded Peter of this in Antioch, that the church acknowledges Jews and Gentiles are ultimately saved by faith in God through Christ (Gal. 2:14-16).

understanding of this revelation he hammered out through lengthy investigation and study, and he called it a *mystery* which God unveiled to him personally as the apostle to the Gentiles (Ga. 2:6; Eph. 2:19; 3:1-13).

Paul makes clear he is not the only apostle to understand these things, and that the gospel and its relationship to the scriptures had been revealed to the other apostles and prophets of the early church from their personal knowledge and interaction with Christ himself (Eph. 3:5). He only asserts that his own knowledge of the gospel and its relationship to the scriptures, Christ's life, ministry, death, and resurrection was uniquely conferred to him through revelation by the risen Christ, by the Holy Spirit (Eph. 3:7, cf. Gal. 1:13-2:1). As a result, Paul, more than any other New Testament writer, developed Old Testament themes and ideas in the context of the arrival of the kingdom of God with the advent of Christ, and as a fulfillment of God eschatological purposes. In the epistles of John and Peter, we see similar themes found in Paul's writings. These overlapping ideas indicate that Paul's views were indeed mainstream early church theology, and not wholly innovative Pauline ideas. However, Paul developed many of these themes more systematically and fully than other any New Testament writer. Nevertheless, we do note that both Peter and John speak in remarkably similar ways to Paul on the topics like righteousness, for example (cf. 1 Pet. 1:13-16, 2:9-10; 2 Pet. 3:11-16; 1 John 2:28-29; 3:7-10; 5:18-20). Paul's views were far from dogmatic aberrations of his own devising. Rather, they are a fuller development of the theology and themes recognized as apostolic tradition and preaching in the early church (Rom. 6:17; 16:17; Col. 1:28; 2 Thess. 2:15; 3:6; 1 Tim. 4:6, 13, 16; 6:3; 2 Tim. 1:13; 3:16; 4:3; Tit. 1:9; 2:1; Heb. 5:13; 6:1; 2 John 9, 10) (cf. Act 2:14-39; 42-47; 3:11-26; 4:8-22; 5:29-32 and 13:16-41).

Pauline Treatment of Righteousness and Holiness: Among Old Testament themes that Paul developed as part of the paradigm of the arrival of the kingdom of God in Christ are the concepts of righteousness and holiness, and how they relate to justification on the one hand, and God's redemptive purpose or trajectory for all of creation on the other (1 Cor. 15:20-28; Col. 1:13-20). Paul had the habit of appointing competent teachers to carry the instruction of the disciples forward, and urged his co-laboring leaders to be sure to instruct them in the *holy scriptures*, meaning the Old Testament, as well as the gospel, and presumably the relationship between the Old testament and its fulfillment in Christ (cf. 1 Tim. 3:2; 4:2, 6, 11, 13; 5:17; 2 Tim. 1:13; 2:2, 24; 3:14-17 Tit. 2:1, 3, 7, 9-10, 15). So, when he refers to concepts such as *righteousness* and *holiness* or makes references to the *image of God,* or, as he does in Romans, *being conformed into the image of God's Son,* his readers would be able to supply from their background understanding the necessary interpretive framework from the scriptures. For our purposes, we will mention without excessive comment several Old Testament and Pauline ideas that stand behind *holiness* and *righteousness*.

First of all, as far as the Old Testament is concerned, *obedience* to God is integral to righteousness and holiness. Evangelical Christians are so attuned to the debate over *grace* and *works,* that talk of going on to right conduct is viewed skeptically as an affirmation of works-righteousness. This is the heritage of Augustinianism and Calvinism, which has been rendered almost theologically intractable in the western church.[74] Fundamentally, however, God demanded that his people, Isreal, both love him and obey him. That is, God demands that his people have a right heart toward him, and engage in right conduct before him as his representatives to the world around them (cf. Deut. 6:4-5; 7:9;

---

[74] Schaff, 1887, 46-49, 53-54, 55, 57, 62-63, 66, 112-115, 145, 149, 160, et. al.

10:12; 11:13, 22; 19:9; 30:16; Josh. 22:5; Isa. 56:6; Dan. 9:4). It is not enough to love God alone without right conduct. It is not enough to technically obey his commandments but not have a right heart toward God. Both are required simultaneously in the Old Testament to be in proper relationship with God. The absence of either or both is enough to make fellowship with God impossible, and to render any worship ritual null. God demanded the correspondence of both in the lives of his people for worship and relationship (cf. Isa. 1; 58).

In other words, God demanded a right heart for producing right conduct. The core of Israel's historical enmity with God was not having a right heart toward God, while still outwardly engaging in empty religious ritual (cf. Isa. 1; 58; Mal 1-3). What had been a problem for Paul, once a law keeping Pharisee, continued to be the problem for many in Judaism, and it was out of this God delivered him through the power of Christ and the Holy Spirit (cf. Rom. 7:24-8:4). Technical performance, when not matched by genuine inward devotion and holiness of heart toward God, was for the Old Testament people of God of no value. If the prophets complained about anything in Israel, it was that Israel's worship and religious practice did not always correspond to a genuine heart right with God (cf. Ps. 50:7-15; 51:16-17; Isa. 1:10-20; 58:3-14; Jer. 6:19-20; Joel 2:12-14; Mal. 1:6-14; 2:13-16; 3:13-14). Right conduct is not a peripheral issue to fellowship with God but at the heart of what God requires, because when it is acceptable to him, it comes from a genuine heart of devotion and love for God. Ritual and religious practice are never an end in themselves; instead, righteousness (right, ethical, and moral practice) are the fruit of a genuine relationship with God. This is the fundamental Old Testament teaching on holiness, that integrity is the correspondence between a right heart and right conduct, love, and obedience.

Paul confirms his new covenant perspective is the same as the Old Testament by his early treatment of the topic in Romans 2-3, where God is looking for the right conduct that it is essential to the survival of a relationship with God (Rom 2:5-11; 3:23-31). Paul is speaking at this point in Romans about the foundational principle of fellowship or reconciliation to God, where a right heart doing right things is critical to relationship with him. Despite Paul's unshakable conviction that it is *only* by grace that we are justified before God (Rom. 5:1-2; Eph. 2:8-9; Gal. 3:1-6; 5:1-6), he never allowed *grace* to become an excuse for habitual moral failure or refusing to adopt righteousness as consistent right practice or conduct (cf. Rom. 5:20-21; 6:1-2). Indeed, after warning the Galatians not to adopt law keeping for achieving righteousness, but rather to rely on God's grace at work through the Spirit in them, he further warns them that freedom from law is not an excuse for the flesh to run wild (Gal. 5:13). An overarching idea early in Romans 6, is that those who have been justified by grace cannot then continue in habitual sinning. How can they, Paul asks, when justification is morally transformative, putting to death the old life and self, leading to resurrection into new life in Christ (Rom. 6:1-10)?

Paul denies that the justified believer might cavalierly go on habitually sinning because grace will overflow it, applying the remedy of God's pardon (Rom. 6:1-2). Paul warns his readers that such conduct will inevitably lead to the death and dissolution of the relationship with God (Rom. 6:23). Why? Because habitual sinning comes from a heart that is not right with God. Habitual disobedience results in a fractured relationship with God, not because our relationship with God or salvation is secured or lost because of our conduct, but because "bad company corrupts good manners" (1 Cor. 15:33). The presence of persistent sinning in our lives leads to moral dissolution, and is the result of a heart problem. Something sinister lies behind bad conduct, something inwardly wrong, that is inconsistent with fellowship with God (1 John 1:5-7). It is at variance with holiness consistent with knowing God and walking in fellowship with him. John remarks that if we claim to have fellowship with God but walk in darkness (habitually sin and disobey him) we lie (1 John 1:6).

Bad conduct is the sign of a bad heart, a heart not right with God (cf. Matt. 7:17-18; 21:18-19; Luke 6:43). Jesus' battle with the Pharisees was often over the appearance of righteousness, versus its sincere possession inwardly, so he condemned insincere piety (Matt. 23). Righteousness. then, is the result not of right religious observance, but of a right heart with God, especially in Jesus view. In this way, Jesus' teaching, as he overtly says in Matthew 5, is not at variance with the law and prophets, but a fulfillment of them. When Paul invokes right conduct in his epistles, or corrects bad conduct in the churches, he does not set aside grace, but deals with conduct generally under the rubric of his expressed theology of *righteousness* elsewhere, that God's grace provides both moral transformation through justification (Rom. 5), and power through the Spirit to secure good character and good conduct (Rom. 8:1-4; Gal. 2:19-21; 5:13-25).

Ephesians 4:17-24 is an example of Paul doing just that, where he warns his reader to not return to conduct that is uncharacteristic of those who belong to the body of Christ (Eph. 4:29-32), and who represent him (Eph. 4:23-24). He argues that since they have been morally changed at justification into the image of God, namely his holiness and righteousness (Eph. 4:24), we ought to reflect those attributes in our conduct and dealings with one another (Eph. 4:25, 29. 32).[75] Elsewhere, he argues that through the indwelling Spirit, believers may go on to righteousness of conduct and mature godly character (Rom. 8:1-4). If it is through the power and influence of the indwelling Spirit that right conduct is attained, arising from an initial mortal

---

[75] We should notice how Paul's treatment of holiness has application to relationships and unity in the church, the underlying theme of this passage, and arguably the whole letter.

transformation occurring at justification (Gal. 5:16, 18, 24-25), then not only are we initially changed by grace through justification and pardon by God, but through the Holy Spirit at work in us God perfects holiness by grace as well. Both salvation and perfection depend on God's grace (Rom. 8:1-4, cf. Eph. 2:8-9; Gal. 5:16-25).

Furthermore, by advancing the idea that holiness comes from the inward working of the Spirit in the life of the believer, Paul upholds the scriptural principle that right conduct comes from a heart where the right inward dynamics are at work or are in play. In the Old Testament, this is seen as sincere love for God. In the New Testament love is certainly not excluded but endorsed as part of the inward environment of those who obey God, but that also includes the indwelling Spirit (John 14:21; 15:10; 1 John. 2:3; 3:22, 24; 5:2-3; 2 John 6; Rev. 14:12). To love, Paul adds the eschatological promises of the scriptures concerning the impartation of the Spirit to God's people, particularly in connection with the new covenant, at which time the Spirit would be given so that God might write his righteousness (law) into their hearts as a result of giving his people a new heart, and a new S(s)pirit, and by forgiving their sins, and wickedness (justification) (Jer. 31:31-34; Ezek. 36:22-28). Therefore, we see in Pauline theology of justification and righteousness, of character and conduct, the dynamics of a righteousness God sought to instill in his people Israel as part of the old covenant. By promising a new covenant, involving pardon of sins, moral cleansing, a new heart, and a new S(s)pirit, as well as moral transformation, God's promise to impart the kind of moral momentum in his people toward uprightness of character and conduct, Paul celebrates as now available in Christ (Gal. 2:19-21, cf. Jer. 31:31-34; Ezek. 36:22-28). Paul found that morally transformative justification and the impartation of the Spirit answered to these promises of a new covenant, as well as to achieving God's goal of a people whose right conduct arose from right heart with him.[76]

Paul concluded, in Romans 2-3, that both Jews and Gentiles have hopelessly failed to produce the righteousness God is looking for in terms of conduct (all have sinned), the one by failure to obey the law, and the other by a failure to follow innate moral awareness, so that both are in the same predicament before God, and are sinners in need of justifying grace (Rom. 3:9-26). Paul's argument is moving toward the conclusion that both Jews and Gentiles suffer from a heart problem in need of correction by the grace of God. Jews *and* Gentiles are in need of transformative justification for salvation to gain right-standing with God, and both need the power of the Spirit to succeed in righteousness (character and conduct) (Rom. 3:21-26, cf. Rom 7).

Romans 6 lays down the centrality of right conduct and its *attainability*, initially as a result of a moral and spiritual transformation in justification through union with Christ (Rom. 6:1-11).[77] Nevertheless, the full implications of transformative justification must be fully embraced by the justified believer through decisive faith and ongoing surrender to God, if they are to forsake habitual sinning, and not end up going back to their former practices (οὕτως καὶ ὑμεῖς λογίζεσθε ἑαυτοὺς εἶναι νεκροὺς μὲν τῇ ἁμαρτίᾳ ζῶντας δὲ τῷ θεῷ ἐν Χριστῷ Ἰησοῦ).[78] They are to *count* on the transformed life (where the old life is crucified with Christ, and they have been raised from the dead to the new life of Christ at work in them), a transformation affected in them by the Holy Spirit at justification and in union with Christ, and they are to reckon on its sufficiency, and that it is capable of ultimately delivering on the potential

---

[76] Wesley, Sermons on Several Occasions, 1999, 101.
[77] Cf. Brooks, Scriptural Holiness, 1972, 26-27.
[78] Holmes, M. W. (2011–2013). *The Greek New Testament: SBL Edition* (Ro 6:11). Lexham Press; Society of Biblical Literature.

for the holiness and righteousness that God is looking for in his people (cf. Rom. 8:1-4). After all, that is the basic notion in Galatians 2:19-21; 5:16, 18, 24-25, and Paul's affirmation in Romans 8:29-30 that the goal of justification is to conform God's people into the image of his Son.

Paul's point in Romans 6 (and indeed in Galatians 5) is that it is critical for those who have been so transformed not return to habitual sinning, because sin will enslave them again (Rom. 6:15-18), and the inevitable wages of habitual sinning is death, even for the fallen believer (Rom. 6:11-23). Unchecked sin leads to slavery to sinning and produces death (Rom. 6:23, cf. Jam. 1:13-15). These ideas form the thrust of the second half of Romans 6, where Paul set out the purpose of God through transformative justification, namely, to produce full godliness and holiness of character in those who are willing to live as "slaves of righteousness" (cf. Rom. 6:19-22). Chapters 7 and 8 explain how God will bring all of this about through transformative justification *combined* with the power of the indwelling-Spirit, so that right conduct is linked to a right heart with God producing right conduct.

The Advent of Sin and the Sin Problem: The critical problem of sin that arose in the garden was due to the disobedience of the first pair to the command of God (cf. Gen. 3; Rom. 5:12-14; 1 Cor. 15:20-22). Very much can be said about the consequences of sin on creation. The first pair's retreat in fear from the presence of God is a witness that a change had occurred in them, and their immediate, intrinsic awareness of it. The serious sign of the problem, after trying to clothe themselves, was the severance the relationship between God and the first pair and the impossibility that it might be quickly restored (Gen. 3:8-9). The whole thing had taken moments; the remedy would take far longer than that to enact. Their deep discomfort when God came into the garden that evening was a sign that the damage had already been done, and their awareness of being naked a sign of their shame (Gen. 3:10). They obviously dreaded facing him. And they could not set things right with

God for themselves. The is equally obvious from the passage. It would take a divine initiative, which is seen both in the promise that seed of the woman would ultimately crush the serpent's head, and in the slaying of the animal to clothe them. The Lord indicated by the sacrifice and blood shed that he would act on their behalf to restore the relationship, but also that it would take time to provide grounds for redemption, that its enactment lay in the future (Gen. 3:15).

Both their relationship with God, and their perception of their unworthiness to appear in his presence were indications that something fundamental had changed between them. Subsequent narration confirms the dislocation was occasioned by their rebellion against God's command (Gen. 3:11). A serious alteration occurred in their nature because of their first disobedience, beyond the broken relationship. Shame, discomfort with God, and blame-shifting are indications of an inner dislocation, of which the fracture of fellowship with God was a product. That sin thoroughly corrupted their character, insidiously and demonstrably working its way throughout their progeny is the rest of the story in Genesis and the rest of the Bible (cf. Gen. 6:5-6; Ps. 51:5). David nails it in his psalm of repentance following the Bathsheba and Uriah debacle, in his pleading to cleansed and pardon from his sin, to be restored to fellowship with God, and to have joy returned, his previous "ease" in God's presence (Ps. 51). What resulted from the fall was dislocation of fellowship with God, and the impossibility of its restoration until the dislocation of their inward nature had been addressed. David, even before Christ, had the instinct that if restoration were to occur, cleansing take place, and healing of his fractured nature to occur, the Lord would have to take the initiative, because he could affect it from his side (cf. 2 Sam. 12-23). Paul's theology revolves around this idea that there are two problems that need resolving between men and God, reconciliation through pardon, forgiveness, being set right with God, and the need for moral transformation that leads to a new life that is capable of engaging with

God in fellowship, without the dominance of sinfulness, so that it can go on to produce righteousness (Rom. 5-6; 1 Cor. 6:19-20; Eph 4:17-24, et al.).

The writer of Genesis demonstrates a thorough corruption of human nature in the following chapters, first by referring to Cain's murder of Abel, then by Lamech taking two wives, and the killing a younger man in revenge. Following that, rabid sinfulness takes over and pervades the human race before the flood (Gen. 6). After the flood, the problem was not entirely solved, as Noah's drunkenness, and the challenge offered to the rule of God at Babel bear out (Gen. 4-11). Not only had human beings disobeyed God's command, but they had become sinful, rebellious inwardly, in their nature and attitude, afraid of God's judgment, but not of his rule, no longer possessing rightness of standing with God, and losing a righteousness of character or disposition critical to ongoing fellowship with him (cf. 1 John 1:5-6).

Adam's problem immediately manifested itself as a heart problem, leading to even more disobedience, and a descent into bad conduct for the whole race. No one was doing righteousness, not a single one (1 Kings 8:46; 2 Chron. 6:36; Ps. 14:1-3; 53:1-3; 143:2; Ecc. 7:20; Jer. 17:9; Rom. 3:10-18; Eph. 4:3). No one told the first pair they were naked; No one had to. They just knew it because something changed inwardly (Gen. 3:11). Their avoidance of God was the fruit of a deep consciousness that things between them and God were not as they had been. Whereas in their early innocence, they participated in and actually possessed a measure of the holiness and righteousness which God imparted to them at creation by an act of divine life giving (Gen. 2:7), their first excursion into sin marred that deposit in their nature, thereby creating a barrier to their fellowship with God (Gen. 3:23-24). Not only must the sin they committed be atoned, to set things right with God and affect reconciliation, but a remedy for their corrupted nature was needed (cf. Gen. 3:15, 24). As the hymn writer observed, they needed a double cure – to be saved, to come into in possession of the requisite transformation and endowment of God by grace that would enable them to leave sinning behind, as their past life decisively laid aside, and to find freedom from sins power and control over their nature to regulate behavior, so as to take up a new life, right with God in every way.[79] This idea is basic framework of God promise of a new covenant to replace the old, and it is the framework Paul develops in his soteriology.

The subsequent mushrooming cloud of evil after the close of Genesis 3 also pays testimony to how devastating this alteration of human nature turned out to be, and why after the advent of sin, the relationship between God and his people could not proceed as it had before (cf. Gen. 6:1-8). Implacable differences now existed between God and human beings, differences that cannot be allowed to enter into fellowship with him because of his intrinsically holy nature. The two stood at an impasse with respect to prospects of an ongoing relationship, as John observes, because God is light and in him is no darkness at all (ὅτι ὁ θεὸς φῶς ἐστιν καὶ σκοτία ἐν αὐτῷ οὐκ ἔστιν οὐδεμία).[80] To profess we have followship with God, and to be walking in sin (living in habitual sinful conduct) is a lie, because it is adamantly not possible (1 John 1:6).

Action was required, a remedy to the fracture, so that not only might the infraction be atoned for, but the corruption of human nature needed healing. Because of the way the problem came about, only a divine initiative from God's side could bring about a reconciliation and transformation (cf. John 3:16-18). The impossibility of a self-realized remedy is foreshadowed in the inadequacy of the fig leaves sewn together by Adam and Eve to cover their nakedness (Gen. 3:7). Until

---

[79] *Rock of Ages* by Augustus Toplady.

[80] Holmes, M. W. (2011–2013). The Greek New Testament: SBL Edition (1 Jn 1:5). Lexham Press; Society of Biblical Literature.

God clothed them with the skin of a slain animal, the attempt on their part to redress the transgression was insufficient, because it was God who was offended and needed atoning, and because fig-leaves could not set right the corruption in their hearts (Gen. 3:21).[81] From the outset, as a result of the advent of sin, coming as it did from voluntary human disobedience to the command of God, only God was able to take action to provide the remedy. It was his command that had been broken. It was his holiness that had been offended. And in their current condition, the two had no way back from the corruption that overtaken them, unless God stepped in to provide redemption, which he did prefigured in the first sacrifice, and by making one day the promise that the seed of the woman would crush the serpent's head and right the wrong (Gen. 3:15). In those twin elements, atonement and promise, God set forth the principle of divine initiative, by which *he himself would provide* atonement and redemption, and right the wrong by undoing what the enemy had done in the garden that day – by his own hand working salvation for him (Ps. 98:1; Isa. 59:16; 63:5). Furthermore, he would redeem transform not only humanity from sin, but ultimately all of creation from the fall, the consequences for the material world of adamic sin (Rom. 8:19-21), a redemption and transformation that would begin with those who put their faith in Christ (Col. 1:15-20, cf. 2 Cor. 5:17; Eph. 4:22-24).

This is why only grace can provide salvation for those who are lost and estranged from God, because the sin problem admits only to a divine solution and initiative. Sinners are unable to bridge the chasm between them and God, principally because it is of our own making. A remedy from God's side was necessary. So, it was God who first issued the declaration that he had anticipated the advent of sin and had made provision for salvation through the seed of the woman (Gen. 3:15). In

[81] For a thorough personal Pauline treatment of this read Romans 7.

that declaration, God promised that the results of what transpired would be thoroughly undone, its consequences reversed through the bruising of the woman's seed, and the crushing of the serpent's head. This is, then, what stands behind Paul's theology of grace and restoration, that God has from his side made provision of salvation through Jesus Christ, and that it is both justifying *and* transformative (Rom. 5:1-6:23; 1 Cor. 15:3, cf. 1 Pet. 1:18-23). Because God's plan in Christ is transforming as well as justifying, because through Christ God made provision for those who believe not only to be right with God (justified), but changed by God (transformed), they are able to live differently (go on to right conduct through the Spirit), and to come to a full maturity of godliness (once again fully bearing the image of God) (Rom. 5:1-12; 6:1-23; 8:1-17; 29-30; 12:1-2; Gal. 5:16-25; Eph. 4:22-24).

Grace From Start to Finish: Paul seems to find impossible a claim to be right with God without righteousness and holiness subjectively experienced in justification and also being developed as conduct and character in the believer's life.[82] There is no dichotomy in Paul between what later Reformed and Calvinistic theology calls *imputed* and *imparted* righteousness disconnected from an authentic subjective

---

[82] Cf. Keener, Galatians: New Cambridge Bible Commentary, 2018, 97-112. Keener wrestles with Paul's view of righteousness and the view that it is simply another way to say simply *justified* or *justification*, made right with God (in one's standing with him) (N.T. Wright et al.). Keener concludes that even though righteousness in Paul is firmly embedded in justification as right-standing with God, it is nonetheless intended to include obedience to God in terms of conduct and right character through the Holy Spirit, or as he puts it, the life of Christ operating in the will of those who have laid aside the old life to embrace a new life through union with Christ. Moral transformation in nature produces moral transformation in conduct, maintained by God's power through the indwelling Spirit or life of Christ ruling the inner environment of the believer's life through surrender (reckoning) to God (Rom. 6:11; 12:1-2; Eph. 4:17-29).

righteousness of the character and conduct in the believer.[83, 84] Paul does not seem to recognize possession of the imputed and imparted righteousness as distinct from actual subjective righteousness, especially in Romans 6 and Galatians 5. The passage we are investigating upholds this conclusion, as Paul reminds his readers that a significant moral change has occurred in their nature through salvation that makes them more like God than they were before, and this is to be demonstrated in the conduct (Eph. 4:22-24; 25-29). At the conclusion of Romans 5, Paul begins to argue this precise point, with a rhetorical question, "Shall we continue sinning (habitually), because God's grace is capable of overrunning sin with forgiveness? After all this would bring glory to God!" (Rom. 6:1-2). The answer is a resounding "God forbid!" Pardon, justification, that makes us right with God, implies and precipitates a moral change. Although we are declared right with God entirely by grace through Christ, Paul argues, that changes occurring in us at justification provide a new moral foundation for a life, affecting changes in character and conduct as we move forward from that starting place with God (Rom. 5:1-2; 6:1-18).

Transformative justification does not make us right with God in a vacuum, that is in only a legal sense, by imparting to us the

---

[83] It seems to me that a great deal of the problem over *imparted* righteousness in the Reformed and Calvinistic theology debate of righteousness vs Arminian views, can be attributed to an insufficiently robust notion of Pauline righteousness as both objectively imputed and imparted by God, as well as inculcated through the Spirit subjectively as character and conduct as a result of moral development. All of it is the result of grace, whether justification on account of Christ, or the development of godliness through the action of the Spirit in us. No wedge need be driven between subjective and objective righteousness, that is how we are viewed by God vs how we are authentically made righteous in our character, experience, and conduct by him through the Spirit. This was John Wesley's foundational contention in his day.

[84] Cf. Keener, Galatians: New Cambridge Bible Commentary, 2018, 115-117.

righteousness of Christ, but it involves a transformation of our nature in order to produce a new creation (newness of life) (2 Cor. 5:17). This is the so-called *imputing of righteousness,* that Paul celebrates in Galatians 2 (Gal. 2:19-21). It is central to a Pauline theology of salvation, that the believer is transformed by God through justification, making the old life, and its ruling principle, irrelevant going forward (Rom. 6:3-10; 2 Cor. 5:17). This new creation is capable of development in righteousness, and although it aims at habitual obedience to God, and the development of godly character, it may nonetheless fail at points and is not flawlessly perfect (cf. Ps. 37:23-24; 1 John 2:1-2). [85] Nevertheless, and this is Paul's point, the justified and transformed believer cannot engage in habitual sinning and disobedience to God, and still be declared just in his sight, no more than the Israelites could claim to be right with God because they were heirs of the covenants and promises of God, and still live in sinful rebellion against him without suffering his rejection and censure. *Paul does not leave open to us a theology of righteousness by virtue of position, that does not also lead to righteousness of conduct and character.* His answer to the question of how subjective righteousness can be achieved, is to present justification (including pardon and transformation) as the starting point, and the Holy Spirit as the source and origin of character development and right conduct through the operation God's grace. Righteousness is therefore imparted *and* imputed, made possible through what Christ did on the cross, at first through justification, and then afterwards through the indwelling power of the Spirit. The effect in the believer is to produce

---

[85] This point explains why Paul constantly challenges his readers to do better morally and in practice. John more explicitly deals with this in his first epistle, where he says, on several occasions, the one who is *born of God* does not go on habitually sinning. However, if we do *sin* on occasion or fail at points we have an advocate with the Father, Jesus Christ to help is put it right and to move on (1 John 1:7-2:2).

authentic righteousness of character and conduct by the same grace at work through Christ and the Spirit in their initial salvation, what we sometimes call conversion and regeneration (transformative justification). As Paul told the Romans, the just shall live by faith, because this thing is from faith in the beginning to faith in its prosecution, and faith will bring it to its final consummation in the coming eschaton (Rom. 1:17).

The fear that Reformed and Calvinist theology has traditionally obsessed over, the encroachment of works righteousness, seems to have not bothered Paul, because he viewed genuine subjective righteousness as character and conduct imparted of God through the power of the Spirit operating in the life of the believer, and, therefore, a product of God's grace (cf. Rom. 8:14; Gal. 5:16-25). After all, this is the core of his argument in Galatians, where Judaizers sought to impose adherence to Jewish traditions and law to perfect righteousness going forward after coming to Christ (and not in order to initially *obtain salvation* as the debate has been historically presented) (cf. Gal. 3:3-6; 5:16-25). The subjective righteousness God is looking for in his people is not possible through mere human effort or devising, but requires the development of character and conduct which only the Holy Spirit can produce in us by his gracious operation and endowment (cf. Rom. 7:24-25; 8:1-4; Gal. 5:16, 18, 24-25). Character as the seat of conduct is, after all, the *fruit of the Spirit*; it come from the presence, power, and inworking of the Holy Spirit, who is its source.

For Paul, then, right standing with God cannot be separated from right conduct, no more than Israel could claim to be right with God while at the same time habitually disobeying him. At some point, without repentance and surrender to God, without a change of heart toward him, God warned them he would abandon the broken covenant (cf. Ezek. 10). Indeed, the threat of withdrawal, under certain conditions, was a part of the covenant in the first place (cf. Deut. 28). This dynamic, the relationship between character, conduct, and right standing with God is most readily seen in the often-repeated injunction that Israel was to both *love* God and *obey* him (Deut. 7:9;10:12; 11:13; 30:16; Josh 22:5; Neh. 1:5; Dan. 9:4). Character and right standing are reflected in obedience and right conduct, and they cannot be separated from one another (cf. Num. 32:11-12; Deut. 1:6; Josh. 14:8-9, 14; 1 Kings 8:23; 2 Chron. 6:14; 19:9; 25:2; Ps. 119:80). Where right conduct is abandoned, and habitual disobedience is at work, right character is missing or eroded, and right standing with God becomes impossible even for those who once followed him (cf. Ezek. 18).

In his self-analysis as a law-abiding Jew, Paul concluded as much. No amount of right conduct (what Paul calls *practice*) could affect righteousness with God for him, or lead to right-standing with God, nor could it produce godly character pleasing to God, even though the law awakened a desire and a consciousness of a need for it (Rom. 7:7-20). The problem of overcoming his transgressions at first, as well as sinfulness in his nature was in need of an adequate solution beyond his own ability to affect a changed in his status with God, or remedy the flaw in his nature that kept him a prisoner to sinning (Rom. 7:24). The turning point for Paul was the realization that the defect lay in his nature, and that the remedy could only be found in connection to union with Christ, by which through God's grace his sin might be forgiven, and his nature transformed in a death to the old life and man, followed by a resurrection to a new life of righteousness (Rom. 6:6-11; 7:21-25). To Paul, transformative justification, through the action of God's grace applying the provision of the cross to his life through the Spirit, was the answer to his dilemma, because by it God was not only able to pardon and restore him to fellowship with God (justification/reconciliation), but at the same time to change him fundamentally in his nature to become a slave to God and of righteousness, initially by delivering him from slavery to sin and sinning (Rom. 6:1-11, cf. Rom. 8:1-4,12-16; 2 Cor 5:17). Paul's point in Romans 6-8 is that not only has a change of status with God occurred, his relationship, his position, his standing with God, and that he has been reconciled to God by grace to have peace with God, but that God has affected a fundamental change in his nature through resurrection to new life in Christ, and that leads to righteousness and holiness (Rom. 5:1-2). This transformation occurs in connection to and is a result of reconciliation to God. His inward nature has been transformed through a death to the old life, and a resurrection to new life in Christ, implanted or created in him by God (Rom. 6:1-23; Eph. 4:22-24).

Paul goes further than that. The new life implanted in him by God through moral transformation in his nature is itself now *supported by God's grace through the indwelling Spirit to produce righteousness of character and conduct by the operation of grace* (Rom. 8:1-4, cf. Gal. 2:19-21). It was not as though Paul only had to make up for the sins he had committed, but he had to effectively address a fault in his nature that bound him over to habitual disobedience to God. He found that by the righteousness of law-keeping, neither could be achieved. Only God, through Jesus Christ, could offer him relief from the sins he had committed, *and* the defect in his nature that bound him over to habitual sinning (Rom. 7:21-25). What's more, God did both through justification by grace that *includes* transformation (Rom. 6:1-11, cf. 2 Cor. 5:17; Eph. 4:22-24). If Paul were to succeed in becoming the godly man he desired to be, in both conduct and character, he needed to avail himself of the remedy that God offers through Christ, that is through grace, in *both aspects* of God's redemptive offer, forgiveness and thoroughgoing moral change (Rom. 7:15, 18-19, 25b; 8:1-4; 12-16).

Habitual right conduct flows from a transformed life, beginning at justification and then through the operation of the indwelling Spirit (Rom 6 and 8). The apostle realized that "right conduct" could not affect salvation (i.e., procure justification – make a person right with God) (Rom. 5:1-2; Eph. 2:5, 8-9). He also realized, through the discovery of another law at work in his members (his human nature linked to the appetites of his body) bringing sin and death, that through Christ, God had made provision for the principle or law of the Spirit of life in Christ Jesus to take over and to work righteousness in him (character and conduct), the very righteousness the law aimed at producing but could not because of the deficiency in his nature (Rom. 8:14) (ὁ γὰρ νόμος τοῦ πνεύματος τῆς ζωῆς ἐν Χριστῷ Ἰησοῦ).[86] This new principle, Paul rejoiced, has set us free from the principle or law of sin and death (ἠλευθέρωσέν σε ἀπὸ τοῦ νόμου τῆς ἁμαρτίας καὶ τοῦ θανάτου), and opens the door to righteousness of character and conduct through the Spirit (Rom 8:1-4). Quite literally, Paul proposes that the righteousness that God aimed at producing through the law is now made possible in those who no longer follow the leadership of the flesh (old life principle) (ἐν ἡμῖν τοῖς μὴ κατὰ σάρκα περιπατοῦσιν), but who live under the influence of the Holy Spirit by following his leadership (ἀλλὰ κατὰ πνεῦμα).[87, 88]

With the condemnation lifted, a nature liberated to new life in the resurrection of Christ, and because the old life is crucified and reckoned dead, it is now possible, Paul realized, for habitual right conduct to flow out of the morally transformed life as a consequence of justification by grace, and where the leadership of the indwelling Holy Spirit in the believer's life is *followed and embraced* (cf. Gal. 5:16). Justification is transformative, and leads to the indwelling Spirit providing a dynamic for holiness for the believer, this is at the core of Paul's theology of personal righteousness (cf. Rom. 6:1-18; 8:1-17). Justification is not merely positional, as many have argued, standing apart and discretely isolated from moral change leading to right conduct (cf. 2 Cor. 5:17). Rather, it

---

[86] Holmes, M. W. (2011–2013). The Greek New Testament: SBL Edition (Ro 8:2). Lexham Press; Society of Biblical Literature.
[87] Holmes, M. W. (2011–2013). *The Greek New Testament: SBL Edition* (Ro 8:4). Lexham Press; Society of Biblical Literature.
[88] Cf. Keener, Galatians: New Cambridge Bible Commentary, 2018, 97-112.

involves a repatriation of the believer into Christ from the world, and inculcates the dynamic of Christ's resurrection to newness life - a thoroughgoing moral transformation of status, nature, character, and life (Rom. 6:1-11; 2 Cor. 5:17; Col. 1:13, cf. Acts 26:18; 1 Pet. 2:9; 1 John 1:5-6).

Grace Stands in Continuity with The Old Testament: Once understood, these connections enrich the whole picture of what Paul is trying to communicate about righteousness and holiness in the context of his gospel. Paul's epistles often assume or lay claim to a common frame of reference with Old Testament scriptures, which believers in the early church possessed or were familiar with from the preaching and teaching of their leaders. Some believers would have previously been Gentile God-fearers in the synagogues, hearing the scriptures read every Sabbath, and were well aware of them.[89] Christian congregations around the Mediterranean basin were often ethnically mixed, Jews and Gentiles, sometimes God-fearers (Gentiles formerly attached to the synagogue), who would have had significant exposure to the Old Testament. Paul's purposeful strategy of beginning in the synagogue when he arrived in a new town almost ensured he would end up with an ethnically mixed church in that location.

Paul wrote to these churches, some with whom he had spent significant time teaching and instructing from the (Old Testament)

---

[89] Paul makes use of this dynamic in Romans 7, where he introduces his illustration of the woman under law who is freed from her husband to remarry only after his death. Paul trades on the knowledge of the Jewish believers and those who were formerly God-fearing Gentile from the synagogues, but who had now put their faith in Christ. Their knowledge of the Old Testament law enabled Paul to make the argument supported by his illustration from marriage. Paul used a similar approach to Jesus, who took to the synagogues to preach the good news. There Paul could trade on their background in the scriptures.

scriptures, encouraging them to keep working out the teaching he had given them, in their daily lives. In his letters, he emphasizes these scriptures as foundational for appreciating the ministry and person of Christ, the kingdom of God, and their moral or ethical obligations (cf. Luke 4:21; 24:44-46; John 5:39; Acts 1:16; 8:32, 35; 17:11; Rom. 1:12; 1 Cor. 15:4; 2 Tim. 3:15-17; 1 Pet. 1:10-12). Paul often claimed he had grounded new believers' knowledge of Christ and their experience of salvation in those scriptures, and that he taught the principles of the kingdom of God out of the Jewish scriptures, and that the grace of God and his salvation were anticipated by the prophets in connection with Christ in those same scriptures (cf. Acts 17:2, 11; 18:28; Rom. 1:2; 4:3; 9:17; 10:11; 11:2; 15:4; 1 Cor. 15:3, 4; Gal. 3:8, 16, 22; 4:30; 1 Tim. 4:13; 5:18; 2 Tim. 5:15-17). Paul's teaching, though explicit, was not wholly innovative. Based in the scriptures, Paul discerned righteousness as a matter of a right heart leading to right conduct, and that the Spirit was God's proposed dynamic power at work in them to make that possible. What God promised Israel, in terms of a new covenant and the law written in their hearts and minds, was made real by the power of the indwelling Spirit, just as Jeremiah promised in conjunction with the forgiveness of their sins and wickedness (pardon, justification) (Jer. 31:31-34). Ezekiel also made explicit that God would give his people a new heart and a new S(s)pirit in connection with cleansing them from moral filthiness by sprinkling them with clean water (Ezek. 36:20-28).

As we have seen above, this compositional dynamic of Jewish and Gentile believers, making up many congregations in the early church, was also true of the Ephesian church. It was apparently true of the Roman church. Judaizers seem to taken advantage of this in Antioch, Galatia, and Colossae seeking to rein Gentiles in to adopt Jewish customs and to integrate them into the covenant people of God.[90] To the Ephesians Paul expounds the mystery of the gospel, which was contained, though hidden, in the Old Testament, namely that Jews and Gentiles are to be redeemed together through the one atoning sacrifice of Christ (Eph. 2:11-3:6).[91] In Ephesians 4, Paul goes on to layout the implications of this in terms of the life of the church, its internal relationships, and the character of believers in Christ. Paul is at pains to show that both Jews and Gentiles are saved by God's grace through faith in Christ, and that nothing else is required for Gentiles to be fully integrated into the (new) covenant people of God. Where certain Judaizers argued the customs of the law are needed to promote righteousness in their lives and among the people of God, Paul objected vigorously by presenting the promises of the Old Testament, that God said he would give his Spirit to his people to affect a moral transformation, under the terms of a new covenant, and through the Spirit produce right character and conduct in them (cf. Rom. 8:1-14; Gal. 3-5).

In the passage we are examining, the terms *righteousness* and *holiness* are brought in from the Old Testament (cf. Eph. 4:22-24). Even speaking of the *image of God* alludes to Genesis 1:26-28 in the law. Paul is constantly expounding and teaching the significance of the gospel of Jesus Christ in terms of God's previously revealed plans in the Old Testament scriptures, and its connection with God's future rule over creation, including themes like redemption and holiness, which impact the implementation of God's plans for and in his new covenant people.

---

[90] Cf. Cole, 2008, 14-16; Witherintgon, 1998, 89-107; Hansen, 1994, 14-16; Stott J. R., 1968, 23-27; Barclay, 1991, 45-74.

[91] Note for example that Ephesians 2 deals with the unity of Jew and Gentile believers in Christ under the one sacrifice of Christ Eph. 2:11-22 and that chapter 4 begins with a call to unity based on the intrinsic unity of their faith and common experience of Christ Eph. 4:1-16.

Paul's concepts of righteousness and holiness, how they operate and are achieved, are linked to the Old Testament scriptures, but illuminated by the Christ-advent, and fulfilled in him through his work on the cross, and by his resurrection (cf. Rom. 1:2-4; 3:21; 9:5; 15:4; 1 Cor. 15:3-4; Gal. 3:8, 22; 5:14; Eph. 1:7-10; Col. 1:25-27; 2 Tim. 3:15-17). Advancement in righteousness, for example, which God promised in Jeremiah through a new covenant, where the law would be written in their hearts and minds, in connection with the forgiveness of their sins, and Ezekiel's language of a new heart and S(s)pirit following cleansing, finds its fulfillment in transformative justification through the grace of God by faith for the believer Nevertheless, it must be followed up by an ongoing work of the indwelling Spirit producing authentic righteousness of conduct and character, all made possible only because of Christ's death and resurrection (cf. Jer. 31:31-034; Ezek. 36:22-28; Rom. 5:1-2, 9-11, 20-21; 6:1-13; 7:24-25; 8:1-4; Gal. 2:19-21; 5:13-25). Because it is God that promised to do this himself, and to sovereignly overcome the Israel's previous moral failure and disobedience with respect to his law and covenants, justification and righteousness are *only possible through grace*, because God took the initiative to make them possible when the law failed.

Romans 7 is Paul's autobiographical struggle with the law's ineffectual power to affect the righteousness it demanded, not because the law was at fault (Rom. 7:7, 12-14), but because of a flaw in human nature that demands a remedy (Rom. 7:16-20, 21-22).[92] Paul found that

---

[92] Though some argue that Paul does not intend to relate his own experience, but is entirely parabolic, we say that as a law-abiding Jew coming to Christ, Paul chose to write in the first-person singular precisely because this was his experience, even if there is a rhetorical element in the passage. One cannot ignore the personal level at which Paul speaks, that comes to a head in verse 24 with a cry of dereliction, followed by an equally triumphant and emotional

remedy in Christ through justification and union with him in his death and resurrection (Rom. 5:18-21; 6:1-11). Resurrection to new life in Christ, as a result of justification by grace and faith in God, is the entrance, not only into rightness with God, but into a new life with God of holiness and righteousness led by the Spirit, and into an environment where the grace of God operates in the life of the believer (Rom. 5:1-2; cf. 2 Cor. 5:17; Eph. 4:22-24). Righteousness, Paul opines, cannot be achieved while under the law, it comes only through the power of the Spirit, as a result of union with Christ (Rom. 7:24-25; 8:1-4).[93] Paul encourages the Roman believers that they now *stand* in grace, by virtue of having *gained access* to God's grace when they were reconciled to him by exercising faith in Christ (Rom. 5:1-2). Paul's theology finds that God's promise of cleansing and moral transformation are rooted in Christ, his death and resurrection – all of it, the justification (pardon), the moral transformation, and the going on to right conduct, as well as maturation to godly character (Rom. 5:1-8:4).

Here, then, is the essence of Pauline soteriology, that God has justified us, transformed us, works in us to perfect godliness of character and conduct, and plans to conform us to the image of God in Christ (Rom. 8:29-30). The saving work of God proceeds from grace through faith from its beginning to its end (Rom. 1:17). It was initiated objectively by God in Christ's redemptive work on the cross, and it is initiated subjectively in us through conviction by the Holy Spirit, leading to repentance and justification by faith (Rom 5:1-21). The result of justification is transformation going on to a *present* development in right

---

cry, neither of which can be construed as solely rhetorical. We don't need to argue for "historical present", even if the device is arguably in play, in a passage that is clearly written on such a personal level and bears the marks of Paul's personal experience in Judaism, and after his conversion (cf. Acts 9; Gal. 1-2).

[93] Cf. Keener, Galatians: New Cambridge Bible Commentary, 2018, 113-114.

conduct and character over time (Rom. 6:1-23; Gal. 5:1-25). The future goal is fully-formed godliness in God's sight, in preparation to serve him in eternity (Eph. 4:13-16, 22-24). If *salvation* involved the dynamics of holiness and godliness in the past, and anticipates it in the future, then it is impossible to conceive holiness and godliness as irrelevant to God in the present, as though they are somehow entirely peripheral or unimportant for our relationship with God. Or worse, that we might think that they are entirely unattainable, despite God's command that we are strive for them or move on to them as a matter or daily surrender and engagement. To hopelessly concede that believers are flawed, and incapable of meaningful advancements in holiness of character and conduct in the present is to ignore the command and purpose of God for his people, at first demanded of his Old Testament people, and now reaffirmed in the whole tenor of the New Testament revelation, as the goal and desire of God for his new covenant people.

To reserve meaningful holiness to the "article of death", to quote Wesley, or assert no one is perfect, or are incapable of not committing sin, is to ignore the expressed command of God found in the New Testament, that we must obey his commands, and walk in the Spirit if we want to continue in fellowship with God. Such a notions fails to take seriously the countless exhortations to right conduct and holiness of character from the apostles, and early church leaders recorded there. Wesley, in wrestling with objections to his assertion that God expects those justified by faith in Christ go on to meaningful holiness of life and conduct, asserts that even if some of the holiest of Old Testament saints did *sometimes* commit sin, it does not negate the principle of holiness as the habitual practice of Christian salvation, and a cessation of habitual sinning.[94] He argues that there may be remaining imperfections in the humanity of even the best saints, which are occasions for

[94] Wesley, A Plain Account of Christian Perfection, 1966, 22-24.

temptation and mistakes, but that this does not negate or nullify the purpose and provision of God.

The apostles, Paul in particular, encouraged the saints after initial justification, to go on to righteousness and to spiritual maturity through growth (Eph. 4:12-16; Rom. 5:3-8; 2 Pet. 1:5-11; James 1:4, cf. 1 Cor. 2:14; 3:1-4; 14:20; Phil. 3:15; Col. 1:10, 28; 2:19; 4:12; 2 Thess. 1:3; Heb. 5:11-14; 1 Pet. 2:2; 2 Pet. 3:18; 1 John 2:12-14). In other words, righteousness is not merely right standing with God. Justification implies not only imputed righteousness, but rather the meaningful pursuit and attainment of imparted righteousness as character and conduct, subject to growth and develop by God through the power of the Spirit. Status with God, imputed, or imparted, are by grace, and are to be complimented by an organic development of moral and spiritual character, as well as right conduct, instigated by the Spirit in the lives of those who walk with God in faith and obedience (Rom. 8:1-4; Gal. 5:16-24). Accepting and understanding the notion that righteousness is a matter of the whole man, of right-standing with God, moral transformation, developing character, *and* right conduct, is crucial to grasping the Pauline perspectives on holiness. The implications of this are that salvation involves components of past initial faith in Christ, present faith that leads to spiritual development or growth, and a future consummation of salvation, culminating in the resurrection and transformation of our bodies, which is sometime called by Paul glorification or resurrection.[95] In Romans 5-8, Paul deals in detail with all of these.

For Paul, righteousness in the present life of the believer has a goal or a trajectory, the restoration of the image of God for those who belong to him; it is certainly not static. Salvation is a package deal beginning with repentance and faith at the front end, leading to a final

---

[95] Brooks, Scriptural Holiness, 1972, 41-68.

consummation in the formation of the image of Christ in those who are saved and justified through him at the back end (Rom. 8:29-30). In between is righteousness as obedience to God and moral growth through the power of the Spirit (Rom. 8:1-4; Gal. 5:16-25; Eph. 4:13-24). The typical western dogma of "salvation" consists in a past crisis-experience (past-tense), so that we are considered saved in the present on account of a prior or past faith and repentance. Many consider themselves "saved" on that basis, to not only made right with God, but justified with God regardless of the present state of their faith in God, moral standing, conduct or character, or their attitude to the rule of God in their lives. But this is most assuredly not Pauline (cf. Rom. 6:1-23).[96] In fact, the idea is resisted by Paul as anathema in Romans 6:2, where he says, "God forbid!" Paul speaks of freedom from slavery to sin and abandoning the old life as integral to salvation in the present, or else we will return to a state of alienation from God (Rom. 6:23). So, when Paul writes that salvation is about being transformed by the renewing of our minds (Rom. 12:1-2), about being conformed into the image of God's Son (Rom. 8:29-30), or that justifying (faith) salvation produces a new nature in us that is already created at initial justification in the image of God, reflecting his holiness and righteousness, it is in view grace through faith continuing to work out the implications of initial salvation in terms of maturing and development godliness, which will one day be conformed to the image of Christ (Eph. 4:13-16, 22-24, cf. Rom. 1:17; 8:29-20; 2 Cor. 3:18; 4:7-12, 16-18). Salvation is not static, but moving, vital, living, growing, and developing after an initial transformation, and the dynamic of faith, working by God's grace is behind this movement. Paul lays out, in his theology of salvation, the full scope of what God intended in order to remedy the effects of the fall. It is not a single

[96] If Paul's treatment in Romans 6 addresses anything, it addresses the notion that the state of being justified is not indifferent to conduct and character going forward.

encounter with God involving a religious confession, but rather an introduction into fellowship with God through faith by his grace as a result of transformative reconciliation, which is supposed to be engaged in daily living, and to last a lifetime, indeed eternally (cf. John 10:10).

Paul's Theology of Salvation and Righteousness Answers to the Effects of Original Sin: As scripture progresses, we discover that human sinfulness, the perversion of human nature as a result of the first willful act of defiance, not only intensified but provided an insurmountable barrier to restored fellowship with God. The incompatibility of the absolute holiness of God's nature and the total wickedness of humanity would have made reconciliation all but impossible if it were not for remediation from God (cf. Gen. 6:5; Jer. 17:9; Hab. 1:13; 1 John 1:5). Humanity's moral corruption cannot be overlooked by God, who must be consistent with his own nature, even though he loves those he created, and who are now unable to fellowship with him or restore fellowship on their own initiative, by their own power (Gen. 3:24; Rom. 3:23; 7:24-25, cf. John 3:16-18). Genesis 3 indicates that God anticipated this fracture, and already had a plan in place to remedy it, so he promised that the *seed of the woman,* an early reference to Christ, who would crush the serpent's head (Gen. 3:15). That is, at some unspecified in point in the future, God had made provision for what transpired at the instigation of Satan to be reversed, and to be utterly overthrown through a human representative born to the woman (Gen. 3:15). Paul said, just as sin had entered the world through initial human disobedience, so God appointed a human agent to overcome sin through perfect obedience and atonement through his sacrifice (Rom. 5:12-21; Gal. 4:4).

Jesus' death and resurrection is nothing less than a fulfillment of the promise for the reversal of sin and its effects made in the garden that day. Nevertheless, a personal realization of that reversal and of reconciliation to God can only be affected when God, through grace, applies his provision to those who believe or put their faith in him (Rom. 5:1-2). The result of an application of grace to faith is restoration to God and to fellowship with God, which is to once again have peace with God (Rom. 5:1). Nevertheless, Paul makes it clear, in Romans 6, that an exercise of God's grace in justification presupposes, not a return to habitual sinning, but proceeding toward future habitual righteousness and maturity in godliness (Rom. 6:1-2; 15-23; 8:29-30). Justification exists on a salvific continuum from initial salvation to final glorification, with moral and spiritual development and growth between them, under the supervision of the Spirit.[97] Paul presents the morally transformative nature of justification as the grounds upon which he makes the assertion that those who are in union with Christ, cannot return to a life of habitual sin, of slavery to sinning, but must go on to a new life of slavery holiness and righteousness, of obedience and of moral growth toward final perfection (Rom. 6:1-10). The old life and self are put to death, the control of conduct by the sinful nature is broken, followed by a resurrection, through union with Christ to a new life of consistent and habitual righteousness, where conduct is influenced and controlled by the power of the indwelling Spirit (Rom. 6:3-11; Rom. 8:1-4; Gal. 5:16-25). Paul goes to explain that since God has given the power of the Spirit to those who are no longer condemned (Rom. 8:1), and because they have been justified by faith, and now walk under the direction of the Spirit, that they can expect to meet with genuine success in the enterprise of righteousness as both conduct and development of mature godliness (Rom. 8:1-17, cf. Gal. 5:16-25). It means righteousness and success in righteousness is rooted in the grace of God, because he is the one who is responsible for the provision by the empowering presence of the Holy Spirit, and because it is the Spirit at

---

[97] Cf. Keener, Galatians: New Cambridge Bible Commentary, 2018, 113-114.

work in us that brings about God's program of moral development in our lives (cf. Rom. 1:17).

The elements of Paul's theology answer to the results of original sin reveal in Gensis 3 as immediately pursuant on the first disobedience of the original couple. Wesley concluded, where the problem is two-fold, alienation from God in need of reconciliation, and corruption of our nature in need of restoration to righteousness and obedience, the solution must necessarily be sufficient to both. Pauline theology seems to support this Wesleyan scheme.[98] In this way, Paul's theology of redemption answers to the great effects of the fall and addresses them not simply in terms of forgiveness of past transgressions and right standing with God, but in terms of fallen human nature in need of reconstruction in order to live in genuine fellowship with God (cf. Rom. 6:1-23; 8:5-8; 2 Cor. 4:16-18; 5:17; Eph. 4:22-24; 1 John 1:5-6).

Salvation Is Goal Directed: Paul's theology of redemption sees the redemptive activity of God as goal-directed, as purposeful, as having an end in mind, as aiming at fulfilling his own designs and previously devised plans for creation (Col. 1:13-20). Nothing in creation nor the lives of God's people, whether Israel or Gentiles (cf. Rom. 1:16-17), is random, or without purpose, Paul states in numerous passages. In

---

[98] Of course, Wesley expressed this in a more sophisticated way, and through the lens of his own existential journey of salvation. He employs a similar approach to Paul, in that he capitulates his theology under the rubric of his own experience. That Wesley "arranges" the flowers in his theological vase by using language that recapitulates Paul, as explanation and explication, does not negate his conclusions, or the biblical validity of his observations, where scripture assuredly admits to a "double cure", a remedy for both alienation from God and for restoration of moral uprightness. As we have seen both Old and New Testaments propose that righteousness is a matter of a right heart with God and right conduct, where the former is the foundation for latter. Paul and Wesley are concerned about the same things.

Colossians 1, speaking of Christ in the context of his incarnation, death, and resurrection, Paul goes on to describe the goal-directedness of God's plan. In giving thanks to God for the faith of the Colossians, Paul rejoices that the gospel is "bearing fruit" (καρποφορούμενον) and increasing (in scope and reach) (αὐξανόμενον) throughout the world, just as it was among them (Col. 1:6). In other words, the gospel was producing the results God was looking for, results that Paul saw even among the Colossians. That the gospel is producing something that God is looking for is implied by the metaphor of fruit (cf. John 15:1-17). There is a certain divine expectation that is realized in the gospel, or through the preaching of the good news about Christ when people respond to it in faith. The gospel aims at securing a response of faith to the message, which in turn leads to the salvation of the one believing. The preaching of good news is goal-oriented, aiming at the salvation of those who hear the message.

Still, Paul tells the Colossians, the goal of the gospel is not merely securing a response of faith in God leading to salvation and justification, but that those who believe will "go on to be filled with the knowledge of his [God's] will through all the wisdom and understanding that the Spirit gives" (ἵνα πληρωθῆτε τὴν ἐπίγνωσιν τοῦ θελήματος αὐτοῦ ἐν πάσῃ σοφίᾳ καὶ συνέσει πνευματικῇ) (Col 1:9).[99] This tightly packed sentence exhibits the goal-directedness of God's saving purpose by highlighting that the Colossians should come into an increasing possession of knowledge of the will of God through wisdom and understanding granted to them by the Spirit. Their increasing knowledge of God's will, which is his purposeful activity in them and in creation, is premised on their acceptance of the gospel and gained through the progressive and ongoing impartation of wisdom and understanding by the Spirit. The

---

[99] Holmes, M. W. (2011–2013). *The Greek New Testament: SBL Edition* (Col 1:9). Lexham Press; Society of Biblical Literature.

activity of the Holy Spirit, in that case, is seen as progressively imparting to those who are saved and belong to God, because of the gospel, a deeper knowledge of his unfolding plan or will (τοῦ θελήματος αὐτοῦ). This means that not only does God seem to have a plan but that he is willing to impart the knowledge of that plan to those who have come to know him through the gospel, and to engage them in its execution (cf. John 17:3).

The impartation of the knowledge of the will of God through the Spirit is goal-directed, aimed at empowering and enabling of those who have come to God through the gospel to live a *life worthy of God, to please him in everything* (περιπατῆσαι ἀξίως τοῦ κυρίου εἰς πᾶσαν ἀρεσκείαν ἐν παντὶ ἔργῳ ἀγαθῷ), in order they might actively participate with God in his purposes.[100] How could they possibly please God in everything? The *walking worthy of the Lord* is explained as "in everything [in their lives] pleasing him by every good work" (εἰς πᾶσαν ἀρεσκείαν ἐν παντὶ ἔργῳ ἀγαθῷ) (Col. 1:10). The instrumental dative with the preposition ἐν indicates how or by what means they are to please the Lord, by *every good work* (ἐν παντὶ ἔργῳ ἀγαθῷ). It is by their good works they are to live worthily and to please God (Col. 1:10). Good works that honor and please God are not incidental to their salvation, but the goal of their having put their faith in Christ as a result of the gospel. Paul has piled purpose on purpose here related to their acceptance of the gospel message and God's goals for them.

But Paul is not finished with the goals of their reception of the gospel. By pleasing God or walking (the infinitive περιπατῆσαι) worthy of God in every good work, they will be bearing fruit and growing in the knowledge of God (καρποφοροῦντες καὶ αὐξανόμενοι τῇ ἐπιγνώσει τοῦ θεοῦ) – two more goal-oriented activities expressed as participles, the actions of

---

[100] Holmes, M. W. (2011–2013). *The Greek New Testament: SBL Edition* (Col 1:10). Lexham Press; Society of Biblical Literature.

which attend the walking, or the conducting of their lives in a manner worthy of God and to please him.[101] Furthermore, the result of walking in a way that is worthy of God and pleasing to him, meaning how they conduct themselves in the way they live, is that they will be inwardly strengthened by God, made more able to endure, become more resilient, have greater endurance in trials and testing (Col. 1:11). There is still more. Paul envisions that there will be joyful thanks to God coming out of their experience of God's purposeful saving activity in them. The giving of joyful thanks to God is yet another result of the gospel purposed by the saving activity of God. Not only will God be pleased with the ones he has rescued through the gospel (Col. 1:13), but they will be filled with joy because he has qualified them to share in the kingdom of light with the saints (Col. 1:12). The purpose language keeps stacking up, as Paul continues. Salvation is goal directed, where between initial justification and final glorification, God is at work through his Spirit working out the implications of what it means to have been morally transformed by God, in terms of obedience, and the pursuit of righteousness in character and conduct.

THE IMMEDIATE CONTEXT

By immediate context, we mean the closer context of the passage we are considering, and the section or sections in which it lies as part of the logical progression of Paul's argument; our passage is Ephesians 4:17-29. Paul seems to be developing the theme of unity among believers, which in chapter 4 and verse 4 shifts to the specifics standing behind or supporting unity. Paul's concern for unity at first finds its premise in the overall goals of God's purpose, to restore all of creation to full, unified reconciliation in Christ to himself, so that harmony between God and his creation might be regained (Eph. 1:7-11; 15-23, cf.

---

[101] Holmes, M. W. (2011–2013). *The Greek New Testament: SBL Edition* (Col 1:10). Lexham Press; Society of Biblical Literature.

Col. 1:15-20, cf. Rev. 21). For Paul, God's future and final reconciliation of all things has begun in the present age through Christ's advent, the giving of the promised Spirit, the preaching of the good news of the gospel, and by faith in those who turn to Christ for reconciliation to God (peace with God, ending the enmity) (Rom. 5:1-2, 9-11). The redemption of those who trust in Christ for salvation involves being reconciled to God, a restored to peace with him (Rom. 5:1). Redemption through Christ, then, forms the sharp end of an advanced incursion of the kingdom of God into a world at war with God, anticipating his final victory in the future restoration of all things to him in Christ (1 Cor. 15:20-28; Col. 1:15-20). God's eschatological plans are not entirely future, Paul argues throughout his corpus, but are already at work in the present age, just as Jesus himself taught (Matt. 9:35; 10:7; 12:28; 16:19; Mark 1:15; 4:11; 12:34; Luke 8:1, 10; 9:2; 10:9; 11:20; 17:20-21; 22:29). Jesus professed that he had come with good news of the kingdom's arrival in the present age for those who repent and believe (Mark 1:14-15).

For Paul, the ultimate purpose of God to reconcile all things to himself is already at work in those who believe and belong to the people of God through redemptive pardon of their sins, and to whom God has given the fruit of the kingdom ahead of its full and final realization, an impartation of the Spirit, the presence of God with and in them (cf. Rom. 3:24; 8:23, cf. Eph. 1:13-14; 2 Cor. 1:22; 5:1-5). The idea that the Spirit indwells God's people, is what Paul links to the promises of God to effectively equip his people for righteousness under a new covenant (Rom. 8:1-4; Gal. 5:16-25; Eph. 4:22-24). In this way, by the giving the Spirit to the people of God, the eschatological promise to Israel concerning righteousness written in their nature, and the possession of a new heart, and new S(s)pirit is already at work in those who have been reconciled to God through Christ, and who have been sealed in their redemption and restoration to him by the Spirit (c f. Jer. 31:31-44; Ezek. 36:20-28; Eph. 1:13-14). Possession of the Spirit in the present age means that the saints are equipped by God, through his grace, with the power of kingdom of God for righteousness now, ahead of its full realization at Christ's return.

The apostle seems to make the point that unity in the church, initiated by the action of the Spirit, established by him in the church through a shared, common experience of the grace of God by each member the body of Christ, is served by their personal experience of transformation in salvation. By the transformation of their nature, God has implanted righteousness and holiness in them at initial salvation so that they might thoroughly lay aside the old life of selfish preoccupation and ambition (Eph. 4:17-29). To say there is one body, one Spirit, one hope, one Lord, one faith, one baptism, and one God who is Father of us all and who is over and through all things, and who is all in all, is to acknowledge the divine foundation upon which the unity in the church is established (Eph. 4:4-6). Nevertheless, without a corresponding cooperation by the saints, making every effort possible to support unity, an effort arising from a thoroughgoing moral renewal of their nature, genuine community among them will be in danger of failing, and the goal of unity that sustains and builds the church will not be achieved (Eph. 4:3-6, 13-16, 17-29). That seems to be the flow of Paul's argument, that the unselfishness of the new life they have in Christ is to bear fruit in mutual concern for one another, and thus to provide for the welfare of the church as a whole, as well as the saints individually (Eph. 4:16). In that way, by cooperating with the Spirit, the saints will do their part to keep unity in the church among believers in fellowship with one another (Eph. 4:3, 16). The body/church depends for its thriving and growth on the interconnectedness of believers in the community, an interconnectedness that at its core is an undoing of selfish, human nature, with its old-life self-preoccupation, to be replaced by God implanting in them the morally principled, new-life of righteousness and holiness, which reflect the character of God, and which form the basis of a selfless life of serving others ahead of one's self (Eph. 4:16, 17-21, 22-24, cf. Rom. 12:1-2, 3-21; 13:1-10; Phil. 2:1-11).

Critical to such unity, then, is a personal inner spiritual condition and environment of the heart for individual members in the church, as well a healthy spiritual climate in the church as a whole (Eph. 4:13-16). An otherwise "healthy" church with carnal members suffers problems in seeking to preserve unity, as Paul's first letter to the Corinthians makes plain (1 Cor. 1-2). The dynamic balance between uprightness and sincerity in the saints, in their walk with God, and the overarching spiritual climate of the church as a whole impact what stands behind Paul's body analogy – that each one contributes something to the whole, and the whole to individuals simultaneously, as a function of New Testament fellowship (Eph. 4:1-16).

Paul Builds His Case: As the focus narrows from the God's eschatological goals in chapter 1 to unity among believers in chapters 4, with its practical implications in chapter 4:25-6:9. Paul is making the points that *union with Christ* is the ground of unity among believers, and that God's goal, in any case, is for the final reconciliation of all things to himself, the harmonious reunification of creation to God under his eternal rule (cf. 1 Cor. 15:20-28). Union in Christ and unity in the church anticipate God's ultimate purposes and goals for creation. Paul exults that through the activity of the Spirit in the church and the saints, the power of the age to come is breaking in on the present age, and that the power of the age to come is reflected particularly in the unity of God's people, as well as in their holiness and righteousness by which they represent God's own nature (Eph. 4:17-19; 20-24, cf. cf. John 13:34-35; 15:9-14; Acts 2:42-37; 4:32-37; 1 Thess. 4:9; 1 Pet. 1:22). Therefore, in chapter 2, Paul explains God's plan begins with saving those who are dead in trespasses and sins through his grace, and by a freely given faith to those who turn to God (Eph. 2:1-10), in order that he might create one church, one people of God, one body, one temple, the eternal habitation of God through the Spirit, for Jew and Gentile, all who are joined to one another in mutual and equal fellowship through a commonly experienced union with Christ (Eph. 2:11-22, cf. Deut. 33:19; Is. 2:2-4; 42:6; 45:23; 49:6; 51:4; 55:5; 60:3-6; 66:18; Jer. 3:17).

Chapter 3 explores the idea of the *mystery*, God's plan imperfectly understood in the Old Testament by the prophets, but now thoroughly known through the gospel as a result of Christ's death and resurrection. God has revealed it to the New Testament apostles and prophets. This mystery is that God has created one unified people of God through a shared experience of redemption in Christ (Eph. 2:1-10, 11-22; 3:1-12). The distinction between ethnic Israel and Gentiles has been erased in Christ, and the fulfillment of God's plan, whereby Israel would represent him to the nations resulting in their redemption, has come to fulfillment in Christ and the church (consisting of Jews at first and then Gentiles) (cf. Gen. 12:1-3; Isa. 42:6; 49:6; Rom. 1:16-17).[102]

Paul explains that the lack of clarity for the Old Testament prophets, has since Christ and his death and resurrection, given way to a full realization of how God has unified Jews and Gentiles into one people of God through a shared experience of salvation, not by law, but through grace and faith in Christ (Eph. 2:5-9). Jews and Gentiles form one church, one body of God's people, as a result of a one provision by which

---

[102] In Romans 9-11, Paul will make the point that because there are Jews in the church, redeemed by Christ, and transformed by God's saving power through grace, and because Jews were the first to believe in Christ, God has fulfilled the promises he made concerning the redemption of Israel, and concerning Isreal's eschatological role in his redemptive plan for the nations. Indeed, God has not yet finished with his redemptive initiative toward ethnic Israel, Paul postulates late in Romans 11, and that many will be grafted backing into the vine as a result of God's final moves as the eschaton emerges. It is clear he has something in mind like we read in Zechariah 12:10, when the spirit of redemption will come upon the people Israel as a result of seeing Christ, and realizing the Messiah is the one they had previously pierced (crucified), producing sorrow and repentance, leading to cleansing among the Jews as a people (Zech. 14).

all may be saved, something all believers in the church share in common with one another regardless of their backgrounds, social status, or religious origins. The outcome of this commonly shared salvation is that the people of God, through God's moral transformation and the power in the Spirit, are enabled to produce the good works for which God originally created them, and has recreated them in Christ, and in which he intended all humanity should walk (habitually conduct themselves) (αὐτοῦ γάρ ἐσμεν ποίημα, κτισθέντες ἐν Χριστῷ Ἰησοῦ ἐπὶ ἔργοις ἀγαθοῖς οἷς προητοίμασεν ὁ θεὸς ἵνα ἐν αὐτοῖς περιπατήσωμεν).[103] That is, through salvation in Christ, his people are now capable of acting consistently in righteousness. Chapter 3 closes with an eruption of exultant praise to God for his unfathomable love and mysterious outworkings (Eph. 3:14-21).

So, when chapter 4 resumes the theme of unity of the church from chapter 2, Paul sets out to explore the dynamics of its preservation and promotion from the point of view of the saints themselves, and in the context of their fellowship and interconnections in the believing community. He will explore some very practical implications of unity later, in terms of its effects on specific social relationships between believers in community with one another (Eph. 4:25-6:9). However, at first, he calls on his readers to embrace and exercise gentleness and humility toward one another, and to make every possible effort to maintain the unity that the Holy Spirit has established among believers through the bonding power of peace between them (σπουδάζοντες τηρεῖν τὴν ἑνότητα τοῦ πνεύματος ἐν τῷ συνδέσμῳ) (Eph. 4:1-3).[104] Gentleness and humility underwrite that expenditure of every effort, and

---

[103] Holmes, M. W. (2011–2013). *The Greek New Testament: SBL Edition* (Eph 2:10). Lexham Press; Society of Biblical Literature.
[104] Holmes, M. W. (2011–2013). *The Greek New Testament: SBL Edition* (Eph 4:3). Lexham Press; Society of Biblical Literature.

form the foundation for unity from the perspective of what the saints can do. The Spirit has established peace (unity), but the saints must do their best to sustain, maintain, and not to sabotage it.

Paul is about to go to demonstrate what contribution the saints are to make to unity, by urging the things he mentions later in chapter 4, 5 and most of 6. These practical initiatives can come only from a morally transformed heart and life, through their experience of salvation, whereby God has recreated them with just the right inner conditions in their renewed nature to live in pursuit of righteousness and holiness. The transformation of their nature is nowhere in Paul, or the New Testament, seen as an end in itself, but as the essential groundwork for a new life of obedience to God. Therefore, the Ephesians are to engage these essential qualities in the very practical business of fellowship with one another. Out of the transformation of their nature by God, by which he has implanted in them the beginnings of righteousness and holiness to reflect his own nature and character, they are to begin the project by a demonstration of these qualities to one another in service and mutual concern (Eph. 4:17-24).

Through transformative justification, Paul argues, God has created the right moral and spiritual conditions in their hearts and lives for them to engage gentleness, humility, and tireless efforts at promoting unity among believers in the church (Eph. 4:3; 24-22).[105] By unity, Paul

---

[105] Paul also speaks to the effect and role of these moral changes in connection with those outside of the church, whose understanding is darkened, are separated from God because of ignorance, as a result of the hardening of their hearts, by which they have lost all sensitivity to God and morality, and as a result engage in unrestrained immorality and greed (Eph. 4:17-19). Paul has an eye on the role of their new life and nature with respect to the world outside the church too, as well as their relationships with one another within the community of faith (Phil. 2:14-16). He does not expound on

obviously means promoting peace among believers in the body of Christ, and a unity at first created by God through the Spirit. Their shared experience of salvation through grace, puts everyone on level ground and equal footing in the matter of redemption and reconciliation to God, without consideration of personal merit or status, and serves as the rationale for the humility and gentleness they must exercise toward one another, thereby maintaining unity, mutual support, and concern among the saints (Eph. 2:5-9; Eph. 4:3; 22-24).[106] These qualities of gentleness and humility are going to find themselves expressed in a number of very practical and specific ways in various relationship configurations, and will need to be expressed in their fellowship with one another in the church, in their homes, or other domestic arrangements (Eph. 5:21-6:9). Paul will explore these in Ephesians 4:25-6:9, but, up front, he sets the grounds for unity in the church as the personal redemptive transformation of each one that makes up the body of believers, the church of Jesus Christ.

Paul's approach to unity is to promote the qualities of Christian character his readers will need to regulate their conduct toward one another, to maintain peace, and promote unity in the church. By fronting

---

the former because, arguably, the primary focus of his letter is unity in the church (Eph. 4:3-6, 13-16, 25-31). But there is a sense in which Paul views harmony, peace, and mutuality in the church as a witness to the power of the gospel to the outside world.

[106] Note that early in chapter 2, Paul does something similar to the opening of Romans, where he concludes that everyone, Jew or Gentile, needs salvation, because all are sinners. No matter what, Paul says, *we* all, regardless of background and position, once walked in trespasses and sins, and needed salvation by God's grace (ἐν οἷς καὶ ἡμεῖς πάντες ἀνεστράφημέν ποτε ἐν ταῖς ἐπιθυμίαις τῆς σαρκὸς ἡμῶν, ποιοῦντες) (Holmes, M. W. (2011–2013). The Greek New Testament: SBL Edition (Eph 2:3). Lexham Press; Society of Biblical Literature).

humility, gentleness, and persistent engagement of effort early in his treatment of unity (Eph. 4:3, 1516), Paul clearly proposes that the personal inner character of the saints is critical to unity in the church community, where these qualities are necessary for the preservation of fellowship in the church. At the heart of unity, then, from the side of the saints is character, *the inner environment of the heart before God*. In that case, Paul argues, justification is not merely a matter of right-standing with God, but of regeneration, or newness of life, by which God implants righteousness and holiness in the saints to be reflected or demonstrated in practical ways toward one another, and as an indication of the uprightness of God's own nature (καὶ ἐνδύσασθαι τὸν καινὸν ἄνθρωπον τὸν κατὰ θεὸν κτισθέντα ἐν δικαιοσύνῃ καὶ ὁσιότητι τῆς ἀληθείας) (Eph 4:22-24).[107]

Since Paul goes on to speak of specific attitudes and conduct in the context following this passage, we can confidently affirm that he means for reformed character to impact behavior. His exhortations about moral transformation and purity relate, or should relate, to how they treat one another in the context of their relationships in the fellowship of believers. One example of Paul's meaning in this passage will serve to illustrate this. It is found in his urging those who once stole to steal no more, but to work hard to have something to share with others (Eph. 2:27-28). *Selfishness* linked to an impulse to steal, and which seeks to avoid gain by exertion or hard work, is to be replaced with an ethic of self-imposed labor and hard work, so that reformed members of the community of God's people might be in possession of the means to *selflessly* provide for the needs others in the church (Eph. 4:28). In other words, transformed character must result, or should result in different conduct – outcomes in behavior – and a selfless caring for the welfare of

---

[107] Holmes, M. W. (2011–2013). The Greek New Testament: SBL Edition (Eph 4:24). Lexham Press; Society of Biblical Literature.

others in the church. Every believer should aim at providing for other members of the community, as well as being recipients of the benefaction of others in the church when needed (cf. Acts 2:42-47; 4:32-37; Rom. 15:23-27). Such concern should come from a selfless disregard for social status, ethnic background, Jew or Gentile, or gender (this Paul will address specifically in chapters 5 and 6).

For Paul, these considerations constitute what fellowship in the body of Christ is made of and looks like (Eph, 4:16). The nature of unity is selflessness that produces practical caring for one another in the church, along with encouragement and edifying that provides support (bearing one another's burdens – Gal. 6:2, 10). There is only one body (church, people of God), and one Holy Spirit who works in them, and all share the same hope for the future of salvation and God's redemptive purpose. There is one Lord, who is Jesus, one faith (body of doctrine as well as means for salvation), one baptism (the recognition and testimony of salvation), and one God and Father of all, who is the author of salvation and the architect of redemption (Eph. 4:5-6). All believers are in this together until the end and fulfillment of our hope in Christ.

Nevertheless, Paul observes, the body *is diverse* in the sense that each has been apportioned grace by God (Eph. 4:7, 11-12, cf. Rom. 12:3-8). We are not all the same, and each has gifts, and a unique place to serve God in the church and in his purposes. The strengths of one are not necessarily the strengths of all or others, and the weaknesses of one are not necessarily characteristic of everyone in the fellowship. Therefore, Paul sees the church as one body made up of a diversity of members, where each has its unique place and function, contributing to the health and welfare of the body as a whole, while at the same time as supporting the thriving of each member and part of the body that makes up the whole, they too are strengthened by others (Eph. 4:16, cf. Rom. 12:3-8; 1 Cor. 12:1-12). Now we are at the heart of Paul's concern, and for what arguably stand behind our passage. Believers have been transformed by God to live differently and selflessly compared to the world around them. That is, they are to live in a way that reflects the holiness and righteousness God himself, and particularly as selflessness and graciousness toward other believers (τὸν κατὰ θεὸν κτισθέντα ἐν δικαιοσύνῃ καὶ ὁσιότητι τῆς ἀληθείας).[108] Paul appears to mean a distribution of some gift or gifts from Christ equips each believer in the body uniquely for their role, which must find expression in service and caring toward others (Ἑνὶ δὲ ἑκάστῳ ἡμῶν ἐδόθη ἡ χάρις κατὰ τὸ μέτρον τῆς δωρεᾶς τοῦ Χριστοῦ).[109] This interpretation is confirmed in verse 16, where Paul rounds up the flow of his early argument by saying that each part of the body (each member, each disciple, each saint in the church), exercising their gifts and by participating in their role, makes the body grow and thrive as each one attends to and does their part (Ἑνὶ δὲ ἑκάστῳ ἡμῶν ἐδόθη ἡ χάρις κατὰ τὸ μέτρον τῆς δωρεᾶς τοῦ Χριστοῦ).[110] The mutuality of the supply of resources and benefits to the church, and its individual members, flows from one to the other because of their underlying unity, that is, their interconnectedness with one another, and more especially when each one fulfills their role or does their part (διὰ πάσης ἁφῆς τῆς ἐπιχορηγίας κατ' ἐνέργειαν ἐν μέτρῳ ἑνὸς ἑκάστου μέρους).[111]

Goal Directedness: The goal directedness of God's plan, that the body/church thrives through the interconnectedness of its members, has the trajectory of producing a fully mature/perfect *man* (εἰς ἄνδρα

---

[108] Holmes, M. W. (2011–2013). *The Greek New Testament: SBL Edition* (Eph 4:24). Lexham Press; Society of Biblical Literature.
[109] Holmes, M. W. (2011–2013). *The Greek New Testament: SBL Edition* (Eph 4:7). Lexham Press; Society of Biblical Literature.
[110] Holmes, M. W. (2011–2013). *The Greek New Testament: SBL Edition* (Eph 4:7). Lexham Press; Society of Biblical Literature.
[111] Holmes, M. W. (2011–2013). *The Greek New Testament: SBL Edition* (Eph 4:16). Lexham Press; Society of Biblical Literature.

τέλειον), which Paul further qualifies as consisting in the measure of fullness of Christ's own moral perfection (εἰς μέτρον ἡλικίας τοῦ πληρώματος τοῦ Χριστοῦ) (cf. Rom. 8:29-30; 1 Cor. 15:49; 2 Cor. 3:18; 4:16-18; Col. 3:10).[112, 113] At first he speaks of the church in the figure of a perfect man, but qualifies that to mean a man (the church) reflecting the full/perfect/complete/mature spiritual and moral character, nature, and conduct of Christ himself.[114] In Romans, Paul expresses the same idea as the goal of salvation culminating in conformity of the saints into the image of God's Son, Christ, where his moral character and nature are in view, and which are to be reflected in those who belong to him as a result of glorification at culmination of all things (Rom. 8:29-30). At the beginning of the eschaton, with Christ's return, the saints become trophies of God's grace and redemption, reflecting Christ back into his creation, when at the same time creation will be released from the burden of being subject to the effects of humanity's fall (Rom. 8:29-30 cf. Rom. 8:18-25). So, Paul has the future in view in Romans 8, when God will make all things right at last (cf. Col. 1:15-20). In this way, verse 13, with its elevated statements concerning the goal-directedness of God for his church culminating in a mature representation of Christ, anticipates Ephesians 4:23-24, where the apostle explains that the seeds of this final moral maturation and glorification have already been planted, and are at work, in those who are in union with Christ (ἀνανεοῦσθαι δὲ τῷ πνεύματι τοῦ νοὸς ὑμῶν, καὶ ἐνδύσασθαι τὸν καινὸν ἄνθρωπον τὸν κατὰ θεὸν κτισθέντα ἐν δικαιοσύνῃ καὶ ὁσιότητι τῆς ἀληθείας).[115]

---

[112] Holmes, M. W. (2011–2013). *The Greek New Testament: SBL Edition* (Eph 4:13). Lexham Press; Society of Biblical Literature.
[113] Wright N. T., 2012, 29-33.
[114] Arndt, 2000, 435-436.
[115] Holmes, M. W. (2011–2013). *The Greek New Testament: SBL Edition* (Eph 4:23–24). Lexham Press; Society of Biblical Literature.

Nevertheless, Paul asserts, the outflow or expression of righteousness (character and conduct) is not reserved until the eschaton but is expected to be at work in the saints and in the church in the present age.[116] In particular, it is to be demonstrated in their interactions with one another within the community of faith. For Paul, community relationships and unity in the church are a primary witness to the world of the character of God. Which is what Jesus taught, "By this everyone will know that you are my disciples, if you love one another."[117] Their treatment of one another reflects the holiness and grace of God back into the world. It is a witness to unbelievers when the saints shine as lights in a darkened moral and spiritual skyscape (Phil. 2:14-16). Far from being locked into a perpetual cycle of sinning, Paul argues, the saints have been liberated to becomes slaves of God and of righteousness in the present (Rom. 6:12-14, 16, 18, 22). Righteousness and holiness in the Ephesian context are to be reflected particularly in their relationships with, and treatment of one another.

Paul's holiness rationale seems to be that rather than being under law, the imposition of righteousness by the threat of judgment from God, they are under grace (Rom. 5:2). God will achieve his goals by working in them, at first to transform them morally, and after that to produce what he is looking for, in terms of right character and conduct from his people, through the Spirit (Rom. 6:14; 7:6; 8:1-4).[118] In Romans, the apostle makes it clear that it is through intimacy with (walking with/in, conducting one's life under the influence of) the Spirit that God has made righteousness possible for believers, wherever his people have

---

[116] After all, this is the theology of Paul throughout his epistles, particularly Romans and Galatians, and the assumption lying behind every exhortation to holiness, righteousness, and obedience to the members of his churches.
[117] *The New International Version* (Jn 13:35). (2011). Zondervan.
[118] It is no exaggeration to say that this is the centerpiece of the Pauline theology of holiness of character and conduct for the saints.

laid aside the old life, and embraced new life in Christ (Rom. 6:11; 7:6; 8:1-4, cf. Gal. 2:19-21; 5:16-25). The Spirit, promised in the Old Testament in connection with the coming of God's kingdom and a new covenant, will produce the moral changes that God anticipated in Jeremiah and Ezekiel, going far beyond what the law alone could not produce (Jer. 31:31-34; Ezek. 36:22-28, cf. Rom. 7:7-21).[119]

Everywhere in Paul, what God intends as the ultimate goal of salvation, the reflecting his image in true holiness, is already engaged in the present life of every believer as a result of transformative justification and union with Christ.[120] Such transformation is not static, as though it represents an end in itself, a terminus.[121] For Paul initial justification, union with Christ, and reconciliation with God are not an ending place, a landing zone, but a springboard for a new life in the Spirit that reflects the righteousness of God back into his creation (Rom. 8:29-30; 1 Cor. 13:13; 15:19; 2 Cor. 3:18; Eph. 4:22-24; Phil. 2:14-16; Co. 3:10). That is clearly the sentiment behind out passage. Justification is the beginning of something far greater than mere right positioning with

---

[119] Cf. Keener, Galatians: New Cambridge Bible Commentary, 2018, 149-151.
[120] Cf. Keener, Galatians: New Cambridge Bible Commentary, 2018, 113-114.
[121] Paul never speaks of salvation, whether redemption, the forgiveness of sin, justification, rightness with God, or moral transformation as static or as ends in themselves, even though from the late 17th century this has been more and more the evangelical concept – a once and for all past experience with God that settles it permanently without reference to our relationship or attitude to God in the present. Rather, Paul sees these are starting places for the ongoing work of God in the lives of those who believe, with the goal of which is bringing them to completion, maturity, and final perfection at the return of Christ (cf. Phil. 3:7-14). The process of maturing, development, and moral and spiritual growth are to begin at initial salvation and to carry forward until their consummation in God's final purposes, and they are, as a matter of faith and grace, what salvation consists of, in its broadest terms (cf. Rom. 8:29-30; 1 Cor. 3:1-4; 2 Cor. 3:18; 4:16-18; Gal. 5:22-23; Eph. 4:13; Phil. 3:7-14; Heb. 5:12-14; 1 Peter. 2:2; 2 Pet. 3:8).

God, or of imputed and objectively imparted righteousness.[122] Rather, it is going on from initial transformation to fully reflect and represent the nature of Christ in our own character and conduct as saints of God. Righteousness of character, that consistently produces right conduct, begins in the present (cf. Rom. 6:1-2, 3-23), however, and is driven principally by the impartation of the Spirit to work in those who belong the Christ (Rom. 8:4; Gal. 5:16, 18, 24-25). They have been made new in their nature, that is they have been transformed through a moral and spiritual renewal, with a view to it being a starting place for an *ongoing transformation* of their minds, their thinking, their inward character, to reflect the glory of God through an incremental development and growth in godliness (2 Cor. 3:18; Eph. 4:23, cf. Rom. 12:1-2).

Paul saw *himself* on a continuum, of having been saved by God, transformed, but growing in righteousness through the power of God, so that one day he might be found in Christ having a righteousness conferred upon him through the working of God in his life by faith (Phil. 3:7-14). And while Paul viewed himself as in some sense *perfect in Christ* (possessing a measure of moral perfection), there was room for improvement and growth toward its consummation in Christ at his return and the glorification of the saints (Phil. 3:10-12; 15-16, cf. Rom. 8:20-25).[123] Indeed, he makes the point that those who are mature or are maturing think this way, namely that possessing rightness with God, they must press on to a progressive deepening of righteousness in their character and lives, and in the quest to attain the final prize of God (ὅσοι οὖν τέλειοι) (Phil. 3:12, 15). Believers are by no means to remain in the immature condition of mere justification or initial moral transformation.

---

[122] Cf. Campbell, Paul and the Hope of Glory: An Exegetical and Theological Study, 2020, 260-261.
[123] Fletcher, 492.

To the Ephesians he writers that their natures have been seeded with righteousness and holiness from God, which reflects God's own righteousness and holiness in their lives and conduct. This implantation supports the changes now occurring in their minds due to ongoing renewal by God (ἀνανεοῦσθαι δὲ τῷ πνεύματι τοῦ νοὸς ὑμῶν).[124] These moral changes must find expression in their lives as conduct and obedience to God, as a reflection of his character to the world on the one hand, and to one another in the church on the other. In this way, verse 13 joins hands with verse 24. Verse 24 explains how the foundation for maturing godliness will reach is final goal, beginning with the laying aside of the old life to embrace the new life implanted in them by God. The implications of this change, and its ongoing development, is that they are to live a different life in every practical way, the nature of which Paul will soon speak (Eph. 4:25-6:9). There are, then, implications to the moral transformation by which God has implanted a new moral condition in the hearts of those who believe, and these implications impact the believer going forward in terms of obedience and character development. By working out these implications and obligations, arising as they do from moral transformation and possession of the Spirit, God builds a witness to the world, and maintains unity in the church among believers.

All this begins with a change in the disposition of their minds, a transformation in the very core of their nature. However, this transformation must embraced by acceptance on the part of the believer, by a *reckoning* that puts off the old man, and puts on this new man of holiness and righteousness, only then will their conduct reflect consistently the character of God – at first because of an initial transformation of character or nature, but then as a result of walking in

---

[124] Holmes, M. W. (2011–2013). *The Greek New Testament: SBL Edition* (Eph 4:23). Lexham Press; Society of Biblical Literature.

the Spirit, which leads to moral development and maturity in godliness (Eph. 4:24, cf. Rom. 6:11; 12:2).[125] Of this change, Paul says, God has implanted genuine righteousness and holiness in them, in their nature, through the transformation of their minds. This amounts to a recreation of their natures as a result of union with Christ.[126] Paul lends substance to his affirmation in 2 Corinthians 5:17 in this passage, that all things have become new, the old has gone. He summarizes here what he elsewhere describes in detail. What stands behind moral success for believers going forward is a subtraction of the old life and nature (through crucifixion with Christ), and the implantation of new life in them (through union with Christ in his resurrection) (Rom. 6:1-11; Eph. 4:22-24). However, this change must be accepted and engaged by *reckoning on it,* by embracing it at the level of the will and the mind, as a total surrender to God, or here in Ephesians by putting off the old man, and clothing themselves with the new man (Eph. 4:20-24, cf. Rom. 13:14).

Paul's readers are to go beyond initial, transformative justification to embrace fully the new life of Christ in the Spirit, and to apply it to their moral development and conduct, just as he said to the Romans, and to the Galatians earlier.[127] They are new because the old life is gone, and the Spirit of God has implanted in them the new life of Christ (cf. Gal. 2:19-21), conceived in them by the Spirit with righteousness and holiness as its moral foundation (Eph. 4:23-24). Their lives, then, cannot

---

[125] Cf. Wright N. T., 2012, 31-32, 167.

[126] This is the point Paul makes in Romans 6:1-11, that union with Christ, justification, is morally transformative, making the old life of sin and sinning obsolete, and a new, transformed life in Christ of utmost importance. There is a forward movement putting greater distance between the former life of sin and sinning, to go on to the righteousness and holiness of God. That is the theme of the rest of Romans 6, that God's plan has a goal in mind, producing righteousness and holiness toward the goal of eternal life (Rom. 6:12-23).

[127] Wesley, The Works of John Wesley, 1872, 5.

be morally neutral, but are overwhelmingly predisposed toward reflecting the upright nature and character of God, with the goal that God will one day bring them to full moral perfection which will give perfect expression to the full stature of Christ, the image of God's Son reflected back into all of creation by the redeemed children of God (Eph. 4:13, cf. Rom. 8:22-28, 29-30). At last, the intention of God in creation will find its fulfillment in a redeemed humanity that finally does image and represent him to creation (Gen. 1:26-28).

Implications for the Present: The doxological-style passage late in chapter 3, then, seems to provide a transition to Paul's consideration of the essential nature and outworking of the unity he has previously described as essential and intrinsic to the body of Christ. Paul's concern, then, is with the implications and application of transformation in the lives of those who believe, which he considers to be the object of outworking by the indwelling Spirit in their character and conduct – how they walk it out (conduct, consistently act and behave). His particular focus in Ephesians 4-6 is on how transformation and the indwelling of the Spirit impact unity in the church, and the relationships between believers in fellowship with one another in various settings and circumstances (Eph. 4:25-6:9). Chapter 4 seems to mark a transition also to Paul's concern, that, in the believer's life, there should be practical expressions of right conduct consistent with God's own righteousness and holiness, and that it should arise from the new moral dynamics at work in them. He is particularly concerned with how these will affect unity in the church or community of God's people. More specifically, they should positively impact their relationships and fellowship with one another by how they treat fellow believers, so that each is built up and encouraged, and the church as a community thrives (Eph. 4:13-16).

So, laying aside foundational theological principles of salvation (the Pauline soteriology) after verse 24, the apostle goes on to consider the implications of righteousness and holiness at work in them as they navigate various circumstances, relationships and social configurations, including husbands and wives, children and parents, slaves, and slave owners, as well as other interactions. Speaking the truth in love, not allowing anger to remain unaddressed, or the obligation of the thief to become a provider to others, and so on, are all practical expressions of what it means to have put off the old life, to be clothed with the new, and to experience ongoing renewal by God in the attitude/spirit of their minds (Eph. 4:23-24). Paul's upending of the culture of the Greek-Roman world around him by enjoining these principles in the church, will continue through chapter 5, and into the mid-point of chapter 6, and by employing specific, practical examples of its outworking between believers, in a way that traditional social interactions and relationships are infused with new attitudes that reflect the love and integrity of God. It is a fundamental change in natures affecting their attitudes to one another, where even the socially high owe a debt of concern and compassion to fellow believers of lower rank, which Paul calls *mutual submission* (Eph. 5:21). Mutual submission like this does not come from the ethos of Greek-Roman culture in the world around them. It arises from the transforming power of God, and the life enriching power of God's working in them through the Spirit, which encourages believers to put others ahead of themselves in genuine service and concern, a theme repeated throughout the New Testament (cf. Matt. 20:28; Mark 10:45; John 13:12-17, 34-35; Acts 2:42-47; 4:32-37; Rom. 12:3, 7, 10, 16; 13:8; 2 Cor. 13:11; Gal. 5:13; Eph. 4:2, 32; 5:21; Col. 3:13; 1 Thess. 4:9; 5:11; 2 Thess. 1:3; Heb. 3:13; 10:24-25; 1 Pet.1:22; 3:8-9; 4:10; 5:2, 5; 1 John 3:23; 4:7, 11-12; 2 John 5). They are to make no mistake, God's workings in them must lead to mutual submission and concern, even when the worldly models around them differ dramatically, maybe especially so. They must live and act in contrast to them, as a witness to the character of God (cf. Eph. 4:19-19).

Paul saw unity and relationships as a critical witness of Christian moral values to those outside the church.

In the more immediate context, unity must be worked out in present relationships and the interactions between those who make up the church, for the sake of its overall development and growth, for the wellbeing and progress of the of the saints on the one hand, and the church as a body of believers on the other (Eph. 4:13-16). Paul holds in tension the healthiness of the church as a body of believers in fellowship with one another, and that of individual believers, where both depend on the proper functioning and balance of each believer occupying and doing their part faithfully and consistently before God (αὐξήσωμεν εἰς αὐτὸν τὰ πάντα, ὅς ἐστιν ἡ κεφαλή, Χριστός).[128]

Unity is anchored in the working of the Spirit in the church; he has produced it in the first place. Nevertheless, to accomplish the goals God has in mind (full maturity of the church as a body, and of believers personally), a cooperative spirit between believers for the sake of the church is required. According to Paul this arrangement of believers as members of the body, serving one another through caring relationships, brings to bear every benefit and help needed by and for each member of the body to thrive – unity in the church ensures the growth and health of the church as a body, the community of believers, as well as for each member personally (Eph. 4:3-5, 16). Furthermore, unity must be worked out in their daily interactions with one another through constant effort and engagement (Eph. 4:3). Unity is no mere mantra. It is not to be taken for granted. The caring and sharing that underlies it, through intentional relationships between saints, must be constantly and consistently engaged in service and concern for one another. This is what *make every effort* in verse 3 means (Eph. 4:3, 16). Underlying this

[128] Holmes, M. W. (2011–2013). *The Greek New Testament: SBL Edition* (Eph 4:15). Lexham Press; Society of Biblical Literature.

effort is the power of the Spirit among and in them. The specific and practical nature of this unity, of effort and engagement on the part of the saints for the sake of the church, and for each one to thrive, is what Paul will develop from this point on, until almost the end of the epistle.[129]

Conclusion/Summary: Ephesians, one of the loftiest of Paul's epistles in theological scope, underscores a very practical concern for how unity, mutual relationships, and fellowship in the church, and that a unified body of diverse members is critical to the health of the church as a community, on the one hand, and for the thriving of individual saints on the other (Eph. 4:16). By providing a theological foundation for union with Christ (Eph. 1:3-8), for the interconnectedness between believers and Christ, and by considering God's overall redemptive action and purposes to finally unite all of creation through Christ under his rule (Eph. 1:9-10), Paul establishes the principle that God seeks unity at first in the church, and ultimately for all of redeemed creation (Eph. 1:3-10, cf. Col. 1:15-20). In this way, Paul contends, God is working to a plan of his own devising by which he joins believers to Christ and one another in anticipation of the unification and union of all things in creation under his rule in Christ (1:11-12, 22-23). In consideration of this final unification of all of creation under the rule of Christ (cf. 1 Cor. 15:20-28), God has placed a deposit of the age to come in the church and in the lives of the believers personally, the Holy Spirit. He is the seal of their

---

[129] We should note here that the fear of the "works righteousness crowd" who opine that Paul is not establishing a new law in his exhortations to practical right conduct is unwarranted. Paul has already established to a clear degree that the basis for their action toward one another, and uprightness before God, is the grace of God by which they were transformed at salvation, and morally empowered by the indwelling Spirit. It is grace that is working this out in them and in the church as a body of believers in fellowship with one another.

redemption, and of their current participation in what will find ultimate fulfillment in God's plan at the return of Christ (cf. Rom. 8:19-25).

A unified church, Paul contends, made up of diverse people in harmony with one another, where Jews and Gentiles are examples of incompatibility made compatible in Christ, is to be seen as the foreshadowing and initiation of God's overall design from the beginning, where the Old Testament gives only prophetic glimpses into it (Eph. 2:11-3:13, cf. Gal. 3:26-29). Paul discusses what unity looks like in the church, in terms of relationships and fellowship with one another, by addressing specific examples in Roman society, and the households of Ephesian believers (Eph. 5:21-6:9). He speaks of how this unity is to be maintained or serviced in the context of relationships between believers in the church, particularly where the world may have a different view of or practices concerning them. Union with Christ must transformed perspectives and attitudes on relationships between people into something altogether different from the world around them, and they must reflect back into the world the character of God. In that case, if their character and relationships represent God, they must make every effort to preserve unity against the pressures of society, or the world, temptations, disagreements, differences of opinion, and any other pressure that may come against it. Even their own moral or personal failures, or lack of graciousness toward another, or inconsistent engagement of patience, tolerance, humility, gentleness, and love must come under the rule of God and his renewing power in their minds and attitudes (Eph. 4:3, 16, 23-24).

There is nothing disjunctive in the opening chapters of Ephesian, then, where Paul's lofty theology has been sometimes considered separate or apart from the theme of unity, or from the practical exhortations. Chapter 1 underpins his treatment of unity in the church right out of the gate, by establishing the goal-directedness of God's plan for creation in a final eschatological unity of all things in Christ, prefigured in the unity of the church in the present (Eph. 1:3-14, cf. Col. 1:15-20). By encouraging unity among the people of God in the church, Paul argues that there has been a breaking in of the kingdom of God into the present age, which is demonstrated by the power and presence of the Spirit among God's people as a witness to the world in their conduct to the holiness and righteousness of God (Eph. 1:13-23). In Ephesians 4, Paul proposes that the character of God is reflected back into the world by both the upright conduct of saints, and by the unity of their relationships with one another in the church (cf. John 13:35). However, the apostle is anxious also to assert that unity is beneficial for the body, to the community as a whole, and to the saints individually, *as they serve and represent God to the world* (cf. Eph. 1:3-14; 4:13-16; 22-24). He will go on to address this unity, and what it looks like in the specific circumstances, and the social configurations they might encounter in their lives and society, and how they are to work out their obligations to obey God, so as to represent him to those outside of the church (Eph. 4:25-6:9).

Paul's practical, almost mundane, concern for the interactions between the saints in the church belies the working of God through the Spirit behind the scenes so the church might thrive as a whole and the saints personally – growing and maturing into the image of God's holiness and righteousness (Eph. 4:10-16). The goal for the church and the saints is to reflect the holiness and righteousness of God into the world, while moving on to full godliness and moral maturity that will one day represent the full measure of the stature of Christ (a final eschatological realization of God's overall purposes) (Eph. 4:9-16, 22-24, cf. Eph. 1:11-12; 15-23).[130] A church that reflects the character of Christ back into the world in genuine holiness and righteousness must, for success in fellowship, run along the rails of unity in relationships

---

[130] Cf. Fletcher, 492.

among believers, where selfless service and mutual concern for one another give witness to the fundamental difference between the people of God and the world (Eph. 4:17, cf. Phil. 2:14-16).

Earlier theological considerations in Ephesians, then, lay the groundwork for the flow of Paul's argument that considers unity as mutual concern and care among believers, where personal holiness and righteousness reflect the character and nature of God, and that unity is essential to the success of those relationships in the body of Christ. The goal of unity is maturing the saints, and the health and growth of the church as whole (Eph. 4:13-16). Through unity, the working of the parts within the whole, and the supporting structure of the whole for the benefit of the saints, provides the means for supplying sustaining resources to believers, where the Spirit at work in them facilitates the forward movement of church, and saints toward the ultimate goals God has for his people and creation (unifying all things under the rule of Christ in the kingdom of God) (Eph. 1:6-10; 2:14-22; 3:10-13).

In this way, unity in the church, demonstrated by good relationships among the saints, and reflected in their personal righteousness and holiness, prefigures in the present age the divine purpose and plan for the final unification and final perfection of all of creation under the holy rule of God. Understanding the flow of Paul's eschatological arguments, here and elsewhere, helps make sense of a reoccurring insistence in his letters that the saints live and serve one another in unity in his churches. For Paul, unity in the church is part of the "now but not yet" aspect of the coming of the kingdom of God. Having broken in with the arrival of Christ and outpouring of the Spirit, it is already at work among God's people in the present, empowering their lives for godliness, for service to God, and as witnesses to the world, even as they anticipate an eschatological consummation at his appearing (cf. Rom. 8:18-25; 1 Cor. 15:20-28; Col. 1:15-20).

The often remarked upon phenomenon of Paul's epistles, by which some see a hard division between theological considerations at first, and a laundry list of practical concerns later, is only partially true. Ephesians is a transparent refutation of superficial thinking about Paul's epistolary sophistication. As we observed, the letter builds the case for unity from the beginning through a thoroughgoing consideration of the theological underpinnings of unity as the goal directedness of God's purposes (Eph. 1:11-12, 15-23; 1 Cor. 15:20-28, cf. Dan. 7:13-14). Unity as a consideration breaks out at the outset of the letter and is built upon until Paul can address the importance of unity for the church, the body of Christ, more directly. That he goes on to lay out more practical considerations in connection to various relationships between believers, and in circumstances they may encounter, does not undermine the underlying thematic unity of the letter. Indeed, it sets down the concrete ways in which unity in the church might be expressed, and the character of God might be put on to display to the world his glory.

Paul's argument for unity in the church particularly, then, is that God's ultimate goal for all things is unification under the rule of Christ as the head (Col. 1:17-20). Christ, acting as head of the church, his body, Paul argues, is the advanced representation of God's kingdom to the world (Eph. 1:22-23; 4:15-16; 5:23; Col. 1:18; 2:20). How can the church fulfill its mission and role as a witness for God, thrive, or even expect to exist without the headship of Christ or unity between believers (Eph. 4:15-16)? Through unity primarily, the holiness and righteousness of God is reflected back into the present world, bringing glory to God, and signifying the headship of Christ over the kingdom of God. This was, in any case, God's original design and purpose for humanity, to represent God's rule as sovereign over his creation by reflecting his image and likeness back into the world as they took dominion over it in partnership with him (Gen. 1:26-28). The church and people of God have become the advanced expression and representation of God's purpose in anticipation of its consummation at the appearing of Christ.

If we sharply divide Paul's theological concerns from his practical concerns, we will miss Paul's theological framework, woven skillfully throughout, as a development of his core theme (in this case unity). We will be in danger of doing violence to the teaching of the letter to the Ephesians. God's ultimate purposes are anticipated in the union of the saints with Christ through salvation, involving their transformation to reflect the holiness of God back into this present age. And by giving the Spirit as a deposit of what is to come, he has sealed their redemption against their final glorification when he ultimately takes possession of what he has already purchased with the blood of Christ (Eph. 1:17-23). Unity among the saints and the power of the Spirit in the church, provide a way to represent the rule of God to the world as a witness of his character, and at the same time for the church enjoy a preemptive, experimental foretaste of that final unification of creation under God's rule (Eph. 4:10-16). Paul creates theological foundations for his practical instructions to believers and his churches before he offers them, encouraging the saints to work out the implications in specific ways, what God is working in them through salvation and by the Spirit. His epistles, then, exhibit an organic and thematic connection between practical and theological concerns, of which Ephesians is a particularly fine example.

Ephesians 4 marks the transition from the consideration of the purely theological basis for unity to practical implications in the context of the life of the church, and the relationships between believers. Ephesians 4:17-24 seem to delineate the transition where Paul turns his attention to how unity ought to work out in practical terms. Therefore, this section might arguably be viewed as both practical and theological in nature. His readers are to *live* "not as Gentiles..." so that the lifestyles, attitudes, and behaviors of the Roman world and society, with its sensuality and impurity (τῇ ἀσελγείᾳ εἰς ἐργασίαν ἀκαθαρσίας πάσης), might not encroach on *their* conduct, or make their way into the church.[131] BDAG describes this as *conforming to* moral or social pressure.[132] Paul is warning his readers to avoid taking on the distasteful moral attitudes and conduct of the world around them, and allowing it to enter into their personal conduct or way of doing things in the church. In this context, the emphasis is on immorality generally, and may include sexual misconduct in particular.[133] That these are "unclean," or morally pollute the doer, making them unclean to God or contaminated, sinful, wicked, and evil, is clear from how Paul views sin elsewhere, especially when habitually practiced (cf. Rom. 6-7). The personal moral landscape of the mind, heart, will, and life of the individual believer must be dominated by the implanted righteousness and holiness of the new life, followed up by their own decisive and voluntary surrender of their will to God, and the leadership of the Spirit, so that they have put off the old life, and put on the new life (Eph. 4:17-24).

Immorality alienates from God. It separates at a time when God purposes reconciliation and peace with those who belong to him and eventually with all of his creation (cf. Rom. 5:1-2; Rev. 21:1-4). Dissolution of fellowship with God is the consequence of sinfulness, and is the enemy of union with Christ, and unity in the church. The story of Israel is a prime example of this principle. Similarly, immorality and selfishness in the church divide the saints. Therefore, as he transitions to practical concerns, Paul addresses at first the inner environment in their hearts, by which God has transformed them to reflect his own holiness and righteousness (Eph. 4:24), which serves as the foundation for exhortation to practical right conduct that follows. The moral

---

[131] Holmes, M. W. (2011–2013). *The Greek New Testament: SBL Edition* (Eph 4:19). Lexham Press; Society of Biblical Literature.

[132] Arndt, 2000, 141.

[133] Arndt, 2000, 141.

changes that have occurred in connection with their reconciliation to God (Rom. 5:1-8) are also the basis for selflessness in their interactions with one another, and serve as a critical foundation for unity in the church, as well as for their personal thriving through the Spirit.

For Paul, sinful behavior is not just behavior or practice, but a sign of moral corruption, of a moral defect in one's nature. From Romans 6:15 on to then of the chapter, Paul seems to warn that habitual sinning can lead to a reintroduction of corruption into our nature, away from God, and, even if we once believed but have fallen away, to death (cf. Rom. 6:15-23; Gal. 5:19-21). Habitual sinful conduct, for Paul, and the Bible generally, is the result of some pollution in human nature, something morally wrong that needs addressing or redemption by God (cf. Ps. 51:1-12). Unaddressed sin, Paul warns, leads to habitual sinning, even after justification (Rom. 6:1-2, 15), and will become the cause for a reintroduction of corruption into our nature, which he characterizes as obedience or slavery to sin, leading to death (Rom. 6:20-23). Such slavery has a way of producing ever growing expressions of disobedient and sinfulness (cf. Gen. 6:5; Ps. 51:1-12; Jer. 17:19; Rom. 5:12-21; 6:1-23; Gal. 5:19-21). Both dynamics are at work simultaneously, whereby sin as corruption of nature begets sinning, and sinning hardens into moral corruption (Rom. 6).[134]

No observer of human nature and in the present age can deny that this dynamic is at work in humanity, manifested to a frightening and increasing degree in the last days.[135] It is the thesis that stands behind

---

[134] This is, after all, the point Paul is making in Romans 6, as he lays out his case for changed conduct after initial, and morally transformative justification.

[135] Interestingly enough, N.T. Wright, in *After You Believe,* argues for the same dynamic at work in the transformed Christian life, whereby the moral changes brought about by salvation through the Spirit, producing moral purity, when

Genesis 6, where the Lord says that he will not always do battle with men over their sinfulness (Gen. 6:3). Paul also warns the saints in Rome, and the Corinthians too, that sinning can produce corruption and a falling away from God, even for those who once served him (1 Cor. 5:6-8, cf. Heb. 10:26-31). In other places he cites examples of this and the danger (1 Cor. 5:1-5, 6-8, 13; 1 Tim. 3:6-7; 2 Tim. 2:17-18; 25-26). Outside the church, moral ignorance is described in our passage as a progressive darkening of the understanding or minds, a deepening fog of non-apprehension of God for those who practice immorality (ἐσκοτωμένοι τῇ διανοίᾳ ὄντες) (Eph. 4:18).[136] In the world, increasing fogginess occurs with respect to God's existence and holiness, so that people do know or perceived God as God (cf. Rom. 1:18-32). Practicing sin has a way of numbing one's sensitivity to immorality and to corruption, blinding the eye of one's awareness of their lack of moral uprightness or integrity, masking the seriousness and extent of one's moral depravity (οἵτινες ἀπηλγηκότες).[137] So, Paul posits that the saints and the church are to reflect the holiness and righteousness of God back into that darkened moral fogginess, in order to demonstrate the character of God, and reveal to those who have no concept of uprightness or of a morally pure God, the creator of all things, whose purpose is to reunite all things under his rule, and that they are being invited into fellowship *with him*.

---

engaged through consistent right practice, produce ever increasing godliness toward final glorification at the return of Christ. He is making application, of course, of Pauline theology found in passages like 2 Corinthians 3:18 and this one.

[136] Holmes, M. W. (2011–2013). *The Greek New Testament: SBL Edition* (Eph 4:18). Lexham Press; Society of Biblical Literature.

[137] Holmes, M. W. (2011–2013). *The Greek New Testament: SBL Edition* (Eph 4:19). Lexham Press; Society of Biblical Literature.

Hardened by the darkening of their minds toward morality and God, and estranged from him, Paul says, the world becomes increasing unresponsive to God and to goodness, as people give themselves over increasingly to all kinds of wickedness (ἐσκοτωμένοι τῇ διανοίᾳ ὄντες, ἀπηλλοτριωμένοι τῆς ζωῆς τοῦ θεοῦ, διὰ τὴν ἄγνοιαν τὴν οὖσαν ἐν αὐτοῖς) (cf. Rom. 1:24-25).[138] For believers and the church to behave in the way the Gentiles of Roman-Greek culture behaved, is to leave the people outside of the church without a witness to the holiness and the righteousness of God, to leave them unchallenged about salvation, and the impending judgment of God on sin. Becoming sinful or acting disobediently to God, and betraying his by nature by our sinful conduct compromises the church's mission to the world. Since it is conduct that is perceived and measured by those outside of the church, the saints are obligated to see to it that in every practical way, their conduct is consistent with the new nature representative of God's, which he implanted in them by the Holy Spirit (τὸν κατὰ θεὸν κτισθέντα ἐν δικαιοσύνῃ καὶ ὁσιότητι τῆς ἀληθείας (Eph. 4:24).[139] So, Paul, having established the grounds for changed conduct, a transformed life guided by the Spirit, will now address some of the more mundane and practical circumstances and relationships in which it must play out in full view of the world.

We made a considerable effort to trace the authorship of Ephesians, and its background because during our study we will want to compare what this epistle says about holiness with other known Pauline writings on the same topic. Confidence in the Pauline authorship of Ephesians is, arguably, essential to a proper appreciation of its flow of argument, and understanding its concerns is best appreciated from confidence in

---

[138] Holmes, M. W. (2011–2013). *The Greek New Testament: SBL Edition* (Eph 4:18). Lexham Press; Society of Biblical Literature.
[139] Holmes, M. W. (2011–2013). *The Greek New Testament: SBL Edition* (Eph 4:24). Lexham Press; Society of Biblical Literature.

the Ephesians as the original recipients. Both Pauline authorship and a knowledge of the background to the epistle will help us ground our conclusions firmly in an objective biblical landscape, and to see if they properly belong there, rather than asserting our interpretations *ex nihilo*. Furthermore, we have sought to demonstrate that Ephesians holds together by a closely reasoned argument for unity in the church, based upon the saints' union with Christ through salvation. This unity Paul puts in the context of God eschatological purpose, to bring his church and its people to a maturity that represents the full measure of the stature of Christ (Eph. 4:13).

God's goal-directed purposes in Christ were initiated in the garden through the promise of the serpent bruiser, who would undo all of had transpired with respect to the introduction to sin and its consequences into God's creation, over which he had placed human beings to represent his rule (Gen. 3:15). Having summarized the purpose and plan (Eph. 1:9-10), Paul asserts that, by union with Christ (Eph. 1:4), the saints preemptively participate in God's purpose by reflecting his holiness and righteousness into this present age (Eph 4:22-24, cf. Phil. 2:14-16). Through the Holy Spirit, by which they have died to old life of sin, and are made a live to live a new life in union with Christ, the reintroduction of the character of God has taken place, and the reestablishment of their role in reflecting God back into the world has begun (Eph. 4:17-24). Union with Christ implies and requires unity among believers, because by it the saints reflect holiness and character of God back into the world as God's witnesses (Eph. 2:11-22). Their moral transformation, and ongoing moral development, has repatriated them into the kingdom of God, and reinstated their role as God's representatives, or witnesses to the world. In 2 Corinthians 5, Paul calls the saints Christ's ambassadors through whom God is making his redemptive appeal to the world (2 Cor. 5:21-22).

Still, failure of unity in the church or tensions in relationships among believers mars the witness and belies an authentic representation of God's character. As the Lord complained to Israel, the nations around them profaned his name on account of them, and the way they acted (cf. Ps. 50:21; Isa. 29:15-16; 52:5; Ezek. 18:19-20, 25-29; 20:9, 33:17-19; 36:16-21, 21-23; Mal. 2:17; 3:13-15). The moral transformation of the saints, and that which is taking place in them, must support their witness to the world around them, where unity in the church, as each one makes every effort to exercise gentle humility with patience toward one another, is its most indisputable sign (Eph. 4:3, 13-16). [140] Selflessness arises out of a morally transformed life to produce the witness God intends to the world of his holiness, because their attitudes and conduct are so different from the world around them (Eph. 4:17-24). Unity is more than an assent to a principle or noble idea. It consists in the conduct of the saints, including their own morally upright behavior, whereby they treat of one another rightly in the context of fellowship with one another in the community of faith, so all are built up personally, while the church is enriched corporately at the same time (Eph. 4:16).

---

[140] Cf. Stott J. R., 1979, 25.

CHAPTER TWO

THE GOAL-DIRECTEDNESS OF SALVATION

Ephesians 4:17-24, right out of the box, exhibits a certain goal directedness for initial salvation. In this somewhat transitory passage under our consideration, Paul finalizes the foundation for the practical exhortations to the Ephesians that are coming. He will provide them with specific examples from their mundane lives and relationships as to how their conduct ought to reflect that they are new-creation people, with a new nature, transformed by God and led by the Spirit (cf. Rom. 8:1-4; Gal. 5:16, 18, 24-25). He is concerned that they should give evidence to this by their daily conduct and in their interactions with those who are still *walking in trespasses and sins* (Eph. 2:1). They should particularly exhibit holiness in how they interact with one another in the context of their fellowship in the community of faith (cf. 1 Cor. 1:10). By referring to their former way of life, and that are being made new in the attitudes of their minds (ἀνανεοῦσθαι δὲ τῷ πνεύματι τοῦ νοὸς ὑμῶν), Paul establishes the difference between those who are in union with Christ and those who are still dead in trespasses and sin (Eph. 2:1; 4:17-19).[141] The former are improving morally in their reflection of the image of God, and the latter are retreating into further moral darkness (Eph. 4:17-19, 22-24) (see below). Alluding to chapter 2, those in union with Christ are no longer walking in trespasses and sins, nor are they under the control of the prince of the power of the air (Eph. 2:1-2), having darkened minds, and being insensible to morality and sin (Eph. 4:17-19). Through union with Christ, they have crossed a threshold, a boundary that separates their life and conduct from those around them, whose

---

[141] Holmes, M. W. (2011–2013). *The Greek New Testament: SBL Edition* (Eph 4:23). Lexham Press; Society of Biblical Literature.

minds *are* darkened and insensitive to morality, the holiness of God, and to sin, because they give themselves to the pursuit of ungodliness with increasing greed for more (Eph. 4:17-19).

There has been a moral movement in connection with their salvation, Paul contends, from the point of their realization of sin, repentance, and pardon, leading to justification, the result of which is they must leave the old life behind (Eph. 4:22). In other words, salvation is inherently directional (cf. Ga. 3:1-3; Col. 3:9-10). It entails deliverance from sin and moral transformation, whereby the old life is forsaken, and a new life is taken up. This movement is away from the old life to new life in Christ, and the new life is a morally transformed one that is designed to reflect the holiness and righteousness of God through changed conduct that builds on character as it matures toward full godliness (Eph. 4:13-15, cf. 1 Cor. 13:11-12; 13; 2 Cor. 3:18; 4:16-18; 7:1; Col. 1:28; 2:19; Phil. 3:12-14; 2 Tim. 3:17). Salvation is not static, a past transaction, setting us right with God, but a moral transformation that turns its back on the old life to embrace a new life that reflects the holiness and righteousness of God implanted as the redeemed nature of the new believer (Eph. 4:20). They are to now being made new in the attitudes of their minds, implying a new direction, a new way conducting themselves going forward (ἀνανεοῦσθαι δὲ τῷ πνεύματι τοῦ νοὸς ὑμῶν).[142] In other words, justification, initial salvation, is inherently directional, with a starting point beyond which those who come to Christ must advance and grow. In his letter to the Romans, Paul will make this even more clear with an extended treatment of moral transformation leading to changed conduct, and a life of obedience to God assisted by the indwelling power of the Spirit (Rom. 6-8).[143]

---

[142] Holmes, M. W. (2011–2013). The Greek New Testament: SBL Edition (Eph 4:23). Lexham Press; Society of Biblical Literature.
[143]Cf. Osborne G. R., 2004, 182-202.

IMPLIED FORWARD MOVEMENT

Realizing that Paul is encouraging his readers to advance from initial salvation to go on to righteousness and holiness that reflects the character of God, helps make sense of the rather abrupt introduction of what some may see as a discordant note – the exhortation to *no longer* (μηκέτι) conduct themselves as Gentiles do, that is to live like unsaved people in the world around them (μηκέτι ὑμᾶς περιπατεῖν καθὼς καὶ τὰ ἔθνη περιπατεῖ).[144] As we have said, Paul is drawing on the idea that the unsaved Gentiles still live or conduct themselves in trespasses and sins, and implores the Ephesians to no longer live like that (Eph. 2:1-4). Speaking of Gentiles, Paul says, their conduct is regulated by what he calls an empty mindedness (ἐν ματαιότητι τοῦ νοὸς αὐτῶν), which exists in a state of being darkened (ἐσκοτωμένοι τῇ διανοίᾳ ὄντες).[145, 146] Paul is about to draw a contrast between the inward condition of the hearts and minds of those who are walking in *trespasses and sins,* and those who have been sealed with the Holy Spirit, as a result of redemption, who have adopted a new life characterized by the righteousness and holiness that reflects the nature and character of God.

Without Christ, Gentiles conduct their lives oblivious to God, thoughtlessly with regard to true morality. Their minds are undirected, fruitless in concepts of goal directed morality, or of living in purposeful morality, or with godliness at its core (cf. Rom. 7:7-21).[147] This appears to be what the apostle means by *with emptiness of their minds,* where the preposition with the dative may imply something of an instrumental

---

[144] Holmes, M. W. (2011–2013). The Greek New Testament: SBL Edition (Eph 4:17). Lexham Press; Society of Biblical Literature.
[145] Holmes, M. W. (2011–2013). *The Greek New Testament: SBL Edition* (Eph 4:18). Lexham Press; Society of Biblical Literature.
[146] Merkle B. L., 2016, 138-139.
[147] Arndt, 2000, 621, Cf. Merkle B. L., 2016, 137.

sense – they are conducting their lives by means of a certain moral empty mindedness. Implying why they are living this way, Paul remarks that they are in a state, a condition (Greek perfect), of their minds having been darkened, where the condition persists from the past into the present. The idea is stative, those who walk (conduct themselves) in *trespasses and sins* do so because of the moral state and condition of their minds.

For them to be darkened in their minds, obviously alludes to an inability to see or perceive what Paul is encouraging his readers to adopt, a new life of which the controlling principles are the holiness and righteousness from God.[148] They give no thought to God at all, or the redemption he offers. Paul uses synonyms for the mind here (νοός, διάνοια), where he is thinking of their habitual way of thinking, what their minds are focused on, what they go about doing or thinking about all day, how they see life and themselves, and where morality and redemption are not even in the frame at all.[149] Their condition is such that they are alienated from life of God, because they are ignorant in themselves of righteousness and redemption (διὰ τὴν ἄγνοιαν τὴν οὖσαν ἐν αὐτοῖς), and their ignorance is the result of having empty, darkened minds, which have no moral sensibility.[150]

Their empty-mindedness and darkened outlook is the result of a lack of a particular or specific understanding, or a comprehension of morality at a fundamental level, the level of their conscience, of their hearts.[151]

---

[148] Arndt, 2000, 932.
[149] Cf. Arndt, 2000, 234.
[150] Holmes, M. W. (2011–2013). *The Greek New Testament: SBL Edition* (Eph 4:18). Lexham Press; Society of Biblical Literature; cf. (Brooks, Ephesians Outline and Unfolded, 1984), 175-177.
[151] Cf. Stott J. R., 1979, 176-175. Note: Paul testifies that God awakened his moral awareness through the law, and he immediately realized the law could not produce what the law demands (Rom. 7).

The apparatus that controls their moral compass and will is faulty, and they are insensible to what is right and wrong, what is holy or sinful because their hearts are calloused, or turned to stone, implying mental "dullness", "obstinacy", "stubbornness", and "insensibility" (διὰ τὴν πώρωσιν τῆς καρδίας αὐτῶν).[152, 153] Gentiles, those who are still in *trespasses and sins*, having become calloused, now give themselves over to immorality and sin, in order to practice every unclean thing, with an increasing greed for more (οἵτινες ἀπηλγηκότες ἑαυτοὺς παρέδωκαν τῇ ἀσελγείᾳ εἰς ἐργασίαν ἀκαθαρσίας πάσης ἐν πλεονεξίᾳ) (cf. Rom. 1:24-25, 28-32).[154, 155] The moral condition of those who do not belong to Christ is getting worse, and there is a willfulness in it that comes from a decision to give *themselves* to sin with ever increasing abandonment (παρέδωκαν τῇ ἀσελγείᾳ).[156, 157]

As Paul contends in Romans, the human moral condition and alienation from God is not static. In general, it is getting worse, where wickedness and a desire to practice immorality is increasing more and more as the desire for it deepens; that is Paul's evaluation of the moral

---

[152] Holmes, M. W. (2011–2013). *The Greek New Testament: SBL Edition* (Eph 4:18). Lexham Press; Society of Biblical Literature.
[153] Arndt, 2000) 900; Robertson, 1933, Ephesians 4:18.
[154] Holmes, M. W. (2011–2013). *The Greek New Testament: SBL Edition* (Eph 4:19). Lexham Press; Society of Biblical Literature; The New English Bible (NT 1961, 2nd edition 1970; OT 1970).
[155] Robertson, 1933, Ephesians 4:19.
[156] Cf. Rom. 1:18-32. Paul uses the same term παρέδωκαν in Romans 1, where is it God who gives them over to their sinning and to the consequences as a result of their refusal to acknowledge him, even though knowledge of him is inherently available in creation (Rom. 1:18-23). Here Paul also lays the blame at the feet of those who give themselves over to sin, with a greed for more and more, having hardened their hearts to God (διὰ τὴν πώρωσιν τῆς καρδίας αὐτῶν) (Holmes, M. W. (2011–2013). The Greek New Testament: SBL Edition (Eph 4:18). Lexham Press; Society of Biblical Literature).
[157] Merkle B. L., 2016, 140.

condition of humanity (cf. Rom. 1:18-32).[158] There is movement in the wrong direction, and away from God into greater depths of sinfulness, and ultimately to judgement – "the wrath of God is being revealed..." – and it is against willful, deliberate, stubborn mindedness (Rom. 18-20).

There is an increasing descent into depravity, so that the moral condition of the race is becoming worse (cf. Gen. 6:5-9; Jer. 19:9-10; Rom. 1:24-32). Increasing moral turpitude is exacerbated by a pervasive moral insensibility in people whose minds have been emptied of a consciousness of moral purpose; they are mentally darkened to moral perception. Paul views the human race as moving in only one of two directions, either away from God and toward judgment, or toward him, to eternal life, and to righteousness that reflects God back into creation (Rom. 8:29-30; 2 Cor. 3:18; 5:17; Phil. 2:14-16). In any case, no one is morally static; if they are not moving on to godliness, they are growing worse.[159] Salvation does not, and cannot consist in attaining a static position of rightness with God, without growth and movement toward moral perfection and mature godliness that reflects the character of God in the image of God's Son (Rom. 8:29-30; Eph. 4:13-16).

Moral insensibility is a defect in human nature that Paul will contrast to the new life the Ephesians have in Christ, which has already been endowed with righteousness and holiness by God, so that they are moving away from the life they once lived when they *walked in trespasses and sins*.[160] At this Point, Paul is contrasting the moral

---

[158] How could we doubt this in the early part of 21st century America, and western culture.

[159] This is the *whole* point of Paul treatment of grace in Romans 6, in terms of their future conduct and development in light of the exercise of God grace, and what that implies.

[160] In Romans 1 Paul treats this topic at length in order to conclude that humanity is utterly lost and without God. To a great degree, moral

condition of those who live in the world without Christ, and the Ephesians who have been brought into union with Christ and into fellowship with God through redemption, and the difference it ought to make in the way they live and conduct themselves going forward (cf. Eph. 2:3-10).

Gentiles, in Paul's way of speaking here, are those, who, unlike his readers, are still walking in *trespasses and sins,* are living in habitual disobedience to God, and in compliance to the ruler of the kingdom of the air, who is at work in the disobedient (Eph. 2:1-2). Since his readers, and he himself, have been brought out from under that tyranny, through the redemptive power of God, and are sealed by the Spirit, they must set themselves on course to new life, with a new nature reflecting a righteousness that represents God (Eph. 2:1-10; 4:17-24). They are to adopt it, sign on to it, and reckon on it (to use Paul's language in Romans 6:11) by counting on or fully embracing the death of the old life, controlled by the flesh, and leaning totally into the newness life they have in Christ, as a result of spiritual and moral resurrection, the transformation that took place when they were justified by God's grace (Rom. 6:3-10, Eph. 4:22-24; cf. 2 Cor. 5:17). His readers are not to imitate the people around them, adopt their ways, or fall into their patterns of behavior or conduct, because they are incompatible with the new life of Christ in them, and the leading of the Spirit who dwells in them (Eph. 4:23-24, cf. Rom. 6:1-23; 1 Cor. 6:18-20).

Clearly, then Paul alludes to the pursuit of a new and different life, with different attitudes and conduct which reflect the character of God's holiness and righteousness for those in union with Christ (Eph. 4:24).

---

consciousness and awareness of God has been seared and those who willfully, continually sin, with a desire to do so more and more, have lost their moral sensibility, and no longer respond to their conscience. Cf. Stott J. R., 1979, 137; Blaikie, 1909,151; Wood, 1981, 62.

Movement from the old, rejected life of sin, by which the old self controlled by the flesh is laid aside in order to embrace the new life of Christ, brought to birth in them by the Spirit, and by which they have been made inwardly new, leads to new, right conduct and attitudes. As a result, they are now to be governed morally by the Spirit (Gal. 2:19-21; 5:16, 18, 24-25), so that there is a new controlling principle at work in them (Rom. 8:4). This is what Paul calls in Romans 7 the *law of the Spirit of life in Christ Jesus*, which replaces the *law of sin and death,* that previously held them captive to sin (Rom. 7:21-8:4). He will later speak of being changed in the attitudes of their minds, of what is effectively a reversal of their former moral insensitivity and hardened disregard for God and to his righteousness, to increasing appreciation of and maturity in godliness (Eph. 4:23-24). *The law of the Spirit of life in Christ Jesus* will move them in a new direction of obedience to God (walking in the Spirit, under his influence and direction), of the development of integrity of character in righteousness and holiness, of reflecting more and more the glory and character of God (2 Cor. 3:18).

A moral transformation has occurred that has at its core the goal of changing the outcome of their lives, of setting them on a different course toward righteousness, obedience, and fellowship with God. There is in this not only a moral development of those who are in union with Christ (Eph. 4:13), but a growing intimacy of relationship with God (Eph. 4:24). We will soon see that the final end-goal is even more significant, but for now we should notice that Paul has in mind a movement away from the former life, which they witness continually in the Gentile world about them, and toward a new life that reflects the holiness of God back into that world as a witness to him (cf. Phil. 2:14-16).[161] What is at stake here, is the forsaking of one way of life to embrace another, the going in

[161] What that looks like in practical terms is what Paul will turn to in the rest of the chapter until round chapter 6 and verse 9.

one direction to forego going in the opposite direction, an exchange of the lack of a moral consciousness for moral awareness through the enlightening of their minds by God, the rejection of a life of moral powerlessness for a life of holiness and righteousness through the power of God, and to be freed from alienation from God for intimacy and fellowship with him (Eph. 4:19-24, cf. Rom. 7:21-8:4; Gal. 2:19-21; 5:16-24).

IMPASSIONED APOSTOLIC PLEA

So, what induced Paul to make an impassion plea to his readers, at this stage in the argument or the rhetoric of his letter, to not live like the Gentiles (Eph. 4:17)? There is nothing in the letter, except possibly the focus on unity, that hints of a moral problem in Ephesus. Both the pathos and the way he frames the segue into the next part of his argument betray some sort of urgency or serious concern on his part regarding the saints of the Ephesian church or possibly, arguably, some sort of disturbance and disunity that requires addressing. We probably should not attempt to over develop the narrative behind Paul's remarks. We simply do not know what is at play in the church. We do know that he is transitioning to a more practical treatment of unity in the church with respect to various situations, circumstances, and relationships between believers in the context of their social roles or families (Eph. 4:25-6:9). Whether Paul is giving general exhortations and instructions is hard to say, but on balance, the emphasis on unity seems to indicate he has something particular in mind or is addressing something specific. It is possible that attitudes or some conduct in church, particularly as it relates to relationships and fellowship between believers concerns him, and do not represent the *righteousness and holiness of God,* to which they have been renewed through the one who re-created them in Christ (Eph. 4:24). That some behavior, attitude, conduct, or how they related to one another is more reminiscent of how Gentiles in the world conduct themselves is a possibility (Eph. 4:17, 23). Is there any external support for such a notion?

Problems in Ephesus: Arguably, four external sources help build a picture of the Ephesian church, and its situation. We will try to tackle them in a sort of chronological way. They are Acts of the Apostles, remarks about Paul's time in Ephesus found in Corinthians, instructions to Timothy, the temporary pastor at Ephesus, and John the Apostle's letter to the seven churches in Asia. Acts give us background to the planting of the Ephesians church on Paul's third missionary journey, even though that was not his first stop over in the city. Luke's account straddles the chronology, in that in 1 Corinthians Paul addresses his experience in Ephesus before returning to Jerusalem, when he writes the letter from Ephesus. After the letter, Paul will visit Corinth as part of a tour of the churches further north in Macedonia. He returned by going back north through Macedonia, and descending to Asia through Troas, on his way to Jerusalem (Acts 20). He bypassed Ephesus because he didn't want to be delayed there (Acts 20:16), but he arranged a meeting with the Ephesian elders and leaders at Miletus (Acts 20:17). There he addresses them, and rather pointedly speaks of the challenges they will face in the future, warning them they will never see his face again (Acts 20:25). The letter to the Ephesians was written when Paul was "in chains", that is he is already in Roman custody, expecting to appear before Caesar's court in Rome (Eph. 6:20).[162]

His opening plea, not without some sense of urgency or intensity, is for the Ephesians to "no longer" live as the Gentiles. Ben Merkel, quoting Andrew Lincoln, notes that the combination of "I say and witness in the Lord," has the effect of, "I solemnly declare" (λέγω καὶ μαρτύρομαι ἐν

[162] Merkle B. L., 2016, 4; Turner, 1994, 1222; Wood, 1981, 16; Eusebius., 1890, 134.

κυρίῳ).[163] He could be hinting at either a moral defection beginning to take place in the church or among the saints, or the danger of imminent moral defection. Had Paul detected signs of moral attrition in some believers in Ephesus? Or, is this a general exhortation to maintain moral uprightness against the pressure of the world around them? It is not uncharacteristic of Paul to warn his churches of such dangers in a general sense. The mention of "Gentiles" could be a reference to some who might be modeling their behavior more on the world around them and not on principles consistent with the new creation in them. Paul could be simply warning his converts not to be lured into returning to the lifestyles and attitudes which, after all, through union with Christ, they left behind. Is Paul being prescriptive, or proscriptive?

It is hardly deniable that the opening clause, rendered by the NIV, "So I tell you this, and insist on it in the Lord" arrives hot to the page without prior warning.[164] The inferential particle, translated by the NIV as "so" (οὖν), can be construed as a reference to what he has said up until this point, about unity in the church. Since he is about to give the grounds for unity in the church as the personal moral and spiritual uprightness of believers who comprise the community of faith in Ephesus, and since what is now broached is that they should *refrain from* conduct more consistent with Gentile lifestyles than those in union with Christ, one might conclude that some sort of a breakdown has occurred, arguably moral, that is threatening the unity of the church. If Paul's exhortation is more casual, as it might be argued, it certainly does not appear to be so at first blush, with Paul's "I tell you this, and *insist* on it in the Lord." The NIV seeks to convey Paul's strong prohibition

---

[163] Holmes, M. W. (2011–2013). *The Greek New Testament: SBL Edition* (Eph 4:17). Lexham Press; Society of Biblical Literature; Arndt, 2000, 619; Merkle B. L., 2016, 137; Wood, 1981, 61; Stott J. R., 1979, 174; Turner, 1994, 1239; Wuest, 1997, 106.

[164] *The New International Version* (Eph 4:17). (2011). Zondervan.

against imitating the world around them, and it consists of a strong insistence that they are "to no longer walk [conduct themselves] as Gentiles" (μηκέτι ὑμᾶς περιπατεῖν καθὼς καὶ τὰ ἔθνη περιπατεῖ).[165] So, the strong language of *telling them* and *bearing witness to this in the Lord,* amounts to the giving of a serious instruction, prohibition, or warning, maybe something of all three, to the church in the presence of God, and can hardly be considered innocuous or a pedestrian exhortation. Something in Paul's mind, something he knows, seems to have elicited an unexpectedly strong insistence to the Ephesians that they no longer act like worldly people.

Another striking feature is Paul's use of the adverb *no longer* (μηκέτι). Although not necessarily so, it could imply Paul is censuring something that is taking place in the church or among the believers in Ephesus, that is starting to occur or is in imminent danger of breaking out in the church. A warning that they should no longer behave like the world around them, surely indicates that the apostle fears attrition. Whether or not it has begun, or his warning in remedial, we cannot tell. For that we need information from outside of the epistle itself, and even then, our conclusions will be conjectural. Nonetheless, this much seems clear, Paul is encouraging the Ephesians to recommit themselves to a life of holiness and righteousness that represents God and is consistent with the moral and spiritual changes that have occurred in them as a result of salvation (justification and regeneration) (Eph. 4:22-24). The way he frames this, along with the urgency of his appeal, seems strongly to suggest he is seeking to head something off, even if he is not issuing a warning for some to return to right attitudes and conduct. The context of his exhortation appears to be Paul's concern for unity in the church. His strong urgency, coupled with the

---

[165] Holmes, M. W. (2011–2013). *The Greek New Testament: SBL Edition* (Eph 4:17). Lexham Press; Society of Biblical Literature.

similarly weighty earlier language, "...make every effort to maintain the unity of the Spirit through the bonds of peace" (instrumental dative with the preposition ἐν), leans toward some sort of corrective or appeal for a change in conduct, or warning of some danger of attrition which might affect unity in the church, as well as its thriving (ἐν τῷ συνδέσμῳ τῆς εἰρήνης). [166] Is there external evidence for these conclusions or speculations?

From Acts, we know that Paul faced some of his most perilous struggles and fiercest opposition from the tradesmen in the town (Acts 19). We also know that Ephesus was one of Paul's longest stopovers, and that he developed some of the closest relationships of his ministry among the Ephesians, particularly the elders and leaders of the church (Acts 20:17-21:1). He speaks of his experiences in Ephesus to the Corinthians, in a sort of offhanded way, to illustrate what he endured as an apostle, and underscoring he would be foolish to go through this if all his efforts were in vain (1 Cor. 15:32). He calls his adversaries *wild beasts,* wild animals (ἐθηριομάχησα), where Paul is using a metaphor based on the arena, underscoring the struggle he was having against people who opposed him (Acts 20:19).[167] Whether Paul is speaking exclusively of those who outside the church who opposed him, like Demetrius or the Jews, or alludes to confrontations in the church, it is hard to tell, but on balance from context he seems to be speaking of external pressures (1 Cor. 15:29-32). Nevertheless, Paul's Ephesian mission was tumultuous, fraught with what Luke calls *obstinate Jews* in the synagogue who *refused* to believe and maligned to the gospel message, believers, and the church (Acts 19:9). Paul set up shop in the lecture hall of Tyrannus for the rest of his time there. Despite success with the gospel, and extraordinary miracles, when a collection of books

---

[166] Holmes, M. W. (2011–2013). *The Greek New Testament: SBL Edition* (Eph 4:3). Lexham Press; Society of Biblical Literature.
[167] Arndt, 2000, 455.

was burned valued at $7,808,000 (by today's standards in the US), the town erupted into riot at the instigation of the tradesmen, and Paul's life was threatened (Acts 19:18-41). To say that Paul's presence and ministry in Ephesus was divisive is to understate the case. While Ephesus was one of Paul's greatest successes, it became one of the most challenging of his ministry and life. People either hated Paul, or as is the case of the Ephesian church leaders, they love him dearly. The point is Paul's time in Ephesus was tumultuous, difficult, emotional, contentious, and mentally exhausting. The church at Ephesus was founded in an environment of theological contentiousness with the Jews, and social and even religious war with the Gentiles in that part of Asia.

It is little wonder, then, that Paul, intending to make a timely visit to Jerusalem for Pentecost, chooses not to stop over in Ephesus (Acts 20:16). However, not wanting to miss the opportunity to say a proper goodbye, and issue a commission to his dear friends and leaders in the Ephesian church, he summonsed them to Miletus. His commission to the leaders takes the form of a polemic (defense) of his ministry among them (Acts 20:18-27), and some rather shocking or surprisingly intense warnings of what will come to the church after his departure, and as time goes on (Acts 20:29-31). He calls for the Ephesians leaders to watch over the flock, to guard them against heresy, false teaching, and exploitation by false teachers and leaders (Acts 20:29-31). He warns them that *savage wolves* will come in on the flock (λύκοι βαρεῖς), meaning unscrupulous leaders whose goal is to secure a following and exploit the church and its people for their own ends, without any concern for their welfare (Acts 20:29). While we might not realize it, this warning from Paul impinges directly on concerns he expresses in Ephesians 4:11-16 for the church, its unity, thriving, and growth through morally upright conduct expressing support and concern for one another (Eph.4:16). These leaders whom Paul is addressing, appointed by God, should have as their supreme goal and motivation the thriving and growth of the church (Eph. 4:11-12, 16). Nevertheless, prophetically, Paul warns the Ephesians, "I know that savage wolves are going come in the church after I have departed." With striking certainty, which leaves no room for ambiguity of meaning, Paul states the impending danger (ἐγὼ οἶδα ὅτι εἰσελεύσονται μετὰ τὴν ἄφιξίν).[168]

His emphatic use of the first-person pronoun only adds to the weight of his warning, "I *know...*" (ἐγὼ οἶδα). The church is in for a rough ride in the near future and is in danger of being exploited by unscrupulous leaders who will come in from outside, ingratiate themselves with the congregation, and do them harm. Even more shocking is Paul's prediction that people already in the church, arising to positions of leadership and influence, will distort the truth to secure a following for themselves (ὀπίσω ἑαυτῶν), while at the same time betraying sound doctrine to do so (Acts 20:30). In both instances, whether from outside or from within, these leaders are going to exploit the believers in the Ephesian church, possibly in competition to one another, threatening a serious disruption of church life. The result will be division, the disintegration of fellowship, disenfranchisement of some, and fragmentation of the church to gather around leaders who are seeking the following. It is the very definition of disunity and dysfunction in the body of Christ, and is diametrically opposite to God's design of functional unity, mutual concern, and the thriving of the body as a whole through mutual support, fellowship, and caring (Eph. 4:16). What will be at play, under those circumstances, will be the selfishness and the self-will of those who do not live as Paul has suggests here in Ephesians 4, laying aside the old life and embracing the new life of righteousness and holiness that reflects the character and nature of God (Eph. 4:22-24).

---

[168] Holmes, M. W. (2011–2013). *The Greek New Testament: SBL Edition* (Ac 20:29). Lexham Press; Society of Biblical Literature.

These false leaders will be living for themselves and promoting their own agendas, for their own benefit, and not that of the church or the saints.

If we are wondering how that turned out, we can go to 1 and 2 Timothy, where Paul gives instructions to the temporary or interim pastor, Timothy, concerning the church. A picture emerges of a church that has problems, not least among them is contentious quarreling and debate over doctrine and genealogies (1 Tim. 1:3-4). Timothy was sent to Ephesus by Paul to get a handle on what seems to be an increasingly deteriorating situation in Ephesus, just as he had predicted. Many of the things Paul said in 1 Timothy, particularly about women teaching or occupying leadership roles, have been the source of great debate and much anxiety.[169] Nevertheless, Paul addresses a particular set of circumstances in Ephesus which were not wholly unanticipated by him, but which, if left unaddressed, will result in the loss of the church altogether (1 Tim. 2:11-15). A perilous level of disunity exits in the church, in which some of the women appear to be playing a key role in the disruption, eliciting Paul's strong response.[170] Ephesus is one of the churches that ranks high on Paul's list of important successes, along with Galatia, Thessalonica, Philippi, and Corinth. Since he spent the greatest amount of continuous time in Ephesus to establish the work there, he is not content to see it fall apart.

---

[169] It might be interesting to consider the role of Artemis worship in Ephesus, to create a prominent societal presence of influential women, who now in the church are, for reasons Paul only hints at, are causing problems through argumentative speculation or teaching. The evidence is probably too light to draw a solid connection, but the possibility is intriguing.

[170] Cf. Witherington, The Problem with Evangelical Theology: Testing the Exegetical Foundatiuons of Calvinism, Dispensationalism, Welseyanism, and Pentecostalism, 2016,95-105; Keener, Paul, Women & Wives: Marriage and Women's Ministry in the Letters of Paul, 2004, 101-132.

So, what were the problems in Ephesus, exactly? From the instructions given to Timothy, we can build a picture of the issues in the church faced by the young pastor. Rather like listening to one end of a phone conversation, it behooves us to be circumspect with our speculation. Still, some things are quite clear from Paul's warnings and instructions to his *son in the faith*. Right out of the gate, in his first epistle to Timothy, in chapter one and the third verse, Paul reminds Timothy that when he went on to Macedonia, he left him in Ephesus to "*command certain people* not to teach false doctrines *any longer* or to devote themselves to myths and endless genealogies."[171] The problem appears on the surface to be *certain people*, who have arisen to a place of influence and arguably put themselves forward as leaders (seeking a following, perhaps), and they are teaching questionable doctrine, along with what Paul flatly calls myths, and endless genealogies. Later Paul calls these myths *godless*, and *old wives tales*, which oppose the good teaching that Timothy has been following from Paul (1 Tim. 4:6-7). BDAG notes that *myth* refers to speech, conversation, narrative and story, "without distinction of fact or fiction" and that stands opposed to "λόγος, the truth of history."[172] For Paul, who grounds his gospel in the historical reliability of the Old Testament and the authenticity of the incarnation of Jesus, including his ancestry, as well as his death and resurrection, this is a serious threat to the church (cf. Rom. 1:1-4; 1 Cor. 15-1-58). Later, in his second epistle, Paul warned Timothy of the proclivity of people to turn aside to myths in the last days (2 Tim. 4:4), and he warned Titus, on a similar assignment to Timothy, to rebuke indolent saints, so that they will not be tempted to be drawn away by Jewish myths and human commands (Tit. 1:12-14). It seems that what

---

[171] The New International Version (1 Ti 1:3–4). (2011). Zondervan.
[172] Arndt, 2000, 660.

Paul predicted to the leaders in Miletus had become a strong tendency in the Ephesian church.

It seems clear that sound doctrine is under threat, and *certain people* have arisen to places of influence in the church, possibly the *savage wolves* of his earlier prophetic warning or leaders arising among them seeking a following, who are introducing false doctrine, and making use of myths and genealogies to the detriment of the church (1 Tim. 1:3-4). Certainly, from the *no longer* that the false teaching, and contention over genealogies were already under way at the time of Paul's writing the first epistle to Timothy, and were poisoning the Ephesian church, creating disunity. Paul goes on to speak of *promoting controversial speculations,* which clearly implies that the false teachers were causing division and disunity in the church by promoting quarreling over debatable matters, something he confirms toward the end of the letter (1 Tim. 6:2c-5). There are quarrels, controversies, and constant (perpetual or unending) friction between people in the church (1 Tim. 6:4). The result is envy, strife, malicious talk, evil suspicions, and constant friction (1 Tim 6:4). Ephesus is a church that is disintegrating, just as Paul had warned the leaders in Miletus it would soon be under threat of doing so. What Paul speaks of is continual argumentativeness in the church as a result of these false teachings, myths, and speculative genealogies (διαπαρατριβαὶ). The effect was to bring the church to brink of ruin because of the depraved minds of men who have stolen away the truth and supposing godliness to be the means of profiting themselves (διεφθαρμένων ἀνθρώπων τὸν νοῦν καὶ ἀπεστερημένων τῆς ἀληθείας, νομιζόντων πορισμὸν εἶναι τὴν εὐσέβειαν).[173] This is why Paul sent Timothy to Ephesus, to get on top of this mess.

---

[173] Holmes, M. W. (2011–2013). The Greek New Testament: SBL Edition (1 Ti 6:5). Lexham Press; Society of Biblical Literature.

These statements to Timothy, that some have rejected the truth (1 Tim. 1:19-20), as well as warnings about uneducated women assuming teaching and leadership roles (1Tim. 2:9-15; 3:11) (which may have been the source of some of the error or argumentativeness), indicates that the church was in trouble. Paul's council, that women should be worthy of respect, temperate, and not malicious talkers, paints a picture of good deal of unrest. Some were advocating legalism with respect to food, or forbidding marriage in favor of holy celibacy, no doubt (1 Tim. 4:1-5). In 2 Timothy, Paul even hints at one of the elements of false doctrine plaguing the church, that certain people were teaching that the resurrection had already taken place, something that was spreading like gangrene in the church, and was destroying the faith of some (2 Tim. 4:18). He calls these false teachers, those whose consciences have been seared with a hot iron, hypocritical liars, deceiving spirits, and taught by demons (1 Tim 4:1-2). When such things occur, Paul observes, it is an indication we live in the latter times or days, near to the coming of the Lord (1 Tim. 4:1).

In case we are inclined to play down the severity of Paul's characterization of these false teachers and their followers, he says they have abandoned the faith, are followers of deceiving spirits, and their teachings are doctrines of demons (1 Tim. 4:2). This can hardly be considered a pedestrian or passing church disagreement. Rather it is a serious breakdown of fellowship and unity, and signals defection, and disruption. Timothy had landed in a hot bed of controversy, in a church with a serious failure of fellowship fueled by greed and posturing leaders seeking to promote themselves, along with their own interests. The apostle encouraged Timothy to no longer be timid (2 Tim. 1:7). He should not let the older leaders run over him because he is young (1 Tim. 4:12), but in his dealings with the people of the church, unlike the troublemakers, he must treat each one with respect and gentleness (1 Tim. 5:1-2; 2 Tim. 2:25-26), yet firmly, and with pastoral authority. He must correct and rebuke where it is necessary (1 Tm, 5:17; 6:3-5; 2 Tim.

2:14; 4:2-5). He is to never to tire of reminding the Ephesian believers about the truth and warning them solemnly before God not to quarrel (2 Tim. 4:16). Paul predicted something like this in Miletus, and his epistle to the Ephesians, with its emphasis on unity, certainly seems to be aimed at the historical situation in the church, as far as we may discern it from these indicators in his letters to Timothy.

Nor should we miss how Paul describes the principal characters in this drama, who are responsible for the disintegration of the church. They are hypocritical liars, profiteers, legalists, argumentative, self-promoting, and constantly creating friction between fellow believers in the church! They are men and women of flawed character, acting in the flesh and not under the leadership of the Spirit, promoting their own authority and fighting with one another over trivialities (cf. Eph. 4:17-24). Their conduct does not represent the righteousness and holiness of God, and their attitudes and the way they behave is more like the Gentiles in the world around them, than like God who has saved and transformed them (cf. Eph. 4:17-24). The cause of the breakdown in unity is attributable to the moral failure of those who are responsible for promoting false doctrine and strife in the fellowship, as well as between believers, for their own gain and securing a following. The church is not thriving. It is not building itself up in love (ποιεῖται εἰς οἰκοδομὴν ἑαυτοῦ ἐν ἀγάπῃ).[174] The opposite is taking place; it is tearing itself apart.

Approximately thirty years or so later, John, writing to the church at Ephesus, commends them for doing well, for working hard, and for their perseverance (Rev. 2:2a). It seems, maybe, that the church had done battle with false prophets, and wicked people, by testing those who claimed to be apostles but are not, but are false (Rev. 2:2b). They hated the works of the Nicolaitans, an apostate group of which we cannot

---

[174] Holmes, M. W. (2011–2013). *The Greek New Testament: SBL Edition* (Eph 4:16). Lexham Press; Society of Biblical Literature.

speak with precision now, but may have had connections to the false teachers that infiltrated the church, or from the leaders seeking to develop groups of followers, about which Paul had warned them (Rev. 2:6). There is a remarkable synchronicity in John's letter when compared to Paul's warning in Acts 20, and his impassioned instructions to Timothy. Maybe the church had gone to war against the false teachers and leaders seeking to raise up followers by dividing church loyalties and creating allegiances. The church had excelled again in enduring hardships, not growing weary in their service to God (Rev. 2:3). However, something was wrong, and John puts his finger on it, their devotion to God, their passion or enthusiasm, their first-love fervor had dissipated, and they had settled into a more tepid fellowship with God (Rev. 2:4). John spent his final years in Ephesus, according to Irenaeus.[175] Toward the end of his life, John the elder, as he called himself, unable to preach, constantly reminded the Ephesian believers to love one another, a similar call to unity found in Paul's epistle 30 years prior.[176] Revelation provides corroborating evidence for our conclusions about the situation in the Ephesian church that Paul addresses.

If we are right about this, whatever disunity or disruption the church at Ephesus suffered, it was largely the result of *ravenous wolves* disguised as sheep, motivated by greed for gain and by a perverse misuse of "godliness", or by *false teachers* arising from within the church, rejecting truth and adopting novel doctrines or teachings in an effort to secure to themselves followers (cf. Acts 20; 1 Timothy).[177]

---

[175] Harrison, 1975, *The Apostle John*.

[176] Tasker, 1996, 593.

[177] Ignatius' letter to the Ephesians, if authentic, in chapters 7 and 9 hints at some of the same problems still existing in the church some 10 years after John, and as addressed by Paul to Timothy, (The Epistle of Ignatius to the

Quarrelling and dissention in the church was obviously growing or had taken a firm hold among the congregations that made up the Ephesian church, or so it seems from Paul's description. Disunity and fractured relationships threatening to break up the church, rather than building it up and edifying believers, had developed, brought into question the church's progress, at least in Paul's mind, and maybe even its continued existence. So, Paul left Timothy there to provide some continuity to his ministry, and he left for Macedonia, because his continued presence in Ephesus had become too polarizing for the town.

This would not have been the first time Paul had feared for his labor, that it had been in vain and was under threat from defection to less scrupulous leaders, claiming to be (super) apostles. He feared for the Corinthians, the Galatians, the Thessalonians, and expressed a prophetic concern for the Ephesians that there might be catastrophic attrition, even defection in the near future (cf. Acts 20:25-31; 2 Cor. 11:1-11; Gal. 1:6-9; 3:4; 4:17-20; 5:7-8, 9-12; 1 Thess. 3:5). It may not be too much to say that when Paul expresses to the Corinthians that among his burdens in ministry, he has continual concern for the churches (2 Cor. 11:28), he means these kinds of things were always on his mind. Indeed, the roles of Timothy, Titus, and Silas seems to have been visiting the churches established by Paul to bring back reports of their progress, and to give the apostle some peace of mind over them and their progress (1 Cor. 4:17; 16:10; 2 Co. 1:19; 2:13; 7:6, 13; Phil. 2:19; 1 Thess. 3:2, 6; 1 Tim. 1:3-7; Titus 1:5).

Paul's Proposal for Threats to Unity in Ephesus: The root issues facing the church and believers in Ephesus arguably appear to be

---

Ephesians, 1885), 52-53. Cf. Beacham, A. D. (January 2025) *Ephesians: The Victory of Prayer for the Church*. In Bishop's Blog - https://iphc.org/gso/2025/01/07/ephesians-the-victory-of-prayer-for-the-church/.

selfishness among leaders, self-focused ambition, carnality (greed), and strong assertive personalities undermining sound doctrine, all of which are disrupting healthy fellowship between believers, or at the least are threatening unity in the church. That these things are antithetical to the gospel and its values, as well as to sound doctrine and are a threat to unity in the church, is obvious. But Paul will make an even more fundamental point. They are contrary to the renewed life of Christ for those who have been brought into union with him, into whom God has sown the seed of genuine holiness and righteousness, at first through regenerative justification, but also through the ongoing power of the indwelling Spirit, something he argues at length in Galatians and Romans (Eph. 4:22-24m cf. Rom. 6:1-16; 8:1-17; Gal. 2:19-21; 5:13-25). What is going on in the Ephesian church, if 1 Timothy is an indication, represents more of the values, character, and conduct one might find among Gentiles in secular, Roman society. Instead of providing a witness to the people around them of the righteousness and holiness of God, disunity in the church, infighting, disputes over doctrine, quarreling, and endless friction, resulting in factionalism, and disintegration of relationships are sending the opposite message. They are to reflect the holiness and righteousness of God, Paul argues, to be representations of him and his character to unbelievers (Eph. 4:17-24, cf. Phil. 2:14-16). But right now, they are not doing so. They are behaving like Gentiles, by which Paul means secular, unbelieving members of Roman society, and this type of thing, Paul argues elsewhere, damages the witness of the church and the gospel. In our context, however, Paul seems to be focused on the internal fracturing of the church, the breakdown of precious fellowship between believers, maybe more than their external witness per se.

Now, of course this is arguable, and depends upon the conclusions one draws from the internal evidence for Paul's overarching theme for his letter, and whether or not he is the author, or whether the letter was in fact originally written to the Ephesians. The evidence we have cited above, and the earlier discussion of the context of this epistle, along with seeking to establish the recipients and author, all seem to strongly point in the direction of Pauline authorship, and that the Ephesians were at least its intended, original recipients, even if it was circulated widely among other churches after that. In any event, even if some are not convinced by our historical analysis, the internal contextual analysis greatly supports church unity as an overarching theme. Paul began with God's purpose of unifying all things in Christ and under his rule and went on to show believers are in union with Christ, thereby initiating the eschaton in the present. For example, they are sealed in their present redemption by the Spirit, who guarantees their final and complete delivery into God's possession in the future (Eph. 1:13-23). A unified church ought to reflect such union with Christ, through unity with one another, and by edifying and encouraging relationships. What that looks like in the context of specific societal conventions, institutions, and circumstances, Paul will take up from Ephesians 4:25 on, almost through the end of the letter. So, in order for the character of God to be seen in the world beyond the church, the saints must behave differently within the church, and among themselves, and reflect his holiness and righteousness at first in their dealings with one another through unselfishness and upright character and conduct. The nexus in which they behave rightly to one another, and in which they have an obligation to reflect the righteousness of God in their conduct and character, is the internal workings and interconnectedness of the saints in fellowship with one another in the church, so that it might support itself, and build itself up in love. A proposition like this is bound to affect their external witness to the Gentile world around them. Verse 17, then, opens with the premise that the internal relationships of the saints *in the church*, and their moral and spiritual characters, should be markedly different from how Gentiles behave and interact with one another *in their spheres of life and commerce* in the world outside of the church (cf. Eph. 2:1-3).

Paul sets up an antithesis here, whereby he contrasts the character of the Gentile world against what ought to be the character of the saints, in whom God has implanted a new life. Gentiles are estranged from God, because their minds have been darkened to him and to the concept of the kind of moral uprightness that is represented by the holiness of God (ἐσκοτωμένοι τῇ διανοίᾳ ὄντες, ἀπηλλοτριωμένοι).[178] They have no perception of God or of his righteousness. It is hidden from them, because the *god of this world has blinded them to it* (2 Cor. 4:3). But the saints ought not to behave toward one another in a way that is more reflective of how Gentiles behave, whose minds are shrouded in darkness where God is concerned.

Paul's comparison of their behavior to Gentiles would, no doubt, have been shocking to the Ephesian, whom Paul loved dearly and who dearly loved him. It was a sharp rebuke, arriving somewhat unexpectedly on the page without any softening cushion. He is implying that currently the Ephesians conduct may be reflecting something that looks more like unsaved Gentile behavior, than that of people whom God has renewed through union with Christ. The "no longer" is a dead giveaway that the situation is not merely theoretical or hypothetical, but that actual problems exist in the Ephesian church as a result of bad conduct producing disunity. And when we read 1 Timothy, we can believe it!

It is, then, scarcely arguable that when Paul speaks of *reflecting the righteousness and holiness of God,* he has in mind that the saints in Ephesus ought to be displaying godly character, first of all, to *one another in pursuit of edifying and supportive unity in the church*, and encouraging them to provide a good external witness to the world, as

---

[178] Holmes, M. W. (2011–2013). *The Greek New Testament: SBL Edition* (Eph 4:18). Lexham Press; Society of Biblical Literature.

important as it is to Paul, is secondary.[179] The context seems to use *Gentiles* as a foil for their current conduct, a pejorative example, designed to bring them around to a modification of their current conduct for the sake of the unity of the church (Eph. 4:16-17).[180] The extended and more focused treatment of unity from later in chapter 2 through chapter 4 and verse 24, strongly leans in the direction of an internal focus, on developing and maintaining good relationships between the saints that build up the church, and that ensure that every believer is supplied with what they need to thrive as a member of the body (Eph. 4:3, 13-16).

So, what exactly is Paul proposing, and what does he insinuate about the current state of affairs? We have already shown that Paul alludes that members of the Ephesian church are behaving badly, and we have proposed that there is external evidence that the disruption he predicted in Miletus was indeed at work in the church. The church is struggling to maintain unity or harmony of relationships at the very least, or else much of what Paul says is of the nature of a general exhortation to unity. However, the abrupt reprimand in verse 17 appears as a serious challenge to those who, in the context of Paul's pleas for *making every effort to maintain unity* (Eph. 4:3-5), are acting badly, more like the world around them than like people in whom the character of God has been sown through regenerative union with Christ (Eph. 4:17-21). Paul proposes that they make a conscious decision to abandon the old life, and fully adopt the new life implanted in them by God (καὶ ἐνδύσασθαι

[179] Cf. Brooks, Ephesians Outline and Unfolded, 1984, 172.

[180] No longer (μηκέτι), Ephesians 4:1, 17! Cf. Wood, 1981, 61; Brooks, Ephesians Outline and Unfolded, 1984, 172-173; Bruce, 1961, 90-91; Westcott, 1906, 65.

τὸν καινὸν ἄνθρωπον τὸν κατὰ θεὸν κτισθέντα ἐν δικαιοσύνῃ καὶ ὁσιότητι τῆς ἀληθείας).[181]

That Paul is speaking to those who claim to be and are in fact believers is axiomatic. He calls them saints and faithful at the beginning of the letter (τοῖς ἁγίοις τοῖς οὖσιν [ἐν Ἐφέσῳ] καὶ πιστοῖς ἐν Χριστῷ Ἰησοῦ).[182] Paul is not reprimanding them for total attribution, but rather, like John thirty years later, he is calling them to return to a time when their devotion to God was better, and their surrender to the Spirit produced better results, in terms of unity and fellowship among the saints (Eph. 4:3). The "no longer" (μηκέτι) arguably points to a time when they did better than they are right now. The apostle's call is to return to the devotion and attitude they once held to, when they had decisively laid aside the old life in favor of adopting the new life through union with Christ (Eph. 4:23-24). The apostle is making an appeal for them to renew themselves to the implications of that regenerative experience of justification, and to the time when they came to Christ and were morally and spiritually changed by God. At that time, they forsook the old life for a new life of holiness and righteousness that reflected, in their conduct and relationships with one another, the inner change that had taken place, and which reflected God, his character and nature (cf. 2 Cor. 5:17). He calls them back to a better time, to a *fresh recognition* of the new life of Christ that ought to be at work in them, for producing the fruit of holiness and righteousness that God is looking for in his people.[183] This new life is to be expressed in there conduct toward one another in the church, so that the church, the community of believers and worshippers, is a place where each part does it work, and everyone is

---

[181] Holmes, M. W. (2011–2013). *The Greek New Testament: SBL Edition* (Eph 4:24). Lexham Press; Society of Biblical Literature.
[182] Holmes, M. W. (2011–2013). *The Greek New Testament: SBL Edition* (Eph 1:1). Lexham Press; Society of Biblical Literature.
[183] Cf. Stott J. R., 1979, 175.

supplied with the resources they need to love and serve God, so that the church builds itself up in love (Eph. 4:16).[184]

The nature of Paul's proposal, how it reflects a consistent Pauline theology of moral and spiritual renewal/development involving the Holy Spirit's initial and his ongoing working in them, we will explore in the next chapter. So, we will conclude this section with two observations that are critical. First, Paul is calling saints and faithful believers to *renewal and a fresh commitment* to the new life imparted to them at the time of their original, regenerative union with Christ at justification, and to faith in Christ for salvation (cf. Rom. 6:1-16; Eph. 2:5-9). He is encouraging them to more fully take up something that had already occurred and taken place in them, but which they need to reaffirm by a fresh application of faith, and by a reengagement of attention and assent of the will – principally through some definite change of mind and attitude under these present circumstances (cf. Rom. 12:1-2). This is something of a call for a definite reckoning on the death of the old life, and on resurrection to new life, as he puts in in Romans 6, even if he uses different terms here to the Ephesians (Eph. 4:23-24, cf. Rom. 6:1-11).

No matter how we approach this text, we cannot deny that Paul is calling *believers*, whom he calls *saints* and *faithful*, to apply *fresh faith* (reckoning), and to adopt and appropriate a renewed attitude of surrender and acceptance to the implications of the moral and spiritual changes which initially occurred at regenerative union with Christ. He does much the same thing in his discussion of the conduct of believers after transformative justification in Romans 6, where what is at stake in a proper view of God's grace and of sin (cf. Rom. 6:1-11, 12-16).[185] Two

---

[184] Cf. Brooks, Ephesians Outline and Unfolded, 1984, 172.

[185] It is Paul's repeated call for believers to go on to renew their commitment to new life in Christ, through a death and resurrection, or the putting off of the old

things ought to stand out. Paul is not pedantically exhorting his reader to a general moral renewal, but to a categoric application of the death of the old life and of resurrection to new life, which is imparted at salvation, and under these current circumstances where their current conduct is affecting unity in the church. They are to reaffirm or rededicate themselves to the principle of pursuing holiness and righteousness of character leading to right conduct which reflects the character of God. Secondly, the urgency of his opening remark is found in a context calling them to more rigorously engage unity in the church. This underscores that his proposal is somewhat remedial, a corrective which he expects his readers to engage to remedy what is currently going wrong and affecting unity in the body of believers, rendering the church less effective in its purpose of building itself up in love (Eph. 4:16). There is a definiteness, an urgency that requires a decision, a surrender of the mind, an acceptance of new attitudes toward one another, a change to their current conduct through decisive surrender to God. Paul is calling for them to apply and fully embrace, through a decision of the will, what has previously been done in them through the saving work of the Spirit at justification.[186]

What Paul proposes then, in the current crisis, is a reapplication of faith to appropriate and better engage the new life of Christ in them, the life of union with Christ that had its origin in the transforming power of the Spirit at justification, but in a new context of reestablishing the

---

and the taking up of new life, combined with Wesly's personal experience of struggling with assurance of salvation, and sensing his lack of power to go on to holiness without the aid of something from God, that led him to a theology of a *second blessing*, of subsequent spiritual renewal, and of definite, post-conversion commitment to God that leads to a successful pursuit of holiness.

[186] Note: Paul exhorts them to change their conduct and attitudes by reminding them of what has already taken place, and that they have been remade in the image of God (Eph. 4:22-24).

character and conduct of the saints to safeguard unity in the church, and to preserve its function.[187] We can then, tentatively reach back to verse 3, and say that by "make every effort to maintain the unity of the Spirit..." Paul is calling on them to engage a fresh application of faith that lays aside the old life of selfishness, greed, self-will, to more fully embrace the new life of Christ implanted in them, which consists of righteousness and holiness that reflects the character of God (Eph. 4:22-24). The nature of the *effort* is the application of faith to the proposition that the old life that reflects Gentile conduct has been crucified with Christ, and that they have been raised with new life in Christ to conduct that reflects the holiness of God.

Paul's treatment of saints revisiting their original experience of moral and spiritual transformation at justification in Ephesians is essentially the same as his treatment of the same principle in Romans 6. The one has as its focus a restoration of unity in the church, the other a critical avoidance of a misunderstanding of the limitless grace of God (Rom. 6:1-2, 15). In Romans 12:1-2, Paul engages the same idea, that the saints ought to present themselves to God fully and wholly, as a living sacrifice, in order to do the will of God and be effective in serving others in the church. In Colossians he tells his readers, whom he calls faithful brothers and sisters in Christ, that they have been circumcised in Christ, that is the life of the flesh has been cut away by God, that they have been buried with Christ in order to be raised to new life in him (Col. 2:11-12), and that they are to engage a fresh application of the power of God that saved them to resist the impulse to go back to the rules and conduct of the old life (Col. 2:20-23). Rather, they are to apply the power of a transformed life by setting their hearts on things above and not on things that belong to the earthly realms (of their former life), because they have died to those things, and been raised to a new life hidden with

---

[187] Cf. Brooks, Ephesians Outline and Unfolded, 1984, 148-150, 166-171.

Christ in God (Col. 3:1-4). Again and again, in various ways, Paul asserts that believers take a decisive step to engage the new life given them in Christ at initial salvation, and to consciously (by reckoning) apply what has been done in them through union with Christ, at the time of their justification, to make certain the old life is decisively defeated, and the new life fully engaged, under the guidance of the indwelling Spirit, so that he might produce the fruit of righteousness in them.[188] This then in Paul's proposal, that the Ephesians address the break down in unity in the church by abandoning the old life, represented by the way Gentiles live, and to reaffirm their commitment and apprehension of the new life they have in Christ, and apply it to their conduct toward one another, so that they reflect the holiness and righteousness of God (Eph. 4:23).

IMPLEMENTING HOLINESS

They did not learn to live that way from being in Christ, Paul says (Eph. 4:20). Paul contrasts what arises, in terms of conduct (cf. Eph. 4:19), from the darkened and insensitive minds of Gentiles, with conduct that ought to arise from the enlighten minds of believers who have been raised to new life in Christ (Eph. 4:21-24).[189] The NIV seeks to

---

[188] This is the essence of Welsey's theology of the second blessing. For reasons that can be found in his personal experience, and how he viewed the problems of assurance of salvation and going on to holiness as two related but different aspects of salvation, John Wesley took up Paul's insistence that we "go on to" through a decisive surrender to God, subsequent to initial salvation, for growth in godliness to develop a theology sanctification more particularly and specifically. Despite developments in the later holiness movement that created a deep division between salvation and sanctification, which Wesley did not teach or intend, it can be demonstrated that Welsey viewed salvation and sanctification, though distinct, as wholly and integrally linked to the saving work of Christ, and existentially contiguous in the life of the believer, and are not separable.

[189] Merkle B. L., 2016, 139.

render into softer English what appears a little terse in Greek, "You have not thus learned Christ" (ὑμεῖς δὲ οὐχ οὕτως ἐμάθετε τὸν Χριστόν).[190] Paul's observation forms the apodosis (the *then* clause), rendered first, of a conditional sentence. The protasis consists of "If indeed, you listened (heard)[191] and were taught in him consistent with the truth that is in Jesus" (εἴ γε αὐτὸν ἠκούσατε καὶ ἐν αὐτῷ ἐδιδάχθητε, καθώς ἐστιν ἀλήθεια ἐν τῷ Ἰησοῦ).[192] Although when rendered more woodenly in English it seems awkward, the basic idea is clear, that Paul is suggesting that his readers should know better if they were in fact listening like they should, and were as a result instructed in the truth that is in Christ. That Paul is offering a correction and even a reprimand is further supported by the emphatic position and use of *you* (ὑμεῖς), which has been fronted in the apodosis, that itself has been brought forward ahead of the protasis for emphasis.

The NIV renders this as an indicative, that blunts the force of the expression, whereas Paul originally presents a conditional sentence that assumes they were listening and learned how to live in Christ, according to the truth, but which also calls into question their current conduct. We might render it loosely, "I know this is not the truth you heard, and not what you were taught in Christ, to live like Gentiles." Paul strongly suggests that they are not behaving in a way that is consistent with what they had learned and heard concerning the truth that is in Christ – what he had personally taught them (cf. Acts 20:25-28, 32-35). He proposes that if they had properly heard and were accepted what they were taught, not only general morality, but what is consistent with the truth that is in Jesus, then surely they must know that behaving like

---

[190] Holmes, M. W. (2011–2013). *The Greek New Testament: SBL Edition* (Eph 4:20). Lexham Press; Society of Biblical Literature.
[191] Arndt, 2000, 38.
[192] Holmes, M. W. (2011–2013). *The Greek New Testament: SBL Edition* (Eph 4:21). Lexham Press; Society of Biblical Literature.

Gentiles is not appropriate for those who claim to be in union with Christ, and in whom the Holy Spirit has affected a moral transformation (Eph. 4:20-21, 22-24). In the next verses, Paul will give the content of what they have learned in Christ, the truth about the basis of conduct consistent with a transformed life (cf. Eph. 4:22-24).

Holiness Is Not Theoretical: What is at stake here is implementing holiness, conduct consistent with the morally and spiritually transformed life for those who belong to Christ. Righteousness is not a theoretical inner condition of a believer's soul or spirit, or merely a matter of one's right standing, or position, in the sight of God, of righteousness imputed and imparted. Rather, righteousness is holiness ensconced in the transformed heart and life, leading to an expected, consistent, and habitual practical outflow from the sanctified believer's life.[193] Paul observes that the new man has been created in them

---

[193] Flattening out the notion of righteousness to mere "rightness with God", a declaration of justification or rightness in God's sight, while ignoring the call from the New Testament for righteousness of spirit/transformed nature/character and conduct, in the sense of moral purity of heart and habitual practical living, is a sad development and an effort to recast the righteousness in Paul's theology It ignores expectations in scripture that those who belong to Christ are called to *act consistent* with their new transformed life. This call is not a matter of benign indifference to the New Testament writers, whether Jesus, Paul, Peter, John, or the writer of Hebrews. Rather, it is a matter of urgency and imperatival force, with warnings of the imminent danger of apostacy for those who do not take heed (some examples of which Paul names in his letters!). Dynamics of a Pauline proposition that (and John) expect habitual right living/conduct arising from the transformed Christian life ought to be fully explored in exegesis of his epistles. Wesley lamented denial of the possibility of the meaningful pursuit of righteousness, in terms of a purity of heart producing consistent/habitual right conduct for the saints, blaming a prevailing theological premise, in his day, that even saints are flawed and broken, and cannot be expected to achieve consistent

according to the true righteousness and holiness of God, so they should consciously take firm hold of the new self, and engage it through the Spirit (Eph. 4:23-24). Since they have been transformed in nature, they must go on be transformed in conduct (cf. Rom. 6:1-11). At the heart of Paul's treatment of this theme in Romans 6, the apostle's concern is more precisely unveiled, that those who are in Christ, and who have put to death the old life in Christ's crucifixion, and have been raised to new life in his resurrection, must go on to conduct consistent with the righteousness of God (Rom. 6:1-23). They cannot return to the life of habitual sinning because it will lead to a life ensnared once again to slavery of sin as principle, creating once more an environment in which carnality rules the will and produces sinful conduct – the ultimate result of which is death (Rom. 6:23). In Ephesians he addresses the same idea by reminding his readers that conduct their reflects the way Gentiles live their lives is not what they learned from the truth that is found in Christ; it is not what they had heard or were taught by him (Eph. 4:20-21)! On the contrary, they were taught to lay aside the old life, and to fully embrace or to actively take up the new life they have in Christ which produces practical right conduct, the fruit of an inward righteousness established in them by God through union with Christ (Eph. 4:20-24). Holiness and righteousness (moral transformation through union with Christ) as conduct must be implemented and applied to their practice

---

results in holiness. Arising from an Augustinian two-nature proposition in answer to Pelagius, such pessimism, Pelagius asserted is not consistent with the imperatives of New Testament theology. We have no choice, given Paul's theology of holiness, and his moral expectations, but to grapple with the practical implications of New Testament demands for right conduct, and to discern the relationship between such expectations, the transformed nature and character of believers, moral growth in moving saints to greater maturity in godliness, and of their daily conduct guided by the indwelling Spirit.

or walk with God, particularly, in this case, to their relationships with one another to promote unity in the church.

Verses 20 and 21 contain a first-class conditional sentence, which assumes for argument's sake that the statement in the protasis (the *if* clause) is true, and, that under those conditions, the statement in the apodosis (the *then* clause) will inevitably follow.[194] Paul has *fronted* the apodosis (the *then* clause), presumably for emphasis, "You have not learned this from Christ [apodosis], if you were in fact listening, and allowed yourselves to be properly taught the truth that is in Christ [protasis]" (Eph. 4:20-21). Indeed, his statement is striking, coming off the description of the kinds of conduct that results from the moral blindness and insensitivity of Gentiles. The adversative conjunction sets up a contrast between Gentile conduct, which Paul challenges as inappropriate for them as believers in union with Christ, and conduct that flows out of a morally transformed life, where everything has been made new in Christ (Eph. 4:17-19, 20-24).

You Were Instructed in Holiness: For Paul to say bluntly, "That's not the way you learned to live from Christ!" (Eph. 4:20), implies he is saying the kind of conduct they are currently engaging in is not consistent with the truth in Christ (Eph. 4:21), or in which the Ephesians had been instructed by Paul and now Timothy (cf. Acts 20:18-21, 27-28, 32; 1 Tim. 2:8-10, 15; 3:1-13, 14-16; 4:16; 5:22, 24-25; 6:3-4, 10-11, 13-16; 2 Tim. 2:15-19; 22; 3:1-9; 4:3-4). The *no longer,* followed by *you didn't learn this from Christ,* further crystalizes the sense of remediation in Paul's treatment of the topic in this passage, arguably offering a corrective to what has already begun to or is in danger of creating disunity in the church. That a certain amount, even dangerous levels, of disunity are in fact occurring is confirmed in the apostle's letters to Timothy, supported by Paul earlier warning to the Ephesians leaders that

---

[194] Cf. Wallace, 1996, 691-694.

they were in danger of encountering these things soon after his departure (Acts 20:28-31).

To say that this is not what they learned from Christ, is also to encourage them to implement the principles and teaching of what *they **have** learned from Christ,* the truth that is in Jesus (Eph. 4:20-21). The content of what they learned with respect to Paul's more focused point here is found in verses 22-24. The implications for unity for the church, and how that might look in specific relationships and circumstances, is the topic of what follows from verse 25 to at least chapter 6, and verse 9.[195] So, what exactly is it that they have learned from the truth that is in Christ, with respect to how they should conduct themselves?

Holiness Means Living Consistently With The New Life We Have in Christ: Before we turn to that consideration, let's note that this is not unlike Paul's concern in Romans 6, where the conduct of those who have been justified by God's grace, through faith, should follow the leading of the Spirit, and live consistently with the new life they have in Christ (Rom. 8:1-14). In Ephesians 4, the same idea is in the bullpen, even if the application of right conduct is more specifically aimed at promoting unity in the church. There is no qualitative difference in Paul's argument, logic, or flow of thought between the two instances, where he addresses the conduct of believers who are in union with Christ and are led or sealed by the Spirit (Eph. 1:13-14, cf. Rom. 8:1-4; Gal. 2:19-21; 5:16-25). Paul is addressing his readers, and encouraging them to engage holiness in their lives, in the sense of the habitual pursuit of righteousness as conduct premised on changes that have occurred at justification and union with Christ. In Romans 6 union with Christ is identification with him in the death of the old life controlled by the

---

[195] Cf. Brooks, Fingertip Holiness 35; Brooks, Ephesians Outline and Unfolded, 1984, 163-207.

desires of the flesh, and in his resurrection to a new life, which he will go on to explain is controlled by the Spirit, so long as they walk in surrender to him (Rom. 8:1-4). In Ephesians 4, Paul reminds his readers who, arguably, appear not be behaving as they ought, to reevaluate what they have learned in Christ, that they must do away with the old life, by putting it off, and take up the new life that has been implanted in them by God, and that is consistent with his own holiness and righteousness (Eph. 4:20-24). In both instances, Paul is asking his readers to more fully sign on to an internal reality that has taken place in them as a result of union with Christ, that is they have been transformed and are renewed to new life in Christ, which consists of the pursuit and implementation of righteousness in their conduct (Rom. 6:12-23). In other words, by encouraging the Ephesians to *put off* and *put on*, Paul is saying something similar to what he told the Romans, they must reckon on the death of the old life, and on a resurrection to new life. They are to apply faith to proposition that through Christ, in union with him, they are new creations, the old as gone and the new has come, and they are to conduct themselves in a way consistent with that reality (cf. Rom. 6:11; 2 Cor. 5:17; Eph. 4:20-24).

Holiness is not a theory, or a merely an unfulfilled desire for the future eschaton, it is something that must be engaged in the present, and to say differently is to fall into the trap which Israel fell into, not obeying God and losing connection with him on account of reigning and habitual sin in their lives. Paul says we have been reconciled to God through grace, we have peace with him, that is a relationship in which fellowship takes place, communion with God (Rom. 5:1). Romans 6 warns us that under those circumstances, we cannot return to habitual sinning by trading on God's grace, without the consequence of becoming slaves to sin and sinning again, and that will only lead to death (Rom. 6:15-16). Sin will ruin the relationship, because there is *no darkness in God at all,* and if we say we walk with God in fellowship while habitually sinning, we are liars, John warns (1 John 1:5-8). If with

Augustine we capitulate, and accept sinning as more or less inevitable because of our humanity, even for believers, then we fail to comprehend Paul's point, his soteriology, his theology of salvation and sanctification, that God has empowered us through the Spirit to gain meaningful traction in holiness, as long as we walk in fellowship with and surrender to him. And although our humanity is imperfect, as Paul's expanded epistolary exhortations indicate, and the present passage confirms, it does not mean that we have to return to our former slavery to habitual sinning, and to the control once exercised over us by the old life.[196] John encouragingly acknowledges that if we do sin we have an advocate and sacrifice to put things right with God, but that those who are born (again) of God do not practice habitual sinning (1 John 2:1-2, 4, 29; 3:6, 9; 5:18).

Hebrews also warns us that holiness is vital to see God (Heb. 12:14), and that God is making holy those whom he has *perfected* by the sacrifice of Christ (Heb 10:10, 14). First, that means that final holiness comes from the grace of God at work in us, and secondly the final harvest of righteousness is the result and consummation of God progressively improving what he redeemed and transformed initially at salvation. The writer evokes themes consistent with a Pauline theology of salvation and sanctification. Also reminiscent of Paul, Hebrews says that we are trained by God's discipline in order to reap a harvest of righteousness and peace ultimately, so that the righteousness at work in us in the present, capable of improvement through the working of God now, will come to its fullest and most complete expression in the future eschaton (Heb. 12:11, cf. Eph. 4:13). These ideas evoke what Paul said about himself to the Philippians, that while he had *gained Christ*, and God was working out his salvation in him (Phil. 2:12-13), more work still

---

[196] Cf. Rev. Josh Smothers, "Just because you inherited it, doesn't mean you have to practice it!" in a series *Emotionally Healthy Discipleship*, Wilmington NC: Wilmington First Church, Wednesday Night Bible Study, September 3, 2025.

needed to be done for that perfection to reach its culmination in a resurrection to the full righteousness found in Christ (Phil. 3:7-14). The apostle appeals to what he has attained in Christ, with a view to what has yet to brought to final completion (cf. Gal. 2:19-21).

So, there is new life at work in us, offering the prospect of genuine obedience to God, and acceptable, concrete righteousness in the present, but that is also capable of moral and spiritual improvement, culminating in a consummation that reflects the full measure of the stature of Christ (Eph 4:13, cf. Rom. 8:29-30). This is the tension in which the New Testament holds morality and final perfection for the believer. This tension is what Wesley recognized when he classed sinning as intentional disobedience and rebellion against God and battled with what he called the *enthusiasm* of those who tried to represent his doctrine as *angelic perfection* in the present.[197] Wesley wanted nothing to do with unrealistic claims about holiness that invited slander on the doctrine he preached. Wesley attempted to be consistent with Paul when he taught that *Christian perfection* is an upright condition, capable of improvement, and though not fully perfected in this life, it does, nonetheless, provides a meaningful reflection and demonstration of the righteousness and holiness of God through personal character, integrity, and right conduct.

IMPLICATIONS OF RECREATION TO BE LIKE GOD

What is the nature of *this truth* that is in Jesus, which Paul alludes to in this passage, and applies to his current concern for the Ephesians and their church (Eph. 4:21)? How did they learn Christ in a way that addresses Paul's concern for them not to conduct themselves as Gentiles do (Eph. 4:17, 20)? The content of what they learned and the

---

[197] Tyson J. R., 1986, 268-277; Wesley, The Works of John Wesley, 1872, 411-415.

truth that is in Jesus is found in verses 22-24, consisting of what is now recognized as a fundamental Pauline theological construct, the old life has been done away with, and saints ought to be moving forward under the impetus of the new life with which they have been endowed in Christ (Eph. 4:22-24, cf. Rom. 6:1-11) (a fuller exposition of this passage is below). In Romans this new life is part of the grace-endowment of God in which they now stand as those reconciled to God, and by which they are resourced to live out the new moral implications of justification, to go on to mature godly character (Rom. 5:1-8).[198] They received grace initially, and by it gained entry into the environment of grace in which they now have been ensconced (stand), where God freely resources their spiritual development and a moral progress, as well as their service to him and to one another (Rom. 5:2; Eph. 4:16, 22-24). Their redemption through a morally transforming experience of justification is directional, away from the old life, which has been crucified with Christ, and going in the direction of the moral development (godliness, maturity, Christian character) of the new, that is of the resurrection life of Christ implanted in them by the Spirit (Rom. 5:1-8; 6:8-10). From now on the Spirit is going to guide and empower them toward righteousness of character and conduct. He will resource the moral and spiritual development of their lives, something provided freely by God to those

---

[198] Paul is quite literally making the point in Romans 5 that those who are justified and reconciled to God (have, through union with Christ, entered into a relationship with God, supervised by the indwelling Spirit going forward), now live in the environment of grace, the supply of God resources designed to move them on toward development of Christian character. Romans 5 affirms that the exercise of God's grace in justification is supposed to be an initiation into the *environment of God's grace,* in which through the constant provision of God, the believer is to go on (forward – directional) to godliness in character, and in the integrity of practical Christian living (Rom 5:1-5).

who walk in faith with him, and in surrender to the leading of the Spirit (Rom. 8:1-4, 14). This is the definition of grace (cf. Rom. 1:17)!

No Room In Paul's Teaching for Moral and Spiritual Stasis: Their lives are not to be morally (or spiritually) static.[199] Neither should they allow themselves to be drawn back into the habits and conduct of the old life (Rom. 6:1-2, 15-16; Eph. 4:17).[200] We might even tentatively say that Paul rejects moral stasis as the enemy of spiritual growth and maturing godliness. No Christian can fulfill the design of God, expressed here in Ephesians 4, attaining the fulness of the stature of Christ (Eph. 4:13), in Romans as being conformed to the image of God's Son (Rom. 8:29-30), or elsewhere as participation in his resurrection, or glorification, or as being found to have the righteousness of Christ, unless they are growing, progressing, or moving forward in moral and spiritual development, and walking in surrender to the Spirit (Rom. 8:1-4; Gal 5:16, 18, 24-25), or deepening their relationship with God through consistent fellowship (Eph. 4:13-15, Eph. 5:9; cf. Rom. 6:22; 7:4; 1 Cor. 3:1-4; 15:42-44; 2 Cor. 3:8; 4:16-17; Gal. 2:19-21; 5:16, 22-23; 6:9; Phi. 1, 6, 11, 25; 3:12; Col. 1:10-14, 28; 2:19; 4:12; 2 Thess. 1:3). There is a right way to conduct one's life after union with Christ, after justification, and its transformation, and it is in resurrection to newness of life that is

---

[199] Cf. Wright N. T., 2012, 27-71; Board, 22-27; Brooks, Pardon, Purity, and Power,10-11, 14-16; Drysdale, 1955, 16-18, 32-36, 58-61, 78-83, 105-109, 147-150, 155-160.

[200] I think this was the dilemma of John Wesley, and to a degree of his brother, Charles. John recognized that God demanded purity of heart and life from his people, and that the New Testament expects moral development in them. John knew this even before Aldersgate but could not find peace with it until then. It was a driving consciousness of the need to go on to purity of life and conduct, to moral growth and maturity that at first undid him, and then later produced the theology of a second blessing.

the opposite and antithesis of the old life shackled to sin and sinning (Rom. 7:24).[201]

In Romans Paul speaks of a shift away from slavery to sin, and towards becoming slaves of God and of holiness. He obviously means that justification is the launching pad for a positive and essential movement forward in fulfillment of God purpose for those who are justified, and leads to the development of Christian character, integrity, and consistent right conduct (cf. Rom 6:1-10, cf. 2 Cor. 3:18; 4:16-17; 5:17). He asks the question up front, *what is going be the direction of our lives after we are justified and reconciled to God, will we remain in sin,* that is in a state of habitual sinning, producing sinful behavior (Rom. 6:1-2)? Resoundingly, no! God forbid (Rom. 6:2)! Is the Christian in moral and spiritual stasis after union with Christ,[202] justified, declared right with God, but still somehow bound to the old life, hoping that the grace of God is sufficient to make up for the constant moral failure that ensues (Rom. 6:1)? His question meets an immediate and strong repudiation, *God forbid*! Union with Christ has moral and spiritual implications for us, and for the transformation of our nature, whereby the old life, and the old self that once controlled it, the decisions we made, and the kind of person we were becoming, because the old life has been crucified by our union with Christ, and by participation in Christ's death (Rom. 6:3-4). Furthermore, the death of the old life has implications with respect to our participation with Christ in his resurrection to new life (Rom. 6:5, 9-10), so that we too have been raised to new life, a life in which sin no

---

[201] Drysdale, 1955, 14, 16-18.

[202] Note Paul's description of justification, as being baptized into Christ, into his death and resurrection. It is a full moral and spiritual participation in Christ, his sacrifice on the one hand, bringing the dominion of sin and sinning to an end, and in his resurrection to bring about a new life of moral and spiritual victory that leads to genuine holiness and righteousness through the Spirit (cf. Rom. 7:4, 6).

longer has mastery over us, not in our nature, character, conduct, or destiny (Rom. 6:5-10; 12-23). New life must go in a new direction toward the development of righteousness and holiness in character and conduct, that is righteousness ontologically and practically; this change and its implications are designed to bear fruit to God (Rom. 5:1-8; 7:4, 6, cf. 2 Cor. 3:18; 4:16-17; 5:17).

We Cannot Continue to Live in the Environment Where Sin Rules: It is not quite as J. H. King has framed it, *shall we allow sin to remain in us,* although we ***fully*** appreciate his point.[203] Rather Paul asks shall *we remain under the control of sin*, habitually sinning, counting on God's grace to bail us out (Τί οὖν ἐροῦμεν; ἐπιμένωμεν τῇ ἁμαρτίᾳ, ἵνα ἡ χάρις πλεονάσῃ;)?[204] His question is about our living environment after justification. Are we to remain in the environment of sin, of its control and its dominance (ἐπιμένωμεν τῇ ἁμαρτίᾳ).[205] Since we are in union

---

[203]Let us not too readily lay aside the impact and perspective of two or more generations of holiness preaching and homiletics, which attempted to follow Paul's reasoning for a reaffirmation of the grounds for new life in full renewal, and a rejection of the old life. This was something that resonated with those who heard it and who successfully applied the biblical principle to their lives to profound effect. Surely, they caught the essence of Pauline sanctification theology and concern. Nevertheless, let us not then force a homiletic, that upon careful reflection and application to a new constituency of believers, exposes some exegetical concerns, or hermeneutical difficulties. In the end, we all agree that Paul calls for his Romans readers, at the very least, to reapply or more resolutely apply, to their lives through reckoning-faith, by counting on the work God has done in them, the reality of what had taken place in them as a result of union with Christ, implications of which were that they must go on to holiness, and cannot linger or hover around in sin.

[204] King J. H., 1976, 70-80; Holmes, M. W. (2011–2013). *The Greek New Testament: SBL Edition* (Ro 6:1). Lexham Press; Society of Biblical Literature.

[205] Please note that much of the post American civil war theology of sanctification coming out of the holiness movement hung on the question of

with Christ, *we are united to him in the death of the old life through crucifixion and raised to new life in his resurrection* (Rom. 6:1-10), in order to serve God in the new way of the Spirit (led by him) (Rom. 7:6). This is an assertion of purpose, of design by God, that the crucifixion of the old life is supposed to lead to a new life of serving God by the power and influence of the Spirit, and that justification and transformation do not produce a subsequent condition of moral and spiritual stasis in or for the believer. By going in a new direction, and by no longer following the course of the old life, which we have laid aside (Rom. 6:11), we signify that the environment in which we now live in union with Christ is the environment of God's grace that sustains new life and its progress (Rom. 5:2), and by which, going forward, right character develops towards the fulfillment of the hope of a final consummation of God purpose of eternal life, and the imago Dei.

This new life is where we live in fellowship with God on account of a reconciliation with God, affected for and in us by justification, involving a union with Christ, both in his death and resurrection (Rom. 5:1; 6:1-11). No believer who has seriously apprehended and decided to "reckon" on the death of the old life, and on the power of new life in Christ can go on pursuing sin, or be engaged in habitual sinning, Paul reasons (Rom. 6:1-10). That is, no believer transformed through justification and union with Christ can seriously consider their lives unchanged by God, when in fact, Paul asserts, in Christ we are new

---

whether the believer will allow sin *to remain in their nature* after justification and regeneration (two-nature theory), often defined as the sin principle inherited from Adam (cf. Rom. 5:12-21). With respect, Paul asks a slightly different question, shall *we remain in the environment of the controlling principle of sin*. His answer is no! The reason he gives is that we have been delivered into a new environment where God's grace is at work in us, resourcing us for holiness as a result of justification and reconciliation to God (Rom. 5:1-2; 6:1-2).

creations from the moment of surrender to God, when our sins are forgiven, and we are reconciled to him (2 Cor. 5:17). Later in Romans, Paul will reiterate the directional nature of salvation and sanctification by saying that those who belong to Christ have not received the spirit of slavery again that stirs up fear of returning to the bondage of the old life, with its threat of judgment on sin and sinning, but have gone on to the adoption of sonship with God, so that they see God as their Father, and anticipate becoming joint heirs with Christ in the new creation (Rom. 8:13-16, 17).

On Our Way to Becoming Heirs with Christ: We have become heirs with Christ through an introduction into new life, and a new relationship to God through the Spirit (Rom. 8:13-17). The change that takes place though justification initiates a new life with a new direction, that Paul calls, in Romans 6, slavery to God. This new life is predicated on being released from slavery to sin and empowerment to become slaves of God, and to holiness and righteousness (Rom. 6:16-18, 22-23). In Ephesians, putting on new life results in new behaviors, new habits, new attitudes, new conduct, and new ways of relating to other believers that involve service and mutual concern to build one another up (Eph. 4:16, 22-24). The point is, this radically new life is oriented in a new direction, and it is quickly moving away from the old life with its slavery to sin, and disobedience to God. The result is a developing new character, and growth in godliness that reflects the holiness of God which he has implanted in those who now belong to Christ.

Paul reminds the Ephesians that they are to move away from conduct that follows the moral and spiritual direction Gentiles are going, to go in the direction of the new life they have in Christ, which was implanted in their natures through a *creation to be like God,* so that they will incorporate the righteousness and holiness of God into their character and conduct (Eph. 4:22-23, cf. John 5:24).[206] For Paul this has practical implications which ought to be reflected in conduct and attitudes, as well as in the ways they relate to and treat one another. He will carefully unpack these in the rest of the book. In Ephesians 4:22-24, however, Paul is speaking of a moral obligation premised on the deliberate and purposeful adoption of the new life they have in Christ, so as to engage right conduct, moral development, and moral uprightness (character) in the present, with hope of finally attaining to the full measure of the stature of Christ ultimately (Eph. 4:13, cf. Rom. 8:17, 29-30).

New life in Christ is predicated on two things, the dramatic moral change that comes from putting off the old life to put on the new, and that the new life must be taken up more resolutely and pursued by those who claim to be in union with Christ. We will talk about what the latter seems to mean in due course. But suffice it to say here, Paul repudiates a moral and spiritual passivity, and urges his Ephesians reader to engage the implications of having been raised to a new life founded on a new creation to be like God in righteousness and holiness. And although Paul does not articulate it *explicitly* in eschatological terms here, he has already indicated the goal of new life is to *be like God,* meaning in the present in character and conduct, as well as ultimately in conformity to Jesus Christ, as God's Son, or the imago Dei (Rom. 8:30). Their union with Christ was never morally neutral, but is in fact morally transformative, and designed to take them on to the practical outflow of right conduct, the development of upright character, to mature godliness which reflects the image and likeness of God back into his

---

[206] Peter makes a similar point about repentance, that it represents movement towards God (2 Pet. 3:9). God does not wish anyone to perish but patiently waits for them to move toward him (εἰς μετάνοιαν χωρῆσαι) through repentance, and thus in his direction, so as to speak. Χωρῆσαι means move from one place to another, to go (cf. Arndt, 2000, 1094).

creation in partnership with Christ, who is even now reigning with God in glory ahead of the full realization of the kingdom of God (Phil. 2:8-11). Their *uprightness now* is the beginning of the final and *realized righteousness and holiness of God to come*, which is to reflect God's own holiness, just as he originally intended in creation (Gen. 1:26-28). They have begun down a road that, compared to the Gentiles in the world around them, is headed in the opposite direction until Christ is morally and spiritually produced in the saints of God. That seems to be Paul's point!

In Romans 8:17, Paul articulates the same idea as joint-heirship with Christ, and as an eschatological consummation of God purposes, begun in creation (Gen. 1:26-28). If humanity was created and designed to reflect God back into his creation, as G. K. Beale articulates its, then the moral and spiritual reclamation of humanity, its recreation in the righteousness and holiness of God, as Paul puts it in Ephesians 4:24, is critical.[207] To live in the image of God, and to reenter the partnership with God in order to fulfill his purpose, there must be a moral and spiritual change, empowerment to go on to full holiness that represents God (Eph. 4:24, cf. Rom. 8:29-30)! That Christ has entered heaven as a glorified representative of humanity, having obeyed God to the fullest extent of his humanity, means that he has assumed the throne and reengaged the divine and human partnership already, by sitting on the throne with God.

Paul clearly articulates this in 1 Corinthians 15:20-28, where Jesus is bringing everything under his control in order, as the supreme representative of humanity, to present it to God to be its divine, supreme ruler (cf. Phil. 2:6-11). What was lost by the man Adam, is reclaimed by the man, the second Adam, Jesus Christ. God's purpose to restore

---

[207] Cf. Beale, The Temple and the Church's Mission: A Biblical Theology of the Dwelling Place of God, 2004.

humanity to their place of divine partnership with God, ruling over creation in his behalf, and in partnership with him, has been both accomplished and initiated by Christ, so that our union with him allows us to become heirs with him, joint heirs with Christ at the consummation and beginning of the coming eschaton. These ideas are not wholly manufactured from new, theological, cloth by Paul, but are part of an underlying New Testament consciousness that Christ has ascended to the throne at the right hand of God, to reign with him immediately in the present, of which the book of Hebrews gives the best explanation in light of Jesus historical sacrifice and resurrection. They are also derived through Pauline reflection on Old Testament themes, from which he received his revelation from God, mentioned in Galatians (Gal. 1:12), where it is Christ (Holy Spirit) who revealed them to him. In passages like Psalm 110:1; and Psalm 8:1-9, Paul found in Christ's victory, and our union with him, a reengagement of our partnership with God, as heirs with Christ (Rom. 8:17), and his original purpose for us to be reflections of his glory and image (Rom. 8:29-30; Eph. 4:24, cf. Gen. 1:26-28; Lev. 11:44-45, cf. 2 Cor. 3:18; 4:18-19; Phil. 2:14-16). Therefore, Paul's idea of union with Christ, with moral implications for our own holiness as a reflection of God's holiness (Eph. 4:24), is critical, and is an initiation into a new partnership with God that will culminate in being conformed to the image of God's Son (Rom. 8:29-30), and reigning with the glorified Son of Man over God's creation (Rom. 8:17, cf. 1 Cor. 4:8; 2 Cor. 4:14; 5:1-5; Eoh. 1:3, 20; 2:6; Col. 3:1-4; 2 Tim. 2:12; 4:18; Heb. 3;1; 9:23; 11:16; 12:22; Rev. 5:10; 1:17).

No Room for Indifference: Morality, for a disciple in union with Christ claiming justification or salvation (cf. Eph. 2:5, 8-9), cannot be a matter of indifference, and certainly not of ambivalence. It is at the heart of the new life, of being a *saint,* and of being *faithful* in serving God

(Eph. 1:1).[208] Upright character and purity of heart is essential to fellowship with God (1 John 1:5-6), and because without holiness no one will ultimately see God (Heb. 12:14). If habitual sinning separated God's covenant people from him under the old covenant, so that they were excluded from the promise of rest (Heb. 3:12-19), the writer of Hebrews argues, then we who are beneficiaries of the new covenant are surely in greater danger of losing our place is we *neglect so great a salvation,* or *trample under our feet the sacrifice of Christ, effectively crucifying him all over again through our rejection, which heaps disgrace upon him and*

---

[208] In a recent conversation with Rev. Josh Smothers about how GenZ experiences morality, Pastor Josh made the astute observation, that while GenZ'ers have a (biblically) faulty and alternative, non-traditional notion, compared to the Judeo-Christian sense of morality, and experience trouble with understanding their guilt, that it should lead to repentance, and a sense that things need to be set right, they do experience the symptoms of conviction and conscience, but interpret them as anxiety and depression. Too often, misdiagnosed guilt is medicated as a mental, emotional, or chemical/hormonal imbalance, and even a disorder, which fails to address the root problem of sin, with its sense of alienation from God. Even if we cannot articulate it, guilt and alienation from God is a common human experience, that manifests itself as a sense of "moral" unease and feelings of guilt. This unease resides at the deepest level of our human consciousness. Even though some cannot identify the root issue of this unease, they do, in fact, experience its symptoms, but are without a convincing philosophical framework, or worldview to find an effective remedy. However, more to the point in this present conversation, it was observed that this has implications for young people who do become Christians. Without moral awareness or short-circuited concepts of morality, sin and alienation from God, growth as a disciple of Christ is undermined, for the very reason that a great deal of Christian growth is moral development, and depends, according to Paul and the New Testament, on moral as well as spiritual maturing to full godliness, and the imago Dei. For me, this is the very reason we need to rearticulate the doctrine of sanctification freshly for this generation, in order for it to resonate with them. (Smothers, Rev. Josh, Personal conversation, September 14, 2025). Cf. Chadwick, A Call to Chriatian Perfection, 1943, 8.

his death on the cross (Heb. 2:1-4; Heb. 6:4-6). These kinds of considerations lie behind Paul's insistence on morality for the saints, and on faithful persistence to the end of the road, if we are to finally inherit what God has promised in Christ (Ezek. 18:24; Matt 10:22; 24:13; Mark 13:13; Luke 9:62; 21:19; Rom. 8:17; 11:22; 1 Cor. 1:8; 6:9-11; 10:12; 15:1-2, 50; 2 Cor. 1:24; Gal 5;1, 21; Eph. 6:14; ; 1 Thess. 3:8; 2 Thess. 2:15; 1 Tim. 4:10, 16, 2 Tim. 2:19; Heb. 2:1; 3:6, 14-15; 4:14; 6:4-6, 12; 10:26-27; 2 Pet. 2:21-22; Rev. 2:10; 21:7, cf. Phil. 1:6, 27-30; 3:12-14; 4:10). Persistence in pursing God and surrendering to him by faith is at the center of the often quoted, w*ithout holiness no one will see God*, and not some legalistic standard of apparent godliness (Heb. 12:14). For Paul, salvation does not consist merely in an initial experience of repentance and pardon, but of a changed life (Rom. 6:1-11). It consists of character and uprightness going forward (1 Cor. 6:19-20), of right conduct coming from a transformed heart that by faith lays hold of God's grace to bring the believer to mature godliness. And, make no mistake, Paul teaches in this passage, salvation aims at bringing godliness to a perfect reflection of the righteousness of God, the image of his Son, to come to the full measure of the stature of Christ (Rom. 8:29-30; 2 Cor. 3:18; 4:6; Eph. 4:13, cf. Gal. 5:16-25; 1 John 3:1-3).[209]

---

[209] The construct of salvation as a once-and-for-all, momentary commitment at an altar or at some moment of conviction, but which has no defining moral power in the life of the person who claims to have been pardoned by God, is belayed by Jesus' parable of the sower. The seed must persist to maturity, without having its roots shriveled up, or being choked out by the wealth and concerns of the world, particularly if it is to achieve final fruitfulness, or be ready for the harvester. It is not the seed's germination that counts, but its persistence to fruitfulness. Augustinian/Calvinism predestination theology teaches that only those predestined by for salvation persevere, which is convenient. It is hard to see which came first, the idea that some are predestined to salvation by God and so cannot fail, or that because some do

The idea that salvation consists of a morally transformative initiation, followed by a life of obedience to God, consisting of moral obligation, and consistent integrity of character after that runs through the teaching of Jesus, Paul, Peter, James, John, and the writer of Hebrews (cf. John 3:3-9). Believers are to be holy, and to conduct themselves as holy people, obeying God, and consistently living uprightly in practical ways every day so as to provide the world a witness to the righteousness and holiness of God (Phil. 2:14-16, cf. Luke 1: 69-75; Rom. 1:7; 6:19, 22; 12:1-2; 1 Cor. 1:2; 2 Cor. 7:1; Eph. 1:1; 2:21; 5:3, 26-27; Col. 1:22; 3:12; 1 Thess. 2:10; 3:13; 4:4, 7; 2 Tim. 1:9; 2:21; Tit. 1:8; Heb. 2:11; 10:14; 12:10, 14;).[210] Some object on the basis of a fear of degenerating into legalism, or works righteousness, and raise accusations of neo-Pelagianism. But surely their fears do not empty the New Testament of its moral imperatives, or of its insistence that

---

appear to fail, they were not predestined to salvation in the first place, and so do not to persevere to final redemption despite appearing to have an experience of salvation! I rather suspect that Augustine formulated his theology in response to Pelagius, by honing it for his rebuttal against him, rather than developing it more thoughtfully from Paul, who everywhere encourages the saints not to become disheartened and to turn away from God or to fall into sin, and insists that final salvation depends on persisting in faith and the grace of God until the end.

[210] Note Hebrews 10:14, where the writer in an almost Pauline fashion, speaks of those who are perfected or made complete (perfect tense – τετελείωκεν) by God, toward, or in view of the goal that they might, without interruption (εἰς τὸ διηνεκές), go on in the direction of becoming more holy. The notion seems to be a state in which development in taking place toward holiness, where a state and standing of perfection with God or in God's view already exists because of Jesus' sacrifice, but where there is also room for growth and improvement in personal character, conduct, and nature. Note the present, substantival participle τοὺς ἁγιαζομένους in the NIV is translated *those who are being made holy or sanctified*. It appears a process is under way leading to holiness, one that is premised on an underlying condition of perfection achieved by God through the sacrifice of Christ on the cross.

disciples of Christ finish the course and go on to be conformed to the image of God's Son (Rom. 8:29-30). Moral pessimism, of the sort advanced by Augustine over Pelagianism, that believers, who still wrestle with the flesh, are too flawed to achieve meaningful holiness in this life, and that we are to expect repeated moral failures or weaknesses in even the stoutest Christian is what Wesley lamented and ultimately rejected. Believers ought to hold out hope, before death, John and Charles believed, for a meaningful experience and expression, in practical terms, of the sanctified life, and should expect God to underwrite it by his grace and power in order to produce in his people what he commands from them.[211] In this way, without acknowledging the ontological error of Pelagianism, Welsey recognized that Pelagius had it right when he said, if God commands us to go on to holiness, it must be possible, and that he must have provided the means to meet the challenge.[212] Wesley considered the accusations against Pelagius, that holiness could be achieved without grace, a slander of Augustine's intemperate and angry rebuttal, by which the man was "bespattered for many ages"![213]

---

[211] Wesley, A Plain Account of Christian Perfection, 1966, 42-46, 51-66, 68-69, 70-72.

[212] Wesley, Sermons on Several Occasions, 1999, Sermon 68, 9. Note: Wesley calls Pelagius a fifth century heretic, whether he is employing sarcasm or not is hard to tell. Nevertheless, he argues that contrary to Augustine's excessively passionate and intemperate attack on Pelagius, Pelagius was not wrong in asserting that God commands holiness, and that he provides the means for its attainment to a meaningful degree, contrary to Augustine, who's pessimism doomed Christian theology for a century to a post-justification, two-natured moral defeatedness.

[213] Wesley, Sermons on Several Occasions, 1999, Sermon 68, 9.

CHAPTER THREE

MORAL AND SPIRITUAL DEVELOPMENT (4:12-16)

In our discussion above, we noted how for Paul salvation is directional in its movement and goals. Noel Brooks, in *Scriptural Holiness,* asserts that Christlikeness, love, and holiness are what we were created and redeemed for. He even says that holiness is what God is aiming for in us and for us, through the action of the Holy Spirit in our lives (cf. Rom. 7:6; Eph. 4:24).[214] In other words, one of the key elements of our growth and progress as disciples is maturing morally toward becoming like Christ (Rom. 8:29), and to ultimately attain to the full measure of the stature of Christ (Rom. 8:29-30; Eph. 4:13). If, by our doctrine and theology, we short circuit moral development and progress in the Christian life, growth toward mature godliness where there is

---

[214] Brooks, Scriptural Holiness, 1972, 37. Noel Brooks also speaks of the ordo salutis (order of salvation), the order of the events taking place in salvation, which includes the idea that logically or necessarily what takes place is applied sequentially or in an progressive order, so that repentance and faith arise before justification, which precedes regeneration (and initiates sanctification – the progressive movement toward mature godliness), sanctification (moral and spiritual development) through empowerment by the Spirit, and glorification (the culmination of salvation from the implanted potential at the beginning to its consummation in perfection of body, spirit, and nature). Glorification is the final reclamation of the physical body to conformed to the resurrection body of Jesus, and to finally bring the process of sanctification to completion by conforming the saints to the image of God's Son in holiness, thus reflecting character of God. In this, Brooks follows Paul own ordo saltus found in Romans 8:29-30. Cf. Brooks, Scriptural Holiness, 1972, 41-50.

progressive improvement, then we have rejected a critical component of the spiritual advancement of discipleship. To say, as Wesley complained and lamented against Augustine, that we are irrevocably flawed and have no power for meaningful holiness in this life, we have contradicted the plain teaching of the New Testament. And contrary to what Calvinists often teach, that righteousness refers only to our *status* with God through faith in Christ, that God imputes righteousness to us, and thus imparts Christ's righteousness into us, the New Testament, does in fact, everywhere encourage the saints to go on to meaningful development of upright character, producing right conduct or behavior.

To be sure we are found having the righteousness of Christ (cf. Gal. 2:19-21; Phil. 3:7-11), but to say at the same time that we are hopelessly flawed, and cannot appropriate it to our character and conduct in such a way that we abandon habitual sinning, and must accept moral imprisonment to persistent or inevitable daily moral failure because of an unresolved flaw in our nature, is to ignore Paul's exhortations and teaching, and repudiate his *God forbid* (Rom. 6:1-2). It is to effectively kite on God grace, something he rejected adamantly (Rom. 6:2). In other words, contrary to an implied passivity in Calvinism (predestination), the New Testament calls for genuine participation and engagement in God's program of moral and spiritual development and practice. That this process moves forward and is empowered by the indwelling Spirit, as Paul argues elsewhere, means that growth and practice come about through the operation of God's grace, and not unaided human effort.

It is categorically not works righteousness, or legalism; it is not Pelagianism, neo-Pelagianism, or semi-Pelagianism. Paul makes this point to the Galatians and brings his argument to its climactic moment in chapter 5 and verses 16-25, where he sets out the action of the Spirit in the lives of those surrendered to God, and walking with him in step and a relationship with God. Where the Spirit is in control, where the believer has surrendered themselves to God, has reckoned on the new life (Rom. 6:11), and walks in daily surrender to the Spirit, Paul claims, the flesh will no longer control conduct, and will no longer be a prisoner to its dictates. We have become slaves of God, and are no longer slaves to sin, sinning, or the flesh (Rom. 6:15-23). That is, Paul says, so long as we walk in surrender to the Spirit, and keep up with him (Gal. 5:16, 18, 24-25). Paul explains to the Galatians that they are capable of going on to holiness without recourse to the law (Gal. 5:16-25). It is a unique relationship with the Holy Spirit, that believers have through union with Christ, not available in the same sense under the old covenant, and resting on an ongoing surrender to God by faith that apprehends the power of the Spirit living in them to make moral development and progress possible.[215] For Paul this is the power of God promised in the Old Testament by which the law, moral uprightness, righteousness, would be written into the hearts and the minds of his people in connection with forgiveness of their sins and wickedness (Jer. 31:31-34). Ezekiel proposes the same thing in a different analogy, that God will replace the stoney heart with a heart of flesh (morally tender toward God), and give them a new S(s)pirit that will enable his people to live in obedience to God, and to be morally upright in their conduct (Ezek. 36:22-28). The key to moral development then, in Pauline theology, is transformative forgiveness of sins, that changes the inner environment of the heart and life, followed by the power of God through the Spirit building a new life of consistent righteousness.

Paul does not seem to know about a static state of being right with God, justified, that leaves the believer morally unaltered or not moving toward the final objectives God has for his eschatological people (Rom. 6:1-11; 2 Cor. 3:18; 4:16-18; 5:18; Eph. 4:13, 22-24; Col. 1:22-23; 3:1-4, 5-15). We saw above how his purposes include a dimension of moral

---

[215] I make this point and cover Paul's argument in Galatians 5:16-24 in more detail in *Help for Holiness*. Evans, Help For Holiness: Rediscovering God's Resources for Practical Sanctification in Galatians 5:16-25, 2018.

development, the goal of which appears to be mature godliness. It is this idea that is captured by Paul's logic in Ephesians 4:22-24, when he uses language about *being created in the image of God,* and *like God in true righteousness and holiness* (Eph. 4:24). He could hardly be clearer, where in the previous section he has spoken of God supplying leaders to the church to oversee its development and growth, so that every part of the body, every member of the church, might benefit from being built up by the resources flowing through the body, and that each believer becomes the conduit to, and a beneficiary of others. When each part does its part, because they are joined properly to one another in authentic unity, each one having put off the old self, and having clothed themselves with the new self that reflects the character of God, there will be a mutual concern for other believers and their welfare, which replaces the selfishness and self-focus of the old life (Eph. 4:11-16, cf. Phil. 2:1-5). The final goal of growth and moral development is the goal of achieving the full measure of the stature of Christ (Eph. 4:11-16, cf. Rom. 8:29). This implies movement, development, growth, maturity, direction, but it also implies God's intention, purpose, and goal directedness. The growth of the church, and the moral development of believers, is not random, haphazard or a matter of ambivalence to him. It is God's purposeful intention and goal for the saints. Paul is concerned with the moral conditions that exist in Ephesus among believers, and that they change and improve the current conditions in the church for the sake of the health of the church and individual members, in order to fulfill God's purpose for his people. His exhortations to put off the old life and put on the new life ought to be seen in this light and against the backdrop of God's intention of bringing the church and its members to full moral and spiritual maturity in Christ.

GOD'S ENDGAME

References like this one, to the *stature of the fullness of* Christ or the *image of his Son,* are another way of saying that God's final goal is for his people to ultimately become like Christ, to be morally and spiritually reflections of God's image and likeness, and to be and to become his representatives to creation (Gen. 1:26-28; 5:1-2; 9:6; Eph 4:24, cf. Rom. 8:29-30; 1 Cor 11:7; 15:49; 2 Cor. 3:18; 4:4; Col 3:10).[216] God's purpose for gifting leaders to the church is to equip the saints so that they may be effective in their role of supporting one another with the resources of God, and so that they might promote the growth of the church and its members into the full maturity of godliness (Eph. 4:7-13). The growth and development of the saints is tied to their connection to the body, the church, and the mutuality of their relationships with one another (Eph. 4:16). Growth for believers personally depends on mutually supportive relationships in the church that edify and build up believers through their daily interactions with one another, a concept axiomatic to Pauline ecclesiology, so that in the context of church life, unity is critical to God's goal of producing mature believers (Eph. 4:11-13, 16).

Now, there is a tendency among contemporary church leaders to leap to a numerical growth index when speaking of church growth, and to fail to fully comprehend that God's endgame is not solely, or even primarily focused on numbers. Surely, it is clear that while expansion of the church's reach is included and implied in Pauline growth-plans to take the gospel into unreached regions of the empire (cf. Rom. 15:20-25), the moral and spiritual development of the church and its members in maturity leading to "the whole measure of the fullness of Christ" is clearly paramount, in terms of the connections the saints enjoy with one another in the body of Christ. That means that forming the image of God in *authentic righteousness and holiness in the character and lives of the saints,* toward a full representation of Christ, is the trajectory of God's efforts for the believers, including implanting the power of the Spirit in

---

[216] (Beale, We Become What We Worhip: A Biblical Theology of Idolatry, 2008)

their lives to support ongoing moral and spiritual development (cf. Eph. 4:13-16, 20-24, cf. Rom. 7:6; 8:1-4).[217]

If God's goals are to be reached, Paul argues, there must be forward movement, a movement toward greater righteousness and holiness, which is what he desires for his people morally in the present, and eschatologically in terms of its fullest expression in the image of Christ ultimately (Eph. 4:13). Once the old life of pursuing sin has been abandoned, the new life must take up the challenge of going after moral progress toward the full realization of what God has planned for the believer in the future (Rom. 6:3-11). Since the new life was originated in union with Christ, by a rebirth into the holiness and righteousness of God, a reflection of his own nature, then it makes sense that it must go on to the goal God has designed for it of fully reflecting him (Eph. 4:22-24, cf. Rom. 8:29). That, however, in Paul's mind, does not mean a *beginning* and an *ending,* without moral development or progression between them! There is, contrary to the view of some, a meaningful pursuit and experience of righteousness and holiness to be appropriated and applied to their daily lives, and to a deeply devotional relationship of the saints with God. And even though there is some incompleteness in it (which Paul admits in Philippians 3:12), room for its further development, or even when there are moral lapses that need forgiveness, correction, and cleansing, it does not follow that the enterprise in doomed to failure and should be abandoned as hopeless (1 John 1:7-10; 2:1-2). That was the argument of John Wesley. That is the whole point of passages like Romans 6, Galatians 5, here in Ephesians 4, and what Paul recounts as his own personal, moral ambition in Philippians 3.

---

[217] *The New International Version* (Eph 4:13). (2011). Zondervan.

There must be, in the present life, prior to the culmination of God's purpose for the believers at the eschaton, a lifetime of moral forward development and maturing (Rom. 6-8; 2 Cor. 4; Gal. 5, et. al.), such that it is reflected in the character and conduct of the saints, particularly, as here, in their relationships with one another in the church (Eph. 4:16) – as well as in other contexts, as witnesses to the world appropriately representing God (Phil. 2:14-16). The point Paul is making to the Ephesians, when he says that that they cannot go on living like the Gentiles, is that this is not God's purpose or goal for their lives (Eph. 4:17). Rather, it hurts the growth and health of the church because of the disunity it engenders through the kinds of selfishness and disruption he predicted to their elders at Miletus would come after his departure (Acts 20:30-31). And now, Timothy was dealing with the fallout of this as the Ephesian pastor, with quarrels, false doctrine, ill-discipline leaders, strong women who taught error, and endless, fruitless debates over trivia, all of which undermined the unity of the church, and disrupted essential connections between the saints. Disunity affects relationships and disrupts the mutual and reciprocal flow of resources through the body, the mutual benefit of which bring to bear God's beneficence to the church, and that makes support available to the body and its individual members for their growth, encouragement, and edification (Eph 4:16). Such behavior and character, leading to disunity, reflect an inaccurate picture of God, whose holiness and righteousness is implanted in the saints when they are brought into union with Christ, and it is more characteristic of the conduct and character of the unsaved world around them.[218]

---

[218] It is now that we can better appreciate the repeated emphasis in chapter 1, which serves as the foundation for Paul's later exhortations, that we are above all things *in Christ, joined to him, belong to him, need to get to know more and more of what we have in him, and what this union with Christ means and*

Once a life of union with Christ begins, there must be moral and spiritual progress trajectory aiming at the target of bringing to full expression what has already been sown into our lives at initial salvation as seed, namely our recreation or regeneration in the holiness and righteousness of God, which ought to reflect him in our conduct and character in the present (Eph. 4:24, cf. Phil. 2:14-16). Progress in moral development (righteousness and holiness as character linked to conduct) begins in the present (cf. Eph. 4:17, 20-21, 24), and aims at being conformed to the image of Christ for the coming eschaton, when all things will be renewed in a new heaven and earth, to become what God originally purposed (Gen. 1:26-28; John 14:1-3; Rom. 8:18-30; 1 Cor 15:20-28; Col. 1:15-20, cf. Isa. 65:18-65:24; Heb. 12:22-29; Rev. 21:1-6). The one is a part and a function, to some degree, of the other. Present moral development of character and conduct, reflecting God back into the world, anticipates final moral perfection reflecting God back into creation. They are joined to one another in God's redemptive action in the lives of his people and church from initial justification until final glorification (Eph. 4:13-16).[219] They cannot be separated, as though current morality and moral development is unimportant or relegated to some spiritual impossibility in the current age, only to be suddenly imparted at death and very near death and morally unimproved saints.[220] Those who are *in Christ* should not expect to be conformed to the *image of Christ* if they are not engaging the process whereby God's

---

signifies, in terms of our character and conduct that reflects the character of God.

[219] Brooks, Fingertip Holiness, 4; Brooks, Scriptural Holiness, 1972, 11, 41-53; Brooks, Bible Validation for Santification, 1975, 15-17; Brooks, Pardon, Purity, and Power, 9-12, 15-16; Brooks, UNIT II SANCTIFICATION, 15-35; Carter & Sauls, 1976,

[220] cf. Wesley, The Works of John Wesley, 1872, 416-423.

grace is moving them in the direction of that conformity into the image of Christ in the end.

The Ephesians are to be like God in true righteousness and holiness because that is what God has implanted in them through transformative redemption and salvation, at their initial union with Christ and when they were saved (Eph. 2:1-10). God prepared his people in advance to do good works, and that is, Paul argues, what we should expect from those who have been morally renewed through the creation of the righteousness and holiness of God in them (Eph. 2:10).[221] Their (re)creation through union with Christ is *according to God*, where the preposition expresses similarity or homogeneity of the character of their new (re)creation (2 Cor. 5:17), supplanting the old, to be consistent with the righteousness and holiness that characterizes the nature of God (τὸν κατὰ θεὸν κτισθέντα ἐν δικαιοσύνῃ καὶ ὁσιότητι τῆς ἀληθείας) (Eph. 4:24).[222] Paul makes it plain that his readers should engage the salvific process of God in their lives, if they expect to personally participate in the consummation of God's purposes for them (Rom. 5:4-5; 8:17-18; 15:4, 19; 1Cor. 1:8; **15:2**, 58; 2 Cor. 3:9-12; 4:16-18; Gal 5:1, 5; 6:9; Eph. 1:4, 18; 4:4; 5:27; Phil 1:6; 3:10-11, 12-14; Col. 1:3-6a, 23, 27, 28-29; 1 Thess. 2:19; 1 Tim. 1:12; 2:10; 4:7-8; cf. Matt 5:48; 10:22; 24:13; Mark 13:13; Acts 20:24; Heb. 3:6, 14; 4:14; 6:11, 18-19; 1 Pet. 1:9; 4:13; 5:10;

---

[221] Note: It is in the context of salvation from a former life of disobedience and sin that Paul speaks of how God has prepared ahead of time that those who are saved by grace should go on to good works, that is right conduct (Eph. 2:10). The saved do not enter a condition of morally stasis (Rom. 5:1-8) but rather take up a life of active right conduct and good works (Eph. 2:1-10). Good works is not a matter of ambivalence or indifference to God, it is part of the ongoing development of the Christian life, where growth in morality of character produces right conduct and obedience to God (called righteousness by Paul quite often).

[222] Holmes, M. W. (2011–2013). *The Greek New Testament: SBL Edition* (Eph 4:24). Lexham Press; Society of Biblical Literature; (Arndt, 2000), 512-513.

2 Pet. 2:20; Rev. 2:26). This process, Paul intimates in Ephesians 4:24, involves the application of a definite moral transformation by God through a decision to put off the old man and put on the new, so that the righteousness and holiness now in them reflect the character of God, and develop their character as maturing godliness, as well as regulating their conduct in the present. Moral development and dynamic is particularly critical in this context with respect to how they treat and relate to one another in the community of faith.

To surrender to the impulses that once controlled their old lives would be to retreat and go backwards, away from God and his goals for them. It would be to back away from righteousness and holiness, and to suffer moral attrition (Rom. 6:1-2). Paul argues that if we have died to sin through union with Christ, we cannot then continue to live in it, or under its power, moving on from justification (Rom. 6:2). A break has occurred between us and our old life (controlled by impulses of the flesh), as a result of union with Christ (Rom. 6:3-11). Union with Christ has seen God reform us with righteousness and holiness as a core, integral component of new life and a transformed nature (cf. 2 Cor. 5:17). In Romans 6:11, Paul encourages his readers to calculate (mentally accept and ascent to the proposition that the old life has died with Christ) (ὑμεῖς λογίζεσθε ἑαυτοὺς) on the new life as sufficient moral grounds to make possible the righteousness God demands form his people.[223] They are to take up this resurrection to new life, where in

---

[223] A mistake that often plagued later holiness theology was that the *new life* we have in Christ is sufficient in and of itself to ultimately produce holiness, whereas Paul makes it clear in Romans 8 and Galatians 5, and elsewhere, that only in partnership with the indwelling power of the Spirit is righteousness attainable (Rom. 8:4; Gal. 5:16, 18, 24-25). Paul conspicuously argues, not that it is the replacement of the old self with the new self that is sufficient for holiness, though it is important, is indispensable even, but that holiness

Ephesians 4 Paul uses the metaphor of putting it on like clothing, as the principle that stands behind their moral development into godly character and conduct (in Romans 7 and 8 called the law of the Spirit of life in Christ Jesus) (Rom. 8:2). The new life requires a repudiation and forsaking of the old life to move forward (Eph. 4:21-22, cf. Rom 6:1-2, 3-11).

With respect to the former way of life controlled by sin, they had been taught to "put it off" or lay it aside and not go back to it (Eph. 4:22). The result is increasing fellowship with God and knowledge of him (2 Pet. 3:18). However, in this case, moral development which reflects the righteousness and holiness of God in an increasing measure, services the life and unity of the church, so that each member is a supplier of the resources of God to other members, and are recipients of the benefits of being connected to the body (Eph. 4:13, 24). The health of the church depends on the moral environment at work in the corporate body, and in the lives of the saints as individuals (Eph. 4:16). The success of the church as a mutually sustaining fellowship of believers thrives when the personal lives of those believers follow the pattern God has laid out for them, and are being lived in obedience to God and the leadership of the Spirit. For this reason, Paul warns them to not live as Gentiles, that is like the world or society morally, because selfishness and disobedience to God puts pressure on relationships in the church. Unity in the church is supported by new life and incorporating new life into how they related to one another with character and integrity – a new attitude of their minds (Eph. 4:23). Paul envisions progress toward more mature righteousness and holiness as right conduct (new life), character (attitudes of their minds), and culminating in full godly maturity (the image of God), which supports the church as a body, and services the

---

requires a partnership with the Holy Spirit and living in daily surrender to his leading (Rom. 8:1-4; Gal. 5:16-25).

fellowship between believers (Eph. 4:16). Selfish ways, and carnal attitudes will sabotage the unity of the church by causing the breakdown of relationships and fellowship.[224]

THE PAULINE MODEL FOR PERSONAL MORAL PROGRESS

Ephesians 4:22-24 presents what is a distinctive Pauline model of personal Christian, moral development, where a transformative experience of justification must go on to produce both habitual or consistent right conduct, as well as maturing character/integrity; these will lead to consistent spiritual development and growth to fully mature godliness, and in turn will reflect or represent the nature and character of God to his creation – his image (Rom. 6:1-8:17; 2 Cor. 3:18; Gal. 5:13-25, cf. Gen. 1:26-28). Although Paul does not explicitly say all of that in this passage, his references to *putting off the old man*, *putting on the new* man, and being *created in the likeness of God's holiness and righteousness* clearly allude to his overarching apostolic model of God's moral and eschatological purposes for the saints, something he discusses in detail elsewhere in his epistles (τὸν παλαιὸν ἄνθρωπον, τὸν καινὸν ἄνθρωπον) (Rom. 6:1-11; Eph. 4:22-24; Col. 3:9-10). Similar language in Romans, Ephesians and Colossians bears witness to a consistent Pauline theology of moral development and imperatives for believers. It provides a Pauline model for understanding ethical necessity (which is key to Paul's exhortations to the churches) based on progressive moral change initiated justification, but more decisively and deliberately considered, adopted, and applied to character, and conduct by faith or reckoning on the part of the believer (Rom. 6:11; Eph.

---

[224] No one who has served in church, or attended church for any length of time can deny the reality of this assertion.

4:22-24; Col. 3:9-10).[225] Paul signals that believers, though transformed by God as a result of justification (Rom. 6:1-10), are to accept and rigorously apply this moral transformation to their lives by an act of faith or reckoning that embraces what is essentially the crucifixion of the old life, followed by a resurrection to new life with Christ, the putting off of the old self, and a putting on of the new self (Rom. 6:1-11; Eph. 4:22-24; Col. 3:9-10, cf. 2 Cor. 5:17).

This is the Pauline theology of soteriological and eschatological redemption. The two are linked by the impartation of the Spirit at salvation so that God's moral goals for his people are met in those who conduct themselves under the leadership of the Spirit (cf. Rom. 8:1-4, 9, 12-17; Ga. 2:2:20-21; 5:16-25). Also, the impartation of the Spirit, Paul innovates in his theology of redemption, is the link between the eschatological future and the present, the kingdom of God to come, and serving God in the present while we await its arrival. He is the downpayment, possessed in the lives of the saints in the present, that guarantees the future, full eschatological redemption of what already belongs to God through justification and faith (Rom. 5:1-2; Rom. 8:19-27; 2 Cor. 1:20-22; 5:5; Eph. 1:13-14). Through the indwelling Spirit, imparted at morally transformative justification, the saints of God preemptively "taste" future fellowship with God, the power, the glory, and the righteousness of the age to come, in their present walk with God under the leadership of the Spirit, and as they serve him in the church (Rom. 8:23; 2 Cor. 1:22; :5:5, cf. 1 John 1:5-7).

Rather than "salvation" consisting, as it often does, in the contemporary sense of primarily a decision made for Christ, it is rather a thoroughgoing shift in moral and spiritual nature, the inner

---

[225] Cf. Brooks, Scriptural Holiness, 1972, 44-47.

environment of the heart, soul, and mind.[226] It is a cataclysmic shift from operating under the influence and in the environment of kingdom of darkness, to living in the kingdom of light and surrendering to its moral influence and guidance through the Spirit. Those who have gone from death to life, from selfishness to union with Christ, from the old creation to a new creation, whereby the old has decisively gone, and the new, equally decisively come, now live in grace and are set on a trajectory to perfection in holiness (Rom. 5:1-2; 6:1-11; 2 Cor. 5:17; Eph. 4:22-24; 5:8; Col. 1:13; 2:11-12, 13-15; 3:9-10, cf. John 3:3-9; Acts 26:18; John 5:24; I Pet. 2:9-10; 1 John 4:13). But the process that leads to perfection, Paul makes clear, is to be engaged in the present, in our daily lives, in our relationships with one another, and in our decisions and conduct.[227] It is not as Augustine conceived it, largely held over for the future, but as Wesley conceived it from the Pauline model, a matter of moral and spiritual engagement in the present through the Spirit. The result of justification is a *new relationship* with God, where we are at peace with him, and no longer at war (Rom. 5:1-2, 10). Justification initiates a *relationship* with God, in which his grace takes over the inward moral and spiritual environment of our lives (Rom. 5:2, 8:1-4; Gal. 5:16, 18, 24-25), and by implanting a new nature in us (2 Cor. 5:17), as well as a changed mind (ἀνανεοῦσθαι δὲ τῷ πνεύματι τοῦ νοὸς ὑμῶν), we are being renewed daily through moral transformation (Rom. 12:1-2; 2 Cor 3:18; 4:17-18), so that God is actively working in us to produce the holiness and righteousness he desires in his redeemed people.[228]

The new relationship with God, initiated at justification, is empowered going forward by the indwelling Spirit for those who are in Christ Jesus, and walk (conduct themselves) under his leadership (Rom.

---

[226] Brooks, Scriptural Holiness, 1972, 44-47.
[227] Wesley, The Works of John Wesley, 1872, 41.
[228] Holmes, M. W. (2011–2013). *The Greek New Testament: SBL Edition* (Eph 4:23). Lexham Press; Society of Biblical Literature.

8:1-4, 5:17). God imparted the Spirit into our lives and hearts along with the thorough regenerative change taking place in our nature at union with Christ (2 Cor. 5:17).[229] His presence and working in us bring to maturity what God has sown in us at the beginning, righteousness, and holiness (Eph. 4: 13, 24). There are enough allusions in the extant Pauline epistles (though it is not our intention to discuss it all in detail here)[230] for us to conclude that Paul's view of the *new covenant* aligns with God's promises to Israel that he would write his law in their *hearts and minds*, and sprinkling them with clean water to purify them, so that, in conjunction with forgiving their sins and wickedness, he would affect a change in their nature by giving them a new heart and new S(s)pirit (Jer. 31:31-34; Ezek. 36:22-28, cf. John 3:9-10). What Paul saw in connection with redemptive union with Christ (Rom 6:1-11), and the impartation of the Spirit (Rom. 8:1-17), was what God promised his people Israel in fulfillment of Old Testament promises, a moral transformation of their human nature, as well as an impartation of a dynamic moral impetus to finally make possible success in the righteousness demanded by the law (cf. Rom. 7). This is why Paul continually sets the activity of the Spirit up as providing the answer to achieving the righteousness demanded by the law, but which it could not deliver (cf. Rom. 7:7-25).

Even if Paul does not provide here an as exhaustive treatment of his theological construct for living consistently in righteousness and holiness as he does in Romans 6-8, it is because in this context the explication of his soteriology is not his main purpose. He is concerned with the unity of the church grounded in maturing godliness, growing saints in fellowship with one another, supporting and edifying one another, so that they, and the church, are continuing to be built up in

---

[229] Wesley, The Works of John Wesley, 1872, 71-72, 74.

[230] Cf. Evans, Holiness Reconsidered: A Fresh Look at the Wesleyan Doctrine of Sanctification, 2016; Evans, Help For Holiness: Rediscovering God's Resources for Practical Sanctification in Galatians 5:16-25, 2018.

love (Eph. 4:3, 13, 16). By mentioning *putting off the old man,* and *putting on the new man,* Paul alludes to what he had no doubt personally taught in Ephesus and treated thoroughly in his letter to the Romans earlier – written from Corinth, while on his way to Jersualem – before he was arrested, being somewhat newly departed from Ephesus. They had learned about Christ, that they must put off the old man and put on the new. His mention of it here ought to have evoked a memory of his personal teaching on the topic of morality and sanctification. Since his letters were quickly in circulation, and he even encouraged churches distribute them, or exchange and share his letters, it is not inconceivable that the Ephesians were already aware of Paul's more in depth treatment by the time they received this epistle years later, while he was under house arrest in Rome.[231] Indeed, references to *putting off* and *putting on* may well serve as shorthand for his fuller explanation elsewhere, and what he means by *the truth they had learned in Jesus* (Eph. 4:21).

Putting Off and Putting On: Using two infinitives (ἀποθέσθαι), *to put off* the old man and (ἀνανεοῦσθαι) *to put on* the new man as complements to the *learning Christ,* Paul refers to the content of what they were taught in Christ (Eph. 4:20-24). They had learned specifically *to put off the old man,* as a figure representing their attitudes and practices coming out of the old life, rooted in a fallen, and previously unregenerate nature, which must now be thoroughly rejected and abandoned, since in Christ, as a result of union with him, they have been be thoroughly transformed in their nature, through a resurrection to new life (Rom. 6:3-10). These are the ways in which Gentiles now walk, those who do not know of belong to Christ. To conduct oneself that way is to betray the new life that they received through union with Christ when they were justified or saved (Eph. 3:5, 8). They must, rather, put on *the*

---

[231] Edwards, 2011, 6.

new man, through union with Christ in his resurrection, out of which a new life of habitual righteousness must and should flow.

The language of *putting off and putting on* reflects the idea of taking off clothes and laying them down or aside, and includes notions of removing something from one location to another, or getting rid of something by moving it away or putting it aside.[232] Paul's reference to the *old man* or *old self,* is clearly a reference to the habits and controlling inner environment of our nature controlled by what Paul's calls elsewhere *the flesh,* sometimes called the carnal nature in theology. The apostle makes a distinction between the character of human nature ruled by selfishness and personal ambition that leads to sin – an element in our nature that predisposes the unregenerate mind and will to habitual sinning and disobedience to God – and sin as conduct, acts of disobedience (Rom. 8:6-7). The latter requires forgiveness, pardon from God leading to justification, the former requires moral reformation or regeneration, a transformation in our nature, through the action of the Spirit, that produces a new creation (2 Cor. 5:17). Justification, in Pauline soteriology (the theological study of salvation), ***is*** morally transformative. It is not, as some seem to teach, morally neutral or virtually ineffectual. Initial salvation involves union with Christ, a participation, in some way related to the mysterious workings of God through the Spirit (cf. John 3:4-9), in his death and resurrection, so that the old life of habitual sinning controlled by a sinful/carnal nature is crucified, and the new believer is raised to a morally and spiritually changed life in his resurrection (Rom. 6:1-10). It is, as Paul instructs, in the later part of Romans 6, a release from slavery to sin and sinning, in order to become a slave to God and his holiness – a life of habitual righteousness and upright character, maturing into genuine full godliness.

---

[232] Arndt, 2000) 123-124.

Slavery to sin and sinning, that is sin habitually engaged, even for those who have at one time experienced the grace of God, Paul argues, leads to death and separation from God (Rom. 6:15-23). In Romans 5:1-21, he explains that the predisposition to sin and habitual sinning is the result of an inherited defect in human nature that makes us enemies of God (Rom. 5:8), because our will is in conflict with God over morality and his rule in our lives, resisting his attempt at regulating behavior through right character producing right conduct, as a result of a right relationship with him (Rom. 5:1-8; 8:1-15). His own painful story is related in Romans 7, in a highly stylized form, in which he tells of the discovery that his powerlessness to conquer sin and sinning was due to a defect in his nature, which left him feeling like he was tied to a rotting corpse (Rom. 7:7-25). The corpse is his sinful and rebellious nature, impervious to every self-generated attempt at reform (Rom. 7:14-23). No matter how hard he tried he could not overcome the *law of sin and death* at work in his nature that inevitably led him into sin and sinning.

A moral law that produces sin and captivity to sinning was at work in his body, as a result of a defect in his human nature, a condition of dominating carnality, of base tendencies characteristic of human nature apart from God and the rule of God (Rom. 7:21-25). To be successful in righteousness or the holiness God demands, Paul realized, would take a *double cure* as it were, the forgiveness of his sins in order to be reconciled to God, and a transformation of the defect in his nature, in order not to remain a slave to habitual sinning. It is the release that caused his outcry in Romans 7:25, "Thanks be to God, who delivers me through Jesus Christ our Lord!"[233] The victory is found in Christ and in union with Christ, in his death to the old life and carnal nature, to lay it aside, to put it off, and in his resurrection to take up, put on, clothe himself with the new life of righteousness and holiness

---

[233] The New International Version (Ro 7:25). (2011). Zondervan.

through the indwelling power of the Spirit, once the condemnation of living under God's judgment has been lifted, and the tyranny of living under the power of the law of sin and death as a slave to sin and sinning has been finally broken (Rom. 8:1-4).

The Apostle Paul is attempting, by way of illustrative figures of speech, to convey the mysterious[234] workings of God through the Spirit that bring about genuine existential change to the lives of those who come into union with Christ at justification. These changes are not merely forensic or of standing and status with God. They evoke organic changes taking place spiritually and in the nature of those who are reconciled to God by his grace, through faith (Rom. 5:1-2). The implications of changes taking place in the nature of those who are now in union with Christ are that they are participants in his death and resurrection, whereby the old life is put away by death to sin and sinning, and a new life is adopted by resurrection to new life, which is set to pursue righteousness and holiness going forward (Rom. 6, cf. 2 Cor. 5:17; Eph. 4:22-24; Col. 3:9-10).[235] The putting off and putting on language of Paul in other places in his letters has at its core an underlying Pauline view of salvation and justification, in which the old life is laid aside, and a new life of moral character and conduct is taken up as a matter of habitual pursuit, obedience to God, and outward practice.

After Romans 6, Paul sets about in chapters 7 and 8 to establishing the theology of a dynamic power of God through the Spirit, whose indwelling presence empowers the believer to go on to holiness of

---

[234] Jesus himself said to Nicodemus that the workings of the Spirit in regeneration are inexplicable from a material or natural perspective, and are perceived by the results, just as wind is invisible to the eye, but perceptible by its effects.

[235] Who can argue that this is not the basic meaning, tenor, and implication of Paul's reasoning in Romans 6-8?

character following initial union with Christ at justification (cf. Rom. 5:1-8). The moral change taking place initially is followed up with the power of God to support and resource the new life through the Spirit (Rom. 5:2; 8:1-4; Gal. 2:19-21; 5:16, 18, 24-25), so that it might be morally and spiritually successful until it culminates in being conformed to the image of Christ (Rom. 8:29-30, cf. Eph. 4:13). Through moral progress and maturing, and of developing character producing right conduct, involving consistent fellowship with God and surrender to Spirit's leadership in daily life, the process of discipleship moves on to greater and greater godliness (cf. 2 Cor. 3:18; 4:16-18; Gal. 5:16-25). The goal of this is to reproduce the holiness of God in his people, so that they reflect his character (Rom. 6:19; 8:29-20; 12:1-2; 1 Cor. 1:2, 30; 2 Cor. 3:18; 5:17, 21; 7:1; Gal. 2:19-21; Eph. 1:4; 2:21; 5:3, 26-27; Phil. 3:7-11; Col. 1:22; 1 Thess. 3:13; 4:3-4, 7; 2 Tim. 1:9; 2:21, cf. Lev. 11:44-45; 19:2; 20:7, 26; 1 Pet. 1:15-16).[236] More of that later. This, then, is a summary of Pauline theology of salvation, not initial salvation, of justification alone, but of salvation from sins committed, from sinning, from a corrupt human nature, of moral and spiritual development, of consistent right conduct, and of being perfected through maturing godliness, to ultimately reflect the image of God, in true holiness and righteousness back into his creation, as we rule with Christ in the eschaton.

---

[236] This is, after all, an eschatological reestablishing of God original purpose for humanity, to reflect the image and likeness of God back into his creation, in the context of working in partnership with God to rule over it (Gen. 1:26-28). This Jesus has already begun at his ascension as the glorified Son of man, the Second Adam having accomplished what the first Adam failed to do. And he has made provision and is making for provision for redeemed humanity to join him in reigning with him in the coming eschaton, so that God's original purpose will carry forward through Christ and in us, whom he has rescued from sin (John 14:1-3; 1 Cor, 15:20-28; Phil. 2:6-11; Col, 1:15-20).

WHAT'S THE POINT?

So, what is the point of justification, of moral reform, of character change, and development, of pursuing right conduct, of walking under the direction of the Spirit, and of engaging in ongoing fellowship with God? What are God's end-goals for the redemption of humanity, both as individuals and corporately? Is God's final purpose related in some way to his original design? Is there some overarching continuity in how he has worked out his purpose from the beginning in the garden, through Israel, in the incarnation of Christ, his death and resurrection, and in his ascension, where he now sits on the throne sharing it with God his Father as the glorified Son of Man? In light of New Testament teaching and theology, particularly teased out by Paul in his epistles, we conclude that there is certainly a connection between God's original purposes and his eschatological goals, and there is an overarching continuity in how he is working them out in human history, both in the overall sense, and in the redemptive sense of what he has recorded of his activity in history in his Word. A thorough treatment of this topic would far exceed the boundaries of this book, but our current consideration of God end-goals for holiness, righteousness, and the moral development and improvement of his people is an integral component of his eschatological purposes, which is to establish a new creation with human beings taking part, but without sin and the effects of sin (Rev. 21:1-4). Therefore, we will engage in as brief an overview as it is possible to make, and still adequately ground our understanding of God's purposes for establishing holiness and righteousness as character and conduct in his people in the present, and how this relates to his final end-game (cf. Rev. 21:1-4).

Original Sin and Broken Relationships: So far, we have focused on the passage, and its context. Now we zoom out, as it were, to take in more of the eschatological landscape to which it is connected, and to ask how it fits into the flow of God's redemptive activity, which obviously has its origin in the garden, when he clothed Adam and Eve in the skins of a slain animal in response to their disobedience (Gen. 3:21-24). Arguably (for some), the most serious consequence of the first sin was its effect on the relationship between God and the first pair of human beings he had placed in the garden. Regardless of the weight one places on the consequences of what followed in terms of human sufferings, and the catastrophic effects on nature, including increasing sin and wickedness that taxed even the mercy of God to near breaking point (Gen. 6:5-7), the banishment from the garden and from free fellowship with God was the most consequential.[237] It ended the closeness

---

[237] I am fully aware that theologians will argue that the expression in Genesis 6 is anthropomorphic in nature, and that the mercy of an infinite God cannot be *taxed* to "breaking point." However, the writer puts it that way in the text, where *nāḥam* (נָחַם) carries the range of meaning regret, change of mind, grief, relent, repent, avenge, compassion, and offering comfort, apparently leaving it to context to determine the precise meaning (Frederick, 2014, page נָחַם (*nāḥam*; Gesenius, 2003, 544; Brown, 1977, 636; Swanson, 1997) #5714). The point is probably that the mercy of God has been strained against his holiness, and that judgment is bound to ensue on the whole human race if a solution to sin and their persistent rebellion is not found. The ark was a solution of sorts, providing an expression of mercy in the midst of judgment on those who would not repent, and prefigured a more permanent solution in Christ, through the intervening election of Israel as God's vehicle in history to enact and finally achieve his redemptive purpose (Gen. 12:1-3). The curse of the serpent that prophetically points to the demise of Satan through the heel-crushing of the seed of the women, though himself bruised, is programmatic for what took place on the cross with Christ, followed by his resurrection (Gen. 3:15). That the end is anticipated in the beginning, where final judgment falls on God's arch enemy, while he offers redemption and reclamation to the first pair, only confirms what unfolds throughout the history of the Bible, on into the New Testament, and anticipates the future purpose of God in putting right what had so dramatically gone wrong. That Adam and Eve were not immediately restored to full fellowship with God, and in fact were banned from his

between Adam and God, the freedom of their interaction, of their fellowship, and community. It placed an intolerable strain on their relationship, and ultimately on God's relationship with humanity as a whole, until God's judgment on their sin was the only response that might retrain it, and reset, as it were to some degree, its rapid growth and development, with all the consequences that this entailed (ct. Gen. 6).

It will not be until the first epistle of John that a succinct and stunningly clear propositional statement of this is recorded in the Word, though the problem of God's holiness and human wickedness is cited constantly as the impediment of the relationship between God and his people. After the ascension of Christ, and near the end of the first century, and about 60 years of early church history, John states figuratively, and brilliantly, "God is light, in him is no darkness at all!" (ὅτι ὁ θεὸς φῶς ἐστιν καὶ σκοτία ἐν αὐτῷ οὐκ ἔστιν οὐδεμία). [238] In contemporary English idiom, we might say, *God is light, in him is no darkness at all, no way!* In Greek, the double negative, unlike in English, is a reinforcement of the negation. The expression is absolute with regard to the holiness and morality of God. There is no moral defect in his nature or being at all, not even in the extreme or slightest.

This fundamental principle is often held up in the Old Testament, concerning Israel, as the reason for their alienation from God, or grounds for their need for reconciliation to God. Because they had sinned, and because God is holy, he cannot simply ignore or overlook their sin (cf. Lev. 11:44-45). The reason for God's demands that Israel

---

presence in the garden, is programmatic of the redemptive process that will take time to unfold and awaited the precise moment in God's plan when it would offer the most efficacious results (Gal. 4:4-5).

[238] Holmes, M. W. (2011–2013). The Greek New Testament: SBL Edition (1 Jn 1:5). Lexham Press; Society of Biblical Literature.

be holy is that *he is holy*, "Be holy *because* I am holy" (Lev. 11:44-45, et al.). God's holiness is the rationale for requiring redemption, because of the diametric moral disparity between God and man. Without rehearsing all the passages from the Old Testament that illustrate or refer to this, intimacy with God breaks or breakdown between him and his people because of their sin and rebellion against him, because of their failure to surrender to his rule, and where he accuses his people of disobedience, hardhearted wickedness, and stiff-necked stubbornness of attitude and will against him.

In order to set down the terms of their relationship with him, and to draw attention to the problem of sin, God made a covenant with his people, where sin and wickedness is viewed as a breaking of that covenant, and the covenant lays down specified conduct that God will not countenance. The law serves as a concrete way of demonstrating to Israel why they have has lost connection with God, because they have strayed morally from the righteousness God demands from them. Righteousness is not an ethereal moral quality of character that is imperceptible or immeasurable, rather it is quantifiable in terms of practical conduct reflecting genuine love for God inwardly, and so is indicative of authentic godliness, integrity and character. [239] The covenant laid out the terms upon which they may interact with God in fellowship and intimacy as a people, as well as individuals, mainly in connection with ceremonial cleanness for worship and observing the ceremonial law, but also as a matter of interacting in communion with God in their personal relationship with him. Not only were they to behave uprightly in terms of outwardly perceived right conduct, but right

[239] This is why, I am convinced, that John Wesley saw sanctification summed up in love, loving God with all of your heart, mind, strength, and soul, and loving others as yourself. This was a way of seeing righteousness as quantifiably recognized in the life of believers, and so as a representation of their upright character and godliness.

conduct was to be linked to an outflow, a reflection of the more important inner state of uprightness where God alone can see it, of the condition of a heart that genuinely, and sincerely loves him. Since the covenant included the law, as a codification of what morality and obedience looked like, and of what it consisted, right conduct demonstrated not that they had "earned God's favor", but rather that they loved God and were in right relationship with him. The law was not the means to secure God's favor, as much as the means of expression of righteousness that reflected their close relationship with him, as well as their authentic love for him.[240]

Reconciliation and Peace: Sin breaks the connection between God and people, human beings (Gen. 3:8, 23-24; Deut. 32:19; Judg. 10:13; 1 Sam. 8:7; 15:23, 26; 2 Kings 17:20; 2 Chron. 24:20, 24; Job 33:10; Ps. 44:9; 60:1, 10; 78:57-59; 108:11; Isa. 1:4; 54:67; Jer. 2:13; 6:8; 7:29; 12:7; 16:11; 17:13; Lam 3:21-22; Ezek. 8:12; 14:5; Hos. 5:4; 7:10; Matt. 15:8; Rom. 5:8; Col. 1:21).[241] For that reason, the Bible consistently, Old and New Testaments, represents the paramount human need as reconciliation to God, the restoration of the relationship,

---

[240] I am convinced that this what Paul had in mind in Romans 7, when he expresses his discontentment with law-keeping, and realized that his attempts to be a law-keeper only served to underscore that there was a problem in his nature. He found he was not right with God inwardly, and he needed a remedy for a flaw in his nature that could only be addressed by Christ (Rom. 7:21-25). Also, this was the intention, I believe, for the command in the garden to not eat from the tree of the knowledge of good and evil. Not because the tree was anything, but because to obey God demonstrated love for God, and ongoing obedience was a sign of the health the relationship as well as their inner integrity and uprightness in God's sight.

[241] Interestingly, Ezekiel 14:5 and Isaiah 49:14 provide the flipside of sins alienating effect, in that God drove Adam and Eve from his presence in the garden because of sin, but in Isaiah and Ezekiel the people have just as certainly deserted or abandoned God; they have *forsaken him*.

and the reestablishment of fellowship.[242] In the Old Testament the Lord constantly implores his people to repent and return to God (Deut. 30:1-3; 2 Kings 17:13; Neh. 1:8-9; Isa. 1:18-20; Jer. 3:12; 4:1-2; 8:5; 18:11; 23:22; 24:7; 25:5; 26:3; 31:18; 35:15; 36:3; Lam. 3:40; 5:21; Ezek. 18:30-32; Hos. 3:5; 6:1; 12:6; 14:1-2; Joel 2;12; Hag. 2:17; Zech. 1:3-4, 16; 8:3; Mal. 3:7). Reconciliation rather than the destruction of humanity is what God seeks (cf. Isa. 1:18-19; Ezek. 18:30-32; 2 Pet. 3:8-9). In describing himself to Moses, sequestered in the rock as God passes by, the Lord

[242] This is best represented by the formula express in something like these terms, "I will be your God, and you will be my people" (Gen. 17; 7; Ex. 6:7; Lev. 26:12; 1 Sam. 12:22 1Kings 6:13). Sometimes, it is rendered in terms of God dwelling with his people, where the pillar of cloud and fire or the glory over the mercy seat of the ark are considered the tokens of God's presence dwelling among his people, and where the mercy seat becomes part of the throne-room furniture of God reigning over them, his footstool attached, as it were, to the throne in heaven (Ex. 25:22; Num. 7:89; 1 Sam. 4:4; 6:2; 2 Kings 19:15; 1 Chron. 13:6; 28:2; 2 Chron. 5:13-14; Ps. 80:1; Isa. 37:16; 99:1, 5; 132:7; Isa. 66:1; Lam. 2:1; Ezek. 9:3; 10:4, cf. Matt. 5:25; Acts 7:49). The tabernacle was constructed to give God a place to dwell among his people (Ex. 25:8; 29:45-46; Num 5:3; 35:34; 1 Kings 8:13; 2 Chron. 6:2, 18; Ezra 6:12; Ps. 68:18; 85:9; Joel 3:17; Zech 8:3). The Lord even told Moses that he would speak with him from the mercy seat of the ark and would dwell there among his people and walk about their camp (Deut. 23:14). The idea of God dwelling among his people occurs frequently in the earliest days of Israel redemption from Egypt and expresses God's intentional goal for his people to live in his presence and in fellowship with him. This is recapitulated in the prophets as God's eschatological goal for Israel as a result of redemption and reconciliation to God (Isa. 51:16; Jer. 7:23; 11:4; 24:7; 30:22; 31:1; 32:38; Ezek. 11:19-20; Rom. 9:25; Heb. 8:10). Finally, in the context of final redemption and eschatological consummation of all things, John states that God's purpose or end-goal for the new heaven and earth is that he will now be the God of *all of* his redeemed people, both Jews and Gentiles, and they will be his people, now that the new has come and the old has passed away (Rev. 21:1-4, cf. Zech. 2:11; 13:9; 2 Cor. 6:16). This is further expressed in terms of the removal of all that is sinful, wicked, evil and in rebellion against God's rule Rev. 21:5-8).

leads with his mercy and compassion, his grace and willingness to pardon, and not with judgment and wrath, although he declares these to be inevitable for the persistently wicked (Ex. 34:6-7).[243] In other words, how God views himself and describes himself when Moses could not look upon his glory is that he is first of all full of mercy, grace, and compassion, willing to forgive the sinner, and to restore them to himself. How God reveals himself to us is that he is loving and compassionate (John 3:16); it is how he sees himself with respect to his relationship with human beings. The leading edge of God's dealings with humanity is not a desire to bring judgment and destruction on them, but forgiveness and pardon, to bring reconciliation and restoration of fellowship (cf. John 3:17; Rom. 5:1-2). Paul, in particular, highlights this in connection with justification, the action of God by which he declares right with him those who have put their faith in Christ, so that due to his pardon and forgiveness, we now have *peace with God* (Rom. 5:1). That means restoration of relationship, reconciliation to God, where hostilities between us have ceased and fellowship or communion has been established (cf. Rom. 5:6-11).

In Colossians, reconciliation to God, first of humanity, but also of all of creation through Christ, is God's overall goal, so that all things in the end, at the conclusion of God's redemptive activity, will be fully restored

---

[243] This self-revelation of God to Moses entered into the corporate consciousness of Israel, as the character of God, and is often cited or quoted throughout the Old Testament. It is recapitulated in the famous conversation of Jesus with Nicodemus, that God so loved the world that he gave his one and only Son, that whoever believes in him will not perish (especially important that this comes first as in Exodus 34), but have eternal life (John 3:16). Jesus went on to clarify the point, and so reinforce the declaration in Exodus, that God did not send his Son into the world to condemn the world, but rather that the world, human beings, might be saved (John 3:17). Later John renders this revelation propositionally stating in his first epistle as "God is love" (1 John 4:8, 16).

to him in proper and right relationship (Col 1:15-20). That the fall of human beings into sin has precipitated a consequential "fall of creation" under its dominion is tackled by Paul in his enlightening theological treatment in Romans 8. There God is said to have subjected creation to the frustration and suffering of human defection from him (Rom. 8:20, cf. Gen. 3:14-19). But this subjection of creation to the consequential effects of sin on account of human defection is held in tension, Paul says, with the prospect of its final liberation from bondage to decay when the children of God are ultimately liberated from *their* mortality, when they are adopted physically into the resurrection of Jesus with new bodies (Rom. 8:23). Creation will participate in that liberation to immortality alongside the children of God (Rom. 8:21, cf. Rev. 21:1-4).

Colossians 1:15-20 makes clear that this is God's end-goal to liberate all of creation through the redemptive action of Christ, so that all things will come under his authority in the way he originally intended when he commissioned the first Adam to represent him (Gen. 1:26-28). Prior to this, Paul highlights, this program of eschatological restorative reconciliation has *already begun* in those who have been rescued from the kingdom of darkness and brought into the kingdom of light (Col. 1:13). Paul's use of light and darkness is similar to John's where he contrasts the world of sin that binds human beings to evil and wickedness (Eph. 2:1-3), and the kingdom of God that liberates them to holiness and righteousness. Paul clarifies that it is through transformative salvation, which he calls redemption, that we are rescued from the kingdom of darkness and transferred into the king of God and light. This, he asserts, involves the forgiveness of sins, that is the action of God to remedy the moral condition of the human race that stands as an impediment to communion between them and God (Col. 1:14). Rescue or redemption of sinners involves a moral calculation whereby their sins are pardoned by God. However, elsewhere, Paul makes it equally clear that it involves a moral transformation as well, whereby those who are justified become new creations in Christ - the old life has passed away, and everything has become new (2 Cor. 5:17).

It is this idea that stands behind Paul's reasoned argument in Romans 6, that following the exercise of God's grace in justification, those who now belong to Christ *must* forsake the old life of sinning to adopt the new of righteousness and obedience to God (Rom. 6:1-11). The reason for this is that not only have they been reconciled to God, on account of the pardon of their sins, so that they stand justified before him, but because they are now in union with Christ, participating in his death to sin (the influence of old life of sinning as a habitual lifestyle), and his resurrection to new life (the habit of living in obedience to God because of the leading of the Spirit) (Rom. 6:8-11). They have been raised with Christ to a new life, they have become new creations, they are morally and spiritually different people than they were before. For Paul, this is the nature of justification. It is not merely a declaration rightness with God; it is a transformation beginning the process of sanctification and of becoming like God, of being holy because he is holy (cf. 1 Pet. 1:15-16).[244] Salvation for Paul is at the same time pardon for sins, reconciliation to God, the beginning of fellowship with God (through the indwelling Spirit), and a moral transformation that initiates the process that has its goal in producing in them or conforming the saints to the image of Christ, that they might reflect his moral perfection and glory in the new creation that is to come (Rom. 8:29-30; Eph. 4:13, 24, cf. 1 Cor. 13:12; 2 Cor. 3:18; 4:16-18).

The beginning of the Christian life then consists of pardon and reconciliation to God, and involves a restoration of a relationship with him through a recognition of what makes peace with God possible, namely, faith in Christ (Rom. 5:1-2). Although we were alienated from

---

[244] Cf. Brooks, Scriptural Holiness, 1972, 44-47.

God and were his enemies – enemies in our minds (inwardly, dispositionally) and our conduct (sinful conduct, disobedience, rebellion) – we have now been reconciled to him to be ultimately presented to God without blemish and free from accusation – pardoned *and* morally transformed (Col. 1:21-22). The moral component of our alienation, that humanity is morally corrupt, which Paul brings out in Romans 5, cannot be ignored. It is not merely our standing before God that must be addressed, that we are guilty of disobedience and sin, but that our nature is immorally opposed to God, and resistant to his rule on account of a predisposition toward sin and away from righteousness (Rom. 7:21-25). Until our sins are forgiven, and we are morally changed, we cannot be reconciled to God or have fellowship with him. Our enmity against God consists in our rebellious disposition and aversion to him – minds as well as our actions (sins) – and is the result of the corruption of our nature; that is what makes us sinful and wicked (Gen. 6:5-6; Jer. 17:9; Rom. 7:21-25). While sins require pardon, sinfulness requires more than forensic justification. It needs radical moral transformation and reclamation. Paul argues, in Colossians 1:21-22, that God has done both, and in Romans 5:1 that the result is that we now have peace with God and stand in right relationship with him in the environment where his grace operates in our lives to produce and mature moral uprightness through the Spirit (Rom. 5:2).

Reconciliation to God, for Paul, is far more than the moral realignment with God, or a positional change, as it has often been represented in systematic theology, laying down an underdeveloped soteriology. John Wesley was not the first to recognize this of course, but he was the champion of a theology that sought to grapple with the Pauline idea that justification includes meaningful moral transformation, which begins a life of discipleship consisting of the equally meaningful prospect of going on to holiness and righteousness. They may be genuinely engaged, Wesley believed against the prevailing skepticism of his day, by those who profess faith in Christ and to go on to serve him. Moral impotence and thwarted moral development, Wesley argued, is not what scripture intends by its teaching, particularly in the New Testament. We might say that John the Apostle supports Paul's theology of reconciliation and moral transformation that leads to uprightness of character and conduct, when he asserts that moral transformation and integrity are critical to an ongoing relationship with God for those who are born of God (1 John 1:5-7). John argues that to *walk with God* requires that we walk in the light, because God is light. His figure of speech is clear, God is holy, and we cannot live in communion with him if we do not walk in holiness, and certainly not if we are habitually living in sin, or walking in darkness. He even says that the one who is born of God does not *going on sinning* or continues in habitual sinning, where he uses the same word Paul uses in his famous Romans 7 soliloquy for *practicing sin* (πᾶς ὁ γεγεννημένος ἐκ τοῦ θεοῦ ἁμαρτίαν **οὐ ποιεῖ**) (1 John 3:9; 5:4, 18).[245] John is not addressing something else. He is speaking of something that is at the heart of Pauline soteriology, that justification must go on to produce a changed life, with a different moral outcome, supporting altered conduct, and consistent upright behavior as its demonstrable fruit.[246] Paul's concern in Romans 6 runs parallel to John's in his first epistle, that those who are born of God, or in union with Christ, who have been justified through faith, and are reconciled to God, so that they have peace with him, must walk it out in true holiness and righteousness (Rom. 8:1-4; Gal. 2:19-21). In this way, reconciliation to God presuppose the need for consistent

---

[245] Holmes, M. W. (2011–2013). The Greek New Testament: SBL Edition (1 Jn 3:9). Lexham Press; Society of Biblical Literature.

[246] While we do not have time to examine John's first epistle here, it is themed around love as demonstrable fruit of salvation in terms of practical living, both with respect to God and with respect to how we treat and deal with one another in the community of believers. John's theme is not unlike what we have observed Paul addressing in Ephesians.

up-rightness of character and conduct for fellowship with God to survive (cf. Rom. 6:23).[247]

---

[247] I do not intend to revisit here the matter already addressed above in response to the thunderous sound of objections warning that this will lead to works righteousness, or that we are in danger of Pelagianism or semi-Pelagianism. If Paul intends that the righteousness God seeks comes from the operation of the grace in which we stand (Rom. 5:2) as a result of reconciliation to God (Rom. 5:1), and through the power of the Spirit who dwells in us (Gal. 5:16, 24-25), because we live in surrender to God by faith (Gal. 2:19-21), drawing upon his resources for this enterprise (Gal. 5:22-23), then I cannot see how accusations like these are consistent with a Pauline theology of faith from first to last (Rom. 1:17; 9:30; Gal. 3:11, cf. Heb. 10:38), or, as in Galatians, God's grace producing, through the Spirit, the life that goes on to righteousness (Gal. 5:1-25), not by resorting to law, but by adopting the power and leading of the Spirit (Rom. 8:1-4; Gal. 5:16, 24-25).

CHAPTER FOUR

YOUR KINGDOM COME!

For a good while now theologians have recognized that the writers of the New Testament see the advent of Christ's incarnation as the initiation of the kingdom of God in the present age, though without its final full consummation. The idea of the *nearness* of the kingdom of God can be paradigmatically seen in Mark 1, where its imminence in the preaching of John the Baptist, and then of Jesus, are introduced at the outset of his gospel, in a section that serves as a prologue similar to John's gospel (Mark 1:1-15). John the Baptist offered himself as the voice of one *crying in the wilderness* for God's people to make preparation for the imminent arrival of the kingdom of God, and John's ministry was seen by Jesus, and the church, as a fulfillment of the promise that *temporally* Elijah would precede the coming of the Messiah/LORD to get things ready for his arrival (Mark 1:1-6, cf. Matt. 3:1-6; 11:7-15; 17:10-13; Luke 1:14-17, cf. Mal. 3:1; 4:5-6). Mark, and Matthew make the connection to John the Baptist's fulfilling the prophecy about Elijah coming as the messenger ahead of the arrival of the LORD, by describing, in one of the few biblical descriptions of the physical features and dress of a character, that he wore a camel's hair garment, secured around his waist with a leather belt, and he ate locusts and wild honey, just as Elijah is described to have clothed himself (Matt. 4:4-5; Mark 1:6, cf. 2 Kings 1:8). The gospel writers present the ministry of John the Baptist, baptizing people for repentance and faith, as preparation for the imminent arrival of the kingdom of God at the appearing of the Messiah, so that the appearance of the Messiah is the signal that the kingdom of God had finally come.[248]

THE START OF SOMETHING BIG!

As an integral part of his preaching, John insisted that there was *one coming **after** him*, whose sandal-thongs he was not worthy to stoop down to loose, and that although in the present he baptized them with water, the one coming ***after*** him, implied in the near future, would baptize them in the Holy Spirit (Mark. 1:7, cf. Matt 3:11; Luke 3:16; Acts 1:4-5). The kingdom of God is near (imminent), John insisted (Matt. 3:1). When interrogated by the religious leaders, John asserted that he did not see himself as the Messiah, but as a voice crying out in the wilderness, seeking to prepare the way for his appearing (John 1:19-28, cf. Luke

---

[248] Confirming this analysis is the momentary period of misgiving John experienced while in prison, when he sent disciples to Jesus to have him confirm that he was indeed the Messiah, the one they expected (Matt. 11:1-3). Jesus did not act like the Messiah, in the sense he was not engaged in doing the things that it was popularly thought the Messiah might do, principally making war on Rome and establishing Israel's kingdom (cf. Acts 1:4-8). Israel was looking for a new Maccabean uprising led by God's champion. Jesus' answer was to have John's disciples witness to John about evidences they saw of the kingdom of God breaking in upon the world in fulfillment of what Isaiah prophesied in chapter 61. And then he said that those who were not offended by his "methods" and strategy for bringing about the kingdom of God would be blessed (Matt. 11:1-6). Jesus then confirmed to those around him that John was indeed the Elijah-figure promised in Malachi, who would come ahead of the imminent arrival of the kingdom of God to prepare God's people for the appearing of the LORD as king (Matt. 11:7-15). In this way, Jesus reinforced John's original impression, by confirming that John had been right about him (John 1:29-36), while also, in his characteristic approach to revealing his identity, indirectly confirming that he really was the Messiah, demonstrated by his actions, preaching, and miracles, and that this also signified that the kingdom of God had in fact come, just as Isaiah predicted (Isa. 61:1-6).

3:15). He did not see himself as the reincarnation of Elijah, when asked (John 1:21). But his role was clearly to fulfill the prophecy of "Elijah's" reappearing immediately prior to coming of the Messiah, as Malachi predicted it (Mal. 3:1; 4:5-6).

John's favorite self-identification was with Isaiah's voice crying in the wilderness (in the desert place where he baptized), and that it was time to *prepare the way* for the coming of the Lord, which he set forth as the need to repent and turn back to God (John 1:26-27). Two prophetic streams conjoin in his person and ministry, and they come to a climax when John recognizes Jesus as Messiah at his baptism, because he saw the Holy Spirit come to rest on him bodily in the form of a dove, and heard the voice of God affirming that Jesus is "...***my*** beloved Son...", and that he was pleased with him (John 1:32-34). This led to an equally dramatic moment, when John, seeing Jesus crest the Judean hills, coming near to where he was baptizing in the Jordan, cried out, "Behold the Lamb of God that takes away the sins of the world!" (John 1:29, 36). John admits that he recognized Jesus in this way because of a revelation from God that he would know the identity of the Messiah when the Spirit came down and rested on him (John 1:32-34). John, then, self-consciously stood temporally prior to the arrival of Jesus, and the inauguration of his ministry at his baptism, proclaiming the imminence of his arrival and, just as importantly, the kingdom of God, when God would bestow his Spirit on his people (cf. Matt. 3:11; Mark 1:8; Luke 3:15-16). John said, while he baptized in water, that the one coming after him would baptize them in the Holy Spirit, signifying that he realized that with Jesus' appearing the kingdom of God had also come, just as God had promised it would, with an outpouring of the Spirit on all his people (John 1:33-34, cf. Matt. 3:11; Mark 1:7-8; Luke 4:15-16; Acts 1:5, also cf. Num. 11:29; Isa. **32:15;** 32:1-29; 44:3; 59:21; 63:11, 14; **Ezek. 36:27**; **37:14; 39:29; Joel 2:28-29**; Hag. 2:5; Zech 6:8).

It is Luke who really develops the theological implications of John's statements about Jesus coming after John the Baptist, that he would baptize his disciples with the Spirit at Pentecost (Acts 1:4-5, 8; 2:1-4, 16-21, 38-39; 19:1-6). Nevertheless, Mark, no less than Luke, presents John's teaching in light of what was going on in the first century church at about the time he was writing his gospel. Roger Strontad's observations, in his *The Charismatic Theology of Saint Luke,* thoroughly explores Luke's historical-theology of the Holy Spirit as a main theme in Luke-Acts.[249] In it, he traces Luke's recognition of a breaking into the world and present age of the Holy Spirit at the birth of Jesus, where the characters of the narrative are filled with the Spirit, and speak out under his inspiration, something he calls prophetic speech, a pattern that carries over from the Old Testament, where those filled with the Spirit almost inevitably speak prophetically under his anointing (cf. Num. 11:24-29; Sam. 10:5-7, 9-13).[250] The idea that the Holy Spirit would come upon all of God people, and that they would become "prophets" was first articulated by Moses in Numbers 11:29, Stronstad observes. But a similar idea, that in connection with the future kingdom of Israel and of God, God would pour out his Spirit on his people universally is articulated again in Isaiah, Ezekiel, and by others, particularly in Joel (Isa. 11:2; 35:15; 42:1; 44:3; 59:21; 61:1; Ezek. 36:27; 37:14; 39:29; Joel 2:28-29). These writers associate the universal outpouring of the Spirit with the coming of the Day of the Lord, and the consummation of God's end-time purposes – that is with the *coming of YAHWEH to his people* – and its arrival is to be marked by an outburst of prophetic activity inspired by the Spirit among God 's people generally (Isa. 37:32; 59:20; Jer. 29:10; 31:2; Hos. 6:3; Hag. 2:7; Zech. 14:5; Mal. 3:1).

---

[249] Stronstad, 1984.

[250] Stronstad, 1984, 13-20, 36-39, 42-46, 79-80.

Luke, Stronstad also observes, sees the infilling or baptizing in the Spirit as vocational, so that his coming upon people equips them for serving God with supernatural power in the present – to accomplish impossible things for God (cf. Judg. 3:10; 6:34; 11:29; 13:25; 14:6, 19; 15:14; Sam. 10:5-7, 9-13; 11:6).[251] When it came to finding language to explain what was happening in the early church with respect to the Holy Spirit at Pentecost and afterwards, Luke found what he needed to look no further than the Old Testament, where the elders of Israel, Sampson, Saul, David, and others were filled with the Spirit, spoke prophetically, and were empowered to act supernaturally in situations beyond their natural ability. In this way, Luke demonstrates the theological significance of the Holy Spirit's breaking in as indicating that with the arrival of Christ, the kingdom of God was no longer temporally remote, but had come spatially, even if not yet in its fullest expression. It was now, but not yet.

The Holy Spirit brought the kingdom of God to bear on the current age for the sake of God's redemptive purpose, Luke demonstrates, and he is probably influenced by Paul's theology and teaching, where the Holy Spirit is the *deposit* in the current age of the fulfillment of God promises for the final consummation and realization of the kingdom at Christ's return. More about Paul's view later. What we need to see here is the tension between the coming of the Spirit as a signal of the arrival of the kingdom of God at the end of time, in the present age and world, against its final realization or consummation held over for the future at Christ's return. This is why Jesus said that his disciples would receive power when the Spirit came upon them, and would become his witnesses, ultimately to the ends of the earth, because through the Spirit the gospel and the kingdom of God are brought to bear on humanity in the present age – and in his own words, the gates of hell will

---

[251] Stronstad, 1984, 63-70, 82-83,

not prevail against his church (Matt. 16:18, cf. Act 2 1:4-8). Jesus portrays the kingdom of God as advancing on the kingdom of darkness in the present age and putting irresistible pressure on it until it collapses with his return in glory (cf. Col. 1:13).

At the same time, Mark presents the arrival of Jesus proclaiming the same message as John, "The time has come, repent and believe the good news, because the kingdom of God has come near you" (Mark 1:15). If we miss the critical Markan elements of Jesus' reported proclamation, then we miss the most critical part of Mark's opening, that Jesus himself declared that the time for the kingdom's arrival had come at that moment temporally, that the kingdom's arrival is *no longer future,* the time of fulfillment had come (Πεπλήρωται ὁ καιρὸς). Jesus literally declared that the time for the kingdom's arrival had come at that moment, alluding to the promises made by God in the Old Testament through the prophets, so that the coming of the LORD and his kingdom is in the process of fulfillment before their very eyes! His arrival was not just another prophetic visitation, as the people later speculated prior to his crucifixion (Matt. 21:10-11), but the coming of the messianic king promised to David to sit on his throne, and to rule over God's kingdom in his behalf forever as his representative (2 Sam. 7:8-16; Ps. 2:1-12; 110:1; Isa. 7:14; 9:6-1; 11:1-16; 42:1-9; 61:1-11; Dan. 7:13-14; Zech. 12:10; 14:1-9, cf. Matt. 22:4; 26:64; Mark 12:36; 14:62; 16:19; Luke 20:42; 26:69; John 14:1-3; Acts 2:33-34; 5:31; 7:55-56; Rom. 8:34; 1 Cor. 15:20-28; Eph. 1:20; Phil. 2:8-11; Col. 3:1; Heb. 1:3, 13; 8:1; 10:12; 12:2; 1 Pet. 3:21-22; Rev. 5:5-7). Whereas John the Baptist looked forward to a time when the kingdom would *soon* break through, Jesus proclaimed that *it had broken through into the world with his arrival*, and particularly with the inauguration of his ministry. With Jesus, the kingdom of God was *spatially near* (Mark 1:14-15; Luke 4:21). Jesus' message was that in his presence, the kingdom of God was spatially proximate, and available to all who would repent and believe, or needed healing and deliverance from oppression. It was, according to John's gospel in particular, accessible through a personal relationship with God through him (John 1:14-18; 14:6-9; 17:1-3, 6-8; 20:30-31).

In some way, we might view Jesus' propensity for touching people or being touched by people for healing, as symbolic of the spatial nearness of the kingdom of God, and how its arrival and power could fundamentally change the ordinary lives of the people of Judea and Galilee in the present. Also, its arrival has changed our lives too, who believe in Christ, and belong to him, becoming his disciples. Where *we live,* through the power of the Spirit in the church and in us, we are Christ's body, the church, representing the continued presence of Christ in this age, bearing the power and mission of the kingdom to lost humanity as he once did (cf. Acts 1:1, 8). This is why the church is called to touch the lives of people inside and outside the church in concrete and practical ways through service. Luke describes how this worked in the early church in Acts, and Paul's epistles call on the saints to serve one another with true humility and concern for the welfare of others, because that above all things represents the power of the kingdom of God pushing back against the power of darkness in this age, rescuing lost people from slavery to sin, and alienation from God (Rom. 12:3-8-9; 13-14, 16-18; 13:8-10; 2 Cor. 8:14; 9:12-15; Gal. 5:13; Eph. 4:28-29; Phil. 2:1-5, 25; 4:10-19; 1 Tim. 5:3-5; Tit 3:14; cf. Acts 1:8; 2:42-47; 4:32-37; 6:1-7).

Pauline Theology of Overlapping Worlds: The confluence of the divine and human natures in the Messiah, clearly set out in passages like John 1:1-3; Romans 1:1-3; Philippians 2:6-11; Colossians 1:15-20; Hebrews 1:1-4, and so on, is captured by John's description of the incarnation of the Word, who is fully God, but who *dwelt* or *tabernacled* among us as a human being (John 1:14). The incarnation of the Word somehow brought God into the world, perfectly revealed, and capable of close and personal interaction with human beings in a material cosmos (John 1:1-3, 14-8; John 14:9, Gen. 3:8).[252] Paul, in his letters, brings out the same truth as gospel dogma, that Jesus was fully God before his incarnation, but laid aside the free exercise of his divine prerogatives to become a human being and a servant of humanity, particularly through his death on the cross (Phil. 2:6-8). In him, that is in his humanity, the fullness of the divine nature and essence of God dwelled bodily, Paul said (Col. 1:15-20). In the earthy body and humanity of Jesus, the full-blown deity of God nonetheless dwelled and lived in mystical union with his humanity (cf. Gen. 3:15; 2 Sam. 7:11-16, 18-19, 27-29; Ps. 2:6-7; Isa. 7:14; 9:6-7; 11:1-3; 42:1-4; 52:13-53:12; 61:1-3; Dan. 7:13-14; Matt. 1:16; 18, 20-21; 22-23; 3:17; 17:5; Mark 1:11; 9:7; Luke 1:30-33, 34-35, 39-45; 2:8-12, 15-20; 3:22; 4:14-21; 9:35; John 1:1-3, 14-18; 3:13; 5:17-19, 36; 6:57; 8:16, 28, 54; 10:15, 30, 38; 12:28, 49-50; 14:6, 9-11, 20-21, 31; 16:15, 28; 17:1-3, 5, 21, 24-25). Jesus was, as far as his earthly nature was concerned, from the lineage and family line of David, the fulfillment of all that God promised concerning David's future kingdom (Rom. 1:2-3, cf. 2 Sam. 7:1-17). But as far as his *fuller* nature was concerned, he was declared and demonstrated to actually and also be the Son of God, and fully divine, when the Holy Spirit raised him from the dead (Rom. 1:3-4).

These are ideas Paul obviously had revealed to him by the Holy Spirit during the time between his conversion and his involvement in the church at Antioch, and to which he refers in Galatians (Gal. 1:11-2:10). Paul's understanding came about because of *revelation* from *Jesus Christ,* but also out of his Old Testament background, no doubt, so that by the help of the Spirit, he processed the messianic passages against the story of Jesus' life, ministry, death, and resurrection (Ga. 1:11-12). His growing discomfort, to which Jesus referred on the Damascus Road

---

[252] In a sense reminiscent of God's fellowship with Adam in the garden, only better (Gen. 3:8).

at his conversion as kicking against the goads, may even be an opaque reference to a growing conviction in Paul's mind and heart concerning Christ in light of his persecution of Christians, and as a result of a tugging at his conscience (Acts 26:14).

Paul's aversion to the disciples of Christ was almost pathological, and Luke describes him as "breathing out murderous threats against the disciples of the Lord" (Ὁ δὲ Σαῦλος ἔτι ἐμπνέων ἀπειλῆς καὶ φόνου εἰς τοὺς μαθητὰς τοῦ κυρίου...) (Acts 9:1).[253] Paul describes himself as putting many Christians in prison, opposing them in their trials, and affirming his hatred at their executions (Acts 26:9-10). He obsessively hunted them down from synagogue to synagogue, trying to stamp out the church, and to eradicate belief in Christ altogether (Acts 26:11). But his conscience was already being assaulted by God, it seems, because of conviction by the Spirit no doubt, making him uncomfortable even while he was persecuting the church (Acts 26:14). Paul's pre-conversion personal spiritual struggles are described vividly in Romans 7, where he is in mental and spiritual agony over not being able to achieve, by law-keeping (including his fanaticism), the righteousness he desired, and which he believed God required. That Christians claimed to have found acceptance with God through Christ, something he could not achieve, must have galled him greatly prior to his conversion. On occasions, even after his long service in the gospel, Paul mentions his prior persecution of the church, in which we still see hints of discomfort and an unsettled spirit over how he had previously treated the disciples of Christ (Acts 22:1-21; 26:14; 1 Cor. 15:8-10; Gal. 1:13-15; Phil. 3:6-11). Even before he changed, something was stirring in him; he was already evaluating his own experience and was dissatisfied with it. So, Paul had come to his conclusions about Christ as a result of a dramatic

[253] Holmes, M. W. (2011–2013). The Greek New Testament: SBL Edition (Ac 9:1). Lexham Press; Society of Biblical Literature.

turnaround of his heart and mind, and an equally radical transformation in his thinking, as a result of reconciliation to God (cf. Rom. 5:1-2).

In any case, there is no doubt that Paul was aware of the gospel traditions concerning Jesus' birth, baptism, the miracles, his claims, and about his resurrection, even before the Damascus Road experience. After his conversion, he left out for Arabia and did not immediately consult the apostles in Jersualem (Gal. 1:17). We can surmise that he wanted to work things out for himself, and that this is what he refers to when he says that his gospel was revealed to him by Jesus (Gal. 1:12). It is not too much of a stretch to think that that Paul needed to process what he knew about Jesus through his knowledge of the scriptures, in order to be thoroughly convinced of the authenticity of his claims, and the claims of the church, that he was the Messiah. He added to his conversion a vision as the foundation in scripture that would support his convictions, and allow him to develop his theology thoroughly under the inspiration of the Spirit (2 Tim. 2:15; 3:14-15, 16-17). Paul's investigation and conviction became the unshakable and ever-present foundation of his preaching and writing about Christ and the kingdom of God, using both direct quotations, but even more prolifically, allusions to the scriptures pregnant with theology and eschatological significance. When he did go up to Jerusalem to see Peter personally and to talk with him, he later met privately (κατ' ἰδίαν) with the other leaders and James. He did so, according to his own confession, by revelation (κατὰ ἀποκάλυψιν) (urging of God) to make sure that he was preaching the gospel accurately (μή πως εἰς κενὸν τρέχω ἢ ἔδραμον), and by laying down before the apostles and leaders of repute (δὲ τοῖς δοκοῦσιν) in the church at Jerusalem his theology and preaching (καὶ ἀνεθέμην αὐτοῖς τὸ εὐαγγέλιον ὃ κηρύσσω ἐν τοῖς ἔθνεσιν) (Gal. 1:18; 2:1-2).[254]

The result was the church leaders verified and confirmed that Paul was indeed accurately preaching the gospel to the Gentiles, and that it reflected the same gospel being preached to the Jews in Judea (Gal. 2:6-10).[255] The issue had arisen because of Judaizers sowing doubt concerning the issue of circumcision in the Gentiles churches belonging to Paul (Gal. 2:3-5). He and Peter no doubt talked about the life and ministry of Jesus, his death and resurrection, and testified to their own post-resurrection encounters with him, Peter soon afterward, and Paul more remotely on the Damascus road (1 Cor. 15:1-8).[256] It is likely that they spoke of Jesus ascension, and his assumption of the throne at the right hand of God, which was by then an established doctrinal tradition

---

[254] Holmes, M. W. (2011–2013). The Greek New Testament: SBL Edition (Ga 2:2). Lexham Press; Society of Biblical Literature.

[255] It is of critical importance for moderns to know that in the view of the church in Jersualem, Paul was preaching the same gospel and teaching an accepted and endorsed dogma concerning Christ. The much later academic assertions that Paul highjacked early church theology does not comport with the New Testament. This is true, despite two things developing later on, that, as James observed, Christians in Jersualem found a new appreciation for their roots in Judaism, and as Peter observes about Paul's epistles, Paul develops his theology in light of the Old Testament more thoroughly than any of the other apostles. Luke is the only other New Testament writer who so thoroughly grounds his historical observations and theological ideas in the Old Testament. Paul provides what is the most complete exposition of the theological implications, connections, and understanding of Jesus life and ministry, his death and resurrection as it relates to the Old Testament, and particularly to God's redemptive and eschatological purposes and outworkings for humanity, and a new creation.

[256] Paul displays, in what is an old church "creed", a close knowledge of Jesus' post-resurrection appearances, to which he appends his own testimony of an encounter with the risen Christ.

in the early church (cf. 1 Cor. 15:1-8; Phil. 2:6-11),[257] even before Paul's conversion (cf. Acts 2:22-24, 32-36; 3:17-23, 4:8-12; 5:29-32; 7:55-56). In his teaching and epistles, Paul fully endorses the orthodox ideas current in the first century church coming out of Jesus teaching and ministry, and applies his unique awareness of how Old Testament scriptures are fulfilled in the new covenant gospel tradition (Mark 16:19; Luke 22:69; Acts 2:33-34; 7:55-56, cf. Rom. 8:34; 1 Cor. 15:20-28; Eph. 1:20; Phil. 2:8-11; Col. 3:1; 2 Thess. 2:1-12).

Paul is the one who more thoroughly and systematically makes the theological link between the prophetic tradition in the Old Testament concerning the Messiah, and the narrative of Jesus appearing, death and resurrection, followed by his ascension to the throne to share it with God his Father (cf. Matt. 19;28; 26:64; Mark 14:62; 16:19; Luke 22:69; John 1:51; 3:13; 6:62; Acts 2:33; 7:55-56; Rom. 8:34; Col. 3:1; Heb. 1:13; 10:12; 12:2). Peter endorsed Paul's epistles, admitting they contain things hard to understand, and which false teachers twisted like they do *the rest of scripture* (ὡς καὶ τὰς λοιπὰς γραφὰς) (i.e., the Old Testament) (1 Pet. 3:15-16, cf. 2 Pet. 1:20-21). Peter's statement, *the rest of the scriptures,* is astonishing for a Jew like him to make. He would not have asserted it lightly, since his phrasing clearly puts Paul's epistles into the scriptural tradition of inspired writings from God, and which Peter attributes, in chapter 1, to the inspirational breath of the Holy Spirit carrying the writer along (1 Pet. 1:21-22). His comment is a not-so-subtle assertion that the writings of Paul were to be considered authoritative for the church and believers, on a par with the Hebrew scriptures (2 Pet. 3:16). Peter, a lot later than their earlier conference, is still endorsing Paul's gospel and theology in the highest terms.

---

[257] Thought to be earliest known creed of the first century church, and an early church hymn, likely to have preceded Paul's conversion.

Paul went on to develop his theology of the kingdom of God breaking in with the appearing of Christ, and in particular with the outpouring of the Spirit on God's people, as God's preemptive deposit of the future, fully-realized kingdom of God, bestowed to indwell the lives of the saints in the present (Eph. 1:13-14; 4:30; 2 Cor. 1:20-22; 5:5). In a passage early in his epistle to the Ephesians, speaking of believers sealed with the "deposit" of the Spirit against their final and full redemption in the eschaton, Paul said that we should expect to experience in our lives, in the present, the exercise of the same power of God that not only raised Jesus from the dead, but exalted him far above all things, and that placed all things under his feet (Eph. 1:18-23, cf. Matt. 28:18). Paul is alluding to Jesus' enthronement as the glorified Son of Man, whom he calls the Second Adam in his treatment of the same topic in 1 Corinthians 15, and who now rules in heaven as he prepares the kingdom to turn over to God (1 Cor. 15:20-28, cf. John 14:1-3). He has been exalted above every principality and power in heaven, earth, under the earth in Philippians 2 (Phil. 2:8-11). In other words, Paul was promising, for those sealed with the Spirit, for whom the guarantee of God's final, future redemption is vouched safe by their possession of the Spirit, that they can expect, in their present lives, to experience the provision and power of the risen and reigning Christ to be expressed and manifested in them (Eph. 1:18-19).

For Paul, two worlds and two ages have collided in the glorified Christ, who has risen victoriously from the dead, and ascended to assume his place on the throne at the right hand of God. The future kingdom of God is already at work through the Spirit in the church in the present age, following the pattern of Jesus own ministry, and is being supervised by the reigning Christ as he advances God's final end-plan or purpose, until the glorified Son of Man is ready to present the entire kingdom to God so that he will be all in all (1 Cor. 15:20-28). Jesus will do, as the Second Adam through his flawless obedience, what the first Adam failed to do because of his disobedience. He has taken dominion over what God entrusted to him, to administer it is partnership with God, by representing him in his likeness and image, until it is time for him to offer it up to God as the supreme ruler over all of creation (1 Cor. 15:25-28, cf. Gen. 1:26-28). There is, then, an overlapping, a coincidence of the material and present age with the coming of the final, but in some sense still future, realization of the kingdom of God. Through the Spirit, the power of God and God's rule is already at work through his people in the church, so that God is bringing about through them his redemptive purposes by preaching the gospel, while anticipating Christ's return (cf. Acts 1:1, 4-8, 11; Eph. 1:15-22). Jesus has already dispensed the Holy Spirit to the church for believers, as promised in the Old Testament, and now the power of the coming kingdom is at work in them in the present, preemptively enacting the rule of God and his kingdom among those who belong to him in the church.

FINAL REDEMPTION HELD IN TENSION

Paul believed that the appearing of the kingdom of God in the present age, through the arrival of Jesus' ministry and now the power of Spirit at work in the church, is available as a personal redemptive experience for those who believe in Christ. By this, Paul meant that God has made provision for entry into the kingdom of God by an exercise of faith, as a result of justification for those who believe (Δικαιωθέντες οὖν ἐκ πίστεως) (Rom. 5:1).[258] This justification is reconciliation to God, that is peace with God through Jesus Christ our Lord (εἰρήνην ἔχομεν πρὸς τὸν θεὸν διὰ τοῦ κυρίου ἡμῶν Ἰησοῦ Χριστοῦ). It is a reestablishment of the relationship lost in garden, something that positioned humanity, Paul says, as enemies of God (Rom. 5:8, 10). Through Jesus, and by the exercise of faith, that enmity is ended, and there is peace with God, or

[258] Holmes, M. W. (2011–2013). The Greek New Testament: SBL Edition (Ro 5:1). Lexham Press; Society of Biblical Literature.

as John puts it, fellowship with him (cf. 1 John 1:5-7). Those who now belong to God, also have access by faith to God's grace to undergird and support their ongoing fellowship and relationship with him (Rom. 5:2). Indeed, locatively, they stand in a different environment than before, that is, in God's grace-environment, where his action and activity in them and through them supports their moral and spiritual growth toward mature godliness – the kind Paul speaks of elsewhere as the stature of the fullness of Christ (Eph. 4:13), as the inward man being renewed (2 Cor. 4:16-18), going from glory to glory (2 Cor. 3:18), or being conformed to the image of Christ (Rom. 8:29-30). This spiritual and moral relocation from an environment of sin, and the control of the flesh producing sin, represents a genuine and authentic moral and spiritual change, the kind Jesus called being born again, and Paul calls becoming a new creation in Christ, so that old has gone and the new has come (2 Cor. 5:17).

Elsewhere, Paul speaks of this new state of affairs as being *in Christ,* or as a deliverance out of the dominion of darkness (ὃς ἐρρύσατο ἡμᾶς ἐκ τῆς ἐξουσίας τοῦ σκότους), and a transfer into the kingdom of the Son God loves, or his beloved Son (τοῦ υἱοῦ τῆς ἀγάπης αὐτοῦ) (Col. 1:13).[259] His explanatory remark that follows this wonderful declaration is that it is in him we have this redemption, and that this redemption involves the forgiveness of sins (Col. 1:14). Salvation through pardon of sins ***is*** God's rescue (ἐρρύσατο) from the authority of darkness, which means the domain where darkness rules and controls the environment and outcomes. It is a euphemism for the kingdom of Satan, the prince of the power of the air, the ruler of this world's darkness, the spirit who is even now working in those who are disobedient, God's enemy, who exercises control and influence over all who do not surrender to God and his rule (Eph. 2:1-2; 6:12). It is the realm where sin and sinning take precedence.

---

[259] Holmes, M. W. (2011–2013). The Greek New Testament: SBL Edition (Col 1:13). Lexham Press; Society of Biblical Literature.

Nevertheless, God rescuing us from the controlling authority of darkness is not the full extent of Paul's assertion. It is not a net-negative, a rescue away from, but a positive moral and spiritual transfer (placement) of nature and heart into the new environment of the kingdom of his beloved Son for those who turn to God (μετέστησεν εἰς τὴν βασιλείαν τοῦ υἱοῦ τῆς ἀγάπης αὐτοῦ) (cf. Jer. 31:31-34; Ezek. 36:27; Rom. 12:1-2).[260] Typical for the Pauline theology of redemption, there is not merely a net subtraction, a crucifixion of the old life with Christ, nor the mere forgiveness of sins, there is the net positive of justification, or being made right with God, along with a moral change that is aligned with a change of environments, so that the old life is put away in order for a new life of righteousness to begin and flourish (Rom. 6:3-11; 2 Cor. 5:17). In Romans 6, Paul explores this in detail as a crucifixion with Christ of the old life, and resurrection to new life, which the believer must fully embrace as the new way of living going forward, and that ought to be counted on (reckoned on - ὑμεῖς λογίζεσθε) to deliver the goods with respect to the righteousness God is looking for from his people (Rom. 6:1-11).[261]

A new environment of grace implies a new controlling moral principle for a new way of life, in which those who belong to Christ, who are in Christ, are no longer slaves to sin but to God, and to righteousness (Rom. 6:12-23). The notion that we are in Christ corresponds to what Paul describes elsewhere as *standing in grace or* having been *rescued from the authority of darkness, and transferred into the kingdom of his*

---

[260] Holmes, M. W. (2011–2013). The Greek New Testament: SBL Edition (Col 1:13). Lexham Press; Society of Biblical Literature; (Arndt, 2000), 625. (Harris M. J., 2012), 31.

[261] That after all is Paul's point in Romans 7, with his semi-autobiographical analogy of Jewish law-keeping. He contrasted the moral and spiritual fruitlessness of law-keeping, with the moral and spiritual fruitfulness of new life in Christ animated and controlled by the Spirit.

beloved Son (Rom. 5:2; Col. 1:13). In this way, Paul uses locative language as a description of the magnitude of moral and spiritual change that has taken place at justification (when the redeemed are forgiven of their sins), so that there is an extraction from the realm where the authority of darkness controls a person's life and conduct, and a transfer to an environment of God's grace, the realm of the rule of his Son, as the king over God's kingdom (Col. 1:13), where the control and outcomes are now determined by their relationship to God through the Spirit (Rom. 8:1-4; Gal. 5:15-25). In Romans 8 and Galatians 5, Paul develops this line of thought in terms of the indwelling Spirit. If followed and obeyed, they will no longer live under the tyranny of the flesh, and its passion, but rather produce the righteousness that God is looking for in his people, leading to the fruit of the Spirit, attributes characteristic of maturing godly character (Rom. 5:3-7; 8:1-4; Gal. 5:16-25).

Consistently, Paul points to new moral outcomes coming from significant moral changes taking place in those who now belong to Christ, because their lives are no longer aligned to the flesh and the spirit of this age, or controlled by the spirit that controls those who live in disobedience to God (Eph. 2:1-2). This realignment is spiritual and moral relocation to the sphere of God's kingdom, where he rules, and where his gracious provision operates to give his people moral and spiritual traction, even if they still live physically in the present age and a world of materialism and rebellion against him. What that means in a practical sense is that there will be a change in outcomes, of conduct, of fruit, of character development, and increasing integrity for those who walk in alignment with God by exercising faith in him, and who follow the leading of his Spirit (Titus 2:12-15). When those who are justified by faith are set at peace with God, it is not a momentary ceasefire, a past experience of temporal reconciliation, but the beginning of an ongoing relationship, in which we are no longer slaves to sin, to the old life, or to the spirit of this age. Rather we have become slaves of God as a result of morally transformative justification, of righteousness, and of his rule through the Spirit dwelling in us. It means that to that if we suffer and endure through patience, character and godliness are formed in us, which in turn give rise to hope of final consummation the process that forms Christ in us at the imminent return of Christ (Rom. 5:3-5).

Present Character Development Gives Rise to Hope for Final Godliness: For Paul, present character development, with deepening integrity, leading to maturing godliness, also give rise to hope (Rom. 5:4). Hope is the quality of Christian confidence that does not make us ashamed to live godly lives (Rom. 5:5), because it looks forward to the ultimate realization of God's purpose for our spiritual and moral growth, which is God's plan for us to reach the full measure of the stature of Christ, and for us to be conformed to the image of his Son (Rom. 8:29-30; Eph. 1:13). In Romans 5 and 8, Paul shows that God has in mind the final goal of producing the image of Christ in us, morally and spiritually, in order to reestablish his original purpose for humanity in the *imago Dei* (Gen. 1:26-28), and by making us representatives of and partners with God in reigning over his new creation (Matt. 19:28; Rom. 8:17; 1 Cor. 4:8; Eph. 1:18; 2 Tim. 2:12; Rev. 5:10; 20:6; 22:3-5). This is the end-goal of the process of redemptive transformation and moral development beginning at justification, and of the forgiveness of sins in the present. At the same time, God's ultimate purpose for humanity, full and final godliness that represents and reflects his own, is commensurate with the renewed conditions he will establish in a new heaven and a new earth, where his rule is unchallenged by sin, and the old order of this present world has passed away (Rev. 21:1-8; 22:3-5, cf. Rom. 8:29-30; 1 Cor. 13:12; 2 Cor. 3:18; 4:16-18; Eph. 4:13).

For Paul, the two aspects of God's divine end-game coincide in the final redemption of humanity and of creation (Col. 1:13-20). His goal is to reconcile all things to himself Col. 1:19-20), that is everything belonging to creation, so that Christ will be the head and Lord of it all. He is, after all, Paul says, the firstborn of it all, its Lord and king, and he holds all thing together by his power (Col. 1:15-16). He, Christ, is its creator, a role he shared with God the Father as the divine and preexisting Son (John 1:1-3; Col. 1:16), and he will become its ruler in God's behalf as the glorified Son of Man, the perfect representative of an imperfect humanity, the Second Adam, in whom all of the fullness of God dwells bodily, so that was lost by man's disobedience will be reclaimed by Jesus', the Son of Man's, obedience and sacrifice on the cross (Col. 1:19-20).[262]

Creation awaits with groaning and yearning the coming final and unopposed rule of God, when restoration will occur, anticipating its release from bondage to a lost humanity at war with God, and the consequences of that rebellion on its materiality (Rom. 8:20). Paul asserts that the object of that anticipation is the appearance of the final revelation of the saints in their true nature as the *sons of God*, that is a redeemed humanity belonging to God whose bodies are glorified, so that the whole man is redeemed, and perfected (Rom. 8:19-21). Paul's point is that at the revelation of the *sons (children) of God*, at the time of the consummation of God's purpose for redeemed humanity, creation will participate in its own reclamation and redemption, to full renewal, to exist under a new order, the unopposed rule of God (Rev. 21:1-8; 22:5-7).

In reality, those who are in Christ, relocated into grace, and who live by the power of the Spirit in reconciliation and fellowship with God are

---

[262] Paul sees the role of Christ as already begun with his ascension to the throne at his glorification and "coronation", to sit at the right hand of God (1 Cor. 15:20-28; Phil. 2:8-11). Just as the kingdom of God has broken into the world to redeem it with the first appearing of Christ, the risen Christ has assumed his place on the throne as ruler over it, establishing the a link between the rule of God in heaven and on earth among his redeemed people (cf. Isa. 66:1), and in anticipation of his final future rule in a new creation.

already *children of God* (both Paul and John make this point) (Rom. 8:18-25; 1 John 3:1-3). They are justified, redeemed, and transformed, relocated into the kingdom of God's beloved Son, having come out of the kingdom of darkness, so that their status as children of God and citizens of heaven is in the present, as they live under the rule of God through the indwelling Spirit, even before the kingdom's final consummation and revelation in the eschaton. Though they are not fully known in this age or by the world, they are, Paul says, already *citizens of the heaven*, awaiting the changing of their base and materials bodies to be fashioned like Jesus glorious body (Phil. 3:20-21), a transformation Paul speaks of elsewhere as coming with the final appearing of Christ and the beginning of the eschaton, when the trumpet of God sounds as a signal of its arrival (1 Cor. 15:50-59). The political affiliation (τὸ πολίτευμα) of those who belong to Christ is not this material world under the curse of sin and earthly rulers, but it is heaven (ἐν οὐρανοῖς ὑπάρχει), serving as an anticipatory deposit in their lives and hearts through their connection to God by the indwelling Spirit, and from where they earnestly expect a savior to come (ἐξ οὗ καὶ σωτῆρα ἀπεκδεχόμεθα), the Lord Jesus Christ (κύριον Ἰησοῦν Χριστόν). He will, when he comes, transform their bodies (ὃς μετασχηματίσει) and bring them into the final redemption hoped for by all creation (Phil. 3:20-21, Rom. 8:19-21).

The two things are held in tension in Pauline theology, present salvation, with its justification and rightness with God in the present through faith in Christ (Rom. 5:1), along with the ongoing work of the Spirit in the present, perfecting what God has transformed beginning at justification (2 Cor. 5:17), and what is to come in the eschaton with the return of Christ, the final, future redemption of the bodies of those who belong to Christ, in order for them to be animated by same Spirit who is already at work in the saints perfecting them in godliness (1 Cor. 15:50-58). The future will bring the culmination of the redemptive perfection and purpose of God, which is already at work in the saints through the moral and spiritual transformations occurring in and because of salvific justification. Somehow through the Spirit, those who belong to Christ are already in possession of and participate in that future glory, which is final perfection, through an increasing measure of growth in character and godliness ahead of time as a result of God's grace working in them, and as the Spirit lives in them and works out God's purposes for their lives (2 Cor. 3:18, cf. Rom. 1:16-17; 5:8-21; 8:1-4; Gal. 5:15-25; Eph. 1:13-23; 4:17-24; Phil. 3:20-21; et al.).

Paul links the liberation of creation from its disadvantaged position and condition as a result of human sin and rebellion against God (Rom. 8:20), to the final and full liberation of the children of God from *their* mortal condition, which is subject to physical death (Heb. 2:17-18), when they are finally glorified (Rom. 8:22-23). There is a coincidence between the glorification of the saints and the creation of a new heaven and earth, whereby creation "anticipates" the former as a sign and indication of the arrival of the latter (Rom. 8:19). When the new creation of justification for the saints presently culminates in the full realization of a new creation through the glorification and resurrection of their bodies, Paul teaches, there will be a realignment of even material creation under new conditions and the rule of God (cf. Isa. 11:1-9; 65:17-25; 66:1-2). The two will coexist in the harmony of God's originally intended plan, with Christ as their human-divine representative on the throne, the Second Adam leading the race to do what the first Adam failed to do, take dominion in God's behalf as his representative, to model him to creation in God's image and likeness (Gen. 1:26-28, cf. 1 Cor. 15:20-28; Heb. 2:17-18).[263]

This is the object of the sincere hope of those who God is even now perfecting through the Spirit in the present, which Paul mentions in

[263] Cf. Beale, The Temple and the Church's Mission: A Biblical Theology of the Dwelling Place of God, 2004, 365-393, 395-402.

Romans 5 as character development toward God's final goals for a redeemed humanity. The children of God also anticipate perfection, their final liberation from every consequence of the fall in their own human physicality, with groanings similar to those of a creation under the burden of human failure and its consequences (Rom. 8:23-24). At that time *their* material bodies will be finally redeemed into the full experience of the kingdom of God, into which they were first introduced through justification, and that is being worked out even now in the present with fear and trembling, as they surrender to the working of God in them (Rom. 5:1-2; 8:1-4; Phil. 1:6; 2:12-13). At the same time, Paul says, creation also will also undergo the redemption for which *it* also longs, a redemption from the consequences of *their* sin and rebellion against God, with all the suffering and misery that followed (Rom. 1:18-32; 8:20-21, cf. Gen. 6:1-8). There is, then, a coincidence, an alignment if you will, between the redemption of humanity, and the full restoration of the people of God spiritually and materially, with the final renewal of creation in a new heaven and a new earth at the time of Christ's return in glory (Rev. 21:1-8; 22:5-7).

It is, Paul says, the object of God's plan to bring all of creation into the final liberation and restoration of a redeemed humanity under the headship of Christ, and to be fully reconciled to God (Rom. 8:19; Col. 1:19-20). Nevertheless, and this is Paul's point, it is a transformation that has begun in the saints with their salvation and reconciliation to God (Rom. 5:1). It includes relocation into the grace of God and the kingdom of his beloved Son immediately (Col. 1:13-14). Those who are reconciled to God by faith, have been relocated by the Spirit into the kingdom of God *in the present*. They are in Christ at a time when creation is still broken, even though the program of restoration has begun in them. Paul contends, on account of *new creation*, the old has passed away for those who are in Christ in anticipation of the final and complete renewal of all things (2 Cor. 5:17, cf. Rom. 8:18-24). Justification and reconciliation to God by faith anticipates this final restoration, not for the saints alone, but for all creation as well.

The revelation of *the sons of God* (τὴν ἀποκάλυψιν τῶν υἱῶν τοῦ θεοῦ), *the children of God,* in their glorified bodies, adopted out of the fallen world and finally raised to be like Jesus' in a glorified body, means that just as they were born in the earthly and mortal image of the first Adam, with the full ramifications of his original sin and its subsequent consequences, they will also bear the image of the heavenly man, the Second Adam, the Son of Man, now glorified in heaven, serving as their representative before God, and interceding for them in anticipation of their future participation in his resurrection to glorified, new life (1 Cor. 15:20-28). Through him, and in union with him in his resurrection, that they will be introduced in the full ramifications and privileges of a new life in Christ beyond initial justification (1 Cor. 15:42-49; Phil. 3:20-21). We will not all die, Paul assures his Corinthian readers, but when the trumpet sounds and Christ returns, we shall *all* be changed, in a moment, in a flash, when the perishable shall put on imperishability, and the mortal immortality (1 Cor. 15:53). Death will lose its sting and power over them, and over creation (1 Cor. 50:55). In 1 Thessalonians 4, Paul speaks of the return of the Lord, and in a similar fashion that the dead and living in Christ will both be caught up together into the air to be with the Lord forever (1 Thess. 4:13-17). More importantly for our consideration, is that morally transformative justification, with its union with Christ in death to the old life and resurrection to new life, not only anticipates the fuller expression of what is to come with Christ's return, but actually, in Paul's theology, begins it, by placing a deposit, a seed, beginning the new life of Christ in them to be experienced in connection to our present walk with God in the Spirit (Rom. 8:1-4). The new life has been initiated at justification, and is progressing through the power of the Spirit toward God's goal of perfecting it at the return of Christ, and in anticipation of a new creation to come. For Paul, kingdom transformation has begun, and even though its final realization is future, those who are in Christ are to live as people of the kingdom of God presently, in true righteousness and holiness, and in surrender to the rule of God through obedience to the leading of the Spirit.

When Paul speaks of the *revelation of the sons of God*, for which creation longs, the redemption that involves the adoption of their bodies into the kingdom of God, finally completing what was begun in justification, he means to link the final redemptive divine endgame for creation with the consummation of his redemptive action and purpose for those who have been justified by faith, morally changed, and who even now have been relocated into the kingdom of God, and into the environment God's grace, where the Spirit operates and provides the influence, rather than the flesh (Gal. 5:16-18). They now come under the rule of God through the Spirit. Paul sees the program of God's final redemption of all of creation already underway in a redeemed humanity, who have been reconciled to God by faith, and who stand in grace (Rom. 5:1-2). The kingdom of God has broken into the present age and world, and is operating in those who belong to Christ, pushing back violently against the kingdom of darkness, so that even the gates of hell cannot prevail against it (Matt. 11:12; 16:18; 21:31, cf. Eph. 6:10-13). There is an inexorable movement toward God's intended purpose and end for all of creation, something already reflected in the salvation of those who have been reconciled to God by faith, and who, as a result of justification, have already become new creations in Christ – the old has gone and the new has come (2 Cor. 5:17). In the present, this reality finds itself expressed as a process toward the development of godliness in those who belong to Christ. Even if at the same time their physical bodies succumb to material dissipation, their nature and character, their inwardly renewed personality and life in Christ under the power of the Spirit, improves more and more toward the character of holiness and righteousness that God is seeking to develop in them (2 Cor. 4:16-18). Paul talks of going from glory to glory, as a metaphor for the development of Christlikeness in an increasing measure in those who have been transformed by God, but are in need of perfecting, and maturing in godliness over time in the present (2 Cor. 3:18).

Coming back now to Ephesians 4:13-16; Paul speaks of the church as the instrument of God's support for the developing spiritual and moral lives of the saints, as each one does their part in serving one another, so that all are edified, and all make progress toward the goal God has in mind, the fullness of the stature of Christ, both for the church and for the saints (Eph. 4:13-16). While the end has not been reached, the process is well under way (cf. Rom. 8;29-30; 2 Cor. 4:16-18). It began with the appearing of Christ, and is now advancing and undergirded by the impartation of the Spirit at Pentecost. He is the great *paraclete* promised by Jesus, to lead his disciples into all truth, and in whom Paul sees the power of God for godliness and righteousness for believers (Gal. 5:16-25). So, when Paul speaks of hope in Romans 5 and 8, he doesn't mean a vain longing, but a confidence and anticipation of certain outcomes in God's purposes, which he says have begun in those who are justified, namely, their moral development through patience in suffering that produces character (Rom. 5:3-8, cf. Phil. 3:12-14). It is the hope of a final consummation, culminating in being conformed to the image of God's Son (Rom. 8:29), grounded in the knowledge that since we have born the earthly image of the first Adam, we will be found one day in the heavenly and glorified image of the Second Adam (1 Cor. 15:15:49).

This means that in Pauline thought, the arrival of the kingdom of God in Christ and with the Spirit, promised earlier by God, has already occurred, even if it has not yet reached its final and full expression – but will inevitably with Christ's return. The kingdom's appearing and its future full realization are held in tension, so that the kingdom's arrival in Christ, his ministry, death and resurrection, is pushing back against the kingdom of darkness in this present age and world (Matt. 11:12; 16:17-20), relocating those who come to Christ into God's kingdom, to come under the rule of God as transformed and redeemed children of God (2 Cor. 5:17). At work in the present, the rule of God has begun, even if it has yet to find its final and full expression in a renewed creation in which the physically glorified saints will play their part (Rom. 8:19). If the kingdom of God is at work in the saint and in the church already, holiness and righteousness, the power and leading of the Spirit are signs that mark that kingdom as present and at work in the world. The renewal has begun as redemptive transformation for those who were once bound to sin but have been forgiven and changed by God to become like Christ (2 Co. 3:18; 4:16-18, cf. Rom. 8:29-20). This moral and spiritual transformation has begun something that will come to its final consummation in the future.

Through the Spirit, the future has been seeded in the present into the lives of those who belong to God, who works with them to bring about their development into the full image of his Son (Rom. 8:29-30; Eph. 4:14). They belong to the kingdom of God, and the presence of the Spirit in them represents the rule of God in their lives (Rom. 8:9-11). His rule in them in the present, Paul says, is the guarantee of the future resurrection of their mortal bodies, to which he will give life *because of the righteousness* that is even now being formed in them by the Spirit (Rom. 8:10-11). It is a righteousness not of their own devising, but comes through the Spirit, and thus it is by grace, the grace in which they stand, and into which they were relocated in Christ when they were justified by faith (Rom. 1:17; 5:1-2). It is a righteousness that begins through spiritual transformation and a relocation into Christ (2 Cor. 5:17), but is being developed and matured through the Spirit in them, as they walk in surrender to the rule of God and in obedience to him (Rom. 8:1-4; Gal. 5:16-25).

Nevertheless, those who belong to Christ must work out their salvation with fear and trembling (Phil. 2:12), in cooperation with God in their development toward the goals and purposes he has in mind for them. God brings to bear the power of his kingdom in their lives (Paul would say through the Spirit at work in them), to work and to act to accomplish his purpose, their moral development, until it is perfected at the appearing of Christ, so that they might be a reflection of the image of God back into his creation (Phil. 2:13, 14-16). So, the future fullness of God's purpose for the saints is held in tension with a preemptive progress and process in the present. They are, however, one and the same substance, though not of the same order of magnitude. It is a matter of degrees, Paul says, and not of substance or nature (2 Cor. 3:18). God is working in the saints what he intends to produce in its final full glory, the righteousness of God reflecting him as a redeemed humanity. Their present and final renewal anticipates a fully renewed and restored creation. At the moment, then, a redeemed humanity is representing God to a broken creation, in a wicked age that is in rebellion against God, among whom they shine as lights in a darkened sky (Phil 2:14-16). So, for Paul, the enterprise of redemption is held in tension between what God has done in the present, and its completion in the future, between a new creation as a result of transformative justification, sustained by the power and presence of the Spirit in the present, who seeks to develop godliness in those who are redeemed anticipating their future conforming to mature godliness, and into the image of God's Son (Rom. 8:29-30; 1 Cor. 15:48-49; 2 Cor. 3:18; 4:16-18; Eph. 4:13, 22-24). The future is already at work and being realized in the present, with the Holy Spirit as the seal or deposit of God, and who guarantees God will finally bring to full redemption those who are *ALREADY* his redeemed possession in Christ (Eph. 1:13-14).

HEAVENLY PREPARATIONS

What we have discussed immediately above is the "earthly" side of the kingdom of God, as it relates to the effects of its breaking into the present age, and the results on those who now enter into it through faith in Christ. It would be a mistake to miss Paul's theology of what the "heavenly side" looks like, corresponding to a contemporaneous activity in heaven, while the church acts in cooperation with the kingdom of God on earth (Phil. 2:12-16), in the power of the Spirit, to accomplish God's purpose and Christ's mission (cf. Matt. 28:19-20). Action on the plans of God are not just taking place on earth in the present age, but they are also taking place in heaven, Paul argues in 1 Corinthians 15:20-28, and in Philippians 2:9-11 (cf. John 14:1-4). Corresponding activity is taking place in heaven, as the Spirit is working out the plan of the kingdom of God in and through the church in the earthly realm (1 Cor. 15:24-28, cf. John 14:2-3). When the disciples asked Jesus, after his resurrection, about whether the kingdom was coming immediately (provoked by a previous conversation about the coming *baptism in the Spirit* that Jesus promised) (Acts 1:4-5), he told them that the times and season of God purposes, and of their consummation were not for them to know, and lay in the hands of God (Acts 1:6-7). Their role, however, was to receive the power that he had promised them, when the Spirit came upon them, and to become his witnesses (that is continue the mission of proclaiming the good news of salvation) throughout the world (Acts 1:8). His subsequent ascension into heaven before their very eyes, meant that he too was to take his place at the right hand of God in the time between his ascension and return. He was to assume *his* role as reigning Lord and King, and to engage the work of bringing the kingdom of God to its final and full revelation, when he will return in *like manner* (as his ascension) at the time set by God (Acts 1:4-8,11).

What Jesus called making preparation of "a place for you", ahead of his return to retrieve the saints to be with him wherever he might be in the future (John 14:1-3), Paul describes as Jesus presently engaging the a heavenly process of subduing all of the enemies of God, ending with the final enemy, death, so he might hand over the entire kingdom to God at some future point known only to God (1 Cor. 15:24-28, cf. Ps. 110:1). Along with Paul's parallel passage in 1 Thessalonians 4, Paul lays out the theological implications of Jesus' own teaching about his departure and return (John 14:1-3), particularly with respect to what we now commonly call the *rapture of the saints* (1 Thess 4:17). In John, Jesus spoke of returning after a hiatus to retrieve the saints (John 14:1-3). In the Synoptics, where the context is his reappearance with respect to historical Israel, and the prophecies and promises of God to his covenant people, Jesus speaks of his coming in glory and power to overthrow the enemies of God, and to bring final judgment on sin and the wicked (Matt. 16:27; 24:30; 25:31; Mark 8:38; 13:26; Luke 9:26; 21:27). Writing to the Thessalonians to answer related but distinct concerns, Paul addresses the former and the latter respectively (1 Thess. 4:13-17; 2 Thess. 2:1-11). Paul adopts the scheme Jesus sets out for his return for the saints, and to bring judgment on the world, where they appear not to be entirely temporally coterminous. Paul allows Jesus' scheme to exist with some tension in these two elements as part of the entire eschatological program of the Day of the Lord, something which, apparently, he addressed earlier in greater detail, and more explicitly in person to the Thessalonians (2 Thess. 2:5).

Paul is able to do this because of his eschatological awareness of the broader end-time program of God with respect to the coming of the Messiah, Jesus, first of all to die and rise from the dead, the outpouring of the Spirit signaling the temporal arrival of the kingdom of God as promised, and the mission of the church in the power of the Spirit, commission by Christ prior to his promised Parousia at the end of time to bring judgment. For Paul, an eschatological program involving a process or progression of events leading to the consummation of God's purposes was not a stretch.[264] It had already begun with the incarnation,

---

[264] We should note that the Old Testament also holds the eschatological future in this same tension. Beginning with Genesis 3:15, where the seed of the woman will bring redress to the fall of man at the temptation of Adam and Eve

resurrection, and ascension of Christ, and with the outpouring of the Spirit. Paul detected clear hints of God's programmatic eschatology in the Old Testament, upon which he expounds in Romans 9-11 (with regard to Israel's placed in the redemptive scheme), and in Ephesians 3 (where he explains how God made room from the outset to include Gentiles with Israel in salvation). The Revelation of John confirms such a scheme of developing and intensifying events, especially very close to final judgment, and this only serves to show that the New Testament church had a more eschatologically nuanced theology, in many ways, than our own.[265] Indeed, Jesus' repeated predictions of his impending arrest and death to his disciples, his caution to people not to tell what he had done by way of healing, along with his "cryptic" teaching in parables were all part of a process by which the kingdom of God broke into the world in the present without the immediate political overthrow of Israel's enemies, or the final judgment of God coming at that time (Acts 1:6-7). Jesus' claims to be the Messiah, Son of Man, and Son of God without immediately making war on Rome and Israel's enemies

---

by crushing the serpent's head but also suffering injury in the process. We trace certain dual aspects to the Messiah's coming and rule by which he will suffer rejection but will ultimately triumph. Some elements of this are: The rebellion of God's people against the king he has already determined to set up on his holy hill of Zion, spoken of in Psalm 2, the death and resurrection of God Holy One in Psalm 16, the humble and anointed Servant of the Lord, who comes not as a conqueror, but gently and with meekness to bring justice in Isaiah 42, or as the one who will offering himself for the sins of the people in Isaiah 53. Also, there is the Messiah, the Anointed One who will be cut off in Daniel 9, and be left with nothing, and whom Israel will finally recognize as the one they pierced in Zechariah 12:10!

[265] If we are willing to accept a "premillennial" eschatology, we may even see in Revelation a focus arising in ongoing processes of divine judgment designed to finally bring Israel into the knowledge of salvation through Christ, the one whom they "pierced" (Rev. 7, 11, 12, 13, 14, cf. Zech. 12:10; 14:1-3).

shocked the religious leaders, who refused to accept his claims and so endanger their own political standing with Rome. To advance against the kingdom of darkness prior to final judgment and its full, future implementation, in order that salvation might be made offered in the present age to those who repent and believe (Mark 1:14-15), was an idea that did not occur to Jesus enemies, but Jesus consistently maintained it was in *their* scriptures (John 5:39). Consideration of Jesus' approach to his mission only serves to underscore that Paul was on the right track with respect to his eschatology.

Jesus at Work in Heaven Preparing for His Return: Paul views Jesus in heaven preparing for his return, serving both as intercessor for the saints (a universal first-century church perspective), and as the agent of God's victorious kingdom, subduing all things under the rule of God in preparation for his arrival to finish the job. His descriptions are among the most explicit depictions of Jesus activity between his ascension and Parousia in the New Testament, with the possible exception of some passages in Hebrews (1 Cor. 15:20-28). Paul says that Jesus must reign until he has put all his enemies under his feet, along with the last enemy, death (1 Cor. 15:25-26). Paul's allusion to Psalm 110:1 – which Jesus himself raised at one point to the Pharisees – appears deliberately ambiguous. The clause "...until *he* puts his all *his* enemies under *his* feet," is virtually a quote of the Psalm, where God is the one doing the "putting."[266] Paul often does this with his eschatology, he recasts Old Testament prophecies and promises as fulfilled in Jesus, either by

---

[266] Ps. 110:1 (LXX Ps. 109:1) "ἕως ἂν θῶ τοὺς ἐχθρούς σου ὑποπόδιον τῶν ποδῶν σου." 1 Corinthians 15:25 "ἄχρι ⸀οὗ θῇ πάντας τοὺς ἐχθροὺς ὑπὸ τοὺς πόδας αὐτοῦ" where the 2nd person singular pronoun is replaced by the 3rd person (Tan, R. K., deSilva, D. A., & Hoogendyk, I. (2012). *The Lexham Greek-English Interlinear Septuagint: H.B. Swete Edition*. Lexham Press; Holmes, M. W. (2011–2013). *The Greek New Testament: SBL Edition*. Lexham Press; Society of Biblical Literature).

allusion or sometimes in direct quotation where the originals refer to YAHWEH. Paul ambiguously, even pointedly, has Jesus as the one acting to bring about the subjection of his enemies; he is the one doing the "putting".[267] In 1 Corinthians, Jesus is the active agent of the kingdom, subduing the enemies of God, where the reign of God's appointed Messiah *has begun* and is underway in anticipation of a future resurrection of the saints, but each in the right order (ἕκαστος δὲ ἐν τῷ ἰδίῳ τάγματι), Christ first, and then *when he comes,* those who belong to him (ἔπειτα οἱ τοῦ Χριστοῦ ἐν τῇ παρουσίᾳ αὐτοῦ) (1 Cor. 15:20-23).[268] Paul's point appears to be demonstrating that the eschatological reign of Christ is underway, and in want of nothing but its final consummation at his return – Parousia (ἐν τῇ παρουσίᾳ αὐτοῦ) (1 Cor. 15:42-58).

Such a consummation of the kingdom of God at Jesus' Parousia, bringing the renewal of all creation in heaven and earth (Col. 1:19-20, cf. Isa. 65:17), Paul asserts, will come as the result of Jesus completing his role as the glorified Son of Man, the Second Adam, so that the kingdom of God will finally be subsumed under the unopposed rule of God (1 Cor. 15:25, cf. Isa. 66:1-2). Having taken dominion as God's human representative of a redeemed humanity, and presenting the kingdom to God, God will assume authority over it without opposition (1 Cor. 15:24-28). In a curious statement, Paul says that even the Son will be subject to God (1 Cor. 15:28). Paul obviously means in his role as the Second Adam, because Jesus serves in heaven as the incarnate representative

---

[267] There is an interesting instance of Paul changing up the Old Testament, without obliterating its basic meaning, in Ephesians 4 where the Lord taking captives captive, doesn't receive gifts, but gives gifts to men. Paul has changed the direction of the giving from the earthly to the heavenly, to the earthly from the heavenly realm (Eph. 4:7-8, cf. Ps. 68:18); cf. Farrar, 1909, 487; Soards, 2011, 333.

[268] Holmes, M. W. (2011–2013). *The Greek New Testament: SBL Edition* (1 Co 15:23). Lexham Press; Society of Biblical Literature.

of a redeemed humanity, which he has saved and brought into the kingdom through reconciling justification by which they now stand *in grace,* and in fellowship with God (Rom. 5:1-2, c f. 1 John 1:5-10). He has become, as the writer of Hebrews puts it, the representative of a redeemed humanity, calling them his brethren (Heb. 2:5-18), anticipating their final inclusion in the role God originally assigned humanity over creation (Gen. 1:26-28). Now with Christ as the captain of their redemption and the author of their inclusion, they can engage the role God has for humanity as the remnant representing the whole, and in whom God's purposes come to fulfillment (Ps. 8:1-9).

As it stands, Jesus was made a little lower than the angels by incarnation and is now crowned with glory in heaven, and one day every knee will bow and every tongue will confess Christ is Lord over all creation (Heb. 2:9, cf. Phil. 2:9-11). In Paul's eschatology, those who belong to Christ through justification, are already part of the kingdom of God in the present age by virtue of a relocation into Christ (cf. 2 Cor. 5:17; Phil. 3:20-21) – which means they stand in grace (Rom. 5:1-2), and have been transferred from the kingdom of darkness into the kingdom of God's beloved Son (Col. 1:13). They are even now under the rule of God as they follow the Spirit (Rom. 8:1-4). Charged by God originally to multiply and take dominion over creation, to rule over it as his representatives in his likeness and image (holiness and righteousness – cf. Eph. 1:4; 4:24) (Gen. 1:26-28), the sons of God through redemption (Rom. 8:9-14), and led by the Spirit, will ultimately become coheirs with Jesus of the new creation, and so fulfill the original purpose of God for humanity (Rom. 8:14-17).[269] Jesus is in the process of bringing about

---

[269] Cf. Beale, The Temple and the Church's Mission: A Biblical Theology of the Dwelling Place of God, 2004. Beales' book is a thorough treatment of the theme of God's presence and fellowship with his people, beginning with the garden and ending in the new heaven and earth. He argues that God's efforts

what God originally intended for the human race, and will ultimately accomplish as their representative, what they so spectacularly failed to do. As the Second Adam, and on behalf of a redeemed humanity, as their representative, through obedience to God, even to the point of sacrificing his life on the cross (Phil. 2:6-8), Jesus has completed the mission assigned to the first human pair by God (Gen. 1:26-28), and is in the process in heaven of bringing it to completion (1 Cor. 15:20-28) in anticipation of the inclusion of the entire redeemed people of God to reign over a renewed creation (Rom. 8:18-24; Eph. 1:13-23; Col. 1:15-20).

So then, this is another one of those Pauline tensions, where the joint action of God and Christ are seen as fulfillment of God's prophetic promises. They act together in complete synchronicity to accomplish the end-goal of God's redemptive purpose as Christ initiates and engages the rule of God over creation, a role which God originally assigned to humanity.[270] Jesus acts in man's behalf, and represents a redeemed humanity doing what God originally ordained for humanity to do, while also acting as the divine Son of God ruling over his creation as sovereign and Lord representing God (Gen. 1:26-28; Isa. 9:6-7; 11:1-9;

---

to establish a people among whom he would dwell is programmatic of his overall redemptive intentions and purposes. Israel at first, and the church as the temple in which God dwells by his Spirit is the precursor to a new, united heaven and earth in which God dwells in eternal closeness and communion with his people (Re. 21:1-8). The temple serves as a type of what it means to live in fellowship and relationship with God, and reminds us of the original plan of God in the garden, where he engaged in fellowship with humanity. It also anticipates the reinstatement of that state in the new heaven and earth ultimately, but better (Gen. 3:8; Rev. 21:1-8).

[270] It was a hallmark of Jesus ministry, as presented by John, that Jesus did nothing without the approval and engagement of the Father, and that the Father worked entirely through him, because they shared a unity of purpose, of being and of nature. Paul is able to make use of this idea in his eschatology.

Ps. 2:4-12; 8:1-9, cf. Dan. 7:13-14). In Jesus is the quintessential divine-human partnership and cooperation, which was first rolled out in the garden, but now at the level of the incarnation of the divine in human flesh (John 1:14, cf. Col. 1:19). To accomplish and rescue the failed mission, Christ came so that through his victorious obedience (Heb. 2:10-11), he might undo original disobedience and provide redemption for those caught up in the consequences of the fall (Rom. 5:12-21; Eph. 1:18-23; Col. 1:13-20; Heb. 2:10-11). In the divine-human Jesus, God has vindicated his original plan to include humanity as partners in ruling over his creation (Gen. 1:26-28; Ps. 8:1-9; 1 Cor. 15:20-28; Phil. 2:6-11; Col. 1:15-20), while acting himself as supreme ruler over all that he created, just as he first intended (Ps. 8:1-9). Jesus united both the rule of God and the rule of man in divine partnership through his person as the Word that was *made flesh* (John 1:1-3; 14, cf. Eph. 1:18-23; Col. 1:15-20). Through his redemptive incarnation, death and resurrection, he invites a redeemed humanity to once more unite with God's original purpose on the basis of their reconciliation to God through his grace that justifies them, sets them right with God (Rom. 5:1-2), but that also provides for their full moral, spiritual and, ultimately, physical reclamation from the fall and its consequences (Rom. 6:1-23; 8:1-17; 2 Cor. 5:17). This is the divine endgame.

The Future Kingdom Already Engaged in the Present: Nevertheless, Paul sees that even now, by engaging in the kingdom of God in the present, and through surrender to God in salvation, what is yet to come to its completion at the Parousia of Christ may already be engaged in the present through reconciliation and fellowship with God (Rom. 5:1-2), particularly in an experience of the indwelling Spirit for the believer (Rom. 8:13-17). Paul's adjustment of the text in 1 Cor. 15, then, seems to be Messianic in the light of Jesus incarnation, death, resurrection, and ascension, in order to change the camera angle from the heavenly throne room view of Psalm 110:1, where God is the mover, to the ascended and enthroned Son of Man, the risen Second Adam, as the mover who is in the process of bringing the kingdom to its consummation (1 Cor. 15:25-28). Jesus even now is at work accomplishing, in his exalted place, the work and role assigned originally to humanity. He has preemptively begun the rule of God on the heavenly side, something Paul reiterates in Ephesians, Philippians and Colossians with reference to the connection of the saint have with Christ in his heavenly role and place, even while they live in obedience to his rule on earth and in this age as partakers of the kingdom of God (Eph. 1:3, 20; 2:6; Phil. 3:20; Col. 3:1). Thus, there is a process underway, whereby Christ is working from both the heavenly and earth perspectives to bring about the full expression of the unopposed rule of God to all of his creation. He is in heaven bringing about the purpose of God by overseeing the historical progress of events that will lead to his return, as well as working in the church to bring the kingdom of God to bear on a lost humanity in need of salvation (cf. John 14:1-3). Consummation of God's endgame is not the discrete and quick event anticipated by Jesus' disciples or the religious leaders of Jesus' day, but a series of events, and a process leading to a final, climactic moment of his Parousia in glory and power.

John, in Revelation, gives us a similar visionary view of this with the Lamb that looked like it had been slain, taking the book with seven seals, and opening it so as to unfold the plans and purposes of God in history which lead to final victory and judgment (Rev. 5:6-8:1). Paul's treatment of Israel as the historical covenant people of God (Rom. 9-11), the descendants of Abraham, to whom God's promises were made (Gen. 12:1-3) (along with David (2 Sam. 7:8-17)), makes it abundantly clear that God fully intends to be true to his word. Those among the Jewish people who recognize Jesus as Christ, serving as a faithful remnant, as they often did in Old Testament, will represent the whole nation in God's redemptive scheme, and will be the objects its fulfillment in terms of the promises and covenants he made to the patriarchs (cf. Rom. 9-11).[271] In this way, the promises made to Abraham, that through him all of the nations (the Gentiles) would be blessed (Gen. 12:1-2), and reiterated by Isaiah (cf. Isa. 42:6; 49:6), that the salvation of Israel alone was too small a consequence for God's redemptive ambition for his *Servant,* and that he intended to bring the Gentiles into its salvific scope as well (Eph. 2:11-3:12), have come to their fulfilment in Christ and will even more so when at last he brings the unopposed rule of God ultimately to all his creation (Isa. 11:1-16). Paul clearly picks this up in Ephesians 2:11-3:13, where he asserts on scriptural authority from the old covenant, that God fully intended to bring Gentiles into his salvific plan, and to make one people of God out of two ethnicities, Jew and Gentile (Eph. 2:11-22). Indeed, the end of Revelation, where John speaks of a new heaven and earth, a new Jerusalem serving as the temple of God, and a new order for creation (Rev. 21:1-8), Paul anticipates in Ephesians with his talk of Jews and Gentiles as fellows-citizens of the kingdom of God, who through reconciliation to God, and to one another in Christ, have come together to form a new temple in which God will dwell by his Spirit in the future (Eph. 2:19-22).

The Actively Reigning Jesus: Jesus' reign in heaven is not passive. He is not waiting. On the contrary, the New Testament presents Jesus' role in heaven as active intercession for the saints, because he is their high priest representing them to God (Heb. 4:14-16). He is uniquely qualified to serve in this way because he is not ashamed to call them *brethren,* and because he has participated (and still does) in their

---

[271] Paul is not creating his theology out of whole cloth. He is developing the theology of the Old Testament in light of the Christ advent, where in scripture, God appeals to a remnant of those who obey him as representatives of Abraham's descendants upon who the fulfillment of his covenants and promises will fall. Paul's views his ideas in Romans 9-11 as consistent with the Old Testament prophetic scheme of preaching and warning to Israel.

humanity, although he was clearly divine and equal with God (Heb. 1:1-4; 2:10-11; Rom. 1:3-4; Phil. 2:6-8).[272] Indeed, the writer of Hebrews argues that it is only proper and appropriate that Jesus become the perfect captain of their salvation through suffering as a human being, in order to bring them to the glory intended for God's people (Heb. 2:10, cf. Ps. 8:1-10). Jesus not only embraced incarnation (cf. Phil. 2:6-7), but endure human suffering and overcame temptation, experiencing an authentic human life, even though he is the divine Son of God (cf. Phil. 2:8). He is not ashamed to call them *brethren* because he was made like them in his incarnation (cf. John 1:14), and suffered as they do, even in temptation, experiencing human weaknesses just as they do, yet without sinning (Heb. 4:14-16). In this way he is able, on the one hand, to offer intercessions to God in their behalf for grace and resources in the hour of their difficulty (Rom. 8:31-37, cf. 2 Cor. 4:16-18; 12:6-10), and on the other to make preparation for their eventual participation with him in the work of the kingdom of God in the eschaton, so that they might be heirs of God with Christ, coheirs (Rom. 8:17). He can sympathize with them in their struggles and intercede, because he himself has experienced them, and comprehends their human weaknesses as they serve God in the time between the initial arrival of the kingdom of God (cf. Mark 1:14-15), and its final consummation at his

---

[272] Matthew Bridges captures Pauline theology in his hymnody, in the hymn *Crown Him With Many Crowns*, and lines like these: "Crown him the Lord of love; behold his hands and side, rich wounds, yet visible above, in beauty glorified; no angels in the sky can fully bear that sight, but downward bends their burning eye
at mysteries so bright." Godfrey Thring adds a verse of equal theological gravity: "Crown Him the Son of God, Before the world began, And ye, who tread where He hath trod, Crown Him the Son of man; Who every grief hath known That wrings the human breast, And takes and bears them for His own, That all in Him may rest."

return (οὐ γὰρ ἔχομεν ἀρχιερέα μὴ δυνάμενον συμπαθῆσαι ταῖς ἀσθενείαις ἡμῶν).[273]

What the Paul describes in 1 Corinthians 15 is not a passive Christ ruling over the kingdom of God without intervention, engagement or effort, but the active and glorified Son of Man/God at work providing heavenly support to earthly saints, those who are serving God in his kingdom on earth, that is in the present age, fully intending that they be brought through to the full realization of the kingdom of God in the eschaton (Rom. 8:18-25, 32, 38-39). In a great crescendo of emotion, after describing the eschatological consummation God has in mind for the saints and creation, and the intercession of the Spirit to bring to bear the power and resources of God on the lives of the saints in alignment with God's divine plan and purposes (Rom. 8:18-30), Paul erupts into exalted assurances of the final victory of the saints, with guarantees of God's love despite every resistance against the church and the saints in the present age, as they go about their business for the kingdom of God on earth (Rom. 8:31-39).

In 1 Corinthians 15:20-28 and 1 Thessalonians 4:13-17, the apostle lays out an eschatology that embraces the Old Testament, with its predications concerning Israel, and implications for Gentiles, foretold especially by Isaiah (cf. Isa. 42:6; 49:6). Strikingly underscoring Jesus' own description of his departure and return, as they relate to his disciples (the church), Paul enlarges, but maintains, the essential elements of Jesus' description of his return (cf. John 14:1-3; 1 Thess 4:13-17). He will inevitably depart, but he will, with equal inevitability return for his disciples, to take them (παραλήμψομαι) to himself (John 14:3). Paul follows Jesus but declares that at his turn Jesus will first raise

---

[273] Holmes, M. W. (2011–2013). *The Greek New Testament: SBL Edition* (Heb 4:15). Lexham Press; Society of Biblical Literature.

the bodies of the dead in Christ and then will *snatch* (*ἁρπαγησόμεθα*)[274] up those who are alive at his coming (οἱ ζῶντες οἱ περιλειπόμενοι), so that that they will be forever with the Lord (1 Thess. 4:16-17).[275] Paul's choice of ἁρπαγησόμεθα, adds drama to the description, and betrays that Jesus meant that he was returning to *take* his disciples out of the world to be with him, and not simply to *receive* them, as though he is somehow passive.[276] The picture of is Jesus' powerfully intervening in the present moment, interrupting the flow of the world's history to retrieve those who belong to him by *snatching* them out and up into the great company of those who will never suffer separation from him again (1 Thess. 4:17, cf. ἵνα ὅπου εἰμὶ ἐγὼ καὶ ὑμεῖς ἦτε – John 14:3).[277]

In 2 Thessalonians 2, Paul expands on his eschatological scheme by including references to the *lawless one,* an oblique reference to the Antichrist figure, also found in Revelation. There, Paul's eschatology teases out what appears to be Jesus' teaching in the Synoptics concerning his return in glory to establish, by the power of his appearing, the full kingdom of God on earth (2 Thess. 2:3-12, cf. Matt. 16:27; 24:30; 25:31; Mark 8:38; 13:26; Luke 9:26; 21:27; 24:26; John 17:5, 24; Acts 3:19-23). The Pauline perspective is bifurcated, with the eschatological

---

[274] Grab, snatch, forcefully take something from someone, rescue, carry off, seize, drag away, etc. (Arndt, 2000), 134.

[275] Holmes, M. W. (2011–2013). *The Greek New Testament: SBL Edition* (1 Th 4:17). Lexham Press; Society of Biblical Literature.

[276] Cf. NIV and KJV. Earlier or traditional English translations *receive* – GB, KJV, YLT, ASV, NASV (1995), NKJV, LEB; later translations *take* – ESV, NET, CSB, NRSV, TEVNT, NCV, GNB, NOAB; *come and get you* – NLT; *will welcome you* – ISV (splitting the difference, but acknowledging that this is likely an assertion of a more active than passive nature. Paul appears to have intended it as active, and not passive in 1 Thessalonians 4.

[277] Holmes, M. W. (2011–2013). The Greek New Testament: SBL Edition (Jn 14:3). Lexham Press; Society of Biblical Literature.

reign of Jesus already underway, but anticipating a future and final realization for creation and history at the decisive moment of his return. But even then, this "decisive" moment consists of a number of events, even a progressive series of events, leading to the finality of the old order and the establishment of a new eternal order under the unopposed, sovereign rule of God (2 Thess. 2:6, 11-12, cf. Rev. 21:1-8). Nevertheless, Paul sets out an eschatology in which the events that lead to the final realization of the rule of God, and a new order in a new heaven and earth, as already under way because the risen Christ sits enthroned and crowned in glory next to the Father, ruling with him and in his behalf (1 Cor. 15:20-28; Phil. 2:9-11, cf. Dan. 7:13-14). Those who are in Christ, and therefore in the kingdom of God as a result of justification, bringing about their reconciliation to God (Rom. 5:1-2), have already engaged the renewal of God's redemptive plan ahead of the final renewal of all things in Christ (Rom. 8:18-23; Eph. 1:13-23; Col. 1:15-29). For Paul, the incarnation of Christ, and especially his resurrection from the dead, followed by his ascension, have set in motion the event that will lead to the final fulfillment of God's plan, and they serve as the initiation of the kingdom of God in the last days, near the end of time. The outpouring of the Spirit to animate the mission of the church, and that brings to bear now the power of God's future rule upon the lives of those who belong to Christ (for those who have been reconciled to God), is a definitive sign that this initiation has occurred and the process is underway. And, through their experience of the Spirit, the saints are sealed as belonging to God in anticipation of the return of Christ, ultimately to retrieve God's purchased possession, but also to bring about the finality of God's plan, which is that all things must come under the rule of God in Christ (Eph. 1:3-10, 13-14, 15-23; Col. 1:15-20, cf. 1 Cor. 15:25-28).

Though some of Paul's references are difficult to specifically nail down, and he makes mention of things he told the Thessalonians while with them, but does not reiterate them here, there is enough for us to see some correspondences with Jesus' teaching, and the later the vision of John on Patmos, recorded in Revelation. In these passages about Jesus' departure and assurance of return, Paul works out some of the implications of Jesus teaching concerning the prior conditions to his final eradication of evil, and the present world order at war with God (2 Thess. 2:1-12). When word reached the Thessalonians that the day of the Lord had already come and gone (2 Thess. 2:1-2), Paul described the necessity of a prior ascendancy of ultimate opposition to God arising in the world at the instigation of the lawless one (2 Thess. 2:8). He will resist God openly and without disguise, something Paul insists necessarily and logically precedes final appearing of the Christ in splendor (glory – Jesus) to overthrow the kingdom of Satan and of darkness (2 Thess. 2:8). If that has not happened, and at the time of their receiving his letter until now, it had not, Paul insists, then the *Day of the Lord* has not yet come in its final iteration, and we are still living in the in between time of the kingdom of God at work in the present age opposing the kingdom of darkness through the power of God, through the operation of the Spirit in the church, and with hope of Christ's final return to finish the job. That is almost literally Paul's argument in 2 Thessalonians 2. Indeed, it is the final "arrival" of Jesus "at his appearing" that will bring about the destruction of the Antichrist and end his rebellion against God by the "breath of his mouth" and the "brightness of his appearing" (ὃν ὁ κύριος Ἰησοῦς ἀνελεῖ τῷ πνεύματι τοῦ στόματος αὐτοῦ καὶ καταργήσει τῇ ἐπιφανείᾳ τῆς παρουσίας αὐτοῦ).[278]

Coming for the Saints and to Establish the Kingdom: Paul embraces Jesus' teaching that he is both coming for the saints, to retrieve them, and that he will appear to overthrow every resistance to the rule of God. Both elements are intertwined in Jesus' and Paul's eschatology, and

---

[278] Holmes, M. W. (2011–2013). *The Greek New Testament: SBL Edition* (2 Th 2:8). Lexham Press; Society of Biblical Literature.

imply a process and not a single, discrete event. Christ's reign from his ascension until his appearing to overthrow all opposition to God, and to establish the rule of God over all of his creation, is a process. This process, Paul declares, began with Christ's ascension and enthronement, where he is actively engaging from heaven against the kingdom of darkness and those who opposed to the rule of God, pushing back against the consequences of sin and the fall prior to his appearing. That he is doing so mainly through the saints as they do the work of God on earth, and carry out Christ's mission for the church, resourced by the power of the Spirit is axiomatic for Paul (1 Cor. 15:20-28). What is held in abeyance, then, is Christ's return for the saints, and his ultimate overthrown of sin and rebellion against God by his appearing in glory, when the kingdom of God will come to its full and final expression in the unopposed reign of God over his wholly renewed creation (cf. Rev. 21:1-8).

In other words, the eschatological reign of Christ is already at work, reclaiming for God what was lost in the fall. His present work is due to come to its consummation at Christ's return, first for the saints, and then at his appearing to overthrow every opposition to God (1 Cor. 15:50-58; 1 Thess. 4:13-17; 2 Thess. 2:1-11, cf. Matt. 16:27; 24:30; Mark 8:28; John 14:1-3; Acts 1:11). The key, for Paul, is that the kingdom of God is already engaged in the great enterprise of moving God's purposes forward, especially now that Christ sits enthrone with God in heaven, at his right hand. As the saints go about their work of preaching the gospel, and the church serves God in the power and under the leadership of the Spirit (Eph. 4:3, 16), the kingdom of God, under the rule of Christ, is pushing back against the principalities and powers opposed to God's rule in the present, advancing its movement toward the time of Christ's appearing (Eph. 1:10; 2:1-2, 6; 3:8-12; 6:12; Phil. 3:20-21; Col. 1:5-6, 18-20; 1 Thess. 1:10; 4:16-17; 1 Pet. 3:13).

Paul describes Jesus as actively engaged in doing battle with the enemies of God, in the heavenly realms, and on earth through the saints, bringing them into defeat and subjection to God. All of this is in preparation for the day when the kingdom will be presented to God the Father on his throne, so that he will be all in all (1 Cor. 15:20-28). He is, as Colossians 1 states, holding all things in creation together, so that they do not prematurely disintegrate before God can affect his plan, a role, presumably, Christ shares with the Father (Col. 1:16-17, cf. Eph. 1:22-23). A common perception of Christ as passively occupying the throne in glory, awaiting his reappearance on the earth, is rebuffed by Paul's presentation of Christ as subduing the enemies of the kingdom of God ahead of his presentation of the final kingdom to God at the commencement of the eschaton, and holding everything together until that moment. The triumph has begun with the resurrection of Christ, who has appeared before God as the glorified Son of Man, representing the triumphant resurrection of a redeemed humanity. He is the token and first fruits of a final full redemptive harvest of those who, Paul says, will inevitably follow in their turn (1 Cor. 15:20).

Christ's presence in the heaven, as the glorified Son of Man, the incarnate Son of God, represents a glorified and redeemed humanity that belongs to God, and that will in due time join with him to reign (Rom. 10:17). It is a humanity reconciled to God by transformative justification (Rom. 5:1), and that has been relocated into the sphere of God's operations, his kingdom, by the Spirit (Rom. 5:2; 6:1-11). Having surrendered to God's rule through repentance, faith, and justification, they are even now living in obedience to God under the direction of the Spirit, and under the rule of God (Rom. 8:1-4; Gal. 5:16-25).[279] This is

---

[279] If earlier analysis of mine are correct, this is what the law aimed at producing, right hearts, in right relationship with God, doing right things. The law held out as a prerequisite to adherence, loving God or having one's heart

holiness. This is righteousness – lives lived under the influence of God, where a heart made right with God, produces right conduct and produces maturing uprightness in character towards full godliness at the appearing of Christ (Rom. 8:29-30; 2 Cor 3:18; 4:16-18; 5:17; Eph. 4:17-24; Col. 3:9-10). These, righteousness, and holiness, for which Paul passionately argues in Romans 6, are enable through the power of a transformed life in Christ and the indwelling Spirit. They are inculcated through a persistent and faithful walk with God in the present and as the result of a transfer from the kingdom of darkness, living is under the rule of sin and Satan's power over human moral failure and predisposition, into the kingdom of God, where a morally changed life is animated by the indwelling Spirit to serve God. This is taking place for those who are now in the kingdom of God, though still living in this present age, but with hope and anticipation of Jesus finishing his work on the heavenly side, when it will be time to come for them (1 Thess. 4:13-17, cf. Rom. 5:3-5).

The church and believers are connected with both the work of the gospel in the world, which is the role of the kingdom of God in this age, and through their relationship with Christ to the heavenly preparations for a new creation under the unopposed rule of God in the future – where Christ is preemptively reigning at the right hand of God (cf. John 14:1-3; 1 Cor. 15:20-28; Phil. 2:8-11; Col. 1:15, cf. Rev. 19:11-21). It is with great anticipation that the saints await the confluence of both efforts, the work of the gospel going on throughout the world in this present age, and the heavenly preparations, which Jesus said he was ascending into

---

right with God, something than needed clarifying to God's people by Jeremiah and Ezekiel (cf. Isa. 1:2-31; Jer. 31:31-34; Ezek. 36:22-28). Interestingly, when God makes the promise to David concerning Solomon, he emphasizes that before Solomon obeyed him, he must ensure that his heart was in the right attitude toward God, and it is reiterated a number of times in that context. This is an old covenant principle, where technical adherence to the law alone was clearly not enough.

heaven to make, in anticipation of his return on the "day of the Lord." This "day of the Lord" itself, in Pauline theology, consists of a process, a series of events, in which there will be a resurrection and rapture of the saints, followed by the overthrow of the lawless one or man of perdition, followed by the destruction of evil, and the establishing of the rule of God over his creation, unopposed (1 Thess. 4:13-17; 2 Thess. 2:1-12).

The Church Straddling Two Worlds: United to both the ongoing mission of Christ in the present age, and the preparations being made in heaven, it is the indwelling Spirit that connects the two realms with the power and presence of God, God's rule in and among them, if you like, so that believers already, to quote Paul, sit with Christ in the heavenly realms (Eph. 1:3, 20; 2:6). Effectively, those who belong to Christ live and operate in the kingdom of God, as we argued above, and are connected by the Spirit to the future rule of God, so that even in the present the heavenly power and resources of God, which he will exercise in the eschaton, are in some way experienced among and provided to believers in the present (2 Cor. 1:20-21; 3:6; 5:5; Eph. 1:13-23). Through their connection with the kingdom of God, and because of relocation into Christ through justification, the saints straddle two worlds, as it were, the present age in need of the gospel, and in which they serve God and the mission of Christ, and the world to come, where Christ is already reigning and ruling in heaven as their representative (1 Cor. 15:20-28; 42-58).[280] While Christ has ascended, the first-fruits of a risen, and glorified humanity, the saints who are not yet raised and so transformed, must serve God faithfully, laboring without growing weary,

---

[280] This is the idea conveyed in Charles Wesley's hymn when he speaks of the victorious Christ, who wounds are "yet visible above." The glorified Jesus who is the forerunner of a redeemed humanity, reigning in resurrection power even now, while the church serves in anticipation of its final translation and glorification.

knowing that their work in the Lord is not in vain (1 Cor. 15:58; Gal. 6:9-10; Phil. 1:6).

There is, in Paul's view, a continuity between the outworking of God in the church, through the Spirit in this age and world, and the activity of God in heaven advancing his purposes in creation toward the final outcome he has planned since before creation and the fall (1 Cor. 15:20-28; Col. 1:15-20, cf. Gen. 1:26-28; 3:15). They are conjoined through the Spirit, who is the agent of the kingdom and power of God to and the church. He is also the intercessor, along with Christ, for the saints in heaven to God the Father. Because he knows the will of God, he is aware of God's purpose, his intercessions align themselves with God's design in behalf of the saints and the church, as God provides grace and help in their time of need (Rom. 8:23-27). The Spirit both guides and seeks resources for the saints in their role of preparing for the return of Christ, and for a new heaven and earth. He also engages the critical role of aligning the church and the saints with the activity going on in heaven in preparation for the Christ's return to establish the kingdom of God, a visionary insight of which John gives us in Revelation 19:11-21, where Jesus and the saints stand on the cusp of his return in glory, amassed ready break into the world.

This connection means that whatever God's intentions are, the church and believers are participants in what God is doing to bring about his purposes, and that participation consists of engagement in the work of the kingdom of God in the present age, on earth, as well as with the work going on in heaven through Christ, their human-divine representative, the Second Adam. Through the Spirit their earthly efforts contribute to and engage with the heavenly work being done in preparation for Christ's return. Rather than Jesus building gaudy mansions for saints in heaven for them to occupy, his preparations have more to do with making things ready for new heaven and earth, operating under the unopposed rule of God. The efforts of the saints working in unison with the purposes of God on earth are underwritten by the sovereign power of God through the Spirit at work in them (Eph. 1:13-23). The same power is at work in the heavenly realm, where Christ is making preparation for a future new creation (cf. Rev. 21:1-8), and it spills over through the Spirit into the lives of the saints serving God in his kingdom currently breaking into the present age and world. The Spirit of God links the church in the present and material context, with the activity of God in Christ's heavenly preparations for the future new heaven and new earth under the unopposed rule of God (cf. John 15:26-6:15).

At his ascension, Jesus assumed the throne with God, at his right hand (Ps. 110:1; Matt. 22:44; 26:64; Mark 12:36; 14:62; 16:19; Luke 20:42; 22:69; Acts 2:23-34; 5:31; 7:55-56; Rom. 8:34; Eph. 1:20; Col. 3:1; Heb. 1:3, 13; 8:1; 10:12; 12:2; 1 Pet. 3:22). Paul's description of this in Philippians 2:9-11, is that he was exalted and given a name that was above *every* other name in heaven, earth, and under the earth, and that soon every knee will bow, and every tongue will confess that Jesus is Lord (ἵνα ἐν τῷ ὀνόματι Ἰησοῦ πᾶν γόνυ κάμψῃ) (cf. Isa. 45:23).[281] There are clearly two aspects to Jesus' ascension, to reign with God in the present, and to reign with him in the future after the consummation of all things. In the future a time will come when every knee will bow and every tongue confess the Lordship of Christ in all of creation, which clearly in not true in the present, given the rebellion of humanity against God, and the opposition of Satan (Phil. 2:10-11, cf. Isa. 45:23; Heb. 2:8).

Paul's Old Testament background kicks in and he views the exaltation of Christ to his heavenly place at the throne of God, at his right hand, as consistent with the prophecy of Isaiah, that every knee will bow to God and every tongue confess his lordship (Isa. 45:23, cf. Dan. 7:13-

---

[281] Holmes, M. W. (2011–2013). The Greek New Testament: SBL Edition (Phil 2:10). Lexham Press; Society of Biblical Literature. The contingency of the subjunctive, κάμψῃ, has a future or forward-looking aspect.

14). The exaltation of Christ assures the fulfillment of this prophecy in Christ, the divine Word of God, who is God. It is the fulfillment of the Danielic vision of the Son of Man, to whom the Ancient of Days gives his throne, to rule in his behalf, and even to receive the worship that belongs to God (Dan. 7:13-14). The *Son of Man* here is clearly a divine figure, uncreated, and not a creature, because God will not give up his glory to such a being, and refuses to allow Israel to worship what are not gods, but idols and created things. Paul, in Romans, states that this is the problem with humanity generally, it worships what has been created, rather than the creator (Rom. 1:21-25). Isaiah's description of the divine champion, who will bring about the rule of God, is that he is *Mighty God,* the *Everlasting Father, Emmanuel,* God with us, and that of the increase of *his* government, the child that will be born, and the son that will be given, there will be no end (Isa. 7:14; 9:6-7). He will, in fact, possess both divine and human characteristics. He will share in the divine nature of God, as it were, and in the nature of humanity, so that he will act on God's behalf as the *Servant of the Lord,* with both divine prerogatives and human nature conflated into a single Messianic figure. His position will make him uniquely suited to offer himself as the sacrifice for the sins of God's people Israel, an offer of redemption to be expanded to Gentiles, and he will even give up his life, only to be raised from the dead to give redemption, and to see the fruit of his labor in those saved (Isa. 52:13-53:12). He will be both the son of David, and God with us, from the root of Jesse, but possessing the divine nature that entitles him to be called by the titles of God, and receive the worship due only to the Ancient of Days, all without contradiction to the mandate that God alone must be worshipped (Ps. 2:4-9; Is. 7:14; 9:6-7; 11:1-2; 42:1-4; Dan. 7:13-14; Rom. 1:3-4).

Summary: What all of this amounts to is that for Paul, those who are in Christ actually belong to the kingdom of God locatively now. They stand in grace, in Christ, and are participating in what Jesus brought with him at his appearing, when he declared, "...the time has come, the kingdom of God is here" (Mark 1:15). The power of the kingdom of God is mediated to the believer and the church through the Spirit as they live in fellowship with God, and surrender to him and to his leading. Paul insists, those who are in Christ, as participants in the kingdom of God, must live out their kingdom life in a world at war with God and God's rule. They are to live so as to counter it, and as lights shining in the darkened sky of a perverse and cooked generation (Phil. 2:14-16). Paul's own testimony is one of the consequences of living in opposition and resistance to the world and the kingdom of darkness, where he often faced the consequences of pushback against God and the rule of God through hardships and persecutions (2 Cor. 1:5-7; 6:4-5; 11:16-33; Eph. 3:13; 6:20; Phil. 1:7, 13, 17; Col. 1:24; 4:3; 1 Thess. 2:2; 2 Tim. 2:9; 3:10-11, cf. Rom. 5:3; 8:17-18, 36; Eph. 6:10-12; Phil. 1:29; 3:10-11; 1 Thess. 1:6; 3:4; 1 Thess. 2:14; 2 Thess. 1:5; 1 Tim. 1:8; 2 Tim. 1:12; 2:3; 3:12).

Nevertheless, the resources of God's grace in which believers now stand because they are reconciled to God by grace, are made available through the Spirit who dwells in the church and in their bodies as the temple of God in this age (Rom. 5:1-2; Eph. 2:19-22, cf. 1 Cor. 6:19-20; 2 Cor. 6:16-18). The church, and believers are the locus of the presence of God in the world, where once the temple in Jerusalem served that purpose (1 Cor. 6:19-20; 2 Cor. 6:16-18, cf. Rom. 8:10; Col. 1:27). Through the Spirit, message, and work, God's redemption is accomplished and pushes back against the kingdom of darkness that holds so many in bondage to sin and rebellion against God (Eph. 2:1-3, cf. Heb. 2:15). Now, believers are empowered to live as true and authentic representatives of the holiness and righteousness of God (Rom. 8:1-4; Gal. 5:16-25; Eph. 4:22-24; Phil. 2:14-16). In the meantime, Christ is at work preparing for his return, holding things together until that moment, while also working to bring all things under the rule of God (1 Cor. 15:20-28, cf. John 14:1-3; Phil. 2:9-11). Furthermore, he is also interceding, along with the Spirit, from his vantage point at the right hand of God, representing the saints and pleading for the intervention of God with grace and provision for his people as they contend with the hardships of this age prior to his return (Rom. 8:34, cf. John 17; Heb. 4:14-16; 7:25). That the Spirit is seen as contending for the saints fully armed with the knowledge of God's will and ultimate purposes, implies that the church and the believer are at an advantage over those who are not connected the final and glorious triumphant outcome God has his mind (Rom. 8:26-28).

Even now those who belong to Christ, and who are *in him,* have been translated into the kingdom of God, and out from the dominion and authority of the kingdom of darkness operating in this world and age (Col. 1:13). They are already citizens of the ultimate renewal of all things by God, his kingdom, of which they have tasted at their own renewal at justification and reconciliation to God (Rom. 5:1-2; Rom. 8:24-25; 2 Cor. 5:17; Phil. 1:6; Col. 1:27). What is future has been deposited in their lives by the indwelling Spirit's presence (Eph. 1:13-14; 2 Cor. 1:21-22; 5:5), so that they are already participants in the diving nature and plan of God (2 Pet. 1:4), though not yet of its final consummation at Christ's Parousia. They straddle two worlds, the one where they serve God and suffer the same trials Jesus suffered (cf. Rom. 8:17; 2 Cor. 1:5; 2 Tim. 2;12, cf. 1 Pet. 4;13), and the one which Jesus is preparing for the future by his work in heaven, and from which he, through the Spirit, dispenses resources of God's grace to mitigate their hardships and suffering until he comes (Rom. 8:31-39). They are not citizens of the present age, but through their relationship with Christ, have become citizens of the kingdom of God and the guaranteed future renewal of creation under God's unopposed rule (Phil. 3:20-21). It is the view of N. T. Wright that in the new heaven and earth, the two will overlap and interlock with one another (Rv. 21:1-8). God will inhabit not only the heavenly reality of the non-material realm of his dwelling but fully indwell the material realm of a physically new creation, in a way foreshadowed by his presence with Adam in the garden, and by engaging in fellowship with him there (Gen. 3:8, cf. Isa. 65-66; Rev. 21:1-6). Paul contends that this has already begun with the risen glorified Christ in heaven preparing for his return, dispensing the Spirit to the church so that God's people might live and engage in fellowship with God even now in this present age, and taste future glory… in the present.

MEANWHILE IN THE CHURCH AND IN THE SAINTS

In Romans, Paul deals with what the life of the saints looks like in the present under the rubric of a death and resurrection, death to the law and the controlling sinful principle of human nature, along with freedom from slavery to sin in fallen human nature, and a resurrection to new life involving transformation and the inculcation of righteousness and holiness (Eph. 22-24, cf. Rom. 6-8). In Galatians, Paul develops the same theme along the lines of death on the one hand to the former self and way of life (way of living), to be made alive to a new life (way of living) through the empowering action of God (Gal. 2:19-20; 5:24-25). Paul went on to develop the idea of God's empowering as consisting of the indwelling presence of the Holy Spirit in the life of the believer, who will produce in them the fruit of the Spirit when they consistently conduct themselves under his supervision and in surrender to God (Gal. 5:16-25). In the Ephesian the context, Paul focuses, it seems, on the increasing maturity and spiritual development of believers (in the corporate context, the church), where the goal is to reach the full measure of the stature of Christ (Eph. 4:13). Unity is critical to the environment in body of Christ so that the resources and edifying encouragement necessary for growth may freely flow between interconnected members (Eph. 4:11-24). The goal is for the saints to prevail until they have reached the goal God has in mind, that they should come to the full measure of the stature of Christ, be conformed to the image of his Son (Rom. 8:29-30; Eph. 4:13). That a unified church has a role to play in their perseverance through mutual and edifying support one for the other is an important Pauline concept (Eph. 4:16). Their pursuit of the holiness of God and continuation in his grace is linked to their role as vital supporters of the spiritual success of the other members of the church and body of Christ, so that God's goals for his redeemed people may be fully realized in them.

Colossians 3 also has a goal directed sense to it, where Paul instructs his readers to put off the old life and put on the new self (Col. 3:5, 10) in a context where God is moving all of creation toward final reconciliation to God in Christ (Col. 1:13-20). They are to remain firmly established in Christ until the end, unmoved from the hope they have that God will complete his purposes, that is to bring about the reconciliation of all things to himself at the return of Christ (Col. 1:21-23). Paul's idea is that through their unwavering faith in God, they too will find their proper place of inclusion in that reconciliation of all things to God as representatives of him in his image (Col. 3:10). They are to live their lives fully rooted in Jesus, a metaphor suggesting growth to maturity as well as stability, and continue to move toward the goal, implementing in their daily lives what they have been taught (Col. Col. 2:6-7). He encourages the Colossians to *set their minds on things above,* with the implication that this is the goal, and to leave behind earthly things, that is to avoid being distracted and discouraged by earthly attachments and concerns of this life (Col. 3:2). Movement clearly is implied away from one realm more resolutely embrace the other (Col. 3:2). The end goal is to appear with Christ in glory, and when he appears to reflect his glory to all of creation (Col. 3:4).

Having rejected and put off the old life, they must put on the new self, which is *being renewed,* that is in the process of being developed in righteousness and holiness to reflect the image of God (Col. 3:10). It is by engaging the renewal through the Spirit at work in them, that are moving toward that final goal. The sense of forward movement and goal directedness in Paul's exhortations to moral and spiritual growth cannot be missed and should not be ignored, because it has in mind God's final endgame for the saints and creation. Paul consistently portrays the

Christian life, not as a static state of being, simply justified, put right with God, not even momentarily transformed through new birth (imputed/imparted righteousness), but as a genuine organic development and growth toward authentically mature godliness of conduct and character, having *begun* with a morally transformative experience of justification.

Everything we have said so far concerning a Pauline theology of transformative justification, followed by the indwelling power of the Spirit producing right conduct and godly character, in order to produce mature godliness, stands behind what Paul has in mind here. The goal of producing the righteousness and holiness of God in us does not stand in a vacuum. It is not conferred, to use Wesley's phrase, *a little before the article of death*, or even at death, but the Pauline notion that God is at work in us to produce moral and spiritual growth throughout the Christian life is integral to how the believer lives in the present age as a representative of God. The idea that holiness is possible in this present age, and in our ordinary lives as believers is at the heart of Wesley's contention for the second blessing and sanctification. Through the gracious work of God, this new life of holiness and true righteousness must and can have a significant effect on our conduct and character in the present before we die. A Wesleyan theology of salvation is, in its most basic form, the idea that the holiness and righteousness of God are integral to the present life in this world, and furthermore are made possible through the gracious action and provision of God to the believer in Christ.

Where Paul is Going in Ephesians 4:17-24: In our passage, and its related section from 4:25-6:9, Paul employs conjunctions (small words that indicate the relationship between sentences or larger sections of the text) to show the flow of his arguments, or the logic of his address to the Ephesians. At the commencement of this section, in verse 17, Paul uses an inferential conjunction, *therefore* (οὖν), which signals that there is a contingency between what he has said and what he is about to say. “Therefore, this I say and witness in the Lord,” grounds his next remarks in a serious call for the Ephesians to listen and take note of what he is about to say. What he is about to command or instruct is contingent on what he has previously been saying about God’s purpose for the ultimate unity of all things in Christ and in the church. Their union with Christ through redemption involves sealing them by and with the Spirit, and implies the eschatological directedness of God’s purpose for the church and believers. He has *already* given them the downpayment of the Spirit to guarantee what is to come in the future, the goal of which is for them to reach the full measure of the stature of Christ in their moral and spiritual development (Eph. 4:13). We ought to view this as the advanced expression of the rule of God among his people by the Spirit, a preemptive experience of a relationship with God as ruler over his creation and people, where core principles of his kingdom are at work in and among the saints to reflect his own holiness and righteousness back into the world (Phil. 2:12-16). They do not belong even to themselves, they have been bought with a price, and should glorify God in their bodies (1 Cor. 6:19-20). The church is the bridgehead of the kingdom of God into this age, part of the now but not yet proposition of the New Testament.

Paul has already argued that this was revealed mysteriously to the prophets under the old covenant, but more fully and clearly revealed to the apostles and prophets under the new, because of Christ’s incarnation, sacrifice, resurrection, and ascension to rule with God. The kingdom has broken in on the world and the church, with believers as it principal representation. They are politically aligned not with the world, or the Roman empire, but with heaven, of which they are citizens through relocation in Christ (Phil. 3:20-21). Therefore, they ought to display the culture and live by the principles of that alignment with the kingdom and rule of God, in obedience and loyalty to him. Their own reconciliation to God includes God enlisting them in the enterprise and ministry of reconciliation for others (2 Cor. 5:19b). God is making his appeal to the world through them, as far as redemption and salvation are concerned, and they have become his ambassadors to the lost, with a message, not condemnation, but of God's desire for reconciliation and restoration (2 Cor. 5:18-21). Christ has bequeathed the work of the kingdom, to represent God to the world, and to carry out the redemptive mission to the church, to carry it on after his departure, in the power and under the guidance of the Spirit (Matt. 28:19-20; Luke 24:45-49; Acts 1:8). However, this ministry and their representation of God to the world with the message of reconciliation must come with the authentic reflection of his character, in what Paul calls in Ephesians 4, the genuine righteousness and holiness of God by which the new self has been created by God through their *own* experience of transformative reconciliation to him (cf. 2 Cor. 5:21).

For Paul, the character of the saints, and right functioning of the church was imperative as a witness to the world (Phil. 2:14-16). In Ephesians, it appears, Paul addresses the danger of a breakdown in the unity of the church, which he foresaw coming shortly after his departure from Miletus, that not only affects its proper functioning as a healthy body of believers, in which the flow of the resources of the Spirit and edifying relationships build up and fortify the saints for growth and service to God, but that will mar the church's witness to the world as representative of God's character (Eph. 4:11-16).

The *therefore* of verse 17 grounds his remarks in his affirmation of the importance of unity in the church, that they should make every effort to maintain it, because the church needs to build itself up in love, and there should be no hindrance to freely flowing resources of God from one member to another (Eph. 4:3, 11-12, 16). When the apostle says they should no longer conduct themselves as Gentiles, and that they are to lay aside the old life to take up the new, and when we read his warning to the leaders of the Ephesians church in Acts, or his instructions to

Timothy, arguably we are justified in concluding that Paul is addressing pressure on the unity of the church that comes from selfishness, greed, and pride among leaders, which have already resulted in the sacrifice of truth (Acts 20:20; Eph. 4:19; 1 Tim. 1:3, 7; 3:15; 4:1-2, 7; 6:3-5; 2 Tim. 1:13-14; 2:14-15, 23-26; 3:6-7; 4:3-4). So, Paul's *therefore* has as its frame of reference what he has been saying prior to this, and that has coalesced around the overarching topic of unity in the church, that Gentile behavior cannot be allowed to creep back into the church or their lives, because of its effect on relationships between them, and on their witness.

As the argument goes forward, Paul marks his progress in this section and the beginning of the next with two more conjunctions that indicate the relationship between what went before, and what comes next. In verse 21, referring to his previous invective against some in the Ephesians church behaving like Gentiles, using a mild adversative conjunction (δὲ), he reminded them that that this is not how they learned Christ at the beginning, when they first come to know him (ὑμεῖς δὲ οὐχ οὕτως ἐμάθετε τὸν Χριστόν).[282] The current crisis of conduct that is undermining the health and unity of the church is the result of a departure from how they had been instructed at first to conduct themselves as morally transformed believers in Christ. The conjunction sets up the contrast between how things appear to be, based on Paul's invective, "I say this... no longer live like Gentiles..." and his next instructions for them to lay aside the old life altogether, and to more resolutely take up the new life they have in Christ, which is, after all, what they had been united with Christ to exercise (Eph. 4:22-24).

[282] Holmes, M. W. (2011–2013). *The Greek New Testament: SBL Edition* (Eph 4:20). Lexham Press; Society of Biblical Literature.

As believers in Christ, they had learned an entirely different way of life when they heard about Christ and surrendered to him (Eph. 4:20-21a). This new life is guided and informed by the truth that they have learned in Christ (Eph. 4:21b). In verse 22, Paul will go on to describe the content of the truth that they have learned, which in turn will produce a new way to live, practically speaking, through their new knowledge of the truth in Christ (cf. Eph. 4:25-6:9). Verses 22-24 describe the new principle of holiness and righteousness at work in their natures since learning the truth about Christ. The impact of this way of living, by the new principles at work in them through their surrender to and experience of Christ, is far-reaching. In Ephesians 4:25-6:9, Paul lays out the personal and practical details of their daily conduct and attitudes, which they must adopt and practice in their relationships with one another. This change in behavior will have an impact on the unity of the church and their relationships with one another. The implication is that the renewal that has occurred in their nature is to result in more than a few minor moral adjustments, rather it must lead to undertaking a whole new way of life. It is a thoroughgoing change and renewal of their nature to overcome the former sinfulness at work in them before coming to know Christ (Eph. 4:22). It is hard to overstate the Pauline concept of moral transformation which he envisions on coming to know Christ. It is so radical that the former way of life must be abandoned in favor of wholeheartedly embracing the new way of life offered by God by which he perfects holiness in us (Eph. 4:23).

What this new life will look like and how it will work itself out is the subject of the rest of the letter up to chapter 6 and verse 9. In this discussion, Paul will include exhortations about honest and appropriate speech, honesty and integrity, control of anger, refraining from stealing, becoming a productive and contributing member of the church community, resolutely rejecting anger, bitterness, slander, quarreling, and malice, embracing love, compassion and forgiving one another, and avoiding sexual immorality and impurity. They are to live purposefully, knowing God's will, and are to be worshippers so that in the corporate setting, when meeting together, they might encourage and edify one another. Husbands are to love their wives and wives are to respect their husbands. Children should be obedient to their parents, and fathers, in particular, are not to be overbearing and harsh towards their children. Slaves should respect their masters, serving them with integrity, and masters are to treat their slaves with genuine love and compassion, in much the same way God treats them as their Lord and master. These instructions flow out of the entire logic of Paul's discussion on unity, and the fact that this unity has at its core a transformative experience of God that has radically changed those who belong to Christ with respect to their human nature. It is the change of human nature through salvation that creates the necessary inward conditions for them act differently than the Gentiles around them, and to adopt conduct consistent with holiness and righteousness which reflect the holiness and righteousness of God (cf. Eph. 4:24).

ENDURANCE AND FINAL SALVATION: Theologians are often loathed to accept a plain reading of Paul where he appears to present as a contingency to the success of salvation, the cooperation and continued steadfastness of the believer. It is not our purpose to discuss the reasons for this reluctance, except that it is often rooted in a fear of *works righteousness* and the displacement of clear New Testament teaching that salvation is wholly of grace.[283] It was Jesus himself that first suggested that only those, in the face of wickedness and temptation, who stand firm to the end will be saved (Matt. 10:22; 24:13; Mark 13:13). In fact, Jesus seems to make final salvation contingent on endurance to the end (ἐν τῇ ὑπομονῇ ὑμῶν κτήσασθε τὰς ψυχὰς

[283] I have more fully discussed this issue in *Holiness Reconsidered* and *Help for Holiness*.

ὑμῶν).[284] It is clear from the wording of Jesus' statement that he has in mind ultimate outcomes, and is not speaking about securing salvation in the first place. The instrumental use of the preposition and dative (ἐν τῇ ὑπομονῇ ὑμῶν), "by your endurance you will secure your life," is stunningly straightforward (Luke 21:19). Luke's use of κτήσασθε is also stunning, in that it means to gain possession of, to secure, to procure for oneself, to acquire or get.[285] The most natural way to understand this is as something precured or secured, and is conveyed by the NIV's, "...you will win life." The NET Bible notes that although the aorist (κτήσασθε) is the harder reading compared to the future indicative in some manuscripts, in English we are forced to use a future, "you will gain your life," to convey the sense.[286] Jesus' comment has to do with ultimate outcomes, that the final disposition of those who put their faith in God through Christ, are not finally saved based on a past decision, but on the endurance of that attitude of loyal faith and trust in God until the end. There is no implicit compromise of grace because the idea of endurance presupposes the adoption of a position or an entrance into a condition, namely, to have found salvation through faith in God. To endure in a state secured by faith in God cannot conceivably be sustained by enduring in some *other* state secured by merit, by human effort or works (the point Paul makes in Galatians, especially chapters 3 and 5). Jesus obviously means, here, a continuation in the state of faith that has secured salvation initially through the grace of God, that it is by enduring as a matter of faith in God and by confidence in his grace that final salvation is secured to us by God.

---

[284] Holmes, M. W. (2011–2013). *The Greek New Testament: SBL Edition* (Lk 21:19). Lexham Press; Society of Biblical Literature.

[285] Arndt, 2000, 572.

[286] Biblical Studies Press. (2005). *The NET Bible First Edition; Bible. English. NET Bible. The NET Bible*. Biblical Studies Press, notes on Luke 21:19.

The idea that final salvation, that is reaching the goal, is contingent on enduring faith in God and not a past decision alone, persists consistently throughout the New Testament, and is an integral part of how God viewed his relationship with Israel. We have already commented on this above, and elsewhere, so we will not recapitulate it in detail here. Nonetheless, we note that Israel could not look to their historical covenants with God as a basis for an enduring position of privilege and blessing when they were no longer living in obedience to God as he had required and warned to do. Indeed, the covenant reiterated in Deuteronomy 28 completely puts pay to that idea through warnings of curses to come upon his people if Israel if they were to depart from God's law in disobedience, that they would forfeit their privileges and relationship with God under those circumstances. Later Ezekiel spoke very clearly about the righteousness of individual Israelites being contingent on their own enduring attitude toward God, and not on their former righteousness, now abandoned, and neither could they lay claim to the righteousness of their parents or children (cf. Ezek. 18). To live, Ezekiel's expression, they must engage enduring personal righteousness and faith in God (Ezek. 18:25-32).

The writer of Hebrews tackles this same issue in addressing the danger faced by Hebrew believers in Christ, who were about to turn back to Judaism. He writes that they have only come to participate in Christ "if only" or "supposing" they hold to the tenacity and steadfastness of their initial confession and it endures until the end, or until they reach the goal which God has set (μέτοχοι γὰρ τοῦ Χριστοῦ γεγόναμεν, ἐάνπερ τὴν ἀρχὴν τῆς ὑποστάσεως μέχρι τέλους βεβαίαν κατάσχωμεν).[287] The apodosis is fronted for emphasis, the "then" part of the condition, *you have come to participate in Christ,* on the condition, the protasis, that

[287] Holmes, M. W. (2011–2013). The Greek New Testament: SBL Edition (Heb 3:14). Lexham Press; Society of Biblical Literature; (Arndt, 2000), 268.

you *hold fast to your initial confession until the end* (Heb. 3:14). The clear implication is that it is not the initial confession that secures final salvation, but the endurance of that confession until the goal is reached. The whole book of Hebrews is dedicated to this proposition, that these Jewish believers must follow through on their initial commitment to Christ until the end (Heb. 3:6, 12, 14). Paul affirms this idea in Romans 11:22, where he says that his readers must remain firmly in place, or in the state of relying and counting on the kindness or mercy of God for salvation (ἐὰν ἐπιμένῃς τῇ χρηστότητι).[288] Paul finishes his thought with a warning that otherwise (ἐπεὶ) they will *also* (καὶ), like the unbelieving Jews, be cut off (ἐπεὶ καὶ σὺ ἐκκοπήσῃ), or cut loose from the covenant that leads to final salvation (cf. 1 Cor. 1:8; 10:12; 15:2, 58; 16:13; 2 Cor. 1:21, 24; Ga. 5:1; Phil. 2:16; 3:12; 4:1; Col. 1:23; 2:5; 1 Thess. 1:8; 2 Thess. 2:15; 1 Tim. 3:9; 6:12, 19; 2 Tim. 2:19, 7:25; see also Heb. 2:1-3; 3:6, 10-11, 12-14, 4:1; 2-3; 6:4-6; 9-12; 10:19-23, 26-27, 29, 36-39; 11:1-2, 6, 13-16, 27, 35, 39; 12:1-3; 7a, 15, 16-17, 25, 28-29, 13:14, 20-21; Rev. 2:7, 11, 17, 26; 3:4, 11, 21).

Part of Paul's perspective on salvation was that it has an eschatological trajectory toward which it aims and moves. There was both the overall purpose of God to reclaim all of creation through and in Christ (Col. 1:15-20), and within that plan his purpose to reclaim fallen humanity personally and individually through the cross of Christ and faith in him (Col. 1:21-23). The beginning of salvation is to be reconciled to God on the basis of the physical sacrifice (atonement) of Christ on the cross, where we are rescued out of the kingdom of darkness and brought into the kingdom of God morally and spiritually through a transformative experience of justification and reconciliation to God, as a result of pardon for sins (Col. 1:13-14). This reconciliation to God through faith

---

[288] Holmes, M. W. (2011–2013). The Greek New Testament: SBL Edition (Ro 11:22). Lexham Press; Society of Biblical Literature.

in Christ, however, is *if indeed* (εἴ γε) we *remain in the faith* (ἐπιμένετε τῇ πίστει), *steadfast and firm* (τεθεμελιωμένοι καὶ ἑδραῖοι) and are not *moved away from the hope we have in the gospel* (μὴ μετακινούμενοι ἀπὸ τῆς ἐλπίδος τοῦ εὐαγγελίου).[289] Paul bases the final success of the Colossians on their persistent faith, and not being turned aside to the elemental principles of this age, by which he means its vain philosophies and systems that oppose the gospel (Col. 2:8). Their initial faith must be held firmly until the journey is complete, until the end of the road. The perfect participle, τεθεμελιωμένοι, nominative, plural, answering to the subject of the verb ἐπιμένετε, means they are to be hold their faith in Christ as a *steadfast kind of people*, who refuse to turn loose of it. The participle seems to express the idea of a current state of unwavering determination based on originally having taken that position at some point. They are not to be moved from their firm faith, which they adopted at some point in the past, and must hold to it in a state unmoved determination and loyalty to God. This remaining must continue unabated until the end because that is the condition upon which the final of their reconciliation to God depends.

To persistence, Paul adds, what we see in Ephesians 4:22-24, the idea of a progressive development of moral character in the Christian life, where Christ's goal is that through his death he should present us at last as holy and blameless to God (παραστῆσαι ὑμᾶς ἁγίους καὶ ἀμώμους καὶ ἀνεγκλήτους κατενώπιον αὐτοῦ).[290] This then is the goal, reconciliation to God that leads to holiness and blamelessness when we are finally presented to God in the end (Col. 1:22). These themes are consistent throughout the Pauline corpus, that God is working toward eschatological fulfillment of his redemptive purposes, that these involve

---

[289] Holmes, M. W. (2011–2013). *The Greek New Testament: SBL Edition* (Col 1:23). Lexham Press; Society of Biblical Literature.
[290] Holmes, M. W. (2011–2013). *The Greek New Testament: SBL Edition* (Col 1:22). Lexham Press; Society of Biblical Literature.

our reconciliation to God through the sacrifice of Christ on the cross, and that this reconciliation consists in the forgiveness of sins and a moral transformation designed to produce mature godliness in those who are saved (Eph. 4:22-24; Col. 1:22). God's eschatological purposes for creation overlap and interconnect with God's salvific purposes and the final redemption of the people of God (cf. Rom. 8:18-29; Col. 1:13-23). The end is always in view, salvation leads to the goal God has set for it in an eschatological reconciliation of all of creation to his rule, and that redeemed humanity will share the task of ruling over it with Christ.

MORAL MATURING AS PART OF GOD PLAN: The journey to the goal consists of moral a transformation leading to maturing godliness for those who come to know Christ in preparation for their presentation to God, and for their engagement in his future purposes (Eph. 5:27; Col. 1:21-22, 28). The space between initial reconciliation to God and final perfection of the image of Christ is not empty. It must be filled with a growing and deepening of the relationship with and knowledge of God, as Paul makes plain early in chapter 1, where that is not only his prayer, but he states that it is God's pleasure and purpose for the saints (Eph. 1:3-14). A similar growth and development must also take place in their character morally and spiritually, to support and benefit from their increasing knowledge and deepening relationship with God. There is no stasis in salvation. Initial salvation at justification is always aimed at the final trajectory of God's eschatological purpose, the full moral maturity of his people and their consequent involvement in his ultimate purposes for creation into the eschaton. So, for Paul salvation is initial transformative justification aiming at full moral maturity, and it is not just a static state or legal declaration of "rightness with God" in the present. N. T. Wright is surely correct when he says that the justification, or rightness with God, as a result of initial salvation, declares us right with God in the present in anticipation of the final disposition of being right with God in the end.[291] However, it seems to me that for Paul, once faith in God for reconciliation and justification is exercised initially, the basis for continued and final redemption is an ongoing exercise of faith in God, and a steadfast confidence in the saving power of Jesus Christ (Rom. 6:11; 11:22, 1 Cor. 15:2; Eph. 3:17; Col. 1:23, cf. Acts 13:43; Heb. 3:6; 4:14; 6:18-20).

The church is to reach the full measure of the stature of Christ, after all (Eph. 4:13). However, in the meantime, under the current conditions of serving God in this age, the people of God must mature to the point that they are no longer thrown about and deceived by every wind of doctrine, and he cunning craftiness of men who float false doctrine (Eph. 4:14-15). Ephesians 4:14-15 are clearly not eschatological, because what wind of doctrine and cunning craftiness of men will exit in the eschaton? Paul is addressing their current experience and engagement in the church and with one another. An engagement of growth and moral development as a progressive element in their salvation experience in the present certainly has something to do with their endurance, resilience, and fortification against being deceived and sidetracked from ultimately reaching the goal of their redemption (Eph. 4:15). Clearly, Paul has in mind the moral, and even mental development of the saints in their knowledge and wisdom of God, as he puts it elsewhere in Ephesians (Eph. 1:8, 17; 4:13; Col. 1:10, 28; 3:10). Paul views spiritual development to be multi-faceted taking place on many levels of faith, confidence in God, wisdom, knowledge, increasing love for one another, and of moral growth toward an authentic reflection of the image of God. It is undeniable that the apostle sees such development and growth as an essential aspect of a healthy Christian life, and vibrant church community. All of these areas of growth and maturing, as well as the overall progress of the church as a community

---

[291] Wright N. T., 2012, 29-32; Wright & Bird, 2019, 305-306.

of believers, are occurring simultaneously in Paul's model of the believer in healthy relationships with other believers. His letters to Timothy reflect this perspective on the church and how believers and leaders are to interact with one another. Paul encourages Timothy to reignite his spiritual passion and develop his maturity as a believer and leader personally, and to encourage the same in his church people, and to require leaders of the church to live up to their responsibilities (1 Tim. 1:18-20; 2:8-15; 4:1-15; 16, 22-25; 6:2-10, 11-15, 17-19; 2 Tim. 1:6-13; 15-18; 2:1-7, 14-21, 22-26; 3:1-9, 10-17; 4:1-5). Paul holds out this model to all of his churches, and encourages them to follow him as he follows Christ.

In our passage, Paul alludes to similar ideas, where laying aside the old life and taking up the new, in the context of God's renewing of the spirit/attitudes of their minds impinge on their progress in moral and spiritual development (Eph. 4:22-24). He explicitly states that God has created us in and for righteousness and holiness, so that we might ultimately reflect his own likeness back into creation (to use G. K. Beale's phraseology) by representing the full measure of the stature of Christ. The goal directedness of salvation, of unity, and of equipping the church with leaders is to produce the moral development that God seeks for his people, and in the church. In other words, the goal directedness of salvation is not merely for God to reach his eschatological goals for creation, but to reach those goals under the circumstances of his people truly representing him to creation in his authentic image, which, Paul further specifies, consists in righteousness and holiness (Rom. 8:29-30).[292] But they are also to represent God currently, in the in-between time, and act and live

---

[292] This idea has been crystallized in systematic theology as the *imago Dei,* the image of God, where invoking the phrase alludes to the entire theological implications discussed above and that are associated with it.

consistently with the transformation that has taken place in them through reconciliation to God in Christ; now, that is axiomatic in Pauline theology. What they have been made in Christ, and will be ultimately at the consummation of all things is what they are to be and become in ever increasing measure as they serve Christ in the present age (cf. 1 Cor. 13:9-12; 2 Cor. 3:18; 4:16-18).

The echoes to Genesis 1:26-28 are hard to miss. Paul broaches this topic more directly in Romans 8, where he says that all of creation in the present is waiting for the day when the *sons of God* will be revealed to precipitate, as a consequence, in the release of creation from its bondage to the fallout of humanity's sin (Rom. 8:19-21). The goal directedness of *their* salvation and redemption is the longed-for trajectory for all of creation, in anticipation of its own destiny, liberation from the consequences of original sin (Rom. 8:29-30). Since the original destiny of creation was tied by God to the role of humanity as coregents with God, when sin entered the equation, Paul says, creation found itself in bondage to suffering as the consequences of original sin, along with humanity (Rom. 8:20). Furthermore, Paul says, creation's hope for liberation from bondage to the consequences of humanity's sin is connected to the final goal-directed moral and spiritual reclamation of humanity through reconciliation to God in Christ (Rom. 8:19-21). He goes on to explain that the liberation of which he speaks consists in the full and final redemption of God's people through resurrection and glorification of their bodies (Rom. 8:22-25). In this hope for humanity also lies a hope for creation, that it will follow where the children of God go (cf. Col. 1:13-20).

In this way, Paul ties the eschatological hopes of redeemed humanity, in final consummation of their salvation through resurrection-glorification, to the anticipation of creation for its own ultimate liberation from the futility and consequences of the fall. In Ephesians, Paul's idea of the revelation of the *sons of God* in Romans 8 is imbued with substance, *the restoration of the image of God* in true righteousness and holiness, in order that a redeemed humanity might reflect the image of God back into a released, eschatological creation, and to make way for God to finally fulfill his original mandate for creation and humanity together. Now, Christ has ascended to heaven as the advanced representation of a redeemed, risen, reigning, and glorified humanity, to establish on behalf of those who are being redeemed, the reclamation to God original purpose (1 Cor. 15:20-28; Phil. 2:8-11). Paul portrays Christ as the risen, victorious, ascended, and enthroned Son of Man, representing a redeemed humanity that is to follow, and who has begun to reign in their place and as their forerunner, to secure their place (1 Cor, 15:20-28; Eph. 1:13-23; Phil. 2:8-11, CF. Heb. 6:16-20).

There is then an inevitable, intentional moral development included in the plan of justification by grace and faith through Christ, that places those who are saved into the environment of grace, and that lead immediately to the necessity and reality of moral development for the saints (Rom. 5:1-8). This progressive development of moral character is the underpinning of the *hope* of the saints, and it consists in their recognizing that the changes occurring in them right now indicate that God fully intends bring all of this to its final and full expression by conforming them to the image of his Son (Rom. 5:1-5; 8:29-30). God's purpose is not only to impact the church's present witness in this age (cf. Phil. 1:6; 2:12-13, 14-16), but that their experience of moral development and progress might be consciously tied to the eschatological fulfillment of God's purposes for his entire creation in the minds of the saints, whom he is perfecting in righteousness and holiness (Col. 1:13-20, cf. Rom. 8:19). This moral development, Paul argues, is the objective evidence of the believer's hope for the future fulfillment of God plan. Where morally transformative justification leads to a new creation, it must be followed by moral development, the purpose of which is for God to create a people for himself who bear the *imago Dei* in eschaton, in order to represent him to a new creation (Rom. 5:1-5;

Rom. 8:18-30). The saints are being conformed into the image of God's beloved Son as the result of a process initiated at justification and engaged through the indwelling power of the Spirit, seeking the development and maturity of the new life created in them by God (Eph. 4:13-16; 22-24).

On the heavenly side, Jesus has, as the glorified and perfect Son of Man, initiated the rule of God as a morally and spiritually perfect human representative of God. On the earthly side, the saints in the church, and as a community represent the image of God to a still fallen world, in anticipation of the final restoration of creation at the consummation of their salvation in resurrection and glorification – but all in due course (1 Cor. 15:20-21). Their work as God's people is underway; they are representatives of God in true holiness and righteousness in this present age (Eph. 4:22-24, 2 Cor. 5:20). But they await the ultimate fulfillment of God's purpose at the return of Christ, when God will reveal to all of creation what is not entirely apparent right now, that they are indeed the children of God (Rom. 8:20-21).

Reflecting the image of God into creation, through holiness and righteousness is imperative, and at the core of God purpose for humanity, both in the present age and in the age to come (cf. Phil. 2:14-16). For Paul, God's intention and purpose is to reveal *through the church* (God's redeemed and righteous people) the *manifold wisdom* of God, the sheer scope and glory of his plan in Christ for humanity, and for creation, and to vindicate his actions and plan in Christ to the heavenly powers opposed to his rule through an eschatologically redeemed and perfected humanity to become his new creation people who will carry his original purpose forward despite the fall (Eph. 3:10-12). Initial salvation does not result in a static moral state or simply positional 'rightness with God,' but initiates, through morally transformative justification, a change of nature requiring, and capable of, moral development by a process of endurance, believing, and service to God in the present, broken world (Rom. 5:3-5, cf. 2 Pet. 1:5-11). Paul told the Romans that God predetermine and intentionally purposed for those who are in Christ to assume the image of Christ. Final likeness to Christ is connected to God's endgame through God's intentional conformity of the saints to the image of God's Son building on a process of moral development and growth. The language and context in Romans suggests that his intention (προώρισεν) is a *conforming*, where a verbal quality in the adjective seems to imply a finale to growth in them taking on the likeness of Christ (cf. Eph 4:13-15). The culmination, in Paul's way of representing it, seems to be the crowning moment for those who have endured in Christ, when at last they will be established in the fully mature fruit of their growth and maturity in godliness to reflect the image of God's Son, the full measure of the stature of Christ, the image of the heavenly man, the *imago Dei* (Rom. 8:29-30; Eph. 4:13-15, cf. 1 Cor. 15:49; 2 Cor. 3:18).

In Galatians 5 Paul deals with this conforming as coming under the role of Spirit, who is at work in the life of the believer to perfect holiness, to bring about mature godliness, and which Paul represents as the fruit of the Spirit (Gal. 5:16-25). There, Paul makes clear that the dynamic power that stands behind holiness for those transformed by God at justification is the power of the Spirit at work in them, when they follow the leading of the Lord and keep in step with him (Rom. 8:1-4; Gal. 5:16,18, 24-25). The premise of his argument in Galatians seems to be that not only will the Spirit bring about an initial moral change in those who have faith in Christ for salvation, but that the Spirit will also see to it that there is moral development in the saints who have come to know Christ by faith. No need to resort to law-keeping or taking up ritualistic Judaism, because the Holy Spirit will produce the righteousness God is looking for in his people and that is represented by the law (Rom. 8:4). The Galatians do not need to retreat to the law or to Judaism, as had been suggested, to find the means for moral development, because God has endowed them with his Spirit (Rom. 8:9-14). The Spirit, when he is obeyed, that is, when they walk in, are led by, and keep in step with the Spirit, will produce holiness in God's people, leading to mature fruit bearing and godliness, affecting disposition and character (Gal. 5:13-25).

CHAPTER FIVE

TOWARD THE IMAGE OF GOD

Now, we return to our passage, Ephesians 4:17-24, in light of the discussion above. Arguably, Paul has concluded a section on the unity of the church, which began in chapter 1, with an appeal to the responsibility of the saints to maintain a unity established by the Spirit (Eph. 4:3). It is a unity underwritten by God through providing a single means of salvation in Christ for all who believe (Eph. 3:1-11), and a common destiny for all his people to become the habitation of God by the Spirit, regardless of ethnic background (Eph. 2:11-22). To accomplish his goals, he has equipped the church with leaders as a gift celebrating the risen and ascended Christ (Eph. 4:11-16), a dispensation, as it were, from his throne and his position of victory and triumph over death, as well as his assumption of rule over the kingdom of God in heaven (Eph. 4:1-6, 7-12). Grace has been apportioned to each one in the church by God on account of Christ, to do the work of the ministry, so that the church might thrive and grow as each one does their part, supplying the needs of the rest, while also benefitting themselves from the supply that freely makes its way throughout the body (Eph. 4:16). In this way the church grows and thrives toward the goal, which is to come to the full measure of the stature of Christ, that is to be a reflection of Christ, an accurate and mature representation of him in creation (Eph. 4:13). As we have seen, this is the same as Paul telling the Romans that God's goal for the saints in that they be conformed to the image of his dearly loved Son, as a result of the salvific process that leads to consummation of his goals for his people and for creation (Rom. 8:29-30). Paul's eschatological viewpoint is that the church, the saints, have a role to play in the final consummation of all things in creation, which is their hope (Rom. 5:3-8; 8:24-25), and according to God's plan they will reign with Christ, having been conformed to his image – a redeemed humanity is to be restored to a place that fulfills God original purpose for creation (Gen. 1:26-28; Rom. 8:14-24; 1 Cor. 4:8; 15:20-28; 2 .Cor. 4:18; Eph. 1:13-23; 4:13-22; Phil. 3:7-14; Col. 1:15-20; 2 Tim. 2:12, cf. Rev. 22:5).

The new section, that is represented by our passage, opens with two exhortations that fill-out Paul's meaning. Along with the grace of God given to each one to serve God in the church, he has established for every believer the grounds for moral success through a recreation, a transformation of sinful human nature, involving a moral renewal that aims at producing mature righteousness and holiness in them (Eph. 4:23-24). It is at first a transformation of nature (Eph. 4:23-24), and in the end a growth toward a full and mature expression of godliness in nature and conduct that fully represents Christ (Eph. 4:13, cf. Rom. 8:29-30). Therefore, Paul exhorts the Ephesians to lay aside all conduct and attitudes that are characteristic of how Gentiles live, that is, those who do not know or trust in Christ – the people who still live in disobedience to God as they themselves once lived (Eph. 2:1-3). Paul means those who are not believers, and have not been saved or morally transformed by the Spirit, as a result of justification (cf. Eph. 2:1-10). They are, on the other hand, to take firm hold of the new life they now have in Christ, which has been implanted in them by God, and which is characterized by the righteousness and holiness which reflect the moral perfection and purity of God's own nature (Eph. 4:23-24). It is not enough to have been delivered from the old life, that is to have been forgiven and justified, even transformed, if they do not go on to firmly embrace the new life they have in Christ, which is birthed in a righteousness and holiness that reflects the character of God (Eph. 4:22-24, cf. Rom. 6:1-23). Paul went to great lengths to give expression to the idea in Romans, Ephesians, and Colossians, as well as elsewhere, that those who come to a saving knowledge in Christ, *must* go on to take firm hold of the new life they have in him, that is, by leaving the old life behind, and living a new life of surrender and obedience to God (Eph.

4:17-21, 22-24; cf. Rom. 6:1-11; 2 Cor. 5:17). It is not enough to affirm an initial experience of conviction leading to justification, when the transformation that takes place is later rejected and abandoned, neglected, or overlooked (Rom. 6:1-2, 15, 23, cf. 2 Pet. 2:20-22). Paul emphasizes that in Christ's resurrection there is newness of life for the saints, which he describes later in Romans 6:15-18 as slavery to God, or to righteousness and holiness, whereas once they had been slaves to sin and sinning (τίνα οὖν καρπὸν εἴχετε τότε ἐφ' οἷς νῦν ἐπαισχύνεσθε; τὸ γὰρ τέλος ἐκείνων θάνατος) (Rom. 6:17-18, 20-23).[293]

As a transition, so as to speak, between the exalted and high-flying theology of chapters 1-3, and the practical implications for living out the principles of holiness and righteousness in the church as conduct that promotes unity among the saints, and that provides for the interactive flow of God's supplied grace between the saints, Paul reminds the Ephesians that it is necessary for the condition of their own hearts and lives be one of surrender to God, and of rejection of their former conduct and attitudes (Eph. 2:1-3; 4:17). This is after all, Paul reminds them, a matter of conscious and deliberate appropriation of God's provision, whereby the old life has been rejected, and the new life they now have in Christ seized and held on to (Eph. 4:22-24). Here in Ephesians, Paul exhorts his readers to do as he instructs the Romans in chapter 6, to realize what the nature of justification is, that it is morally transformative, and has as its goal a transformed nature, leading to transformed conduct. They are to take hold of this new life by a *calculated decision* that lays the old aside and take up the new. Just as in Romans 6:11, they are to *reckon,* that is, calculate and count on the

---

[293] Holmes, M. W. (2011–2013). *The Greek New Testament: SBL Edition* (Ro 6:21). Lexham Press; Society of Biblical Literature.

power of the new life to deliver what God promises in terms of righteousness through the Spirit working in them (Rom. 8:4).

THE GOAL IS OF THE SAME STUFF AS THE PROCESS

Just as the Holy Spirit is the token in the present of the age to come for the saints, so the substance of initial salvation is of the same character as its final, full consummation in the eschaton. What Ephesians 4 contributes to this picture is that the beginning of the process at initial salvation is not different from the end-goal. The new nature imparted at initial salvation is already created in the image of God in true holiness and righteousness, as a reflection of his nature and character (Eph. 4:24). The goal of transformation, through persistent application of the grace of God, and the consistent, determined cooperation of the saints as they walk in surrender to God, is that through the Spirit, the righteousness imparted to them might become mature godliness that reflects the holiness of God who implanted it in them initially (Eph. 4:13, 24, cf. Rom. 8:29-30). In other words, the original transformation that occurs are salvation imparts a new nature that has the potential for development into a fully mature expression of the image of God, as far as humanity has the capacity to reflect it. Indeed, it is God's goal for it to do so, so that his glory might be revealed to creation in the very humanity he originally commissioned to rule over it in partnership with him, by representing him in his likeness and image (Gen. 1:26-28, cf. Rom. 8:19-21).

In Ephesians, Paul remarks that within the entire sanctifying process, conceived as a movement toward the goal of final consummation in godliness, there is some decisive laying off and some taking up to be done, followed by the need for a willing and conscious ongoing surrender to God (Eph. 4:24, cf. Rom. 6:1-10, 11; 12:1-2; Eph. 2:10; Col. 3:5-10). There is some reckoning and counting on to be done (Rom. 6:11). The believer must not only emphatically embrace God's moral purpose, but by means of grace and the Holy Spirit, have enough faith in God that he can work it out in their lives, even in the present, as a daily, upright walk with God as they follow the lead of the Spirit (Eph. 4:22; cf. Rom. 8:1-4; 29-30; Gal. 5:16-25). Nevertheless, Paul proposes, even after initial transformative justification, and as we walk out the new life we have in Christ, there is some anticipated and further laying off of elements to be done, that might be viewed as flaws in our human nature, or weaknesses in our personal lives (Eph. 4:25-32). In other words, Paul is laying down a rationale that those who are now new creations in Christ, already invested with seed of God's righteousness and holiness, must nonetheless go on to take firm hold of the transformed life of God implanted within them, that they might walk it out in their daily lives, contending against flawed elements in their humanity that may arise from time to time (Eph. 4:25-6:9).

Romans and Galatians engage in lengthy treatments of this idea in terms of the role Spirit dwelling in the life of the believer, providing the influence and momentum toward the maturation of godliness for the believer. Ephesians 4 does something similar, but in a more practical context, under the overarching theme of life in the church that provides for unity among the saints in community with one another. What underlies the connections between the saints in the church is the dynamic of a transformed life under the influence of God through the Spirit, which leads to righteousness of character and conduct, supported by God's grace flowing freely between them as they live in fellowship together (Eph. 4:7-16). Just as in Romans and Galatians, Paul's concern here is that the saints live consistently with the new life that has been imparted to them because they have "been saved" by the grace of God (Eph. 2:8-9), and because God has seeded them with righteousness and holiness that reflect his own nature (Eph. 4:24). The fruit of such lives in terms of conduct, consists in the *good works* for which God created them in the first place in Christ Jesus (Eph. 2:10).

In chapter 2, and verse 10, Paul makes it clear that the anticipated goal of salvation for the those who are in Christ by virtue of faith in him, was that they might produce the good works, which God intended in the beginning (cf. Gen. 1:26-28). The NIV flattens out the original by translating Paul as saying that the saints are God's handiwork, created in Christ (that is recreated, adopted, reinstated) to do good works, which God previously prepared for them to do (Eph. 2:10). Paul uses a stronger language. God previously ordained for the saints to do the good works for which he *created them* in Christ, and which he intends them to *walk out,* or perform as a matter of habitual practice in the present (κτισθέντες ἐν Χριστῷ Ἰησοῦ ἐπὶ ἔργοις ἀγαθοῖς οἷς προητοίμασεν ὁ θεὸς ἵνα ἐν αὐτοῖς περιπατήσωμεν).[294] The saints have been brought into Christ to conduct themselves uprightly in obedience to God, and consequently he expects them to walk out the implications of their salvation in their daily lives. In chapter 4, Paul makes the point that there has been an inward transformation of their nature through Christ that makes what may seem impossible (and is often declared to be impossible), possible. By chapter 4 and verse 24 Paul has brought together right character and right conduct as interdependent elements of God saving initiative for the saints. This is the same Pauline idea of walking in the Spirit in Romans and Galatians, where those who live in surrender to God live under the influence of his leading, rather than the leading of the flesh or carnal nature which they have resolutely laid aside. In Romans 6, Paul describes the outcome of reckoning on the new life as slavery to God, to righteousness and holiness. Paul has in mind practical outcomes in terms of the behavior and conduct for the saints, which are to reflect the inward transformation that has taken placed in them as a result of being justified by faith in Christ, and reconciled to God through grace (Rom. 5:1-2, 20-6:11). Ephesians is not

---

[294] Holmes, M. W. (2011–2013). The Greek New Testament: SBL Edition (Eph 2:10). Lexham Press; Society of Biblical Literature.

saying anything different but uses a different turn of phrase. Paul lays out an expectation that those who are saved will live a habitually new life that is consistent with the transformation of their nature by God. If we can appreciate this core idea, then we will have gone a long way to understanding this passage.

John Wesley appears to have recognized Paul's point. Despite embracing the sanctifying purpose of God (his *second blessing*) through decisive faith as a matter of surrender to God, full moral/spiritual perfection in every aspect of our human nature is not immediately achieved.[295] There is a *walking out* in our daily lives and routines of the implications of initial, transformative justification and a subsequence, conscious, and fuller appropriation of the new life we have in Christ. Wesley spoke of being "liable to mistake," by which he meant we may well be or possibly might be subject to failure or errors due to flaws and imperfection in our humanity.[296] Wesley confirms his understanding of Paul, when he says that even the saved and sanctified cannot do without the constant involvement of Christ in their lives to perfect what God has placed in them by way of a transformed life.[297] Wesley refused to accept the Calvinistic/Augustinian mantra that even the saints are all unholiness and sin. He maintained that real moral transformation takes place through Christ, but that without the constant working of God in us through the Spirit, *left to ourselves,* we will inevitably fall back into sin.[298] He is making the same point Paul makes (in Romans, Galatians and Ephesians), that the transformation of God in us is in need of constant attention by way of reckoning on the new life of Christ implanted in us, and of surrender to the leading of Holy Spirit dwelling in us, who is, after all, seeking to perfect holiness in the people of God. Wesley, contrary to

---

[295] Wesley, A Plain Account of Christian Perfection, 1966, 82.

[296] Cf. Beacham A. D., 1998, 72-73.

[297] Wesley, A Plain Account of Christian Perfection, 1966, 82.

[298] Wesley, A Plain Account of Christian Perfection, 1966, 83.

what we have often heard in exuberant and enthusiastic preaching, never said that after a sanctifying experience, all impediments in our nature to the pursuit of holiness and growth in godliness are removed. So, Paul calls on his readers, in the passage under consideration, not only to lay aside the old life, and to take up the new, but to go on to lay off other habitual behaviors and conduct that may arise from certain flaws in their humanity or as a result of temptations, and to be vigilant against them (Eph. 4:25-32, cf. Col. 3:5-10).[299] The goal is maturation in godliness that reflects the fullness of the stature of Christ (Eph. 4:13). The future eschatological goal consists of the same *stuff* as the present new life inherited through the moral reclamation and transformation of those who are in Christ – namely establishing in them the holiness and righteousness of God that should be reflected in their daily lives in the present (Eph. 4:24, cf. Phil. 2:14-16). Through union with Christ, the saints have already been clothed with the new self, which is created to be like, and to truly (accurately, meaningfully) reflect the holiness and righteousness of God (τὸν κατὰ θεὸν κτισθέντα ἐν δικαιοσύνῃ καὶ ὁσιότητι τῆς ἀληθείας).[300]

A LAUNCHING PAD FOR NEW LIFE

Elsewhere in the Pauline corpus, the apostle works out the principle that if the initial transforming work is rooted in God's grace (Rom. 5:1-2),

---

[299] As a matter of historical record, Paul's strong and acrimonious dispute with Barnabas over John Mark, and subsequent acceptance of John Mark's value to him much later, bears testimony that even Paul's wrestled with issues over which he has to maintain strict control through the grace of God. His "thorn in the flesh" is another example of references to elements in his humanity and physical weaknesses with which he did battle (cf. 2 Cor. 12:7b-11; Phil. 3:12-14).

[300] Holmes, M. W. (2011–2013). *The Greek New Testament: SBL Edition* (Eph 4:24). Lexham Press; Society of Biblical Literature.

and that if it is through reckoning ourselves to be dead to sin and alive to God because we are in Christ this transformed life make moral progress (Rom. 6:11), and if the subsequent daily prosecution of our lives is under the direction of the Spirit (Rom. 8:1-4), then all of it, from beginning to end, is the result of the gracious action of God in us through the Spirit (Rom. 5:2-5). That includes the fruit of Spirit in terms of character (Rom. 5:3-5), and the good works he created us in Christ ahead of time to do (Gal. 5:16-25; Eph. 2:10). It is grace from start to finish (cf. Rom. 1:16-17). As Paul wrote to the Philippians to express this idea, "Continue to work out your salvation with fear and trembling, *for it is God who works in you to will and to act in order to fulfill his good purpose*" (italics mine) (Phil. 2:12-13).[301] Not only is the redemptive and salvific initiative from God, so also is the carrying out of the purpose and the achieving of his goals, including establishing holiness and righteousness in his redeemed people in anticipation of their participation with Christ at the resurrection and glorification of the saints (Rom. 8:18-24, 29-30, cf. Ps. 8:1-9). God works with us over time to perfect what he alone can initiate in those who have fallen short of the glory of God (Rom. 3:23), and he does it through faith that appropriates his grace to initially secure justifying moral transformation (Rom. 5:1-2; Eph. 2:8-9). It is the unique role of the indwelling Spirit to make it happen in the life and character of the believer (Rom. 8:1-4, 13-17; Gal. 5:16, 24-25). Nothing is more is critical to recognize than these dynamics in Paul's "system" of justification and sanctification, that it is God who works it all in us from start to finish (Eph. 2:10; Phil. 2:12-13).

Later Wesleyans, in America particularly, following the theological models coming out of what became known as the *holiness movement,* often left the impression in their preaching that crisis-sanctification (the decisive laying off and taking up, the reckoning of death for the old man

---

[301] *The New International Version* (Php 2:12-13). (2011). Zondervan.

(life/nature/attitude/ practice), and being raised to new life (life/nature/attitude/ practice), was a *landing* place, an arrival lounge, or bus depot, almost automatically resulting in holy living.[302] Paul, however, sees it more as a launching pad for a new life under new management and power through the Spirit (Eph. 4:25, cf. Rom. 6:4-5, 8, 11).[303] It is not the taking away of the old life, as the later holiness movement often emphasized in its preaching, the removal of the hindrance, but engagement of the grace and power of God through the indwelling Spirit that produces right conduct out of renewed character.[304] Justification that transforms is the beginning of a process leading to the full realization of godliness and mature holiness, which Paul often characterizes as glorification and resurrection, and which clearly includes the final reclamation of our physical bodies (Rom. 8:29-30).[305] Paul's laying off and taking up has a decisive element to it, but must be followed by an ongoing process of moral and spiritual development and growth (Rom. 6:19-22; 8:4; 12:1-2; 1 Cor. 6:11; 13:9-10; 14:20; 2 Cor. 3:18; 4:16-28; Eph. 3:19; 4:13-16; Phil. 1:6; 3:12-14, 16; Col. 1:10, 28; 2:2, 19; 4:12; 1 Tim 6:11; Titus 1:1, cf. 1 Pet. 2:2; 2 Pet. 3:18).

Paul's Theology of a Changed Life: Arguably, Ephesians 4:17-24 is transitional from the lofty theology of the early chapters to the practical instruction of chapters 4-6. Bishop A. D. Beacham points out that the passage bridges and unites both what has gone before, and what

---

[302] Cf. Peters, Christian perfection and American Methodism, 1995, 112-113, 129-130, 137, 162, 174.

[303] Cf. Brooks, Fingertip Holiness, 13-15; Brooks, Scriptural Holiness, 1972, 58-64.

[304] J. H. King, early bishop of the Pentecostal Holiness Church, recognized this, and in an article in the Advocate he remarks that once the old building has been torn down, a new building must be erected in its place - King J. H., 1976.

[305] Brooks, Scriptural Holiness, 1972, 43-44.

follows.[306] It seems to stand at the fulcrum of Paul's letter to the Ephesians. By it, Paul seeks to leverage practical Christian righteousness in service to the unity of the church, where right conduct and right attitudes are behind treating one another in the community of faith rightly (Eph. 4:17). Unity in the community, among believers, does not exist in a vacuum, and the Ephesians are to reject the way the world outside the church conducts itself toward others. In Roman honor and shame culture, where honor was perceived to be "in short supply", people tended to see those with advantages or who were well placed as a means to social and economic improvement, to be exploited, and those below them as resources to be used.[307] For the Galatians, just as much for Americans, the way society works would have been deeply engrained in their thinking, but through the gospel those norms have been challenged by the gospel, and the kingdom of God. The difference for the Ephesians, and by extension for us, in how they were to live now compared to those around them. Paul argues, the difference is rooted in the moral-spiritual changes that took place when those who now belong to the community of faith first experienced the regenerative and transformative power of God in justification (Eph. 2:1-3, 8-9; 4:17-24; cf. Rom. 5:1-8:17). Those transformed by God must live differently in conducting their relationships with one another in the church. There must be changes in attitudes and conduct because the inner dynamics of their lives have been altered by God, and are now under the influence and control of the Spirit (Rom. 8:1-15; Gal. 5:16-25).

The yearning for honor and upward mobility has been knocked out by an attitude of humility, love, mercy, kindness, and gentle, selfless service to other believers in the body, the church (Eph. 4:16, cf. Acts

---

[306] Beacham A. D., 2026.

[307] Cf. Witherintgon, 1998, 129-131; Longenecker & Still, 2014, 366; Capes, Reeves, & Richards, 2017, 22-23, 307-308; Witherington, The Paul Quest: A Renewed Search for the Jew of Tarsus, 1998, 44-50.

2:42-47; 4:32-37). Church community life is to be dramatically different from community life in the Gentile world around the church. In other words, a changed life through Christ impacts how the saints relate to and treat one another in their interactions, and as a result the church thrives through the selflessness and interconnected concern of the saints for one another (Eph. 4:16). The apostle is about to get into the specifics from Ephesians 4:25 on, where he will address concrete behavior and conduct, which support the unity argued for in chapters 1-4. But the practical implementation of certain principles of behavior and conduct in the context of Christian community, in chapters 4-6, require a right foundation in the hearts, minds, and attitudes of the saints. Paul reminds them, before he transitions into practical exposition on their conduct toward one another, that this foundation is essential and found only in the redemptive and salvific work of God in them. On the deeply personal level of their experience of the morally transforming power of God, undertaken by him in them by the Spirit, God has underwritten a heart-change that it at the epicenter of their new character and conduct toward one another. This heart change, Paul argues, requires laying aside the former life governed by fleshly impulses (selfishness) (Eph. 4:17-19), to take up a new life governed by godly impulses secured to them by a decisive, personal, daily surrender to God (Eph. 4:20-24).

The second half of Paul's argument in this passage, to which we now turn, consists of an appeal for his readers to *more fully adopt* the way of life they have learned from Christ, in contrast to following the familiar conduct and motivations of the Gentile culture around them (Eph.4:17, 20) (see the earlier discussion). Paul reminds them that the way the world acts is not the way of life they learned when they heard about from Christ. This implies they had both heard the transforming message of the gospel and had been instructed by Paul in the new way of life in Christ (Eph. 4:20-21a). This new life is consistent with the truth that is in Jesus, and its outcome is entirely different from the life of sin, out which they had come, and in which they once walked as children of disobedience (Eph. 2:1-3). Radical changes in their attitudes, and the inner environment of their minds and nature have occurred through Christ, and those changes must be worked out in similarly radical changes of their conduct.[308] It is not possible, Paul proposes, for the saints in the church to continue to act as they once did, like the Gentiles in the world around them conducts themselves (Eph. 4:17-19). The change that took place in them through Christ makes such a proposition impossible to contemplate (μὴ γένοιτο) (cf. Rom. 6:1-11).

Ephesians 4:20-24 makes a similar argument to the one Paul makes in Romans 6, the change at justification, as a result of an application of God's grace, will inevitably produces different outcomes in terms of conduct and character development going forward (cf. Rom. 6:1-11). In Romans 6, he argues that habitual sinning must inevitably cease as a result of a crucifixion with Christ of the old life, and they must move on to a new life, no longer in slavery to carnal desires, but in slavery to God, leading to righteousness and holiness as the result of a subsequent resurrection with Christ to newness of life (Rom. 6:4, 9-11). For Paul these are authentically visceral and organic alterations by God of human nature in terms of the mind and heart through the action of the Spirit, and faith in Christ (2 Cor. 5:17). They are not merely theological propositions of unachievable goals, or religious hopeful yearning. In Ephesians 4, Paul makes the same point, that as a result of a monumental change in us, by which God is making us new in the attitudes of our minds (ἀνανεοῦσθαι δὲ τῷ πνεύματι τοῦ νοὸς ὑμῶν), we

---

[308] A Pauline theology of sanctification does not end with the spiritually and morally transforming power of God, whereby there is a radical change in the heart and minds of the saints. Such a change must lead to practical holiness and righteousness, in terms of right conduct and behavior, as Noel Brooks argues in his important lectures, published as *Fingertip Holiness*. No Pauline theology of sanctification exists without the expectation of practical outcomes in terms of conduct that is consistent with obedience to God.

are to put off, lay aside, the old life, and to put on the new (ἀποθέσθαι ὑμᾶς κατὰ τὴν προτέραν ἀναστροφὴν τὸν παλαιὸν ἄνθρωπον τὸν φθειρόμενον... καὶ ἐνδύσασθαι τὸν καινὸν ἄνθρωπον τὸν κατὰ θεὸν κτισθέντα ἐν δικαιοσύνῃ καὶ ὁσιότητι τῆς ἀληθείας).[309] The operation of God's grace through faith in initial justification and reconciliation to God, Paul says, is not devoid in a present moral development of the intended ultimate outcome, so that godly character is being developed and matured in and for the saints (Rom. 5:1-5; 8:29-30; Eph. 4:13). It is not rightness with God, without the rightness of God at work in us, nature and conduct (Phil. 2:12-13).

Indeed, ongoing character development, through the saving power of God at work in the lives of the saints, is what lays hold of that eschatological hope that one day we will find ourselves conformed to image of God's dearly loved Son (Rom. 8:29-30), and of the consummation of our redemption, culminating in the revelation of the sons of God as authentically children of God. Such a consummation will be marked by the development and perfection of the holiness and righteousness of God/Christ in the saints, who as a renewed humanity belonging to God, will reflect them back into his renewed creation (Rom. 5:5; 8:24-25; 29-30, c f. Gen. 1:26-28). In Ephesians 4:23, as in Romans 12:1-2, Paul identifies the sphere of operation for the morally transforming power of God linked to salvation as the mind under transformation by God. By describing the changes that take place in those who believe as a core reordering of the attitudes and thinking the mind and heart toward God, holiness, and sin, Paul pinpoints where the development of the new life implanted in the saints at justification takes place in our nature, and characterizes its ongoing development under

---

[309] Holmes, M. W. (2011–2013). *The Greek New Testament: SBL Edition* (Eph 4:22-24). Lexham Press; Society of Biblical Literature.

the leadership of the Spirit as the maturing of godliness (cf. Rom. 8:219-30; 12:1-2;1 Cor. 14:20; 2 Cor. 5:17; 3:18; 4:16-18; Eph. 4:13, 23).

LEARNING FROM CHRIST: The apostle introduces his second point (after instructing them not to live like Gentiles) with a statement in the negative that makes a positive point, "But this is not how you learned (were taught) Christ," "This is not what you learned with respect to your new faith in Christ," or "But you did not in this manner learn Christ" (ὑμεῖς δὲ οὐχ οὕτως ἐμάθετε τὸν χριστόν).[310] The NIV attempts to smooth out more wooden English by rendering it, "That, however, is not the way of life you learned."[311] But, in doing so, the NIV omits the reference to Christ by name, who is the subject matter of what Paul argues the Ephesians have learned.[312] It is, after all, not abstract instruction on how to conduct themselves they have learned from Paul, nor are they being encouraged to adhere to a series of propositions for behavior and acceptable conduct as Christians (Eph. 4:25-6:9). Rather, from the context, they are to act in practical ways that are consistent with what they had previously learned concerning Christ, what he demands and represents as the incarnate Son of God. Paul's instruction to the Ephesians about appropriate Christian living had to do with instruction they received about Christ himself as both their example and Lord. That is, they are to act consistently with the instruction they received concerning the nature of their new relationship to God in Christ.

In Paul's mind, there is an appropriate way for believers who belong to Christ to act going forward from initial justification. He addresses this in his other epistles, like Romans, where he explicitly asks how those in

---

[310] Holmes, M. W. (2011–2013). *The Greek New Testament: SBL Edition* (Eph 4:20). Lexham Press; Society of Biblical Literature. Cf. Arndt, 2000, 742.
[311] *The New International Version* (Eph 4:20). (2011). Zondervan.
[312] Cf. Merkle B. L., 2016, 140; Stott J. R., 1979, 178, 179.

Christ should act in response to the exercise of God's grace for pardoning their sins, and whether or not they should continue in the habit of sinning (Rom. 6:1-2). *God forbid, may it never be so*, he replies to such a notion (Rom. 6:2). Their new relationship to God in Christ should reflect what they have been taught by Paul about Christ. Just as Jesus instructed his own disciples in righteousness and demonstrated it by his own life and obedience to God, Paul exhorts his readers to follow what they learned of Christ from him and the gospel (1 Cor. 11:1; 1 Thess. 1:6; 2 Thess. 3:7, 9). It is hard not to see in Paul's instruction here an allusion, possibly subconscious, if there is one, to Jesus' last instructions prior to his ascension, "Go and makes disciples of all nations… teaching them to observe everything I have commanded you" (Matt. 28:19-20).[313]

Ben Merkel notes that the syntax makes the *but you* (ὑμεῖς δὲ) emphatic (by fronting the pronoun), creating a strong contrast between how the Gentiles live and how the Ephesian believers in Christ should live (Eph. 4:20).[314] Nevertheless, the apostle's instruction is not a "net-negative", *abstain from conduct that is like the Gentiles in the world around you*. In what follows, Paul encourages them to adopt or fully take up the new life they now have in Christ, as a result of justification and moral transformation (Eph. 4:24). This is part of the instruction they had learned in Christ from Paul, and it had to do with the nature of this new life, which had been imparted to them at the time of their translation into the king of God, when at the same time the Spirit sealed them as belonging to Christ (Eph. 1:13-14; Col. 1:13). This new life is consistent with the life of those who have come out of darkness into the kingdom of God's beloved Son (Col. 1:13). It is life that is also consistent with the righteousness and holiness of God who rules that kingdom, and it is

---

[313] *The New International Version* (Mat. 28:19-20). (2011). Zondervan.
[314] Merkle B. L., 2016, 140, cf. Liefeld, 1997, 113.

guided by and enable in them through the Spirit as they live under the rule of God (elsewhere obedience) (Rom. 8:1-4; Gal. 5:16-25). Here is a preemptive enactment of the rule of God among his people, just as it will be in the eschaton, implemented by Spirit through transformative salvation and empowered moral uprightness in God's people, those who now belong to the community of faith. Because of this, the righteousness of God is reflected back into his creation by a redeemed humanity, even before the eschaton, that is into the world of this present age as they represent him to a lost humanity in need of God (Phil. 2:14-16, cf. Gen. 1:26-28).

Not only has the new age of the kingdom of God been initiated in the church by the advent of Christ's incarnation, death and resurrection, and by the giving of the Spirit, but by Christ's ascension too (1 Cor. 15:20-28), so that through Christ's rule, the rule of God in heaven is being expressed in the life and ministry of the church, his body, in the present age, to a lost humanity, and to a groaning creation longing for release from frustration of bondage to sin's consequences (Rom. 8:18-24). Therefore, the demonstration of holiness in God's people is essential to the church's mission to the world in the present age because it represents God's character to his creation (Phil. 2:14-16, Matt. 28:18-20). And this witness consists of holiness and righteousness *in them* (that is expressed in their character and conduct), after the fashion of God's own holiness and righteousness, initiated by him through the Spirit, and, through his indwelling, matured and sustain as they live in surrender to God (Eph. 4:13, 24).

Verse 21 tell us what Paul meant by referring to what the Ephesians learned in Christ. It was what he taught them consistent with the truth that is in Christ, at first through the gospel, and then later through instruction as new converts (ἠκούσατε καὶ ἐν αὐτῷ ἐδιδάχθητε).[315] As John Stott suggests, Christ is the teacher, what is taught, the provider and example of the ethos of instruction in righteousness.[316] His readers might be expected to supply the context here, as are we, that sin needed to be pardoned and rejected at first, followed by Paul's later instruction about how those in Christ are expected to go on to holiness and righteousness. Both are critical, the gospel they heard that called them out of sin and sinning, and instruction in righteousness that is to become the pattern of their new life. This is what he reminds them. It is clear from Romans 5 and 6, that for Paul, the exercise of God's grace in the forgiveness of sins does not provide cover for future sinning. Without missing a step, the apostle confronts the notion of remaining in the habit of sinning after extolling the virtue of God's super-abundant grace, capable of overflowing all of our sin to accomplish redemption and deliverance from its condemnation, and to declare us right with God, reconciled to him, and at peace (Rom. 5:1-2; 12-21; 6:1-2). Lest there is some confusion or question about what the future should look like, the apostle rules out the ongoing practice of sinning and, more importantly, he rules in a habitual life and practice of righteousness through a newness of life forged by union with Christ in his resurrection (Rom. 6:4, 9-11). What he taught the Ephesians, while he was with them, beginning with the gospel, and then through ongoing instruction, is that redemption is a life changing proposition that affects the character and conduct of those who belong to Christ. And he has made the same point explicit here in chapter 4 of his letter, by first exhorting them to reject the conduct of those around them, and then to go on to adopt the new life in Christ that God has planted in them, a life consisting of a holiness and

---

[315] Holmes, M. W. (2011–2013). *The Greek New Testament: SBL Edition* (Eph 4:21). Lexham Press; Society of Biblical Literature; cf. Bruce, 1961, 92-93; Liefeld, 1997, 114; Merkle B. L., 2016, 141.
[316] Stott J. R., 1979, 179.

righteousness that reflects God's own holiness and righteousness (Eph. 4:22-24).

As a point of order, so as to speak, we should note that the NIV has not followed the syntax of the original text here, as we noted above. Verses 20-21 form the two parts of a conditional sentence, with the apodosis (the "then" clause), preceding the protasis (the "if" clause), which the NIV smooths over.[317] It seems that the apodosis, the conditionally dependent result, is presented first (cf. Eph. 3:1-2), and followed by the condition under which the assertion might be considered true for the sake of argument.[318] Paul asserts that if the Ephesians heard the gospel, and were subsequently taught the truth as it can be found in Christ, then they have in fact learned the difference between life in Christ and life in the Gentile world around them. He is asserting that his readers are aware, from what they heard, and the instruction they have received from him, that the way those who belong to Christ should live, compared to those who do not know him (Gentiles), and who consequently remain children of disobedience (Eph. 2:1-3), should be different in terms of character and conduct.

There should be, Paul seems to say, no question or dispute over this, because it is something that they have already heard and been taught as fundamental truth in Christ, as an integral principle of Christian life, devotion, and practice. The rhetorical vibrancy of this construction lays down an emphasis on their prior exposure and apprehension of Paul's teaching about the importance of holiness and righteousness for the believer in Christ. The apostle assumes they rightly heard or listened to the gospel, and subsequently allowed themselves to be instructed and

---

[317] Cf. The punctuation of Holmes, M. W. (2011–2013). *The Greek New Testament: SBL Edition* (Eph 4:20-21). Lexham Press; Society of Biblical Literature.

[318] Kostenberger, Merkel, & Plummer, 2016, 442-443.

taught the truth that is in Christ. What he writes now is a reminder of his previous instruction to them concerning morality (εἴ γε αὐτὸν ἠκούσατε καὶ ἐν αὐτῷ ἐδιδάχθητε, καθώς ἐστιν ἀλήθεια ἐν τῷ Ἰησοῦ).[319] If they hadn't missed the point previously about going on to holiness and righteousness, then they will readily comprehend what Paul is about to say to them about taking up the new life they have in Christ, and why he is reminding them to lay aside the old life, represented by the way the world around them conducts itself (Eph. 4:17-19). It is the content of what he taught them in this respect that he will unpack next.

Since Paul assumes, in this (first class) conditional sentence, that they have heard gospel and apprehended his teaching on holiness, he exhorts them to follow through on it by decisively laying aside the old life and taking up the new (Eph. 4:22-24).[320] Paul is not seeking here to re-dig the well, or to exhaustively lay out his theology of moral transformation and godliness. The purpose of the reminder is to set the moral, spiritual, and doctrinal foundation for the practical instructions that follow, which have to do with how they are to conduct themselves toward one another in the connection with their fellowship with one another in the community of faith, and so maintain the unity of the church, the body of Christ (Eph. 4:16). If you like, Paul is going to put the meat on the bones of the earlier instruction for them to "*Make every effort to keep the unity of the Spirit through the bond of peace.*"[321] The unity of the church, the body, has been established by the Spirit, but its maintenance requires the sincere effort of the saints through rigorous cooperation with God. In this way, Paul arranges the room so he can

---

[319] Holmes, M. W. (2011–2013). *The Greek New Testament: SBL Edition* (Eph 4:21). Lexham Press; Society of Biblical Literature.
[320] Cf. Wood, 1981, 62; Utley, 1997, 114.
[321] *The New International Version* (Eph 4:3). (2011). Zondervan.

give concrete examples of what that looks like in terms of their conduct toward one another (Eph. 4:25-6:9).

SUFFICIENT TO GOD'S END-GAME: Mere abstinence from sin, and the removal of the old life is not sufficient to the purpose of God for his people, not personally, corporately, or eschatologically. A certain momentum of moral power and engagement is required from God's people for God's purpose of revealing and vindicating his redemptive wisdom to the powers and authorities in the heavenly realms, and if it to be represented in the present world (Eph. 3:10-12). The revelation of God's redemptive wisdom is something he will specifically accomplish *through his church* (Eph. 3:10). Paul asserts that God's design, which he has already accomplished in Christ, through his death and resurrection, is continuing to be worked out in the lives of the saints, particularly the corporate body of the church as they live in unity with one another, serving God, and representing him to the world around them (Eph. 3:10-12). The unity of the church and the moral lives of the saints are not peripheral, as we often perceive them to be in our common homiletic. Paul presents them as essential to the mission of God, which is to reveal himself to creation, particularly in this age to a world in need of redeeming, and to do so through the church. How the church is perceived and how the saints give moral witness to the character of God is critical to the mission, presently and eschatologically (cf. Rom. 8:18-30; Phil. 2:12-16). In our passage, Paul sets out the moral uprightness and follow-through of the saints as critical to the unity of the church, and therefore to the church's witness and mission.

This is not the kind of project that can be accomplished by the mere absence of sinning, a net-negative, a static religiosity, or by personal piety. Rather, it will require the consistent, faithful, and vigorous prosecution and pursuit of holiness and righteousness by God's people, who are in unity and fellowship with one another as a demonstration of the morally transforming power of the gospel. Unity, and the righteousness and holiness of the saints, provide the vindication of God's redemptive plan accomplished in Christ, and it is shown to be effective to the world through the lives of the saints when they obey God, as well as by the fruit of the Spirit in their character (Rom. 11:14; 15:2; 1 Cor. 9:22-23; 10:24, 31-33; 2 Cor. 6:3; Eph. 4:13-16; Phil. 1:27a; 2:14-16; Col. 3:17; cf. Mark 4:21; Luke 8:16; 11:33; John 5:24; 13:35; 1 Pet. 45:11; 1 John 3:14; 4:20). By these the world will see God in them (cf. Matt. 5:13-16). Religious legalism or moral asceticism is not going to get the job done, without new life and the power of the Spirit to giving expression to the implanted holiness of God (cf. Rom. 8:1-14; Gal. 5:16-25).

The absence of "old life" is not at all the same as taking up the power and momentum of "new life" provided in Christ through his resurrection, and by engaging the grace of the Holy Spirit dwelling in them, which give witness in the world of the power and truth of God in the gospel. *God's ultimate purpose* is that a redeemed and transformed humanity might reflect back into his restored creation, in partnership with God, a true and accurate representation of the image and the likeness of God, and bring glory to him when all things come under his rule and dominion (Gen. 1:26-28, cf. Rom. 8:29-30; 1 Cor. 13:8-12; 15:20-23, 28, 49, 53; 2 Cor. 3:18; 4:16-18; Eph. 1:13-14, 18; 2:10, 21-22; 3:6, 10-12; 4:13; Phil. 1:6; 2:12-13, 14-16; 3:7-14, 20-21; Col. 1:21-23; 3:1-4; I John 3:1-3).[322] In the power of the Spirit, the saints are to provide a witness to the holiness of God for a lost generation to see that same thing in the present (Phil. 2:14-16). The church, clothed with the power of the Spirit, preemptively engages God's mission (endgame/purpose) by imaging him to his creation now, ahead of its consummation in the eschaton, when the sons of God will finally be conformed to the image of his Son,

[322] Cf. Beale, The Temple and the Church's Mission: A Biblical Theology of the Dwelling Place of God, 2004.

and are revealed to a groaning creation as truly the children of God (Rom. 8:18-30). Therefore, Paul points out that the saints have been enlisted to live a new life that represents the holiness and righteousness of God in the present, *ahead of the eschaton*. Holiness, as Wesley pointed out, is by no means held in abeyance until death or the return of Christ, or the future new creation; it is for the church and the saints in the present, as a witness to the power and vitality of God's redemptive power and purposes.

Christ initiated all of this in his resurrection and ascension and preemptively gives expression to the rule of God in his body, the church, though the Spirit dwelling among and in his people. As we have said above, Jesus is leading the charge in this enterprise from his vantage point on the throne, ruling with God as the exalted Son of God/Man (1 Cor. 15:20-28; Phil. 2:8-11). From there he represents his redeemed people to God as he aids them in this enterprise of imaging God to the lost world (cf. Heb. 4:16-16), supporting them through intercessions for those who are working out his mission and purpose in the world (Acts 1:1, 8), and by imbuing them with the power of the Spirit for obedience to his leading (Rom. 8:1-17; Gal. 5:16-25). Christ is working in his body through the Spirit, applying the power of the kingdom of God in service to the mission, but also to the lives of the saints who believed in Christ for their moral and spiritual development and edification in the church. These are the ones who were translated out of the kingdom of darkness by redemption, that is through the remission of their sins, and into the kingdom of God, where the rule of God requires holiness, and the Spirit empowers and gives moral momentum to the saints by his working in and among them personally and corporately, so that as a community, selflessly serving one another, the church might thrive and reach its intended goal of achieving the full measure of the stature of Christ (Rom. 8:1-4; Gal. 5:16-25; Eph. 4:13-16; Col. 1:13).

NEW CLOTHES NEW LIFE: What the Ephesians learned from Christ, then, was that in coming to Christ, they have inherited, through justification and the moral transformation that goes with it at initial salvation, a new life to replace the old (Eph. 4:22-24, cf. Rom. 6:4-11; 12:1-2; 13:14; Col. 3:5). That is at the heart of this passage. God's redeemed people have been imbued with new life (cf. 2 Cor. 5:17), and as a result, the old life may no longer lay claim the controlling interest over their character, conduct, attitudes, or behavior going forward (cf. Rom. 6:1-11). If the controlling moral and spiritual environment of their lives has been transformed by God (and we will soon discuss how and in what way this has taken place), then, Paul argues, by necessity, the outcomes in terms of behavior and conduct must undergo alteration to reflect the holiness and righteousness of God (Eph. 4:24). Nevertheless, the individual believer has a role to play in cooperating with the work of the Spirit of God in them. Paul lays it out here, they must choose to lay aside the old life through an act of determined faith and choice, and to take up this new life with resolution (Eph. 4:22-23, cf. Rom. 6:11).

It is the same line of argument that appears in the early part of Romans 6, and that underlies the rationale of Paul's argument to the Galatians about going on to holiness through the power of the Spirit after initial justification (Gal. 5:16-25). And although the apostle summarizes his theology here in Ephesians 4, elsewhere, notably Romans and Galatians, he lays out his teaching in thoroughgoing detail (Rom. 6:1-8:17; Gal. 2:19-21; 3:1-14; 5:16-25). Because of the inward transformation of their lives and hearts at justification, which amounts to the death of the old life and resurrection to a new life in Christ (Rom. 6:1-4; 2 Cor. 5:17), those who are in Christ must also choose to fully adopt and count on the new life of Christ in them, while at the same time repudiating the controlling principle of the old (Rom. 6:11; Eph. 4:22-24). The one is to be put off or laid aside like clothing, to take up or to be clothed with the new life oriented around a new attitude in their minds affected in them by God and led by the Spirit (ἀνανεοῦσθαι δὲ τῷ πνεύματι τοῦ νοὸς ὑμῶν).[323] Both are critical, the transforming and animating power of God, as well their cooperation, surrender and obedience through walking in step with the Spirit, because now they belong to God through Christ (Rom. 6:4-11; cf. Gal. 5:24-25).

The foundation for the moral change in the lives of the Ephesian, as a result of coming to know Christ, is to be found in an alteration at the fundamental level of their nature, rather a superficial change in conduct and behavior. Whatever Paul goes on to propose as appropriate conduct for the saints in the church after this, to those who are in Christian community with one another, it is not rooted in substituting one code of conduct, that of the Gentile world, for a Christian religious code (like the law or Jewish tradition). Paul proposes new conduct coming out of a visceral change in their nature through the action of God's grace at justification, which he describes in Romans 6 as a union with Christ in his death and resurrection. They have not simply undergone a forensic change in status with God, Paul argues, coming out of Romans 5, but a nature change, by which the old life has been crucified in union with Christ, and they have been raised to a new life in union with his resurrection (Rom. 6:4-7). Indeed, Paul makes the analogy that just as Christ through the cross has died to sin, that is accomplished his mission to break sin and lift the judgment of God on sin by his sacrifice, he also rose to a totally new and powerful life to reign with God in victory (Rom. 6:8-10). So, we too have died in the death of Christ to sin (past and its power to keep us as slaves to sinning) by union with him at initial salvation, at the time of the forgiveness of our sins, and our justification with God. In the same way, our union with Christ in his resurrection at justification has given birth to new life, no longer controlled by the now-crucified-old-life, and its enslavement to sinning.

---

[323] Holmes, M. W. (2011–2013). *The Greek New Testament: SBL Edition* (Eph 4:23). Lexham Press; Society of Biblical Literature.

Rather, this new is controlled by the power of God through the Holy Spirit dwelling in us, the seal and token of our reconciliation to God and fellowship with him (Rom. 5:1-2, cf. Eph. 1:13-14). This new life bears the character of Christ in true holiness and righteousness that leads to eternal life, and we have as a result become slaves of God, that is we have embarked on a new life of obedience to him and his rule over us (Rom. 6:12-23). This life and salvific reality, Paul says, must be taken up consciously and deliberately by a calculation of the will and the mind by those who belong to Christ (Rom. 6:11). It cannot be a matter of indifference to the believer (Rom. 6:1-2). In Ephesians 4:22-24, the apostle makes the same point, by saying that they must lay aside the old life, represented by the Gentiles around them, and take up the new life of righteousness and holiness that reflects the character of God, in service of a subsequent ongoing *change in the attitudes of their minds,* affected in them by God (ἀνανεοῦσθαι δὲ τῷ πνεύματι τοῦ νοὸς ὑμῶν). And this transformation, and their conscious acceptance of it, must bring about a definite, perceptible, moral, and spiritual change in their conduct, attitudes, behavior, and lives.[324] More about that *change* later.

The change of the inner environment in their nature is wrought by God as a result of coming to know Christ and being reconciled to him (cf. Eph. 2:5, 8-9). They were once *children of disobedience,* like the Gentiles, when they were dead in their trespasses and sins, but God *made them alive* (ὄντας ἡμᾶς νεκροὺς τοῖς παραπτώμασιν συνεζωοποίησεν τῷ Χριστῷ).[325] In chapter 2, Paul anticipates what he is going to say in chapter 4 about putting off the old life and putting on the new, by saying that out of the deadness of the life of disobedience and alienation from God, he has made them alive (Eph. 2:5). Life out of

---

[324] Holmes, M. W. (2011–2013). *The Greek New Testament: SBL Edition* (Eph 4:23). Lexham Press; Society of Biblical Literature.
[325] Holmes, M. W. (2011–2013). *The Greek New Testament: SBL Edition* (Eph 2:5). Lexham Press; Society of Biblical Literature.

deadness, especially in a Pauline context, is nothing short of a resurrection that implies a new way of living going forward. Their experience of the old life, which was deadness to God, has been superseded by being made alive by God, to God, to experience a new life of righteousness and surrender to the Spirit, the result of which is being dead (crucified) to the old life and its ways (Rom. 6:3-4). The experience of salvation for Paul's readers is not merely justification or pardon for sins committed previously, but a reclamation from a state of moral and spiritual death to God, and to be made spiritually and morally alive through Christ (where the dative implies union with Christ and instrumentality by which this new life is sustained by their new relationship with him - ζῶντας δὲ τῷ θεῷ ἐν Χριστῷ Ἰησοῦ) (cf. Rom. 7:24-25).[326] An experience of coming to know Christ (faith and grace – Rom. 5:1-2) was the means by which God ushered them into a state of transcendent life (corresponding to coming out of darkness into the kingdom of God's Son as a result of redemption, the forgiveness of their sins – Col. 1:13).

For Paul, redemption, God's reclamation of the sinner from their sin and moral deadness through the exercise of his grace on the one hand, and their faith on the other (by way of the cross), also involves coming into new life as a result of forgiveness of sins (cf. Rom. 6:1-11; 2 Cor. 5:17; Eph. 2:5). This new life is supported by a corresponding translation into a new realm of living that belongs to the kingdom of God, where the Spirit rules and works, so that an ascendancy of the rule of God over the carnal desires of the old life takes root in their present lives and conduct (Gal. 5:16-25; Eph. 2:5; Col. 1:13).[327] Paul's theology with respect to reconciliation to God is salvific, redemptive, and eschatological at the same time. The immediate work of God in those who believe and

---

[326] Holmes, M. W. (2011–2013). *The Greek New Testament: SBL Edition* (Ro 6:11). Lexham Press; Society of Biblical Literature.
[327] Cf. Wright N. T., 2012.

experience new life prepares them for the redemptive fullness of the life that is to come. It is the seal of the Spirit in the present, who is working in them to produce the fruit of righteousness now, and to guide their lives as they walk in obedience to his leading (Rom. 8:1-4; Gal. 5:16-25), the goal of which is mature godliness, which in through the Spirit provides the guarantee that God will finally come after his purchased possession (Eph, 1:13-14) – and that he will ultimately usher his people into the full eschatological experience of eternal life in his presence (cf. Rom. 6:22-23). In other words, their present experience of the Spirit anticipates a future time and place where God will finally dwell among his people as in the temple, and where they will finally reflect or give expression to the mature godliness that God is already at work seeking to produce in their character and conduct right now (Eph. 1:13-23; 2:22; 4:13-16; cf. Rom. 8:29-30; Rev. 21:1-8). So, Paul says, act like those who have be clothed with new life to reflect the righteousness and holiness of God (Eph. 4:22-24), and not like the Gentiles, who are dead in their trespasses and sins.

RENEWED IN THE ATTITUDE OF YOUR MINDS: For Wesleyans at least, Ephesians 4 and Romans 6 present a rather nuanced Pauline perspective on the new life of Christ in those who are in union with Christ.[328] Whereas Paul makes the point in Romans that new life for

---

[328] Note that in Romans 6:3, Paul represents the moral change in those experiencing the grace of God at justification as a baptism into Christ, symbolized concretely by water baptism. The idea of immersion "into Christ" is also the object of the apostle's assertion that believers belong to the body of Christ (the church) because they have been baptized into it by the Spirit (1 Cor. 12:12-13). In similar language in Colossians, believers are translated out the sphere of the kingdom of darkness (rule of the kingdom of the air – Eph. 2:2), to be plunged into the kingdom of God's Son, where God rules, because of the forgiveness of their sins (Col. 1:13). Paul's uses locative and relocative language to figuratively represent moral and practical conditions and changes

those who are joined to Christ, in his death and resurrection, has been established through a radical change in their nature as a result of justification (Rom. 6:3-4), in Ephesians 4, he makes the point that laying aside the old life is essential to being renewed in the attitude/spirit of their minds, and to putting on the new life, created to be like God in true righteousness and holiness (Eph. 4:22-24). A superficial reading may see two somewhat contradicting schemes, whereby moral change is a divine initiative on the one hand, but the responsibility of the believer on the other. Romans 6 presents the old life as crucified, and the new life established at justification, by reason of a moral change through union with Christ, and the pardon of their sins. Ephesians 4 with its use of an infinitive (more about that later), seems to present the laying aside of the old life at the initiative of the believer as grounds for a change in attitude of the mind, and to provide for the adoption of new life (ἀνανεοῦσθαι δὲ τῷ πνεύματι τοῦ νοὸς ὑμῶν).[329] The one presents a divine initiative for

---

at justification, in terms of character, conduct, and relationship to God. To be in Christ is to be relocated out of the world, in alienation from God, and to be delivered from the moral influence and rule of the kingdom of darkness. In Christ, new life is connected to union with Christ in his resurrection, whereas the old life, with its moral ascendancy prior justification, has been crucified in union with his death (Rom. 6:3-4). Nevertheless, Paul also encourages his readers to firmly adopt an attitude of being done with the old life and to fully embrace, and to count on the new life they now have in Christ to produce the righteousness and holiness God is looking for in them (Rom. 6:11). Although the moral changes at justification makes habitual sinning incongruous with new life in Christ, Paul's readers must take responsibility for fully signing on to the moral and spiritual changes that have taken place in them, through an act of the will that adopts a mindset rejecting the old life, and fully embracing the new life with its new direction, and potential for different moral outcomes.

[329] Holmes, M. W. (2011–2013). *The Greek New Testament: SBL Edition* (Eph 4:23). Lexham Press; Society of Biblical Literature.

moral change, and the other the initiative which appears to come from a decision and choice made by the believer. Which is it?

To recast an often-repeated analogy from Noel Brooks, who wrote about *sanctification* in *Scriptural Holiness,* they are two sides of the same coin. In Romans 6, Paul clearly presents a divine side to the moral dilemma and reform of those who come to know Christ by an experience of his grace that justifies them with God (Rom. 5:18-6:10). By God's action in justification, through an exercise of his grace, those who have faith in Christ are reconciled to God, and are relocated into the sphere of God's grace – that is they begin to operate and live in a new sphere of existence consistent with the working of God in their lives (Rom. 5:1-2).[330] This depends wholly on a divine initiative and operation. Paul explores this in Romans 7, where he concludes he can do nothing from his side to initiate his own redemption and moral change (Rom. 7:21-25). He concludes that a fault in his nature makes even lasting or meaningful moral reformation impossible unless God steps in through Christ (Rom. 7:21-23, 24-25). There is, then, a divine side by which God's grace does a work in those who put their faith in Christ. However, there is a personal, human side by which the believer must buy into the work that God has done, and decide to take it seriously, to count on the power of God now at work in them for the outcome he is looking for from his people, which has to do with holiness (righteousness if we are talking more practically). This human dimension, Paul proposes, is a calculation of the will that assents to and fully embraces the death of the old life, as well as resurrection to new life, which take place in those who have put their faith in Christ, and that is the result of the God's gracious action at justification (Rom. 6:11). God's transforming operation at justification, Paul argues, is not a mere declaration of

---

[330] In other places this is a relocation from the kingdom of darkness into the kingdom of God son through redemption, which consists of the forgiveness of their sins (Col. 1:13)

pardon, but a full moral transformation that must be fully accepted and acted upon by those whom God has joined to Christ, in both his death and resurrection (Rom. 6:1-11, cf. 2 Cor. 5:17).[331]

That the post-conversion life of the believer, reflecting a moral change and going on to holiness in character and conduct, is a divine and human cooperation consistent with everything we know about how God works with humanity, and as the scriptures portray it in a divine-human partnership. From the outset of creation, the purpose of God seems to have been to entrust the expansion of his rule throughout (material) creation to the efforts of human beings under his rule as partners, and as they take dominion of it in his behalf (Gen. 1:26-28). That they are to do so in the likeness and the image of God. To reflect God back into his creation sets the enterprise in a moral framework that is consistent with a representation of God's own character (Gen. 1:26-28). Israel was commissioned with this same enterprise to the nations around them, "Be holy because I am holy," where it was an accurate representation of God as a witness that was at stake in how they conducted themselves morally, and in their worship (cf. Lev. 11:44-45).

The incarnation of Christ, succinctly set out in John's "the *word* became flesh and dwelt among us," and Paul's recognition of both the human and divine natures of Christ, something also exquisitely teased out in Hebrews 1, only reinforce God's purposes for creation as coalescing around a divine human cooperation (John 1:14; Rom. 1:3-4; Heb. 2:5-17). Crowning the whole enterprise, Christ has gathered up the entire endgame of God in his own unique personhood as the Son of God and Son of Man through his incarnation (Phil. 2:6-7). Christ has begun the reign of God in his kingdom to represent God, on the one hand, and this human partnership on the other. He has done so by assuming the

---

[331] Cf. Stott J. R., 1979, 179-183.

throne as the risen Lamb of God, after his resurrection and ascension into heaven (see our earlier discussion) (1 Cor. 15:20-28). That there is both a divine and human side to moral change and success in Pauline righteousness and holiness should not surprise us in the least, because it is consistent with the purposes and actions of God throughout his dealings and stated intentions for creation, all the way up to a new heaven and earth, and culminating in the incarnation and enthronement of his Son (Gen. 3:15; Isa. 7:14; 9:6-7; 65-66; John 1:1, 14; Phil. 2:6-11; Col. 1:15-19; Rev. 21-22).

All of this brings us to a Pauline focus on the human side of the divine-human partnership for holiness. Our lengthy discussion on what the Ephesians had been taught with respect to their former way of life, brings us to the statement "to be made new in the attitude of your minds" (NIV). As it is framed in the clause "to be made new in the attitude of your minds" (ἀνανεοῦσθαι δὲ τῷ πνεύματι τοῦ νοὸς ὑμῶν), Paul presses his readers to remember what they had been taught in Christ, that they are no longer morally and spiritually who they were before they came to know Christ (Eph. 2:1-3; 4:17-19, 22-23).[332] Logically, the putting off of the old life, according to what Paul taught, precedes the renewing and the put on of the new self. He implies this by use of the passive infinitive (ἀνανεοῦσθαι), where God is the one who is doing the renewing in connection with their laying aside the old life.[333] They are renewed in the attitude of their minds, because God has/is doing the renewing. *They are not the ones doing the renewing* (cf. Rom. 12:2). Paul's readers (an us) are the subjects of the action of the infinitive, where God is the one who performs it. This is the famous (infamous) *divine passive* we often hear about in commentaries and

---

[332] Holmes, M. W. (2011–2013). *The Greek New Testament: SBL Edition* (Eph 4:23). Lexham Press; Society of Biblical Literature. This is the same sort of argument Paul uses in Romans 6:4-11.
[333] Merkle B. L., 201, 143.

theologies, where God is the one doing the action of the verb, and we are the objects of that action. Renewing is God's initiative, and the result of work of the Spirit, something we are powerless to achieve without him (cf. Rom. 7)!

Nevertheless, the renewing of the minds is linked to their willingness and determination to lay aside the old life, where it is implied that they should now decide to live out the implications of the crucifixion with Christ of the old life, and of the results of having been relocated into him, and into the kingdom of God, to use other Pauline ideas in support of this passage. He is clearly implying that without this attitude of laying it aside, or without their categoric buy-in (a conscious and deliberate decision is indicated) to fully embrace the new life of Christ in them, the old might be allowed to resurface, if it has not been fully repudiated in their thinking, or if they go on living like the Gentiles (v. 17). In that case the renewal of salvation is doomed to fail (cf. Rom. 6:23).

Renewal in the attitude of their minds, in the NIV, is a translation of a *renewal of the spirit of their minds* (ἀνανεοῦσθαι δὲ τῷ πνεύματι τοῦ νοὸς ὑμῶν), where Paul seems to locate the effective change in the will and volitional center of their human personality.[334] At the heart of holiness is the control of the decision making apparatus of human personality, and what sort of an environment it exits in, or by which it is controlled (cf. Rom. 5:2). In Pauline terms, reference to the old life, corrupted by the deceitful desires of the flesh, describes a controlling principle of sin, which results in habitual sinning (cf. Rom 7). Whatever dominates the environment of power or control over human decision making, the will and thinking, is going to produce corresponding character and conduct consistent with either sinful or righteous

---

[334] Holmes, M. W. (2011–2013). *The Greek New Testament: SBL Edition* (Eph 4:23). Lexham Press; Society of Biblical Literature.

properties at work in their nature.[335] Jesus made the same observation, when he said that out of the abundance of the heart the mouth speaks, or that the fruit of wicked or good conduct comes out of the underlying state or condition of the heart (Matt. 5:28; 6:21; 12:34; 15:16-20; Mark 7:17-23; Luke 12:34). The idea of renewal in the center of human personality, to crush the human will controlled by lust and rebellion against God, and to be renewed and surrendered to God, is at the core of Pauline sanctification, and it is an essential concomitant to an initial moral transformation at justification (cf. Rom. 6:4-1). The two cannot be violently separated in our theology, as though right standing with God has nothing to do with going on to character development, or to producing fruit consistent with righteousness in the life of the believer. Can justification stand apart from an obligation to go on to holiness? Paul says, "God forbid!" (Rom. 6:2).

The phrase *spirit of your minds* alludes to precisely that, the center of human personality and decision-making center for the believer. God has, in fact, undertaken a renewal there, through the exercise of his justifying power at initial salvation, because those who are saved are no longer morally what they used to be (2 Cor. 5:17). The infinitive (ἀνανεοῦσθαι) enjoys limited use in the sense of renewal in Greek, but it is clearly what Paul has in mind here from context, where he juxtaposes the morally old self with the morally new self, the former aligned with the conduct of the Gentiles (Eph. 4:17-19), and the latter with the holiness and righteousness of God (Eph. 4:23-24).[336] This premise underwrites this entire passage, in preparation for Paul's practical instructions which follow. Their conduct in the community of the saints, and toward

---

[335] Cf. Wright N. T., 2012.

[336] Arndt, 2000, 68. BDAG notes that the *Shepherd of Hermas* (Rome, mid to late 2nd century) clearly uses this verb in the sense of renewal and refreshing (Hv 3, 12, 2; 3, 13, 2, cp. 3, 12, 3 (Arndt, 2000, 68); Lightfoot & Harmer, 1891, 418).

one another (cf. Eph. 4:16), is to be governed by the renewal of the spirit/attitudes of their minds by God, so that the new life created in them to be like God in true holiness and righteousness might gain ascendancy, to develop Christlike character (cf. Eph. 4:13), and regulate conduct (cf. Eph. 4:3). The putting on and the putting off is Paul's way of exhorting his readers to go with the changes that God is making in them through the renewing of the spirit of their minds, and as a result of leaving the old life behind, so that the development of holiness and righteousness in them might go forward, resulting also in changed conduct (cf. Eph. 4:17).

Leaving aside Ephesians 4 for a moment, we see a similar idea in Romans 12, where the apostle exhorts his readers to present their bodies as a living sacrifice to God (Rom. 12:1-2). To prove (to discover and engage it – expressing purpose) the will of God, to live in obedience to him, the Romans must first be sure that their surrender to God is complete and total, without equivocation (Rom. 12:1). Finding the will of God, and engaging obedience to God requires, in Pauline theology, a prior full surrender to God that refuses to allow the reassertion of the old life, or to permit the world to regain its influence over us.[337] This is a decision which recognizes the implications of justification, that it is a repudiation of sin and of the old life, and involves a surrender to God resulting in moral change (Rom. 6:1-14, cf. 2 Cor. 5:17, c f. Jer. 31:31-34; Ezek. 36:22-28). So, they a cannot, in fact, take back up with the conduct of the Gentiles or the world out of which they came, when they first came to know Christ (Eph. 2:1-3; 4:17). They are no longer their

---

[337] In Romans 12, Paul is saying a similar thing to what he told the Ephesians, that they are not to be squeezed back into the mold of this age, the operating philosophy of this world and it rebellion against God. In Ephesians 4, he instructs his reader not to live like the Gentiles. The remedy in both cases is surrender to God, and acceptance of his renewing power in them, by which they are to lay aside the old and take up the new.

own, they have been bought with a price and owe it to God to glorify him in the use of their bodies (1 Cor. 6;19-20). Paul sees the consecration of their bodies as a living sacrifice to God for righteousness and holiness (obedience to God), which he calls a reasonable (thoughtful) expectation of service, considering what God has done for them (τὴν λογικὴν λατρείαν ὑμῶν) (Rom. 12:1). [338] As a necessary result of justification, those whose lives and conduct no longer reflect the world they have come out of, but rather the kingdom of God into which they have been translated through Christ and by the Spirit, must choose to remain surrendered to God, and to present their bodies a living sacrifice to God, so he may live in them by the Spirit (Rom. 8:1-4). Paul's concern is the same in Romans 12 as in Romans 6, where Paul spoke of no longer being slaves to sin, but of God toward righteousness as a God's goal for his people. God's plan is to affect change in their character and nature to reflect that righteousness in their conduct and demeanor in the present world where they live and serve him as witnesses to the lost (Phil. 2:14-16).

Ephesians 4, obviously, carries the same basic concern. Paul's readers are not to fall back in with the habit of living like the world around them (v 17), but rather to demonstrate, by their conduct, particularly toward one another, the monumental changes that God has made in the *spirit of the minds*, whereby their nature has undergone a recreation consistent with the true holiness and righteousness of God (Eph. 4:17, 22-24). Their new life ought to be supported by a calculation on their part (cf. Rom. 6:11), that they have permanently laid aside the old life, to take up with or be clothed by the new (Eph. 2:22-24).

After all, Paul reflects, the old life, the old man, what they used to be morally in their minds, attitudes, thinking, demeanor and conduct, was not static or a steady state of moral equilibrium, as though they were

---

[338] Arndt, 2000, 598.

neither getting better nor morally worse.[339] The old man, the pre-justification self, Paul argues, is in a state of progressive moral ruination and destruction (τὸν φθειρόμενον κατὰ τὰς ἐπιθυμίας τῆς ἀπάτης).[340] The picture is of something rotting or being progressively despoiled more and more over the passage of time, and in this case of increasing decline toward utter moral ruin.[341] At the same time, the apostle is implying that by putting on the new man, they will be progressively renewed, because the new man created by God in them at justification has the moral properties of the true holiness and righteousness of God himself (κατὰ θεὸν κτισθέντα ἐν δικαιοσύνῃ καὶ ὁσιότητι τῆς ἀληθείας) (Eph. 4:24).[342] The result is that they will advance toward, and achieve the fulness of the stature of Christ (Eph. 4:13), as individuals and as the church corporately, reflecting and representing the holiness and righteousness of God to the powers in the heavenly realms opposed to God, and vindicating his purpose and plan, as well as his divine wisdom (Eph. 3:10-11).

The clue to Paul's logic (and concern) in requiring they *decide* to fully lay aside the old life (τὸν παλαιὸν ἄνθρωπον) is clear, then, from his

---

[339] This argument, that we are no better or worse than the next person, is a big argument against a self-assessment by which Christians see themselves as morally superior to others in general terms, and by which they are therefore perceived by others outside the church as hypocrites. Actually, Paul is arguing for a greater danger. Left unaddressed, sinful nature will inevitably grow worse, and moral corruption only deepens with time. Unless it is repudiated, and transformed by God, the moral condition of the individual only worsens, in step with the moral deterioration of society and culture (cf. Eph. 4:17-19).

[340] Holmes, M. W. (2011–2013). *The Greek New Testament: SBL Edition* (Eph 4:22). Lexham Press; Society of Biblical Literature.

[341] Cf. Arndt, 2000, 1054.

[342] Holmes, M. W. (2011–2013). *The Greek New Testament: SBL Edition* (Eph 4:24). Lexham Press; Society of Biblical Literature.

assertion that the *old life* is in the process of being corrupted by its sinful desires (τὸν φθειρόμενον κατὰ τὰς ἐπιθυμίας τῆς ἀπάτης).[343] Only two ongoing moral outcomes are possible, as far as the apostle is concerned. Either there will be moral renewal through Christ which leads the development and growth of holiness and righteousness in character, which reflect God's holiness and righteousness, or there will be ongoing and increasing moral corruption of our unchanged human nature, because of the unrestrained influence of deceitful desires inherent in the old man or old life (κατὰ τὰς ἐπιθυμίας τῆς ἀπάτης).[344] By failing to recognizing this, that we are not merely justified (saved – Eph. 2:8-9) by faith, but that serious moral changes have occurred in us as a result of faith in Christ, we run the risk of falling back into the old life, which will inevitably result in increasing corruption and moral failure (cf. Rom. 6:15-23).[345] Paul is warning his readers that to escape the culture of the Gentile world, with its sinful corruption and darkened minds (Eph. 4:18-19), the Ephesians need to actively *pursue* the ongoing development of this moral change which has taken place in them through Christ (what they learned). Spiritual and moral passivity for those who belong to Christ presents a serious danger of returning to the life of sin, and sinning (cf. Matt. 13:18-23). The conforming power of the world, seeking to squeeze us back into its mold (Rom. 12:2) must be overcome through a full surrender of our bodies to God as a living sacrifice, and by clothing ourselves in the new life, resolutely and completely (Eph. 4:22-24). There is no room for compromise, and

---

[343] Holmes, M. W. (2011–2013). *The Greek New Testament: SBL Edition* (Eph 4:22). Lexham Press; Society of Biblical Literature, cf. (Brooks, Ephesians Outline and Unfolded, 1984), 181.

[344] Holmes, M. W. (2011–2013). *The Greek New Testament: SBL Edition* (Eph 4:22). Lexham Press; Society of Biblical Literature.

[345] This is precisely the concern Paul addresses to the Romans in chapter 6.

certainly no possibility of allowing the two, the old and new, to coexistence.

The outcome of their new life in Christ, going forward, depends on them embracing, attitudinally and fully, the renewal which has occurred in them through Christ when they came to know him, and when they experienced relocation into him, and out of darkness into the kingdom of God, so that God might reign in them by the Spirit. They must choose to put off the old life as a result of the renewal that has taken place in their minds (Eph. 4:23), if the outcome God intends is to gain ascendancy in them (which is that he might produce his own holiness and righteousness in them) (Eph. 4:24). The second coordinate clause is also governed by an infinitive, "to put on" (ἐνδύσασθαι) the new self, and is logically linked to the instruction to put off the old life. Fully embracing the new life we have in Christ, leads to the outcomes God desires in terms of holiness and righteousness, and it seems therefore, to be logically subsequent or dependent on that previous action of putting off the old (Eph. 4:22-24). To move in the direction of maturing godliness and achieving the goal, the fulness of the stature of Christ, the new life need to be fully taken up by those who have been renewed in Christ (cf. Rom. 6:11)

SUMMARY OF THIS LENGTHY SECTION: Now, it might be said that we are squeezing Paul's analogy too hard based on his ad hoc instruction in Ephesians. Nevertheless, one thing is abundantly clear, Paul views the moral condition of his readers as in a state of flux. It is either improving by the power of God through the Spirit, or it is in danger of deteriorating on account of the prospect of be drawn back into the conduct of the Gentiles around them. I think that we should take seriously that Paul mentions it, and that he may consider it a danger, or sees signs in the Ephesian church of it occurring.[346] The presence of corrupting influence, of a failure to fully lay aside the old ways and life, or embracing new life in Christ, makes them vulnerable to the influence and progressive degradation of the deceitful lusts of the old man or nature. Paul is advocating for their recognition and acceptance of the new morally controlling factors in their lives, a new life that is lives under the influence of the moral renewal of God at first occurring at initial salvation and designed from the outset to lead to the reflection his own holiness and righteousness in them (τὸν καινὸν ἄνθρωπον τὸν κατὰ θεὸν κτισθέντα ἐν δικαιοσύνῃ καὶ ὁσιότητι τῆς ἀληθείας.)[347] The outcome of this recognition, of putting on of the new man, is their future moral development into the full measure of the stature of Christ, and it dominates Paul's exhortation to the Ephesians in this passage. By it, he is making preparation for the practical instructions he is about to give them. The moral landscape of their lives is at the center of this discussion because their interaction with one another and the unity of the church depend on getting it right (Eph. 4:3, 16). Therefore, they are to fully lean into the change God has made in the attitude of their minds that leads to holiness.

The indwelling Spirit, whose presence brings the new life and the power of God to bear on the moral and spiritual success of the saints, is for Paul preemptive, in that it leads to the application of the power and rule of God in the present that anticipates God's future sovereign and unopposed rule over creation. Through the Spirit, the church and the saints already partake of that new life and experience of the God's

---

[346] We have already noted Paul's warning to the Ephesian elders of future dangers, and of the fact that Timothy, as the pastor of the church, was facing some serious problems that were the result of assertive personalities clamoring for recognition and control of the agenda.

[347] Holmes, M. W. (2011–2013). *The Greek New Testament: SBL Edition* (Eph 4:24). Lexham Press; Society of Biblical Literature.

gracious rule that will one day overtake all of creation (Col. 1:15-20, cf. 1 Cor. 15:20-28). Their salvation is more than pardon and justification, or legal, positional rightness with God. It is the inculcation of new life under a new moral principle of spiritual experience, which Paul goes on to say was created to be like God in authentic holiness and righteousness (δικαιοσύνῃ καὶ ὁσιότητι τῆς ἀληθείας). This new life and experience is designed to culminate, through maturation in godliness, in the expression and reflection of the full stature of Christ in them, and in the church corporately (Eph. 4:13, cf. Rom. 8:29-30; 2 Cor. 4:16-28; Phil. 1:6;).[348]

These are the ideas that form the content of what they learned in connection with Christ. Paul is not referring them to a new moral code or tradition by the following instructions after verse 24, despite their practical nature. They are guidelines to how they should live with one another in the church, and serve to describe what new life in Christ looks like in the context of life in the believing community, and as a pathway to unity in the church. He is drawing their attention to the fact that God has *created* (τὸν κατὰ θεὸν κτισθέντα) new life in them with necessary properties, purposefully designed, to authentically (ἀληθείας) reflect the holiness and righteousness of God (δικαιοσύνῃ καὶ ὁσιότητι) back into his creation (cf. Gen. 1:26-28, Rom. 8:29-30; Eph. 4:13; Phil. 2:14-16).[349] It is out of this creation and renewal that the new life is to come and affect their conduct and relationships with one another.

Paul's larger eschatological perspective is that new life in them has been intentionally created by God to authentically reflect his own holiness and righteousness in the present, and to form the foundation

---

[348] Holmes, M. W. (2011–2013). *The Greek New Testament: SBL Edition* (Eph 4:24). Lexham Press; Society of Biblical Literature.
[349] Holmes, M. W. (2011–2013). *The Greek New Testament: SBL Edition* (Eph 4:24). Lexham Press; Society of Biblical Literature.

for a holiness and righteousness to come in the eschaton for those who will be ultimately conformed into the image of God's dearly loved Son, those who will one day bear the full stature of Christ (Eph. 4:13). He is making the point that the future purpose of God has begun presently through the transforming work of the Spirit in them, and it will continue until its final consummation at the return of Christ on the day of the Lord (Phil. 1:6). Paul makes the assertion that the new life of moral transformation in their present redemptive experience is intentionally created/designed by God to reflect in this age eschatological holiness and righteousness, by which a redeemed humanity does and will represent God in his new creation.

The practical instruction that follows is set to flow out of these observations, and the premise that a transformed life ought to produce the fruit of righteousness that reflects the character of God in a renewed attitude of the mind, and in practical conduct, behavior, maturing character, and fruit. If left unchallenged, the NIV's reference to the *attitudes* of their mind might cause us to miss a possible Pauline allusion to the Old Testament, where God promises Israel that in the future he intends to produce righteousness in his people through a change of their hearts, and the implementation of a new spirit in them, both linked to a moral cleansing by the sprinkling them with clean water (Ezek. 36:22-28, cf. Eph. 4:23). Paul's reference to *spirit of their minds*, is clearly a parallel idea to God placing a new spirit in his people, and it is unlikely that Paul missed the significance of this in light of the Spirit's indwelling the new covenant people of God. Furthermore, Jeremiah overtly states that God intended to establish a new covenant with his people to replace the old one, whereby he would write the righteousness of God in their hearts and their minds, again in connection to his forgiveness of their sins and wickedness (Jer. 31:31-34). Paul's theology is of a transformative justification which God promised through the prophets to his people, whereby those who put their faith in God are not only reconciled to him when their sins are pardoned, but are morally transformed with the intention they might conduct their lives differently, and with a vastly better system of support leading to success in righteousness (Jer. 31:31-34). Paul's redemptive scheme involves moral transformation contemporaneous with the pardon and forgiveness of God, and a change in the internal environment of God's people at the level of their nature, that is in their minds and hearts, just as God promised. The outcome is that there will be a change in conduct that leads to genuine success in righteousness. All of this is consistent with what Paul read concerning the promises of God in the scriptures prior to Christ. Through Christ and the power of the Spirit God has enacted what he promised and the prophets foretold. In this way, Paul recognizes a second intention of God promised in the future, that the new covenant is not for Jews only, but also for Gentiles (Eph. 2:11-22, cf. Isa. 42:6; 49:6). It is impossible to miss the good news of the gospel, as Jesus presented it, and as Paul presents it in his letters. God has called us to repentance and faith, as a radical departure from sin, as well as from sinning, in order to be *born again by the Spirit,* so that, as Jesus sought to convince Nicodemus, he can indeed start over again and expect a different outcome (John 3:1-18).

Holiness and Righteousness God's Endgame: Three infinitives (ἀποθέσθαι, ἀνανεοῦσθαι, ἐνδύσασθαι) in this passage carry the weight of what the Ephesians learned from Christ, and give expression to God's goal for moral transformation, which they are to embrace.[350] Brooks in

---

[350] Brooks, Ephesians Outline and Unfolded, 1984, 180; Stott J. R., 1979, 183; Spence-Jones, 1909, 168; Liefeld, 1997, 114-115. A search using ChatGPT reveals that the imperatival, aorist infinitive of indirect discourse is most often used by Paul in the New Testament, some 15-20 times, depending on syntactical interpretation, and 6-7 times elsewhere. The use of the aorist infinitive generally, in indirect discourse, occurs 85-95 times in the Pauline corpus, and 6-10 elsewhere. This gives is strong pattern of Pauline use of the

his commentary on Ephesians, reminds us that Paul's concern at the beginning of chapter four is that they *walk worthy of the calling by which they were called,* were divine passive invoked, meaning called by God.[351] The metaphor of walking is a standard Hebraic metaphor for how a person acts or conducts their lives, and underscores habitual conduct and integrity (cf. Ps. 1). Paul calls on the Ephesians to act and live habitually in ways that are worthy of their new life and relationship with God. They must live *suitably* for what God has called them to be in Christ. That is, those who belong to God and have been instructed in righteousness, God sets apart from the Gentiles, and everyone else who still walks in disobedience to God, influenced by the ruler of this world (the authority of the kingdom of darkness in the spiritual realms opposed to God (Col. 1:13)) (Eph. 2:1-3; 3:7-12; 4:20; 6:1-12).[352] Verse 24 presents an indirect expression of the end-goal of the consistent application of oneself to holiness, that we have might be like God, in character and conduct, authentic holiness and righteousness, which he has, after all, created in us as a result of moral transformation at justification and initial salvation (cf. Rom. 6:3-4; Cor. 5:17).

There are immediate implications in reflecting the righteousness of God by our character and conduct, it is the principal mode our witness to the world and the primary way to represent God to it. That our character impinges on Christ and the gospel message is key to understanding Paul of missiology for the saints to the world outside of

---

aorist infinitive. ChatGPT notes that Ephesians 4:22-24 contains the best example of a "Classic imperatival infinitive sequence following διδάσκω (sic) structure but functioning exhortationally (sic). These are among the clearest examples in the Pauline corpus." They refer back to what Paul previously taught the Ephesians when he was with them. - ChatGPT https://chatgpt.com/c/6999af60-ef14-8331-a026-9568e6c3b10b.

[351] Brooks, Ephesians Outline and Unfolded, 1984, 172-174.

[352] Cf. Arndt, 2000, 94.

the church community (Phil. 2:14-16). But there are also immediate implications inside the church for unity and thriving in the body of Christ, that arise out of selflessness, as the saints freely serve to one another (Eph. 4:16). Still again, there are eschatological implications for the broader purposes of God, by which he is building a church/temple in which he is already dwelling by his Spirit, and in which he will dwell among his people in the new creation, where godliness in the saints has been perfected and reflects God's own character (Eph. 2:22; 4:13). At that time, the church and the saints will represent the full measure of the stature of Christ (Eph. 4:13). Having been conformed into the image of God's Son, they will reflect God's righteousness and holiness back into creation by their character and conduct through their own righteousness and holiness which is authentically like his.[353] Even creation will rejoice in the revelation of God sons as the sign and guarantee of its own liberation from bondage to the fall and consequences of human sin (Rom. 8:18-24; 29-30; Eph. 4:13).

The first infinitive, ἀποθέσθαι, to put off, to lay aside (the old life), provides the content of what they heard and were instructed truthfully in Christ (εἴ γε αὐτὸν ἠκούσατε καὶ ἐν αὐτῷ ἐδιδάχθητε, καθώς ἐστιν ἀλήθεια ἐν τῷ Ἰησοῦ).[354] The third, ἐνδύσασθαι (to put on, to clothe oneself), corresponds with the first as an action complementing the laying aside the old to take up the new life. Both fill out the idea of what the Ephesians had learned from Christ, heard, and were instructed by Paul. The second present, passive infinitive, "sandwiched" between them, expresses the purpose for laying aside the old life, to make way for a renewal in the attitude of their minds by God, followed by being clothed with the new man, created by God "in" true righteousness and

---

[353] Cf. Beale, We Become What We Worhip: A Biblical Theology of Idolatry, 2008, 268-283.

[354] Holmes, M. W. (2011–2013). *The Greek New Testament: SBL Edition* (Eph 4:21). Lexham Press; Society of Biblical Literature.

holiness, "according to God" or consistent with his own nature (Eph. 4:23-24). Daniel Wallace sees the first and third infinitives as infinitives of indirect discourse, that is they indicate the content of what Paul taught the Ephesians with respect to the truth they learned in Christ earlier.[355] He almost opines that they are capable of representing either an underlying indicative, "you have put off... you have put on," or an imperative, "put off... put on."[356] Because the final outcome of this determination is "pregnant with exegetical implications", he suggests caution and "some discussion".[357]

Wallace notes, Burton states that no aorist indicatives of indirect discourse in the New Testament represent an indicative in the corresponding direct discourse.[358] He also observes, however, that Burton offers scant verification of his assertion. Wallace goes on to cite research that has found 150 instances of the aorist infinitive of indirect discourse, of which none appear to represent an underlying indicative, and therefore carry an imperatival force, "put off... put on...."[359] Ben Merkle suggests that the choice of the aorist by Paul is governed by the intrinsic nature of the action represented by the verb, because it approximates the aspectual nature of the tense. *Putting something off,* used for taking off clothes, might more readily be viewed as a whole, and not from the point of view of a process of removing each item.[360] This is a way of saying that the aorist infinitives here represent an underlying command or imperative in Paul's original instruction to the Ephesians, with respect to their moral transformation, by which they are to lay off the old life, to undress themselves of it, and to go on to clothe

---

[355] Wallace, 1996, 605.
[356] Cf. Merkle B. L., 2016, 142.
[357] Wallace, 1996, 605.
[358] Wallace, 1996, 605, cf. Burton, 1898, 53, 154.
[359] Cf. Merkle B. L., 2016, 142.
[360] Merkle B. L., 2016, 142, cf. Liefeld, 1997, 115.

themselves with the new life, created by God for holiness and righteousness.

There appears to be no thought in Paul's instruction that the "undressing" of the old life should go on for an unspecified amount of time, or that it is to be an indefinite process lasting a lifetime.[361] Brooks opines that among Fundamentalists there is a notion that a person "may be eternally saved from the consequences of sinning quite apart from a salvation from the practice of sinning..." which he declares to be entirely foreign to Pauline teaching (cf. Rom. 6:1-23).[362] Indeed, the semantic context implies that Paul means a decisive consent of the mind and will, whereby the believer divests themselves of the old life, and the practice of habitual of sinning like the Gentiles, to be equally decisively clothed with the new to take up habitual obedience to God. Any sanctifying progression in Pauline theology is not of a lifetime of diminishing sin or sinning, but of increasing holiness of character and godliness, producing fruit in terms of right conduct (righteousness of character producing right conduct).[363] For Paul, power for the development of Christ-like character in the life of the believer is not found in a tortuous mortification of the flesh, the slow, painful defeat of sin and sinning, or

---

[361] Note Ben Merkle's interpretation of the aorist participle, κτισθέντα, almost implies that the putting on is contemporaneous and synchronous with the renewing by God, so that the new man is being made new and clothing himself more and more with new life. A straightforward reading of the passage does not give that impression at all, but that they Ephesians are to clothe themselves with the new life that God has created (seeded) in them. Cf. Merkle B. L., 2016, 144.

[362] Brooks, Ephesians Outline and Unfolded, 1984, 182.

[363] This belies conventional evangelical thinking, that moral growth in the believer involves a slow diminution over time of sinfulness, balanced by a growth in godliness. Paul rather speaks of a growth in godliness coming out of a decision to lay aside the old life, so that it no longer claims power to control them, and to secede that power to the Spirit and rule of God in their lives.

indwelling carnal power in our nature (cf. Rom. 7:7-25), but in a renewal of our nature by God that must be fully embraced by those he has justified, transformed, and transferred into Christ, as well as into his kingdom, to come under his rule, and by which they are to mature into full godliness (Eph. 4:13, cf. Rom. 12:2).

Whereas it was asserted in older grammars that the aorist was *punctiliar* in nature and represented a once-and-for-all action, a crisis, something instantaneous, this is no longer the consensus among scholars, who favor an emphasis on aspect in Greek tenses over temporal significance, and who caution that context is key to a proper exegesis of the tense.[364] The aorist, it is argued, represents action that is viewed as a whole without reference to its beginning or ending, even if the nature of the action may indeed involve a process. The present tense emphasizes action that is, broadly speaking, progressive, viewed as ongoing or is repeated from the perspective of how it is portrayed. Agreement on Greek verbal aspect is by no means settled, and there is much debate on nuances so complicating verbal grammar, that it often ignores the simple reality that writers or communicators simply follows the convention or their own instinct when using language, without intellectual angst, minute analysis of linguists, or the hesitancy of contemporary academic speculation. The text needs to be viewed organically, more than it needs to be parsed microscopically.[365]

In a version of the former view of the aorist, the holiness movement has sought to underwrite the theology of sanctification as a subsequent, definite, and instantaneous work of grace, from Paul's use of the

---

[364] Machen, 1951, 81-82; Wenham, 1965, 96; Kostenberger, Merkel, & Plummer, 2016, 289-290, 321; Merkle & Plummer, 2020, 118; Mounce, 2009, 258-259.

[365] Cf. Campbell, Basics of Verbal Aspect in Biblical Greek, 2024.

aorist.[366] It had been claimed that the theology of sanctification as definite, instantaneous, and subsequent to justification, is supported by the once-and-for-all nature of the aorist that commands or describes the action of putting off the old life and putting on the new.[367] Outside of the holiness movement the argument is mostly viewed with disfavor, particularly now. Unknowingly, however, "anticipating" this development, though he employed current conventions with respect to the aorist, Noel Brooks, in *Bible Validation for Sanctification,* argued at the heart of sanctification is a definite consent of the will and the mind, whereby the old life is forsaken, and the new life is taken up. Even without an appeal to the aorist in the former sense, and if we accept current grammatical conventions, Brook's observation still holds, and is in perfect harmony with the explicit version of it in Paul instructions to the Romans, that they *reckon* themselves dead to the old life and alive to the new life they now have in Christ (Rom. 6:11). The outcome is the same, believers are called upon by God to adopt an attitude of mind and will that sets aside the rule of one way of life, with its carnal mindset, to adopt a new one, with a renewed mind, being continually transformed going forward (Rom. 12:2). This much is clear from the context in Ephesians 4, and from what many have concluded are imperatival infinitives.

What Brooks addresses in discussions of Romans 6:11, he imports equally into his analysis of Ephesians 4:22-24. *Putting off* and the *putting on* in Paul is an imperatival call for his readers to make the decision to leave sinning behind, and to go on to the holiness and righteousness of God. They are already disciples, after all, and have

---

[366] Cf. As examples: Hills, 1929; Beacham P. F., 1935, 3; Graham, 1951, 5; Brooks, The Advocate Bible School: Ephesians Oulined and Unfolded: 58. Christian Conversion, 1982, 14.

[367] Brooks, Scriptural Holiness, 1972, 56-57, cf. Brooks, Fingertip Holiness, 11; Tramel, 2009, 148-150.

already been instructed in righteousness on previous occasions by him, now they are encouraged to make sure they act or have acted on that instruction (Eph. 4:20-21).[368] This is precisely what the apostle said in Romans 6:11, but using the language *reckon yourselves,* and in Romans 12:1, *present yourselves to God*. Paul asserts here that the Ephesians were previously instructed by him that they must *choose* to put off the old life and put on the new, if they want to experience an ongoing, progressive renewal of the attitudes/spirit of their minds, or to go on to mature holiness and righteousness. And now he is reminding them of that decision in light of what is to come next by way of practical instruction (Eph. 4:22-24, cf. Rom. 12:2).

MATURING IN HOLINESS AND RIGHTEOUSNESS: What becomes apparent, even clear, is that Paul views the putting off of the old life of sin, and its controlling principle of carnality, as essential to moral and spiritual progress for the believer (Eph. 2:23). His mild, but nonetheless real, albeit somewhat implicit, purpose clause consisting in the second infinitive, expressing the goal of putting off of the old man, should not be quickly or lightly passed over by the reader or exegete (ἀνανεοῦσθαι δὲ τῷ πνεύματι τοῦ νοὸς ὑμῶν).[369] They are to put of the old man, *in order that* God might renewed them in the attitude/spirit of their minds. The logical advancement of Paul's thought should be carefully considered. The first aorist infinitive, providing an imperatival instruction, they must put off the old self, is followed by a present, passive infinitive, *to be renewed,* where the context makes it clear that a subtle but genuine purpose statement is intended. That the success of renewal has some contingency associated with the putting off of the old life, is certainly implied by the syntax, and argument. The laying aside of the old life or

---

[368] Brooks, Bible Validation for Santification, 1975, 48-49; Brooks, Ephesians Outline and Unfolded, 1984, 182-183.

[369] Holmes, M. W. (2011–2013). *The Greek New Testament: SBL Edition* (Eph 4:23). Lexham Press; Society of Biblical Literature.

self is necessary for God to affect the renewing of their minds, where resistance to future, progressive renewal in their minds has been "neutralize" or laid to rest by an act of choice (and faith).[370] The implication of the passive is clear, that God is the one doing the renewing. They cannot renew themselves, even if they do lay aside the old life.[371] It is not the laying aside of the old life in its own right[372] that produces the holiness God is looking for in increasing measure, but the renewing that occurs as a result of God's working in them through the Spirit, as Paul makes clear in other places.

Nevertheless, the old life must be put out of business for the project of maturation in holiness and righteousness to go forward. A decision of the mind and will must be engaged on the part of those whom God has justified (cf. Rom. 6:11). To put it in the vernacular, it is necessary for those who belong to Christ to see to it by a decision born of faith, that the old life, and control exercised by carnality in their nature, does not reassert itself through a return to sin and sinning (Rom. 6:1-11), nor interfere with God's intention and purpose to develop his holiness and righteousness as mature godliness in them, that is in their nature. There appears to be in this expression, a mild contingency, whereby the laying aside of the old life is required to make way for God's work of renewing their minds to proceed without resistance from carnality that once ruled over their minds and will – as it once did when they formerly conducted their lives as children of disobedience, under the authority of the prince of this world (Eph. 2:1-3). All of that must be thoroughly discarded and repudiated by choice (cf. Rom. 6:2, 11, 15).

---

[370] Arndt, 2000, 68.

[371] Cf. Stott J. R., 1979, 182.

[372] In my opinion this has been the historical homiletical, and fatal flaw of the holiness movement's theology of sanctification.

That the second infinitive, ἀνανεοῦσθαι, *to be renewed*, is present tense, means it aspectually hints at something ongoing or progressive. The nature of some verbs, as pointed out so often by grammarians, is atelic, unbounded, and can be conceived as inherently ongoing or progressive in its nature. That ἀνανεοῦσθαι semantically embodies the idea of an ongoing process of renewal, for which the present tense is a fitting mode of depiction, is easily perceived, even in English. Paul does not conceive of renewal as a once-and-done, but a progressive, moral transforming and growth, *coming off of a decision to leave the old life behind*. In Pauline salvific theology, a tension exists between the immediate moral transformation at justification (Rom. 6:3-4), whereby those who are in Christ are a new creation, the old life has gone, and new life begun (2 Cor. 5:17), and the ongoing maturation and growth of godliness in the newly transformed life and nature of the saints (Eph. 4:23, cf. Rom. 8:5-17; 12:1-2; Gal. 5:16-25). Where the decision to put away the old life drives a stake in the ground, and marks the spot from which the decision is made to go on to holiness, God's action of renewal consists in a continual lifetime of refining and maturation. [373] It is essential for us to not blow past the second infinitive, missing the implications of God's role and action in the ongoing moral development of those he has rescued from sin, justified, and transformed.

Paul seems to envision moral renewal as a process leading to maturation in godliness, where no doubt, Christian character and integrity are at stake (Eph. 4:23). That this should not surprise us is obvious to those who pay attention to the unfolding revelation of scripture, where God has been working with his people and individuals from the beginning, and from whom he demands inner integrity in terms of righteousness as the grounds for right conduct.[374] David captures it

---

[373] Cf. Wright N. T., 2012.

[374] This is most notably represented in the Deuteronomic formulae, "If you love me..." you will obey me, keep my commandments, walk in my ways. etc.

in his psalm of repentance, over the Bathsheba debacle, when he addresses not only his need for pardon, but for inward moral cleansing, the restoration of the moral uprightness of his heart, and a restoration to fellowship with God (Ps. 51). Furthermore, the Isaiah's rebuke to Israel in chapter one consists of castigating them for observing the rituals of the temple, but without a heart of uprightness and integrity toward God. Israel's alienation from God lay almost completely at the door of a lack of inner integrity, which resulted in their sin and disobedience, even resulting in post-exilic rebuke from Malachi, and much later, Jesus' rebuke of the Pharisees for the same defect (cf. Matt. 5-7, 23). Inner moral uprightness, with respect to character, is critical to holiness and righteousness in scripture, so that the right practice of devotion to God and right behavior come from a right heart. They cannot stand on their own externally separated from the inner environment of the heart, or relationship to God.

In a telling moment of stunning clarity, through the prophets of the *Old Testament,* God makes plain that the remedy for the differential between religious practice and sinfulness of heart and mind cannot be found in the law, but requires addressing an inner defect of the heart and mind that are opposed to God and desperately wicked (Gen. 6:3, 5-8; Jer. 17:9). The remedy comes from a renewal arising from of a divine initiative, a *new covenant* (Jer. 31:31-34; Ezek. 36:22-28). That cannot be something Paul overlooked in connection with Christ, his propitiatory sacrifice, resurrection, and the gift of the indwelling Spirit, all in connection with the new covenant, and the breaking into this age of the kingdom of God which the gospels portray (cf. Mark 1:14-15). In Romans 7, in what is possibly a stylized template describing the problems faced by law abiding Jews in general, Paul describes his own painful, autobiographical experience of powerlessness, where the law could not affect the moral change, he desired and sought. To this condition, the Lord proposed a new covenant for Israel, whereby he would write his law in their hearts and ***minds*** *in connection with forgiving and pardoning their sins and wickednesses* (Jer. 31:31-34).[375]

In the same sense, Ezekiel speaks of God sprinkling his people with clean water to purify them after their restoration to God, and that he will put in them a new heart of flesh, to replace the stoney heart of resistance and rebellion, and also give them a *new* S(s)pirit, so that they will obey him from an new inner motivation in their nature, and not from unaided human impulse, seeking to keep a written code (Ezek. 36:22-28). Paul identified the problem faced, found in both Jeremiah and Ezekiel, as intractable carnality in his nature that created an inner moral environment that sabotaged every effort at practicing the righteousness demanded by the law (Rom. 7:14-25). Once laid aside, the program of God's renewal can proceed in earnest (Rom. 7:24-25). Paul embraces these Old Testament promises to apply them to the New Testament advent of Christ, and the outpouring of the Spirit (as God also promised), so that through the Spirit, God might affect what he promised his people, cleansing, justifying, and moral transformation. These God intended to apply through a new dynamic (moral transformation and the indwelling Spirit) for moral renewal and empowerment to those who are willing to come under a new covenant, a new way of God dealing with his people (cf. Jer. 31:31-34). Ezekiel portrays this new dynamic as a new heart and a new S(s)pirit, the confluence, arguably, and cooperation of a renewed nature with the divine initiative at work in them (Ezek. 36:22-28). This is precisely what Paul saw at work in believers, and experienced in his own life, a transformative justification, linked to the power of the indwelling

[375] In light of Pauline soteriology, or Jesus' exchange with Nicodemus, at justification there is a renewal that creates a new person, when the life of sin and the old self are rejected to embrace new life by faith in God, and to move forward, expecting different moral outcomes (John 3:3-14; 2 Cor. 5:17; Eph. 4:22-24).

Spirit (Eph. 4:22-24, cf. Rom. 6:1-11; 67:24-25; 8:1-4, 9-15). God promised earlier he would affect his plan to bring lasting moral change to humanity, to reflects his own holiness back into his creation. Quite simply, Ephesians 4 links arms with the promises of God from the earlier scriptures, to take hold of their fulfillment in Christ, through the Spirit.

The laying aside of the old life, unlike the impression left by some holiness movement homiletics, is clearly not an end in itself, certainly in this passage, but a gateway to ongoing renewal and maturation in godliness. This much Paul makes abundantly clear elsewhere too. The choice to lay aside the old life does not aim at producing a void, but at giving room for God to enact his program of renewal which leads to the development and maturation of holiness and righteousness, the establishment of right character and right conduct. We will find ourselves arguing in a circle to discount the importance of a calculated decision needing to be made by every believer with respect to whether or not they are going to surrender to God for ongoing holiness, when justification itself require repentance, which is just as much a decision to turn away from our past sin, in order to trust God for his pardon and forgiveness.

That Paul makes it clear in Ephesians 4:1 our calling to salvation comes from God, and that his readers are to go on to live in a way worthy of that call, obviously means that an ongoing surrender and cooperation with God is envisioned by the apostle in connection with their coming to faith in Christ. If even faith is his gift to those whom he calls, that clearly flattens out objections to works righteousness (Eph. 2:5, 8-94:1, cf. Rom 8:29-30). Nevertheless, God demands something from us in terms of surrender, and that is entirely consistent with the many imperatival commands and injunctions found from the beginning of the Old Testament, starting in the garden, through the full range of doctrinal teaching (like here) in the New Testament. Such surrender does not accrue as a contribution on our part to our salvation ultimately; from

Paul's perspective that much is clear, or else he would not have issued the two infinitival imperatives in our passage in the first place.[376]

After all is said and done, these imperatives are reminders of his previous instructions to the Ephesians that they *must go on* to lay aside the old life and take up the new, if they expect to mature in the holiness and righteousness of God. Likewise, surrender and cooperation by those who belong to Christ in the salvific work of the God through the Spirit is rooted in faith, based on confidence in God's grace that he can manage the program, when those who surrender to him trust him, and walk in fellowship with him through the Spirit (cf. Rom. 1:16-17; 8:1-4; 1 John 1:5-10). It is not, according to Paul, the laying aside of the old life, a net negative, the subtraction of the old life, which leads to holiness. Rather, by laying aside the old life the door is opened to the action of God through the Spirit to affect the renewing of the attitude/spirit of the mind, whereby holiness and godliness are matured progressively throughout the lifetime of the saints who remain surrendered to God.

In the same way, Paul encouraged the Romans to *present their bodies a living sacrifice to God,* in anticipation of avoiding the world squeezing them back into its mold (cf. Eph. 4:17), and so that God might set about transforming them (producing mature godliness in them and their lives) through the renewing of their minds (Rom. 12:1-2). The parallels between Ephesians 4 and Romans 12 ought to be clear, and are staggering. A decision to present themselves to God as a living sacrifice precedes ongoing renewal through a transforming of their minds. In Ephesians, the laying aside of the old life through a decisive exercise of choice precedes the renewing of the attitude/spirit of their minds (Eph. 4:23). That Paul certainly intends for them to lay aside every hinderance from their previous life in sin or under the control of their

---

[376] Cf. Stott J. R., 1979, 182.

carnal nature, to progress in the development of godliness, is obvious. Hebrews captures this sentiment in its great appeal to the Jewish-Christian recipients of the letter, that they should lay aside every hindrance, as well as the sin that characteristically trips them up, in order to run with renewed conviction and determination the race God has set before them (Heb. 12:1-2). There is consistency in Paul over this thing. Surrender to God is required initially at justification, as well as subsequently after justification, as a matter of choice and determination (Rom. 6:11; Eph. 4:23), and they are to be followed by the kind of habitual surrender to God that gives the Spirit permission to order our conduct, and to mature our character in godliness over time, as we live in fellowship with God (walking in the Spirit) (Rom. 8:1-4; Gal. 5:16-25).

Just as important, Paul reminds his readers that he had *previously instructed* them that it is as necessary to *put on* the new life (ἐνδύσασθαι), as it is to *put off* the old. The third of the infinitives, like the first, is aorist, and so is construed as imperatival. Clearly, there is conceptual symmetry in the ideas of laying aside one thing to take up another. God's program of renewal, also conveyed by use an infinitive, appears between the first and third imperatival forms to create something of a chiasm. Moral renewal, ongoing and developmental, by God is at the heart of Paul's exhortation in this passage, in order to resist any impulse to act like Gentiles, and to adopt the lifestyle they had learned from Christ. Renewal is his primary focus and concern here. Ongoing renewal by God is at the heart of his epistle, in many ways, supplying the mechanism and personal dynamics for unity in the church among the saints, as well compliance to the instructions that follow, which promote and support it. In the figure below, we can see a diagrammatic representation of this part of the passage.

Fig. 1

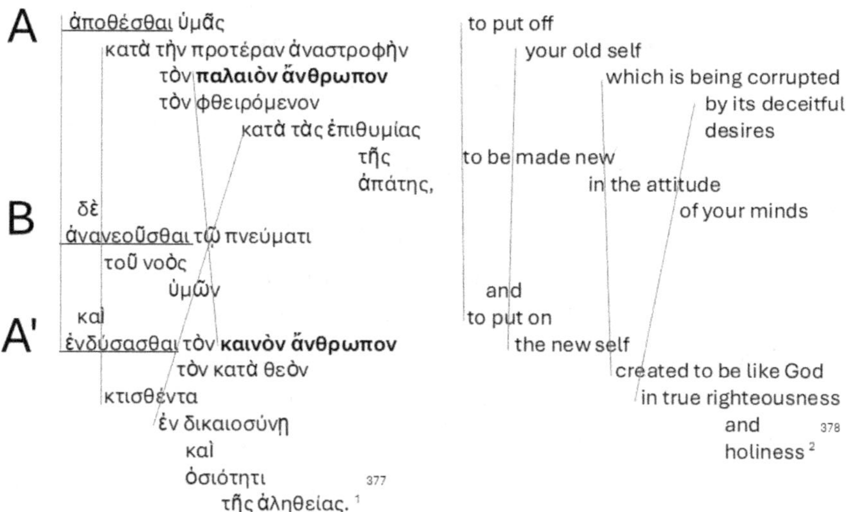

Figure 1 illustrates the symmetry in the latter part of this passage, and may be part of a larger symmetry in the whole. The conduct or Gentiles at the beginning and holiness and righteousness at the end, the old man and new man, and their characters laid out as opposing faces, all point to a Pauline literary structure that enhances the central idea of God's renewing action in the spirit of their minds. In any case, what stands out here is that the infinitives form a sort of chiasm in themselves, with the act of God's ongoing renewal as the central idea. However, for godliness to develop, their engagement is required, putting off the old life and clothing themselves with the new life that God has imparted through justification (τὸν κατὰ θεὸν κτισθέντα), and which he is now bringing to moral maturity, through the ongoing renewal of the spirit of their minds (ἀνανεοῦσθαι δὲ τῷ πνεύματι τοῦ νοὸς ὑμῶν).[377] Looking at the infinitival elements in this way helps us to see more clearly the role played by God renewing of their minds, and that Paul highlights that they are moving away from a deteriorating moral

---

[377] Holmes, M. W. (2011–2013). *The Greek New Testament: SBL Edition* (Eph 4:23). Lexham Press; Society of Biblical Literature.

condition inherent the old life (Eph. 4:17-21). The old life and new life are headed in the opposite directions, the one becoming progressively morally worse, and the other progressively morally more like God/Christ (Eph. 4:13, cf. Rom. 8:29-30; 2 Cor. 3:18; 4:16-18; Col. 3:1-4).

Through coming to Christ, God has laid a foundation for new life to thrive, created (initiated) at justification to reflect his holiness and righteousness (Eph. 4:24) – a life that is now going in the direction of the maturation and perfection of those qualities (Eph. 4:23), leaving behind the increasing moral deterioration of the old life (Eph. 4:22). The Ephesians (and us) must take up the new life as resolutely as they set aside the old one (Eph. 4:24).[378] Again, Paul envisions them as disrobed of the old life, and now just as deftly clothing themselves with the new life of holiness and righteousness that reflects the character of God. That this is aorist, and the aspect of the action is presented holistically, and not as a process of dressing, is seen in the semantic nature of the verb, and supported by textual context. Paul sees the decision they must make as going with, and fully embracing, the renewing action of God, whereby the implanted new life of Christ in them is being perfected through maturing, and so avoiding drifting back into the conduct of the world around them (cf. Eph. 4:17).

They cannot be volitionally neutral with respect to the moral development of their new life in Christ, or as in some evangelical circles, view sin in our nature as an intractable problem, which inevitably produces sinful conduct, something with which we must learn to live in equanimity until the return of Christ. Paul has no idea of the acceptance of the old life exercising its control over the environment of our minds as believers in Christ, inevitably producing sinful behavior (cf. Rom. 6:1-2). Rather, he encourages a resolute adoption of the new life of Christ in them through an attitude of categorical, volitional acceptance, a life, he

[378] Cf. Liefeld, 1997, 115.

says, God has already created in them through an ontological inculcation of his holiness and righteous, but which is also capable of, and requires, developing and maturing over time.

Paul does not teach, here, or elsewhere, resignation of the mind to the old life, or acceptance of sin dominating our nature and life after justification, without it being addressed effectively and head on (cf. Rom. 6:11; 12:2). On the contrary, he encourages an act of definite, volitional surrender to God, not mere acceptance of new life in Christ, but seizing it resolutely, and engaging it through the power of the Spirit in fellowship with God (Rom. 8:1-4). In Ephesians 4:17-24, Paul makes not less than five references to the mind and thinking, the seat of volition and will. The Gentiles, whose way of life (τὰ ἔθνη περιπατεῖ) they must not fall back into or imitate (μηκέτι ὑμᾶς περιπατεῖν καθὼς καὶ), act the way they do because their *minds* are empty (ἐν ματαιότητι τοῦ νοὸς αὐτῶν), and their *thinking* darkened (ἐσκοτωμένοι τῇ διανοίᾳ ὄντες) with respect to the knowledge of God, and the gospel.[379] They are alienated from the life God offers on account of the *ignorance* that is part of the mental landscape of their minds, when it comes to the gospel (τῆς ζωῆς τοῦ θεοῦ, διὰ τὴν ἄγνοιαν τὴν οὖσαν ἐν αὐτοῖς). It is an ontological *ignorance* that is exacerbated by a dullness of thinking or lack of awareness and understanding of God in their hearts (διὰ τὴν πώρωσιν τῆς καρδίας αὐτῶν).[380] In contrast to this state of moral indifference and ignorance, Paul encourages his readers to resolutely and full take hold of the new life created in them by God at justification, or initial salvation.[381] It is a morally changed life which God has resolved ultimately to develop into the full measure of the stature of Christ

---

[379] Holmes, M. W. (2011–2013). *The Greek New Testament: SBL Edition* (Eph 4:17). Lexham Press; Society of Biblical Literature.
[380] Holmes, M. W. (2011–2013). *The Greek New Testament: SBL Edition* (Eph 4:18). Lexham Press; Society of Biblical Literature.
[381] Cf. Stott J. R., 1979, 182.

through a progressive renewal of their *minds* (Eph. 4:23). That this is renewal for both the saints and church as a community of interconnected members, impinges on a central idea of this epistle, making every effort to maintain the unity of body established by God through the Spirit (Eph. 4:3, 13). The moral maturation into the full measure of Christ, God's intended purpose, depends on their cooperation with him, on their laying aside the old life, and just as resolutely and tenaciously engaging the new.

CREATED IN THE IMAGE AND LIKENESS OF GOD: The Ephesians are to put on the new man, which is described by a prepositional phrase as having been created (κτισθέντα - aorist passive) to correspond to God, that is in terms of his true righteousness and holiness (ἐν δικαιοσύνῃ καὶ ὁσιότητι τῆς ἀληθείας).[382] We have already observed this in passing, but it is worth noting here more explicitly. New life has been created by God in us, and according to the logic of Paul's argument in this passage, it has been established by God *prior to the imperative to be clothed with it*. In other words, they are to take up the new life with resolution that God had already established in them.[383] Their resolve to

---

[382] Holmes, M. W. (2011–2013). *The Greek New Testament: SBL Edition* (Eph 4:24). Lexham Press; Society of Biblical Literature, cf. Wood, 1981, 63; Spence-Jones, 1909, 168.

[383] Cf. Merkle B. L., 2016, 144. Note that Ben Merkle makes an interpretive decision in the EGGNT commentary, when he observes, "κατὰ θεόν communicates the standard and refers to the new man *being created according to God's image....*" He presents the aorist participle as aspectually progressive, when both the sematic nature of the verb and the tense, in this context, clearly portray God's creative act holistically. It appears on the surface to be an interpretive observation, not strictly a syntactical one. Paul's imperatival infinitive, corresponding with the first one, put off, assumes that new life has already been established, and that they are to clothe themselves with it, where it is not the process of dressing that is in view, but the idea of

clothe themselves in the new life does not mark its beginning, but their full assent to its development through the power of God, as a result of a similar decision to leave the old life behind.

Now in case some think we are splitting hairs here; the aorist participle (κτισθέντα), from context is temporal, and implies action prior to the infinitives of laying off and taking up the old and new life. There would be nothing to take up unless God had already established new life for them to take hold of, or in the words of Paul in Romans 6:11, to reckon on. Paul's theology of salvation is consistent throughout the corpus, where new life begins at justification, and the old is gone when the new begins, so that those who are in Christ have become new creations (2 Cor. 5:17). In Romans 6, Paul's logic for why those who have been saved by God grace cannot return to a life of sinning and surrender to carnality is that they have been delivered from both by a radical change in their nature through participating with Christ in his death and resurrection (Rom. 6:3-4). A relocation into Christ, spiritually and morally speaking, means death to the old life and the control exercised by carnality in their nature, to be raised to a new life, which he later describes as coming under the control of the indwelling Spirit of God (Rom. 8:1-17). The reckoning of Romans 6:11, therefore, is predicated on God having established new life in them as a result of the exercise of his grace, when they were justified, and reconciled to himself (Rom. 5:1-2). Reckoning on the new life amounts subscribing to the new life with which they have been endowed by God at transforming justification.

---

being clothed in terms of the resulting state. Merkle imports the progressive idea of renewal from the middle infinitive into the second (and the first?), so that Paul instructs them in effect to "be clothing themselves" with the new man, as though it is the process of dressing he is encouraging them to engage, not decisively making room for the divine action of ongoing renewal to take place. It seems better from context to see the putting off and putting on as a decision that opens the way to ongoing divine renewal.

Jesus said something similar to this when he was approached by Nicodemus, and explained his insistence on being *born again*. When Nicodemus expressed reservations, Jesus he said that it was a mysterious, but transformative experience done by the Spirit in those who are willing to accept it from God (John 3:1-14).

The apostle's instruction to the Ephesians, serving as a reminder of what he had already taught them, is that must recognize, by a decision of full acceptance, that God has created new life in them, life that requires their assent and surrender for him to develop its fullest potential for holiness and righteousness (Eph. 4:24). God's creative act, by which he establishes new life in those who believe is rendered here as an adjectival clause describing the new man, with which they are to clothe themselves (τὸν κατὰ θεὸν κτισθέντα ἐν δικαιοσύνῃ καὶ ὁσιότητι τῆς ἀληθείας).[384] Indeed, in more technical terms, it forms an apposition, a restatement of the nature of this new life; it consists of a creation by God that truly, authentically corresponds to his own holiness and righteousness, now imprinted on their nature, so that they are new creations in Christ (cf. 2 Cor. 5:17). Whatever Paul's means by the new self, elsewhere, here he describes it as the creation of God, that authentically represents his image of holiness and righteousness in them (Eph. 4:24).

Nothing is more stunning than this assertion, or its ramifications. If God has created new life in those who belong to him in Christ, a response is required from them, that they must be willing to enthusiastically engage the transformation, to own it fully, to wear it proudly, in order to come under the transforming power of God, who will develop it through a process of renewal into mature godliness which will

---

[384] Holmes, M. W. (2011–2013). *The Greek New Testament: SBL Edition* (Eph 4:24). Lexham Press; Society of Biblical Literature.

ultimately reflect the full measure of stature of Christ (Eph. 4:23-24). In the statements, that the new man is created in the image of God, and that they are to put it on, and that God is at work in them, renewing the spirit of their minds to lead this new life to full maturity of holiness and righteousness, Paul draws together the temporal and eschatological purpose of God, the now and the not yet of the kingdom of God that has broken into this present age, and is already at work in the saints who make up the church.

The process of the renewal of their minds, whereby they are moving in the direction of moral and spiritual maturity (cf. 2 Cor. 3:18; 4:16-18), is founded on a de facto creation of God in them of new life that accords with the image of God or reflects him (κατὰ θεὸν), particularly in relationship to his moral perfection (κτισθέντα ἐν δικαιοσύνῃ καὶ ὁσιότητι τῆς ἀληθείας).[385] It is hard not to see allusion here to the Pauline imago Dei, whereby the divine intention is for his people ultimately to be conformed into the image of his Son, who alone serves in heaven now as the authentic human representation and radiant expression of God to creation and humanity (Heb. 1:1-4). An allusion like this relies upon Paul perception of God's purpose from the Old Testament scriptures, where Adam and Eve were created by God to fully represent him in their shared and united humanity as male and female to image the likeness of God, and serve him by taking dominion over creation (Gen. 1:26-28). By alluding to creation in the use of the aorist participle, *having been created,* Paul sets out the redemptive transformation of human nature through the action of the Spirit in those who believe as God's purposeful reestablishment of his original intention to be more fully expressed in a new heaven and a new earth. The significant assertion that this new creation is according to God, that

---

[385] Holmes, M. W. (2011–2013). *The Greek New Testament: SBL Edition* (Eph 4:24). Lexham Press; Society of Biblical Literature.

is in his image, and that it consists in a true or authentic representation of his holiness and righteousness, clearly points to God's intention to reengage his original purpose of producing a humanity capable of reflecting his image and likeness back into creation.

And yet, the pivotal infinitival clause asserts that in the present God is engaged in the process of spiritual and moral development in the minds (and therefore nature) of those who belong to him prior to the eschaton. Ongoing moral renewal, in which God is engaged with those who fully embrace the new life they have in Christ, and who have fully laid aside the old life represented by the Gentile around them, is anticipatory of its consummation in reaching the full measure of the stature of Christ (Eph. 4:13), or in another place, conformity to the image of God's Son (Rom. 8:29-30). The two are held in tension with one another, the establishment of new life, that is capable of and requires moral growth and development through the renewing efforts of God by the Spirit in those who belong to him, and its final realization in conformity to the image of Christ, and the full measure of his stature (Rom. 8:29-30; Eph. 4:13). This new life, created in them, Paul says, is authentically imprinted with the holiness and righteousness of God, but requires the cooperation of those who belong to Christ, for God to bring it to its full moral potential. Moral growth over time is implied, against the promise of final perfection to come in relation to God's eschatological goals. This is the divine end-game, that God intends to bring to full moral and spiritual perfection what he has rescued from sin and its consequences, beginning with a preemptive redemption and transformation of justified and reconciled humanity in which he is working by his Spirit, to mature the divine deposit seeded in them through his grace at initial salvation (cf. Col. 1:13-20).

Humanity is God's barometer for his redemptive plan (Rom. 8:28-24). His preemptive redemption and moral, and spiritual transformation of those who are in Christ "assures" creation of its own final redemption and perfection, when all things will be ultimately reconciled to God in Christ (Col. 1:15-20). In Christ, what has already begun in redeemed and reconciled believers is a reminder of the divine plan, and the goals God has set of bringing all things back under his reign in his kingdom, so that all things might be fully renewed and restored (Eph. 1:18-23, cf. Col. 1:15-20). So, the ongoing renewal of the saints, reflected in the church and the relationship between believers in the community of faith now, anticipates the ultimate reunification of all things under the reign of God in perfection. It includes bringing to full maturity the current ongoing moral and spiritual development of those saints to achieve the final goal of representing the image of God in the new heaven and earth, where one day they will reign with Christ and reengage the purpose God set to them at creation (Gen. 1:26-28). As we saw above, Christ preemptively reigns in heaven, representing the redeemed saints to God in the heavenly realms, so Paul views the saints, who are live in surrender to God under the guidance of the Spirit (Rom. 6:11; 8:1-4; 12:1-2), as also preemptively seated with Christ in victory (Eph. 2:6). God, who presently works in them, as they represent him to this present earthly age, is connected to them through the Spirit and Christ who victoriously reigns with God. An ontological connection through the indwelling Spirit and the power of a risen life in Christ anticipates and guarantees the fulfillment of God's purposes for them and for creation (Eph. 1:13-23), as he brings them ever nearer the goal through spiritual and moral development (Eph. 4:23-23, cf. Rom. 12:1-2). This is the divine end-game, God's purpose for creation, that it might be reunited to a *redeemed a humanity,* one that is currently in the process of renewal in anticipation of future perfection, so that both humanity and creation together will share the full consummation of a redemption forged by God through Christ, as a result of his sacrifice and victory (Col. 1:15-20; 2:8-15).

Summary: Now, admittedly our analysis might indeed be construed as *microscopic*, and dismissed by some as over interpretation of *supposed* nuances in the text. However, it seems to me that at the very least, there is a flow to Paul's logic, an argument that advances from the conduct of Gentiles, whose minds are empty, futile, and darkened, to the conduct of minds being renewed by God in those who belong to Christ. Their conduct is to reflect the true holiness and righteousness of God, and to be consistent with it. His readers had been previously instructed by Paul, and he reminds them again now, they are to repudiate the former and embrace the latter, by way of a decision and assent of their will. This he characterizes figuratively as putting off and putting on clothing. A similar idea he also expresses by Paul in Romans 6:11. Within the flow of the passage is an implied contingency, that the ongoing renewal of the new life created in them by God, and which they are to decisively embrace, requires laying aside the old life, a life represented by the earlier prohibition against taking back up with the conduct and lifestyle of Gentiles (Eph. 2:1-3; 4:17). That Paul should refer to the new life as something created by God, alludes to the wider Pauline theology of transformation at justification (cf. Rom. 6:1-11; 2 Cor. 5:17), and further implies that he expects God's ongoing renewal of their minds to bring godliness to maturity over time (Eph. 4:13). It is the same idea he expresses in Romans 12:1-2, where there should be a decisive surrender to God to make way for the ongoing renewal of the mind, which will mitigate the possibility of being squeezed back into the mold of the world, and their former way of life. Furthermore, one cannot ignore the eschatological allusions or implications, where Paul states that the holiness and righteousness God has created in them is according to his own characters, and so points forward to his goal of reestablishing the divine image in a redeemed humanity for the eschaton (Eph. 4:13, cf. Rom. 8:29-30; 1 Cor. 15:48-49; 2 Cor. 3:18; 4:16-18; 1 John 3:1-3). From this we can see that nothing said above is, broadly speaking, beyond the scope of the apostle's teaching or in contradiction to it elsewhere. Our close analysis does not override these observations.

Our passage is transitional from the previous section and preparatory for the one to come (Eph. 4:25-6:9). As Paul establishes the principle of unity, in view of God's eschatological purposes in Christ, a fully united, morally, and spiritually mature church and saints, the underlying and ongoing moral development of the members of the Christian community is essential to their conduct and how they treat one another (cf. Eph. 4:3; 13-16). Chapter 4 begins with an appeal for living worthy of their new life in Christ, and in unity with one another (Eph. 4:1, 3). These two ideas appear as something of a thesis statement for the letter. Not just any kind of unity will do; it must be a unity established by God through the Spirit, to be maintained by a diligent effort on part of the saints that make up the community of faith (Eph. 4:3). Moral development by God in the minds of the saints is the foundational dynamic, in terms of the personal energy driving the quest for unity in the church, because it sets aside individual ambition in favor of mutuality of concern and service (Eph 4:16). He will now turn to instructions on how the saints are to engage that unity through careful attention to their relationships with one another in terms of the practical details of living with one another in community (cf. Eph. 4:25). By ordering their own personal lives around the pursuit of godliness, they will find themselves living in a way that honors God in the particulars of their daily routine and their relationships in the church.

So, in preparing to move into those exhortations, Paul briefly reminds his readers of the moral change that has occurred in them through Christ, and that God is engaged in a process of ongoing development toward mature godliness of character, which ultimately is to reflect the full measure of the stature of Christ (Eph. 4:13). The body benefits from mutuality of service and concern, one for the other, when the saints pursue and engage the transforming power of God in their lives personally. Everyone is both supplied and a supplier of the resources of God to others when godliness leads to unselfishness and mutual service among the saints (Eph. 4:16). The result is the growth and health, not only of the saints themselves, but the thriving of the church as a united body of believers representing God to the world.

Critical to engaging this moral development, that supports the unity of the church, Paul asserts that the Ephesians must not fall back into the habits of living like the Gentiles around them (Eph. 4:17). This is not what they learned from the truth that is in Christ (Eph. 4:20). Rather, God requires godliness from his people. They had heard from Paul previously, and been taught, that they are to lay aside the old life to take up the new life they have in Christ (Eph. 4:21-23). He reminds them that laying aside the old life opens the way to God's ongoing transformation in the attitude/spirit of their minds and will, and for God to perfect what he originally created in them by way of transforming justification (Eph. 4:24). Justification was a starting place, but not an ultimate destination (Eph. 4:23-24). It was a transformative prelude to growth and maturation in godliness that leads to the eschatological perfection of the saints in the eschaton, by which they will ultimately reflect the image of God in Christ (Eph. 4:13, cf. Rom. 8:29-30; 1 Cor. 15:48-49; 2 Cor. 3:18; 4:16-18; 1 John 3:1-3). It can hardly be argued that by engaging our analysis, we have strayed too far beyond the basic and fundamental tenor of Paul's argument or intent for this passage.

CONCLUSION

In seems to me, that the problem the post-Wesley holiness movement faced in time, was that it came to view holiness and righteousness as a commodity measured in pints and gallons, mainly as external appearance, which (achieving the evidences of certain quantities of holiness) was conceived as an end in itself. Some saints, comparing themselves to one another, judge the world outside of the church by their own inside (the church) version of holiness. Paul views holiness not as measured in terms of appearance and volumetric units, but as evidenced by unity in the church, and it is at its best when the saints serve one another out of genuine concern. Holiness is quite simply love for God reflected in the love of the saints for one another (a premise in 1 John). In this Wesley was surely right. He and the Methodists sought to practice this kind of love and mutuality in the context of their class meetings. As God develops godliness in his people, personally over time, it contributes to unity and mutual thriving through mutual service and concern (Eph. 4:13, 16). What that might look like in practical terms, Paul addresses until almost to the end of the epistle, after the passage we have been considering. Nevertheless, John Wesley, along with his brother, Charles, sought to implement the spirit of what we have been discussing above in the Methodist revival, as it is expressed by the Apostle Paul in Ephesians, and elsewhere, with John championing the *instantaneous*, and Charles, more and more, the gradual and progressive maturation of godliness over time.[386]

By the *instantaneous*, John reacted against a common view of moral growth as a slow mortification of the flesh, the kind often viewed as characteristic of the early aesthetics, who went to extreme lengths to deprive their bodies and appetites of earthly comfort, with the notion

[386] Tyson, J. R. 1986, 291-301, 303-314.

that this would bring out an impulse for holiness. John Wesley, himself having tendency to rigorous, even religious, discipline, struggled before Aldersgate with two issues, having the assurance of his salvation, confidence in his rightness with God, and a palpable inability to overcome the impulses of his flesh and human nature to go on to what he considered was holiness of life.[387] After his heart was *strangely warmed*, he discovered, in the New Testament generally but in Paul in particular, the idea of *moral transformation,* of *a new creation*, whereby God implants the foundations of holiness of character and conduct in the life of the believer, as a result of justification, through thoroughgoing regeneration as a result of grace and faith (2 Cor, 5:17).[388] Holiness, for John, was not a slow mortification of carnality, but acceptance and full surrender to God in order to experience the impartation of new life that leads to mature godliness. Holiness had a definite beginning in justification, John believed, and in an impartation of new life by God. Wesley, went on to observe that Paul encourages his readers to more resolutely take up that new life, to put it on, having just as resolutely laid aside all thought of or draw to return to the old one, the basis of which is also a decision made in faith, to make room for God to perfect what he has started (cf. Eph. 4:17-24).

Wesley was also a pragmatist, and realized that initial moral change did not automatically inculcate full moral perfection, or result if instant, full maturation in godliness, that growth and development were needed. Nevertheless, Wesley was convinced that moral and spiritual development took place by acting on the deposit of new life that God

---

[387] Outler, 1962, 41-50. In this, Wesly's struggle was not unlike that of Paul, whose autobiographical testimony is found in Romans 7. Wesley sincere quest for salvation and holiness of life all thought his experience in Georgia up to Aldersgate, seem to be emblematic of his theology of a second blessing, a double cure.

[388] Wesley, A Plain Account of Christian Perfection, 1966, 60-67.

implants by his Spirit at initial salvation, or justification (Rom. 6:1-10).[389] Rather than growing away from carnality, a Calvinistic notion, Wesley envisioned the maturing of a new moral impetus, planted in them by God, and that at its core was the new life of Christ at work in those who believe (Gal. 2:19-21).[390] Decisive moral change, arising from the regenerative power of God sets the tone for future growth in holiness, he believed. Even with that, John saw in Pauline theology a role for the believer, in the apostle's language, that of *reckoning,* or *putting off the old life,* and *putting on the new,* of ensuring the old man is crucified with Christ, and of being raised with Christ in resurrection to new life (Rom. 6:4, 8, 11). As a result of the exercise of God's grace at justification, the believer is no longer under condemnation, not of judgment on their sins, and not to continued servitude to the power of sin that compels sinning (Rom. 8:1-4). In Paul's instructions for believers to align their minds and wills with the morally transforming work of God, Wesley saw a second emphasis beyond initial justification, a necessary surrender to God in order to fully embrace this new life.[391]

Paul certainly presented this to his readers as an imperative for future holiness, and Wesley seems to have latched on to the idea. For Wesley this was a *second blessing,* a definite appropriation of already implanted moral transformation (cf. Rom. 6:1-8), whereby the believer signs on and fully embraces this new life as a matter of applying faith and surrender to God, so as to adopt transformation and new life as the determining impetus for the future moral direction and growth of their lives. It is instantaneous, because it involves a fuller appropriation of the new life offered to those who put their faith in Christ, and who engage a *further* resignation of their will to God by which have rejected, stepped

---

[389] Wesley, Sermons on Several Occasions, 1999, Sermon 7, II, 6.
[390] Wesley, Sermons on Several Occasions, 1999, Sermon 7, II, 2.
[391] Wesley, A Plain Account of Christian Perfection, 1966, 28-32; Wesley, Sermons on Several Occasions, 1999, Sermon 14, I, 1-6.

away from, the old life or old self previously controlled by sin in our nature, what Wesley calls “inbred sin”.

Holiness vitally includes moral maturation toward fully developed godliness, and should reflect the character of God even as it develops, no matter what the level of maturity might be in each individual case. The Wesley’s seemed to have recognized this, and comment on it in their journals and letters to one another, and others. Even John, ever the enthusiast for the instantaneous until the end,[392] fully appreciated the need for moral improvement and growth in the grace and knowledge of God. The divine endgame is to forge, in one’s redeemed humanity, a quality of character that represents God, and provides a reflection, the likeness and image, of God back into creation. This will be the ongoing service that the saints will render to God as they reign with Christ in the eschaton. After all, they will one day represent God to his creation in a new heaven and a new earth (Rev. 21-22). Holiness and righteousness are not quantitative; they are qualitative in Pauline theology. So, when we measure it in terms of *how much*, we have lost sight of the purpose of God, which is to re-form his image in those he has redeemed, in preparation for their future service to God, partnering with Christ.

For the contemporary church, this is still a challenge, no less than for the Wesleyan revival, where problems continually arose, and John Wesley either combatted resistance to the doctrine of meaningful moral success in the life of the believer, or extreme versions of it that sought to push the doctrine beyond the biblical boundaries Wesley envisioned (so called angelic perfection).[393] We would say today that John Wesely accepted and worked within the eschatological tension of what is now and what is to come. Despite our veneration of Wesley, by which some

---

[392] Tyson, J. R. 1986, 300.

[393] Wesley, A Plain Account of Christian Perfection, 1966, 51-68, cf. Tyson J. R., 1986, 268-301.

beatify his memory, he was a realist about humanity, and knew that even the *divine deposit* given to the Methodists was not a panacea, and had to be lived out in the real world, where sin and rebellion against God dominate the culture, and the humanity and weaknesses of the saints often create challenges to a consistent pursuit of holiness and right practice. Even a cursory look at Wesley's signature publication, *A Plain Account of Christian Perfection,* reveals these concerns and struggles.

These problems are still the subject of contention, sometimes bitter, and the idea of holiness has sometimes been either abandoned altogether, or reduced to tradition and legalism that measures it by the yard. As a result, those who believe in God's power to sanctify the saints have sometimes lost sight of Paul's original concern for renewal, that they might serve on another in love, and not that they might hold to certain criteria of piety as prerequisites for membership in the community, or as a badge for belonging to the club, an exclusive holiness society.

It can be said with a high degree of confidence that John Wesley believed in two major biblical ideas with respect to holiness. First, God commanded it, and if so, it must be possible to achieve and experience. In which case, he must also have made provision for it for those from whom he requires it. Secondly, Wesley had no use for holiness that did not work itself out in practical, daily living, and in service to God and the saints. He was a practical man,[394] whose holiness had to find tangible expression, and he expected that from those who called themselves Methodists, and even more so from their clergy. His whole life was a testament to both principles. So, Wesley sought to work out his theology of sanctification in terms of what the provision of God might

---

394 Cf. Tyson J. R., 1986, 16-17.

make possible inwardly, and how it might be fleshed out in terms of how believers live practically and externally. Surely, we can see that this is nothing less than the concern that Paul expresses in Ephesians 4 and 5, insisting on inner renewal exhibited by concern for unity in the church through mutual service (Eph. 4:16), as well as practical, sanctified living in every aspect of their lives and relationships (cf. Eph. 4:25-6:18). Upright conduct arises from an experience of the sanctifying power of God inwardly, Paul argues, whereby the old life has been laid aside in favor of taking up the new, so that through the Spirit, God might engage a process of renewal leading to mature godliness. This is the heart of Wesley's doctrine, and not the many extravagant claims, doctrinal aberrations, or homiletic vitriol that arose in the later holiness movement, which sometimes degenerated into a late legalism that crippled so many churches, and cooled the passion of the original revival.

Noel Brooks, whom we have cited a number of times in this book, was a student, not only of Wesleyan thought, but of Wesley's life.[395] Wesley could be quite melancholic, and Charles broody; both could be dogmatic and inflexible, and although Charles was of a quieter and more temperament man generally, he could challenge the authority (and try the patience) of his more passionate brother.[396] Though Brooks admired Wesley greatly, and certainly steeped himself in Wesleyan theology, he sometimes commented in private conversations on Wesley's struggles and obvious weaknesses as factors that sometimes complicated his interactions with others, or led to unreasonable expectations. One such example, Brooks cited one day, was that Wesley had fallen in love with

---

[395] I observed the same principle, that the life and temperament of the theologian is critical to understanding their theology, from Dr. Dan Woods in his lectures on church history, and particularly in connection with the life of Martin Luther.

[396]Cf. Tyson J. R., 1986, 17-19, 268-314.

a good Methodist woman, Grace Murray, who had nursed him back to health, but who, as a result of an intervention by his brother Charles, married someone else, and John Wesley was devasted. [397] Subsequently, he married hastily, late in life, without sharing his plans with Charles, so as to prevent his interference. The marriage was a disaster for any number of reasons, but mainly because Wesley had expected his wife to dutifully fall in behind his itinerary, to endure the hardships of his preaching schedule and its privations. She did not, and they spent excessive amounts of times apart. The relationship failed. It was an error in judgment on John's part, one that arose as a result of his humanity, and not a little naivety. So, when John spoke of even sanctified people being liable to mistake, he knew whereof he spoke!

What the later Wesleyan and holiness movements failed to account for in their subsequent development of a doctrine of sanctification was the *continued humanity of the saints*, and that led to unreasonable expectations with regard to piety, and the condemnation of those who did not meet the commonly perceived standards for holiness. Brooks taught me how to understand Wesleyan sanctification doctrinally, as a product of God's inspiration and illumination of Wesley's mind and reason, but that it was also conveyed to him fully clothed in his humanity.[398] So, we ought to look, not only at what Wesley taught, but seek the biblical basis for ourselves, and reaffirm what we believe from the scriptures. Standing on Wesley's shoulders is one thing, but failing to appreciate the biblical foundations of his arguments and evaluating them for ourselves is another.[399]

What the holiness movement ended up doing, especially in its preaching, was to create an environment where it was frowned upon to

---

[397] Tyson, 1986, 16-19

[398] Cf. Peters, 1995, 15-31

[399] Chadwick, A Call to Chrstian Perfection, 1943, 8.

question or re-evaluate passionately held views or doctrine against scripture, especially when they were held to be inviolable. That off-limits approach persisted well into the late 1990's for many of us. What was not appreciated by the late Wesleyan and holiness movement, was that original Wesleyanism, and its later holiness tradition, in many ways, developed the original doctrinal expressions, positions, nuances, and ideas through a slow drift, beyond Wesley's original assertions, and sometimes misrepresented his doctrine. Once begun, some of these ideas were most effectively concreted in the consciousness of the church by a vigorous homiletic. Even its hermeneutical models changed beyond the core claims and ideas originally set forth by Wesley himself.[400] I would argue that many of these extrapolations were out of step and harmony with Wesley's more cautious claims, especially as he expressed them to Charles at the end of his life, when the two thrashed out whether or not they were on the same page with respect to the essentials.[401]

John questioned Charles as to whether they will go on preaching the original idea, that holiness can be conferred by God, and that new life must be taken up as a matter of a decision to fully embrace definite moral change and practice, or should they simply let it go.[402] What is often not recognized is that in the early days Charles was as invested in Methodism as John, even if later on he differed somewhat on how much emphasis should be given to the doctrine of what John called the *instantaneous*. Charles sought to make more room for emphasis on necessary gradual growth and maturity in holiness, which John readily admitted was necessary.[403] Charles was as deeply concerned about

---

[400] Cf. Peters, Christian Perfection and American Methodism, 1995.
[401] Tyson J. R., 1986, 227-301.
[402] Tyson J. R., 1986, 300, 310-314.
[403] Cf. Peters, Christian Perfection and American Methodism, 1995, 52-53, 228,

teaching holiness as his brother. In later life, his affinity for the gradual process of sanctification (which Brooks also endorses as essential), which he increasingly expressed in his hymns, led John to raise the question of whether his brother was still committed to preaching and representing the *instantaneous.*[404] While John was concerned to not lose the instantaneous side of the doctrine, Charles struggle with the increasing specter of spiritual pride in Methodism, which was incongruous with the true humility of an authentically sanctified life.[405] Charles' voice has all but been ignored by the holiness movement, I think to its detriment. If we are to be Wesleyan, we ought also to hear the voice of the great hymn writer, and hold the affirmations of these brothers in some balance with one another.

John Wesley, arguably, has been selectively mined by certain elements of the holiness movement, leading, quite often, to *imbalance* in doctrine and practice, and a lack of sensitivity to scripture, which in some cases has led to scripture being conformed to doctrine, and not the other way around. The process of renewal and development, clearly represented by Paul in Ephesians 4, as well as Romans 12, foolishly overlooked, missed, or ignored, brought upon the holiness church a great deal of confusion and sorrow. John did not reject the idea of growth either, but his emphasis on holiness as a sanctifying endowment assumed prominence in the movement that came after him, and led it, all too frequently, to miss the equally important side of Wesleyan holiness (in my opinion), growth and maturing in godliness.[406] To cite Noel Brooks, these ideas are not in conflict with one another, they are

---

[404] Peters, Christian Perfection and American Methodism, 1995, 292.

[405] Tyson J. R., 1986, 268-301.

[406] By this I do not mean, what is commonly taught among non-Arminians, maturing *away from sin and sinning.* Paul did not teach this, but rather held to the need for a decisive repudiation and separation from them.

two sides of the same coin.[407] Brooks recognized this deficiency early on, and attempted in many of sermons, as well as in his writing, to remind the church that salvation is not a static event, or series of events. It is a continuum beginning with justification and ending in glorification, that sanctification occurs between the two, and involves both a choice that must be made by every believer, whether or not they will surrender to and go with the plan of God to conform them to the image of Christ, and by embracing growth to mature godliness over time.[408]

It is then, a major premise of this book that the hope of which Paul speaks fairly often, is not a shallow aspiration for God's consummation of all things according to his divine plan, but rather the firm conviction and assurance, that if God is in the process of engaging himself in the ongoing moral renewal of the saints, and if the saints are cooperating with the Spirit, and are conscious of maturing in Christ, they have every expectation that he will bring his plan to its full and final completion in them (Phil. 1:6). There are numerous passages in Paul which bear this out, including Romans 5, where justification is to go on to character development, which in turn provides hope of its final consummation (Rom. 5:1-5). And in 2 Corinthians 3:18, he speaks of progressive improvement as going from glory to glory, where the context makes it clear that he means reflecting the glory of God. In 2 Corinthians 4:16-18, Paul affirms that it is not the progressive regeneration of our physical bodies that counts. Indeed, they are wasting away, while at the same time God is renewing the inner man, redeemed and transformed in his nature through Christ to be like God (Eph. 4:24). A greater weight of future glory will swallow up the hardships of the present (cf. Rom. 8:28; 2 Cor. 4:16-18). In Romans 8, Paul paints a vivid picture of those who

---

[407] Cf. Brooks, Scriptural Holiness, 1972, 43-50; Brooks, Fingertip Holiness, 3-15.

[408] Brooks, Scriptural Holiness, 1972, 41-68.

are led by the Spirit, and walk with God. They are already children of God, who can expect to be heirs of God, and co-heirs with Christ (see the discussion above) (Rom. 8:1-7). He goes on to assure them that nothing will be able to separate them from the love of God that is in Christ Jesus, as he works out this purpose for and in them, as well as for creation (Rom. 8:31-39). In the famous *love chapter*, 1 Corinthians 13, Paul speaks of the supremacy of love, and anticipates that when perfection comes, love will continue. What is temporary and transitory will disappear, at which time the saints will put off the former life of immature Christian practice and character of this age, to put on the moral perfection of full adulthood in Christ (1 Cor. 13:11-12).

Even Peter gets in on this line of thought, when he says that we became sharers of the divine nature, at the time we came to know Christ, and that God is perfecting Christian character in us, whereby, if we embrace it and engage it in increasing measure, we can expect its final consummation, and a rich welcome into the glory to come (2 Pet. 1:3-11). This hope, the writer of Hebrews observes, is an anchor that goes beyond the veil, into the holy of holies, by which he meant the heavenly throne room of God, and is fixed in the reigning Lord Jesus Christ himself (Heb. 6:19). The anchor has already penetrated the glory of what is to come, where Christ reigns preemptively ahead of the coming eschaton (cf. 1 Cor. 15:20-28). We are securely attached to him by faith in God (cf. Rom. 1:17; Phil. 1:6) and through a reconciling redemption, even while we live in this present age. What is to come has been vouched safe to us through our connection to God in Christ, and it is firmly fix as the defining assurance of a final consummation for those who persevere, because they are even now in possession of and living in surrender to the Spirit of God (Eph. 1:13-14).

After all Paul says, in Ephesians, God intends to come after his purchased possession, so he has already put a seal on what belongs to him, the Holy Spirit, whom he promised to his people as a sign and assurance of their final redemption (Eph. 1:13-14). When their bodies are adopted, Paul says in Romans 8, then creation will truly see redeemed humanity for what they are, the children of God, a reflection of his image and likeness (Rom. 8:19-20). This hope permeates Paul, whereby the action of God in the saints presently not only anticipates the future perfection to come, but is the subject of God's effort now, to develop his character in them (Eph. 4;13, 24, cf. Phil. 2:12-13). As he engages the process of developing *his* character in the lives of *his* people, they serve him in the present age as his witnesses (Phil. 2:14-16). The endgame has already been engaged in the rugged day to day battle of life and serving God in an age opposed to him (Eph. 4:17-19), so that reaching the goals God has set for himself, his people, and creation are certain for those who have laid aside the old life, taken up the new, and whom he is renewing in the spirits of their minds day by day (cf. Col. 1:13-20).

BIBLIOGRAPHY

Alford, H. (1865). *The New Testament for English Readers: Containing the Authorized Verson, with Revised Text; Marginal References; and a Critical Explanatory Commentary* (Vol. 2). Cambridge, UK: Deighton, Bell, and Co.

Arndt, W. D. (2000). *A Greek-English lexicon of the New Testament and other early Christian literature* (3rd ed.). Chicago, IL, USA: University of Chicago Press.

Barclay, J. M. (1991). *Obeying the Truth: Paul's Ethics in Galatians*. Minneapolis , MN, USA: Fotress Press.

Beacham, A. D. (1998). *Light for the Journey: A Fresh Focus on Doctrine*. Franlkin Springs, GA, USA: LifeSprings Resources.

Beacham, A. D. (2026, January 20). *General Superintendent's Office*. Retrieved from International Pentecostal Holiness Church: https://iphc.org/gso/2026/01/20/the-preface-to-holy-living-eph-4-17-24/

Beacham, P. F. (1935, October 3). Question Box. (J. H. King, Ed.) *The International Pentecostal Holiness Church Advocate, 19*(23), p. 3.

Beale, G. K. (2004). *The Temple and the Church's Mission: A Biblical Theology of the Dwelling Place of God.* Downers Grove, IL, USA: InterVarsity Press.

Beale, G. K. (2008). *We Become What We Worhip: A Biblical Theology of Idolatry.* Downers Grove, IL, USA: Intervasity Press .

Blaikie, W. G. (1909). *Ephesians.* (H. D. Spence-Jones, Ed.) London: Funk & Wagnalls Company.

Board, R. A. (n.d.). *First Things First.* Franklin Springs, GA, USA: Advocate Press.

Brooks, N. (1972). *Scriptural Holiness.* Franklin Springs: Advocate press.

Brooks, N. (1975). *Bible Validation for Santification.* Franklin Springs, GA, USA: Advocate Press.

Brooks, N. (1982, August 8). The Advocate Bible School: Ephesians Oulined and Unfolded: 58. Christian Conversion. (L. O. Stewart, Ed.) *International Pentecostal Holiness Advocate, 66*(8), p. 14.

Brooks, N. (1984). *Ephesians Outline and Unfolded.* Franklins Springs, GA, USA: Advocate Press.

Brooks, N. (n.d.). *Fingertip Holiness.* Franklin Springs: Advocate Press.

Brooks, N. (n.d.). *Pardon, Purity, and Power.* Franklin Springs: Advocate Press.

Brooks, N. (n.d.). UNIT II SANCTIFICATION. In M. L. A (Ed.), *Focus On Doctrine: A Detailed Study of the Major Tenets of the Pentecostal Hiloness Church* (pp. 15-35). FRanklin Springs, GA, USA: Advocate Press.

Brown, F. D. (1977). *Enhanced Brown-Driver-Briggs Hebrew and English Lexicon.* Oxford, UK: Clarendon Press.

Bruce, F. F. (1961). *The Epistle to the Ephesians.* Basingstoke, UK: Pickering Paperbcks.

Burer, M. H., & Miller, J. E. (2008). *A New Reader's Lexicon of the Greek New Testament.* Grand Rapids: Kregel Pubications.

Burton, E. D. (1898). *Syntax of the Moods and Tenses in New Testament Greek* (3rd ed.). Edinburgh: T&T Clark.

Campbell, C. R. (2020). *Paul and the Hope of Glory: An Exegetical and Theological Study.* Grand Rapids, MI, USA: Zondervan Academic.

Campbell, C. R. (2024). *Basics of Verbal Aspect in Biblical Greek.* Grand Rapids, MI, USA: Zondervan Academic.

Capes, D. B., Reeves, R., & Richards, E. R. (2017). *Rediscovering Paul: An Introduction World, Letters, and Theology* (2 ed.). Downers Grove, IL, USA: InterVarsity Press Academic.

Carter, H., & Sauls, N. (1976). *The Effects of Sanctification on the Humna Nature.* Dunn, NC, USA: Heritage Bible College.

Chadwick, S. (1932). *The Way to Pentecost.* London, UK: Hodder & Stoughton.

Chadwick, S. (1943). *A Call to Chriatian Perfection.* Kansas City, MO, USA: Beacon Hill Press .

Cole, A. R. (2008). *Tyndale New Testament Commentaries: Galatians* (2nd ed., Vol. 9). (L. Morris, Ed.) Downer's Grove, Illinois, USA: InterVasity Press.

Drysdale, J. D. (1955). *Holiness in the Parables.* London, UK: Oliphants Ltd.

Edwards, J. R. (2011). *Romans.* Grand Rapids, MI, USA: Baker Books.

Elwell, W. A., & Comfort, P. W. (2001). Ephesians, Letter to the. In *Tyndale Bible Dictionary.* Wheaton, IL, USA: Tyndale House Publishers.

Eusebius., E. o. (1890). *Eusebius: Church History, Life of Constantine the Great, and Oration in Praise of Constantine.* (2 ed., Vol. 1). (P. S. Wace, Ed., & A. C. McGiffert, Trans.) New York, New York, USA: Christian Literature Company.

Evans, P. F. (2016). *Holiness Reconsidered: A Fresh Look at the Wesleyan Doctrine of Sanctification.* Xulon Press.

Evans, P. F. (2018). *Help For Holiness: Rediscovering God's Resources for Practical Sanctification in Galatians 5:16-25.* Bloomington, IN, USA: WestBow Press.

Farrar, F. W. (1909). *1 Corinthians.* (H. D. Spence-Jones, Ed.) New York, NY, USA: Funk & Wagnalls Company.

Fee, G. D. (1994). *God's Empowering Presence: The Holy Spirit in the Letters of Paul.* Peabody, MA, USA: Hendrickson Publishers Inc.

Fee, G. D. (2007). *Pauline Chrstology: An Exegetical-Theological Study.* Peabody, MA, USA: Hendrickson Publishers, Inc.

Fletcher, J. W. (n.d.). *The Works of the Reverend John Fletcher Late Vicar of Medeley: In Four Volumes.* New York, New York, USA: Carlton and Lanahan.

Frederick, J. (2014). Mercy and Compassion. In D. R. D. Mangum (Ed.), *Lexham Theological Wordbook.* Bellingham, WA, USA: Lexham Press.

Gesenius, W. (2003). *Gesenius' Hebrew and Chaldee lexicon to the Old Testament Scriptures.* (S. P. Tregelles, Trans.) Logos Bible Software.

Graham, L. R. (1951, April 12). Luther Richardson Graham. (H. T. Spence, Ed.) *The International Pentecostal Holiness Church Advocate, 34*(49), p. 5.

Hansen, G. W. (1994). *Galatians: The IVP New Testament Commentary Series.* (G. R. Osborne, Ed.) Downer's Grove, Illinois, USA: Intervasity Press .

Harris, M. J. (2012). *Exegetical Guide to the Greek New Testament: Colossians and Philemon.* B&H Academic.

Harris, M. J. (2015). *Exegetical Guide to the Greek New Testament: John.* B&H Academic.

Harrison, E. F. (1975). John the Apostle. In H. F. C. F. Pfeiffer (Ed.), *The Wycliffe Bible Encyclopedia.* Chicago, IL, USA: Moody Press.

Hills, A. M. (1929, July 18). Sanctification. *The International Pentecostal Holiness Church Advocate, 13*(12), p. 13.

Holmes, M. W. (Ed.). (2011-2013). *The Greek New Testament* (SBL Edition ed.). Lexham Press; Society of Biblical Literature.

Keener, C. S. (2004). *Paul, Women & Wives: Marriage and Women's Ministry in the Letters of Paul.* Peabody, Massachusetts, USA: Hendricksons Publishers, Inc.

Keener, C. S. (2018). *Galatians: New Cambridge Bible Commentary.* (B. Witherington, Ed.) Cambridge, UK: Cambridge Univesity Press.

King, J. H. (1936, June 18). The Mystery of Perfection. (J. H. King, Ed.) *The Advocate: Official Organ of the Pentecostal Holiness Church, 20,* pp. 1-2.

King, J. H. (1976). *From Passover To Pentecost.* Franklin Springs, GA, USA: Advocate Press.

Kostenberger, A. J., Merkel, B. L., & Plummer, R. L. (2016). *Going Deeper into Greek: An Intermediate Study of Greek Grammar and Syntax of the New Testament.* Nashville, TN, USA: B&H Academic.

Liefeld, W. L. (1997). *Ephesians.* (G. R. Osborne, Ed.) Downers Grove, MI, USA: IVP Academic.

Lightfoot, J. B., & Harmer, J. R. (1891). *The Apostolic Fathers* (Vol. 3). London, UK: Macmillan and Co.

Long, F. J. (2016). Ephesians, Letter to the, Critical Issues. In J. D. Barry, D. Bomar, D. R. Brown, R. Klippenstein, D. Mangum, C. S. Wolcott, & W. Widder (Eds.), *The Lexham Bible Dictionary*. Bellingham, WA, USA: Lexham Press.

Longenecker, B. W., & Still, T. D. (2014). *Thinking Through Paul: A Survey of His Life, Letter, and Theology.* Grad Rapids, MI, USA: Zondervan.

Machen, J. G. (1951). *New Testament Greek for Beginners.* Toronto, Ontario, Canada: The MacMillan Company.

Merkle, B. L. (2016). *Ephesians* . (A. J. Yarbrough, Ed.) Nashville, TN, USA: B&H Academic.

Merkle, B. L., & Plummer, R. L. (2020). *Beginning with New Testament Greek: An Introductory Study of the Grammar and Syntax of the New Testament.* Nashville, TN, USA: B&H Academic.

Metzger, B. M. (1971). *A Textual Commentary on the Greek New Testament: A Companion Volume to the United Bible Societies' Greek New Testament (Third Edition)* (Corrected Edition, 1975 ed.). Stuttgart, Germany: United Bible Societies.

Mounce, W. D. (2009). *Basics of Biblical Greek Grammar.* Grand Rapids: Zondervan.

Osborne, G. R. (2004). *Romans: The IVP New Testament Commentary Series.* (G. Osborne, Ed.) Downers Grove, IL, USA: IVP Academic .

Osborne, G. R. (2017). *Romans Verse by Verse: Osborne New Testament Commentaries.* Lexham Press.

Outler, A. C. (Ed.). (1962). *John Wesley.* New York, NY, USA: Oxford University Press.

Peters, J. L. (1995). *Christian Perfection and American Methodism.* Salem, Ohio, USA: Shamul Publishing Co. Inc. .

Robertson, A. T. (1933). *Word Pictures in the New Testament.* Nashville, TN, USA: Broadman Press.

Schaff, P. (Ed.). (1887). *A Select Library of the Nicene and Post-Nicene Fathers of the Christian Church: Volume V. St Augustine: Anti-Plagian Writings* (Vol. 5). (P. Holmes, Trans.) New York, NY, USA: The Christian Literature Company.

Silva, M. (2001). *Interpreting Galatians: Exploarations in Exegetical Methods.* Grand Rapids, MI, USA: Baker Academic.

Smothers, J. (n.d.). Personal Conversations. (P. F. Evans, Interviewer, & P. F. Evans, Editor)

Soards, M. L. (2011). *Understanding the Bible Commentary Series: 1 Corinthians.* (W. W. Gasque, Robert L. Hubbard Jr., & Robert K. Johnston, Eds.) Grand Rapids, MI, USA: BakerBooks.

Spence-Jones, H. D. (1909). *Ephesians in The Pulpit Commentary.* London: Funk & Wagnalls Company.

Stott, J. R. (1968). *The Message of Galatians: The Bible Speaks Today.* (J. R. Stott, Ed.) Downer's Grove, Illinois, USA: InterVarsity Press.

Stott, J. R. (1979). *God's New Society: The Message of Ephesians.* Downers Grove, IL, USA: . InterVarsity Press.

Stronstad, R. (1984). *The Charistmatic Theology of St. Luke.* Peabody, MA, USA: Hendrickson Publishers Inc.

Swanson, J. (1997). *Dictionary of Biblical Languages with Semantic Domains : Hebrew (Old Testament)* (2nd; electronic ed. ed.). Logos Research Systems, Inc.

Tasker, R. V. (1996). John, the Apostle. In I. H. D. R. W. Wood (Ed.), *New Bible dictionary* (3rd ed.). Downers Grove, IL, USA: InterVarsity Press.

The Epistle of Ignatius to the Ephesians. (1885). In A. D. Roberts, A. Roberts, J. Donaldson, & A. C. Coxe (Eds.), *The Apostolic Fathers with Justin Martyr and Irenaeus* (Vol. 1, p. 49). Buffalo, New York, USA: Christian Literature Company.

The New International Version. (2011). Zondervan.

Tramel, T. (2009). *The Beauty of the Balance: Toward and Evangelical-Pentecostal Theology.* Franklin Springs, GA, USA: LifeSprings Resources.

Turner, M. (1994). Ephesians. In D. A. Carson, & R. T. D. A. Carson (Ed.), *New Bible commentary: 21st century edition* (4th ed., pp. 1222-1244). Downers Grove, IL, USA: Inter-Varsity Press.

Tyson, J. R. (1986). *Charles Wesley on Sanctification: A Biographical and Theological Study.* Grand Rapids, MI, USA: Zondervan Publishing House.

Utley, R. J. (1997). *Paul Bound, the Gospel Unbound: Letters from Prison (Colossians, Ephesians and Philemon, then later, Philippians)* (Vol. 8). Bible Lessons International.

Wallace, D. B. (1996). *Greek Grammar Beyond the Basics: An Exegetical Syntax of New Tesament Greek, with Scripture, Subject, and Greek Word Indexes.* Grand Rapids, MI, USA: Zondervan Publishing House.

Wenham, J. W. (1965). *The Elements of New Testament Greek: Based on the Earlier Work of H. P. V. Nunn.* Cambridge, UK: Cambridge University Press.

Wesley, J. (1872). *The Works of John Wesley* (3rd ed., Vol. 6). London, UK: Wesleyan Methodist Book Room.

Wesley, J. (1966). *A Plain Account of Christian Perfection.* Kansas City, Missouri , USA: Beacon Hill Press.

Wesley, J. (1999). Sermons on Several Occasions. Oak Harbor, WA.

Westcott, B. F. (1906). *Saint Paul's Epistle to the Ephesians.* Minneapolis: Klock & Klock Christian Publishers.

Witherington, B. (1998). *The Paul Quest: A Renewed Search for the Jew of Tarsus.* Downers Grove, IL, USA: InterVarsity Press.

Witherington, B. (2016). *The Problem with Evangelical Theology: Testing the Exegetical Foundatiuons of Calvinism, Dispensationalism, Welseyanism, and Pentecostalism* (Revised and Expanded ed.). Waco, Texas, USA: Baylor University Press.

Witherintgon, B. (1998). *Grace in Galatia: Commentary on Paul's Letter to the Galatians.* Grand Rapids, MI, USA: William B. Eerdmans Publishing Company.

Wood, A. S. (1981). *Ephesians. In The Expositor's Bible Commentary: Ephesians through Philemon* (Vol. 11). (F. E. Gaebelein, Ed.) Grand Rapids, MI, USA: Zondervan Publishing House.

Wright, N. T. (2012). *After You Believe: Why Christian Charactrer Matters.* New York, New York, USA: HarperCollins Publishers.

Wright, N. T., & Bird, M. F. (2019). *The New Testament in Its World.* Grand Rapids, MI, USA: Zondervan Academic.

Wuest, K. S. (1997). *Wuest's Word Studies From the Greek New Testament: for the English Reader* (Vol. 4). Grand Rapids, MI, USA: William B. Eerdmans Publishign Company.

www.ingramcontent.com/pod-product-compliance
Lightning Source LLC
LaVergne TN
LVHW020652110826
845149LV00012B/1964

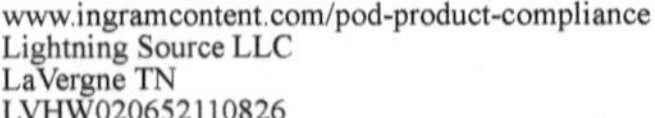

* 9 7 9 8 9 9 5 4 2 1 5 1 1 *